Empire of Landscape

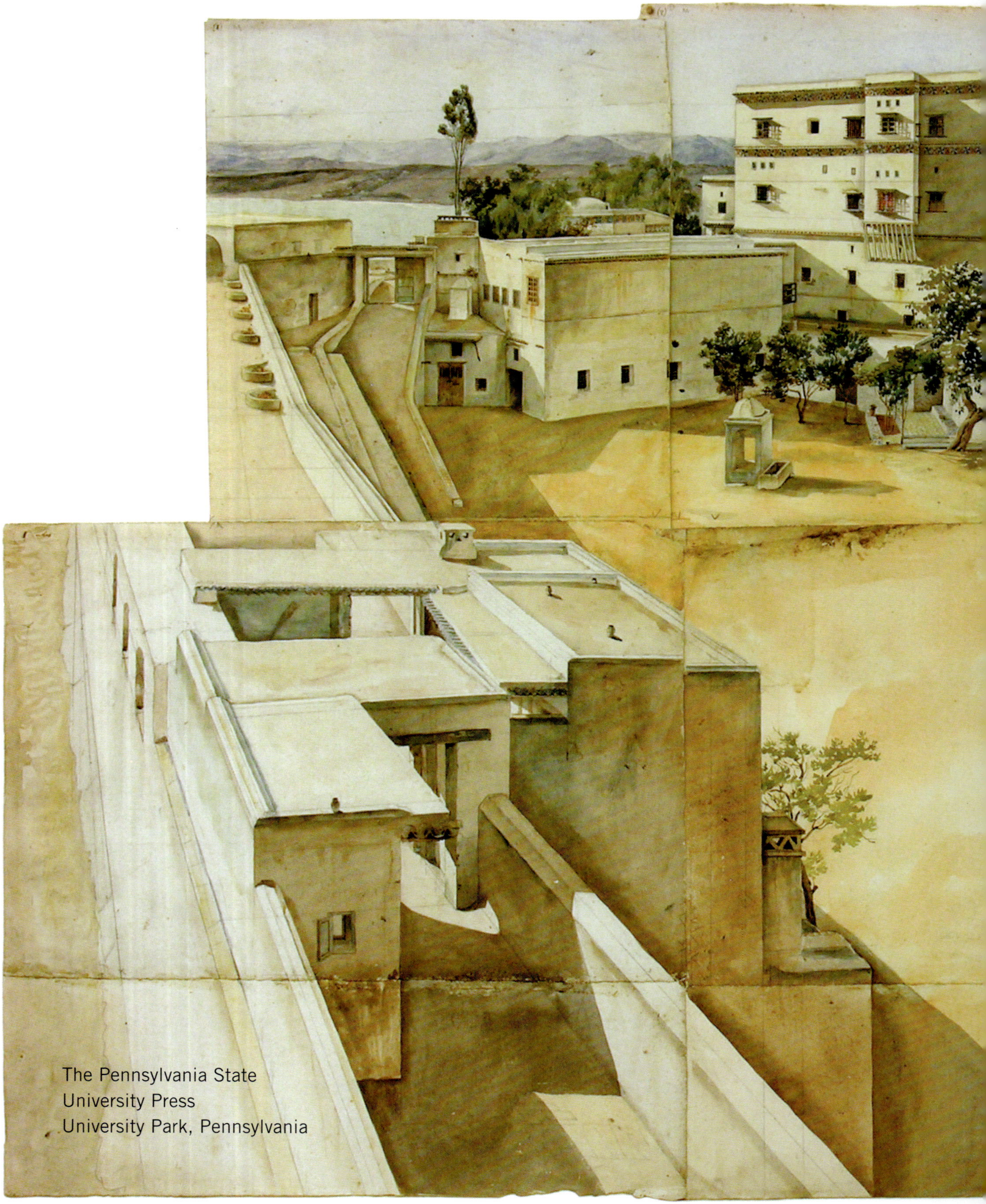

The Pennsylvania State
University Press
University Park, Pennsylvania

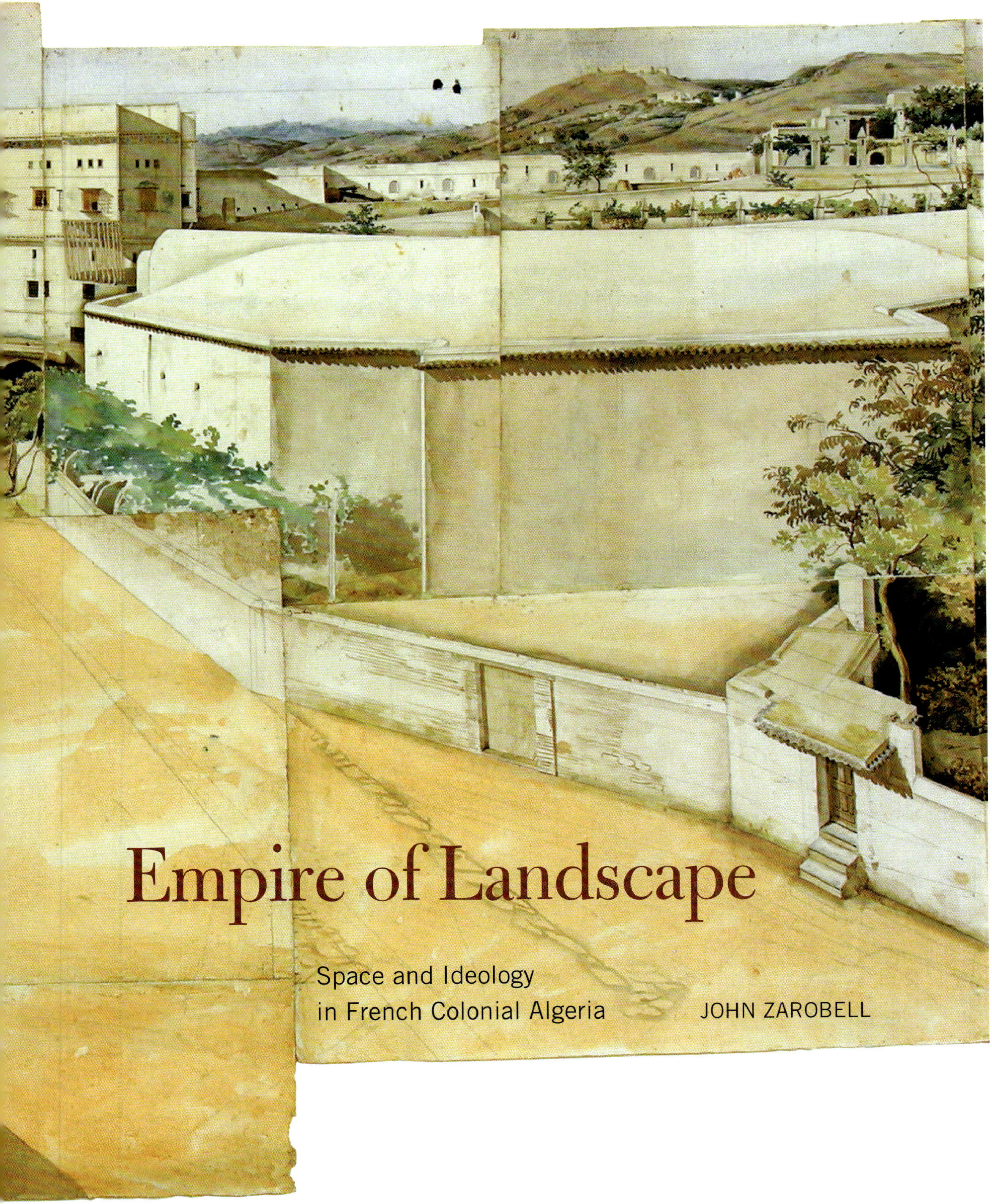

Empire of Landscape

Space and Ideology in French Colonial Algeria

JOHN ZAROBELL

Library of Congress Cataloging-in-Publication Data

Zarobell, John.
Empire of landscape : space and ideology in French colonial
Algeria / John Zarobell.
p. cm.
Includes bibliographical references and index.
Summary: "Explores visual culture and the social history of art
through an analysis of French images of nineteenth-century
Algeria"—Provided by publisher.
ISBN 978-0-271-03443-0 (cloth : alk. paper)
1. Algeria—In art.
2. Landscape in art.
3. Art—Political aspects.
4. Art, French—19th century.
5. Art and society—Algeria—History—19th century.
I. Title.

N8214.5.A4Z37 2009
704.9'43665—dc22
2009014137

Designed by Bessas & Ackerman
Printed in Singapore by Tien Wah Press
Published by The Pennsylvania State University Press,
University Park, PA 16802-1003

It is the policy of The Pennsylvania State University Press to
use acid-free paper. Publications on uncoated stock satisfy the
minimum requirements of American National Standard for
Information Sciences—Permanence of Paper for Printed
Library Material, ANSI Z39.48–1992.

For my three great inspirations:

Jimi Hendrix,

Walter Benjamin,

and Keally McBride

(not necessarily in that order)

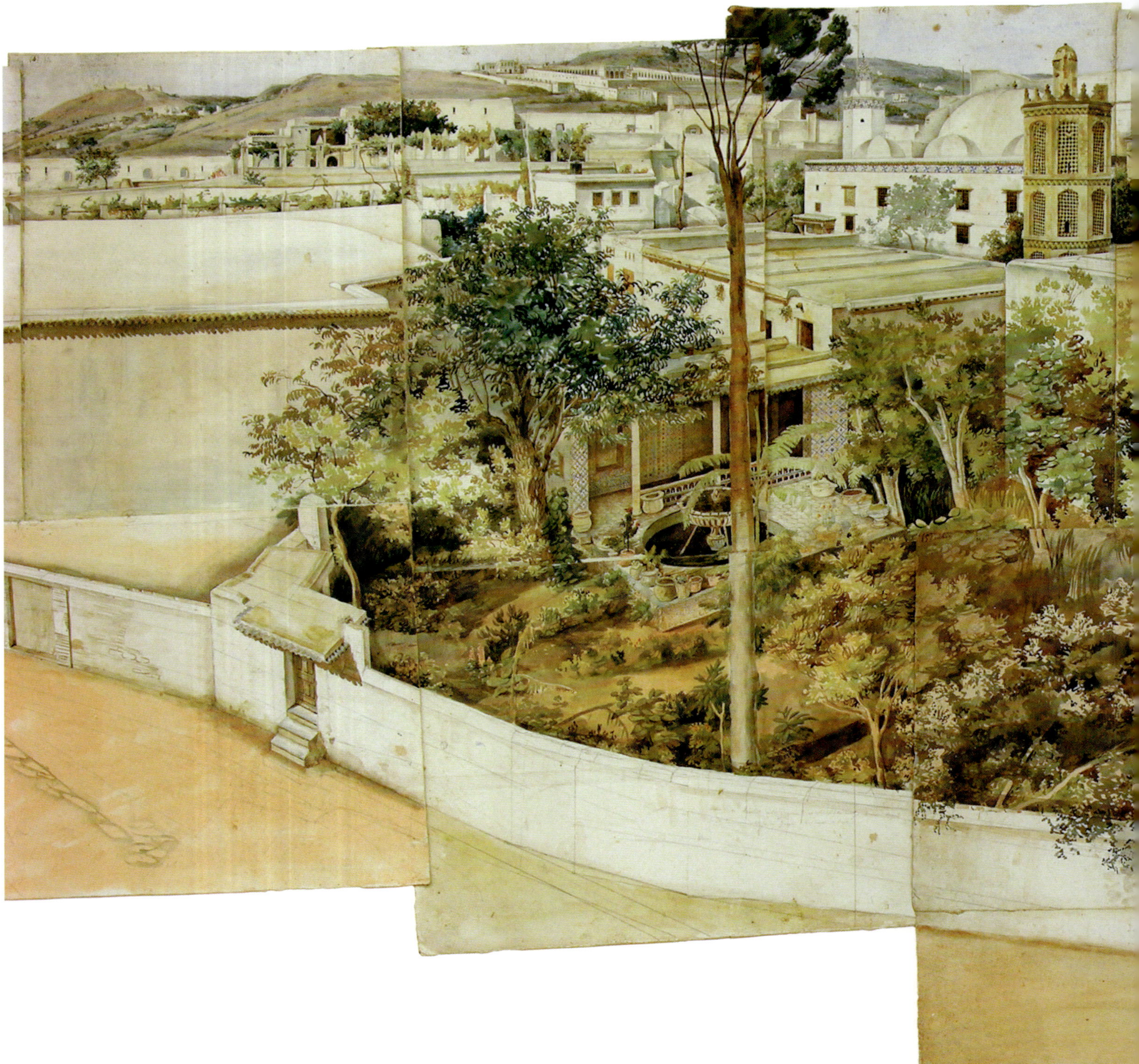

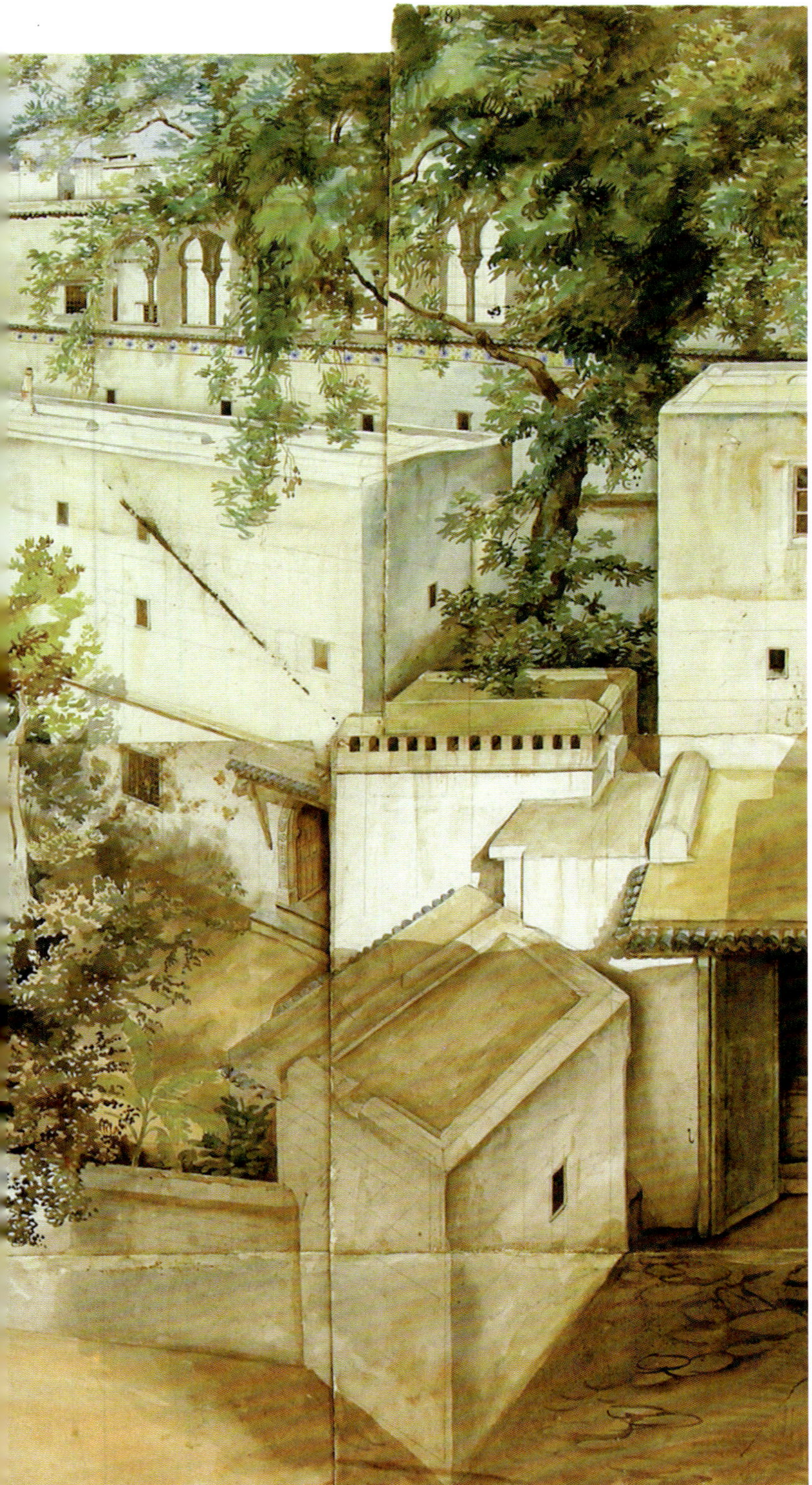

Contents

Illustrations

Guerre, Service historique de l'armée de Terre, Vincennes, France (SAH/D 86). © Service historique de l'armée de Terre.

15. Alexandre-Gabriel Decamps, *Oriental Night Scene*, c. 1836. Oil on canvas, 60.5 × 51.3 cm (23$\frac{13}{16}$ × 20$\frac{3}{16}$ in.). John J. Johnson Collection, Philadelphia Museum of Art, cat. 966.

16. Anonymous, *Atlas d'Alger*, n° 5, "View of the environs of the Fort de l'Empereur." From *Aperçu historique, statistique et topographique sur l'état d'Alger, à l'usage de l'armée expéditionnaire d'Afrique* (Paris: Ch. Piquet, 1830). Bibliothèque nationale de France, Département des Estampes et de la photographie.

17. Anonymous, *Atlas d'Alger*, n° 7, "Interior of a house in the vicinity of Algiers." From *Aperçu historique, statistique et topographique sur l'état d'Alger, à l'usage de l'armée expéditionnaire d'Afrique* (Paris: Ch. Piquet, 1830). Bibliothèque nationale de France, Département des Estampes et de la photographie.

18. Horace Vernet, *Episode from the Conquest of Algeria in 1837; Second Siege of Constantine by Général Damrémont; The Enemy Turned Back from the Heights of Coudiat-Ati (10 October 1837)*, 1838. Oil on canvas, 512 × 518 cm. Château de Versailles et de Trianon, Versailles, France. Photo: Réunion des musées nationaux/Art Resource, New York (Gérard Blot).

19. Horace Vernet, *Episode from the Conquest of Algeria in 1837; Second Siege of Constantine by Général Damrémont; The Columns of Assault Are Set into Motion for the Siege of Constantine (13 October 1837)*, 1838. Oil on canvas, 512 × 1039 cm. Château de Versailles et de Trianon, Versailles, France. Photo: Réunion des musées nationaux/Art Resource, New York (Gérard Blot).

20. Adrien Dauzats, *Second Wall of the Portes-de-Fer. Arrival of the 17th Regiment of Light Infantry (28 October 1839)*, 1840–41. Watercolor on paper mounted on canvas, 63 × 99 cm. Château de Versailles et de Trianon, Versailles, France. Photo courtesy Château de Versailles et de Trianon (Jean-Marc Manaï).

21. Adrien Dauzats, *Third Wall of the Portes-de-Fer. The Chasseurs of the 3rd Regiment and the Soldiers of the 2nd Léger Descend into the Bed of the River (28 October 1839)*, 1840. Watercolor on paper mounted on canvas, 63 × 99 cm. Château de Versailles et de Trianon, Versailles, France. Photo courtesy Château de Versailles et de Trianon (Jean-Marc Manaï).

22. Adrien Dauzats, *Third Wall of the Portes-de-Fer. The Sapeure du génie Indicates by Inscription the Date of the Passage of the Portes-de-Fer (28 October 1839)*, 1841. Watercolor on paper mounted on canvas, 63 × 99 cm. Château de Versailles et de Trianon, Versailles, France. Photo courtesy Château de Versailles et de Trianon (Jean-Marc Manaï).

23. Adrien Dauzats, *Departure from the Portes-de-Fer (28 October 1839)*, 1840. Watercolor on paper mounted on canvas, 63 × 99 cm. Château de Versailles et de Trianon, Versailles, France. Photo courtesy Château de Versailles et de Trianon (Jean-Marc Manaï).

24. Adrien Dauzats, *Passage of the Portes-de-Fer, Second Gorge*, undated. Watercolor on paper, 23.8 × 31 cm. Musée Condé, Chantilly, France (DE 694). Photo: Réunion des musées nationaux/Art Resource, New York (René-Gabriel Ojéda).

25. Adrien Dauzats, *Passage of the Portes-de-Fer, Bottom of the Ravine*, 1839. Watercolor on paper, 23.8 × 30.3 cm. Musée Condé, Chantilly, France. © Giraudon France/The Bridgeman Art Library.

26. Adrien Dauzats, *Passage of the Portes-de-Fer, Departure from the Last Gorge*, 1839. Watercolor on paper, 23.5 × 30.8 cm. Musée Condé, Chantilly, France (DE 696). Photo: Réunion des musées nationaux/Art Resource, New York (René-Gabriel Ojéda).

27. Alexandre-Gabriel Decamps, *Oriental Landscape*, mid-nineteenth century. Oil on canvas, 41.3 × 59.4 cm. John J. Johnson Collection, Philadelphia Museum of Art, cat. 968.

28. Prosper Marilhat, *Oriental Caravansery*, 1835. Oil on panel, 27.5 × 43 cm. John J. Johnson Collection, Philadelphia Museum of Art, cat. 1028.

66. Félix Moulin, *Tomb of the Christian*, 1856. Albumin photograph, 19 × 25.5 cm. From F. Moulin, *L'Algérie photographiée* (Paris: Goubaud, 1860). Service historique de la Défense, Vincennes, France.

67. Le marquis de Courcival, *Hodna-Bou-Saâda, Panorama of the City from the Door of the Fort*, 1861–62. Albumin photograph, approx. 15 × 40 cm. Bibliothèque nationale de France, Département des Cartes et plans, collection of the Société de géographie (We 25).

68. Le marquis de Courcival, *Route from Batna to Biskra: Plain of Ksour and the Camp of the Spahis at Aïn-Touta,* 1861–62. Albumin photograph, 15 × 23 cm. Bibliothèque nationale de France, Département des Cartes et plans, collection of the Société de géographie (We 25).

69. Gustave Guillaumet, *The Desert* (or *The Sahara*), 1867. Oil on canvas, 110 × 200 cm. Musée d'Orsay, Paris. Photo courtesy Musée d'Orsay (Patrice Schmidt).

70. Gustave Guillaumet, *Evening Prayer in the Sahara* (Salon of 1863). Oil on canvas, 137 × 285 cm. Musée d'Orsay, Paris. Photo courtesy Musée d'Orsay (Patrice Schmidt).

71. "Map of Algeria presenting current civil territory divided by *communes* and *douars* constituted by virtue of the *sénatus-consulte*," 1870. Bibliothèque nationale de France, Département des Cartes et plans, Ge D. 4167.

72. Eugène Fromentin, *The Land of Thirst*, undated. Oil on canvas, 103 × 143.2 cm. Musée d'Orsay, Paris. Photo courtesy Musée d'Orsay (Patrice Schmidt).

73. Eugène Fromentin, *The Land of Thirst*, 1869. Oil on canvas, 103.5 × 144 cm. © Royal Museum of Fine Arts of Belgium, Brussels (inv. 3424). Photo: Cussac.

74. Pierre-Auguste Renoir, *Arab Festival, Algiers*, 1881. Oil on canvas, 73.5 × 92 cm. Musée d'Orsay, Paris (RF 1957-8). Photo: Réunion des musées nationaux/Art Resource, New York (Hervé Lewandowski).

75. Henri Matisse, *Periwinkles, Moroccan Garden*, 1912. Oil, pencil, and charcoal on canvas, 116.8 × 82.5 cm. The Museum of Modern Art, New York. Gift of Florence M. Shoenborn (341.1985). © Succession H. Matisse, Paris/ARS, New York. Photo © The Museum of Modern Art, licensed by Scala/Art Resource, New York.

Acknowledgments

For a project that has taken more than ten years to come to fruition, it is perhaps natural that there are many people to thank. Such an enterprise, while individually driven, could not come to fruition without the myriad scholars, researchers, curators, and archivists who have aided me in the process. First, I would like to thank Bob Herbert, who not only opened my mind to the history of art but who followed along my path every step of the way and who inspired me as a wonderful example. His comments and support were instrumental in the production of this work. Darcy Grimaldo Grigsby was the advisor for my dissertation at the University of California, Berkeley. She was a generous and honest reader who did much to influence my study of the topic of Orientalism in general and my research and writing. Thanks are also due to Anne Wagner, Susanna Barrows, and T. J. Clark. All sharpened my understanding of art in France in the nineteenth century and helped me establish a general framework for considering this rich and complex period in a sophisticated and cogent way. To all of these scholars who launched me in my own pursuits, I owe the deepest gratitude.

I have had the chance to present my research in numerous venues and I am grateful to those who have listened to my work and who responded by challenging me with questions and giving me valuable insights. I am particularly grateful to Sura Levine and Susan Canning, who invited me to participate in their College Art Association panel in 2000 entitled "Out of the Academy and into the Arcades." I am also grateful to Susan Buck-Morss and her seminar on Walter Benjamin's Arcades Project held at Cornell University in 2000; the Department of Art and Art History and the Iris and B. Gerald Cantor Center for the Visual Arts at Stanford University; Derek Gregory and the Geography Department at the University of British Columbia; Nina Athanassaglou-Kallmyer at the University of Delaware; and Vojtech Jirat-Wasiutynski and Michael Parke-Taylor, whose symposium at the Art Gallery of Ontario in 2002 provided such a unique opportunity to engage with scholars from a variety of disciplines.

While researching the project, I have met many who have provided me support to make this project possible. Many more discussed ideas with me and extended the scope of my knowledge. I would like to thank you all here. Particular thanks are due to Barbara Wright, Roger Benjamin, Peter Benson Miller, Stéphane Guégan, and Joseph Rishel. I would also like to thank Claire Constans, Valérie Bajou, and Xavier Salmon of the Château et Musée de Versailles; Nicole Garnier and Ramdan Manseur of the Musée Condé, Chantilly; Isabelle Bruller and Jean-Marie Linsolas of the Service historique de l'armée de Terre; Dominique Conte of the Musée des Beaux-Arts, Bordeaux; France Duclos of the Departement des Cartes et plans at the Bibliothèque nationale de France; the curators at the Bibliothèque nationale de France, Département des Estampes et de la photographie; Mme. Pellegrin and Caroline Joubert at the Musée des Beaux-Arts,

Caen; Marie-Claire Adès at the now defunct Musée-Galérie de la Seita; and Mme. Taffin at the Musée des Arts Africains et Océaniques (now the Quai Branly). I should also thank the researchers François Robichon, James Thompson, Luc Demarquest, and Lynne Thornton, the collectors Paule de Domecy and her family, François Bureau, and Fred and Lucy Herman.

I am particularly grateful to the Georges Lurcy Foundation, which funded my year abroad in France, and the Andrew W. Mellon Foundation, which funded both a year of writing and a summer of research. I am also grateful to the Vice-Chancellor for Research at the University of California, Berkeley. It must be said that I could not have completed work on the book without the support of my employers at the Philadelphia Museum of Art and at the San Francisco Museum of Modern Art. My grandmother, Rosemary Lisy, contributed significant resources to help cover the costs of reproductions for the book.

For an art history book, images are of particular importance and there are many who have provided invaluable assistance to me. I would like to thank all of the museums and collectors who have provided me with images. Particular thanks are due here to Barbara Wright and the staff of ACR Éditions, Stéphane Guégan and the Musée d'Orsay, Valérie Bajou and the Château et Musée de Versailles, Caroline Joubert and the Musée des Beaux-Arts, Caen, and Jennifer Vanim and the Johnson Collection/Philadelphia Museum of Art. I am also grateful to the reproductions departments at the Philadelphia Museum of Art and the San Francisco Museum of Modern Art for their assistance with this difficult project.

Finally, I must thank all of those family and friends closest to me who have watched me go through this very long and sometimes harrowing process and who have provided me moral, emotional, and psychological support over the years that it took me to produce this book. If it were not for their encouragement and love, I could never have completed it. Thanks to Keally, Celeste, Theo, Mom and Eric, Rosemary, Richard and Betsy, and all my dear friends and colleagues.

Introduction

Empire of Landscape

The politics, culture, and processes of empire have been much studied, but the means by which imperialism has been—and continues to be—transmitted visually has been examined only in the most cursory way. The publication of Edward Said's *Orientalism* effectively unmasked the discursive structure of the European imperialist project in North Africa and the Middle East. This broad yet in many respects highly detailed account of Orientalist studies, literature, and art between the eighteenth and the twentieth centuries fused Antonio Gramsci's conception of hegemony with Michel Foucault's notion of discursive formations to demonstrate how European and American culture fixed the "other" as a course of study or a subject of art, thereby neutralizing the potential expression of alternative worldviews that might challenge imperialism's legitimacy.[1] Said's work has been questioned and critiqued by many scholars and by the author himself, but the influence of his fusion of hegemony and discourse has only increased in significance and relevance over time.

Numerous analyses of Orientalist painting, particularly concentrating on the nineteenth century, have followed the publication of Said's seminal analysis of Orientalism, resulting in a greater understanding of this ideologically loaded group of images. Studies of Orientalist art began by considering a very broad group of images.[2] Recently, book-length works have developed from extensive historical research and complex, theoretical analyses of Orientalist imagery.[3] Yet despite the ascendance of the study of visual culture, most academic accounts of imperial imagery have focused upon only a small fraction of the pictures that accompanied colonial contact. While some attempts have been put forward to include studies of "popular imagery," meaning broadsides, cheap prints,[4] and the photography generated by colonial encounters,[5] many analyses have been hindered by familiar dichotomies such as self/other, native/exotic, visible/invisible, and so on. Some recent studies have proposed more sophisticated models of contact through recourse to the concept of hybridization,[6] but such a notion leaves out the intentions of many image producers and disavows the unequal distribution of power.[7] Certain images that emerged from colonial contact have survived over time and can be interpreted by historians; other representations, which might have challenged the underlying assumptions of such views, are lost to history. Further, while historians of art have been effective in reading in paintings traces of contemporary political and social developments, no study has considered the way in which colonial imagery not only complements but in fact generates imperial power through an amazing variety of forms. Employing rigorous historical and visual analysis, this book hopes to accomplish as much.

It must be stated from the outset that, while this book follows Said's fundamental premise that a discourse (Orientalism) operates as a real cultural force with political manifestations over the course of history (hegemony, broadly understood), my goal is distinct from art-historical studies of Orientalism, properly speaking. As Said explains, the Orient is not clearly delimited geographically or temporally, so works of so-called Orientalist art could refer to a wide variety of cultures at any point within their distinct historical developments, or even in an imagined or apocryphal history. In this sense, Orientalism as a category of art history is inadequate. While it is useful to describe the irruption of alternative models in the development of the tradition of European painting, Orientalism is not particular enough to serve the purpose of describing the reciprocal development of European culture and the way in which imperial powers in Europe influenced and controlled the cultures referenced in Orientalist art. One of the most significant critiques leveled at Said was that he generalized the West just as much as he claimed the West generalized the East.[8] My response is to follow recent authors and attend to the specifics of the interaction between French imperial machinations in particular locations and the images that negotiated these historical episodes in the mid-nineteenth century.[9] The innovation I propose is to examine in greater detail the way in which images affected—as opposed to merely reflecting—these fundamental social and political changes in France.

Another difference between Said's project and this study is that rather than examining all Orientalist art featuring Algeria and made in France between 1830 and 1870, I focus instead on a single category of images, those that can be productively classed as landscapes. There are two fundamental reasons for this self-imposed limitation. The first is that landscapes have been left out of most examinations of Orientalist art, which have concerned themselves primarily with figurative compositions and problems relating to identity construction.[10] The second reason is that, as will be argued below, depictions of landscape direct attention to the territorial character of French colonialism in the nineteenth century and provide a unique means by which to investigate the relationship of visual representations of the colony of Algeria and the social and political changes that France initiated there.

While it is clear that landscape has played a small role in investigations of Orientalist art, it is also true that examinations of landscape have not played a significant role in the development of art history in the last generation.[11] Of course, countless books on landscape paintings have been published, many of them focusing on nineteenth-century France, but the subject of landscape is a topic whose full implications have been little examined in recent art-historical literature.[12] While many authors have now gone beyond perceiving landscape as merely a category of imagery and have acknowledged it as a category of perception and a historical force, few have formulated a sophisticated model for conceiving the relationship between geopolitical notions of space and landscape representation.[13] Rather, most analyses prize painting over other visual media and primarily consider the way in which politics and society affect the representation of landscape. Those who have broadly considered the social dimension of landscape imagery have examined the way in which artists responded to historical, social, and political changes rather than considering how such transformations are themselves, at least in part, a result of pictorial representations and their apprehension by viewers.[14]

The term "empire of landscape" seeks to account not just for images of power but also for the power of images. My point is that images themselves serve a hegemonic role in society. Of course, images respond to social and historical shifts, but the visual articulation of such transformations alters consciousness and directs perception. New visual media have been continually introduced at a rapid rate from the nineteenth century to the present. As the forms of visual culture multiply, responses to and interpretations of visual media become more sophisticated. By studying a period when visual spectacles became an essential part of modern life—the mid-nineteenth century—it is possible to evaluate some of the fundamental differences between various forms of visual culture and how each one structures our ability to apprehend information visually. Such a project has clear relevance today, in an era when new technologies and visual media have radically altered our perceptual faculties.

Between 1830 and 1870, the French nation experienced unprecedented developments in the spheres of politics, society, economy, and culture. As any French historian knows, 1830 was the year of the revolution that put a constitutional monarch in power, but it was also the birth of France's second colonial empire,[15] which began with the seizure of El-Djezaïr (later renamed Algiers) on the north coast of Africa. While France was, at that moment, administering colonies around the world dating from the seventeenth and eighteenth centuries, the nineteenth century ushered in the period of settler colonialism for France.[16] In the late nineteenth century, European nations greatly expanded their colonial empires overseas and, for France, Algeria provided the prototype for its later colonial ventures. The changes wrought by French domination in this area of North Africa were unquestionably enormous, but France's colonial venture in Algeria also altered French society considerably. There can be no full historical accounting of these changes, but images of Algeria generated by Frenchmen who had experience in the colony offer a window onto this vast historical escapade.

New worlds were opened to French viewers not just extrinsically, through the expansion of France into Algeria and the subsequent imagery that resulted, but also intrinsically, through the profusion of new visual media that allowed French viewers to apprehend the world around them in novel ways. In examining paintings, prints, drawings, photographs, maps, panoramas, and illustrated travelogues from this period, I have become fascinated by the ability of images to transmit certain forms of pictorial truth based upon their particular medium. No one would expect to get the same information from a painting and a photograph of the same subject. The way a viewer perceives information from an image, historical or otherwise, is a product of the underlying principles of the medium itself. In order to interpret a painting, for example, a viewer must be initiated into its pictorial language—such as the ability of relative values to communicate spatial information, the way composition produces pictorial harmonies, or the symbolic importance of color. Attending to the perceptual shifts made possible by new media leads to a more nuanced understanding of the period and its imagery. This investigation of the reception of visual images suggests another role for pictures of the colony in France.

At bottom, a colony is no more than an assertion of control over space backed by military force. Though control of foreign territory is not always colonialism, understood in its proper historical sense, the French colonial experience in the nineteenth century was founded on redefinition of territory. As the ongoing multinational occupation of Afghanistan and Iraq amply demonstrates, military domination alone cannot succeed in convincing the vanquished—or even the population of the vanquishing country—of the legitimacy of such an enterprise. This was equally the case in North Africa in the nineteenth century. In order for a colony to succeed, the character of that place had to be redefined. El-Djezaïr had to become Algiers, the widening area of control had to be circumscribed through borders, and a new name had to be invented: in this case, Algeria. By no means automatic, this development was a process of historical formation. El-Djezaïr was first conquered in 1830, and as the French continued to expand their control, Algeria was christened in 1837. Abd-el-Kader, the leader of the resistance to French domination who did much to unify the region, was not captured until 1847. The pacification of the colony was not complete until Général Randon conquered the mountainous Kabyle region in 1857, and even in 1871 a new anticolonial force emerged. In these years, a profusion of texts about and images of Algeria circulated in France, all connected to this course of events. Numerous scholars have shown how these works were ideologically charged and laden with more or less sophisticated messages about the relationship of France to the colony. The innovation of this study is to examine how these messages were conjoined with the perceptual terms dictated by visual media. Images of Algerian territory not only translated political and social changes in the colony but also suggested the means to apprehend spaces anew.

The term *landscape* has a number of meanings, and most of them apply here.[17] For historians of art, the primary reference is pictorial. It will be useful to say that a landscape is, first of all, a picture of the world. The term *landscaping* suggests that a landscape can be created in the material world. The creation of luxurious gardens and spaces designed for aesthetic enjoyment underlines the fact that nature is a human creation as much as any picture of the natural world would be. Further, the current rise of landscape designers and landscape architects demonstrates a contemporary recognition that spaces, as much as buildings, require human intervention and conception in order to transmit certain experiences. In all of these uses of the term, landscape is a way of framing the world according to aesthetic principles. Whether it is a question of seeing beauty in the world and recording it as a picture, or moving earth in order to achieve a picturesque prospect, landscape is, as Stephen Daniels and Denis Cosgrove have argued, "a cultural image, a pictorial way of representing, structuring or symbolizing surroundings."[18]

There is a certain particularity to the word *landscape* as opposed to *space* or *place.* Landscape is specific and general at the same time. A landscape can be ordered according to any aesthetic principles, but it is always organized, structured, and crafted. Even if it is often perceived as "natural," the crafting of it as such is still a cultural endeavor. It is a means of perceiving the world derived from vision, even the imposition of a visual structure. There is one more meaning of the term *landscape*—the purely metaphorical one—that is not confined to any actual place. In this sense, landscape need not be tied to a material form, such as a picture or a garden. It can be seen as a means of interpreting the world and making it into an identifiable image. This abstraction of the landscape metaphor is telling because it suggests that landscape is fundamentally linked to perception and is applicable to any number of subjects: landscape of the body, landscape of possibilities, and so on.

For the purposes of this analysis, landscape should be contrasted with the inhabitation and productive use of space.[19] It is one thing to live in, make use of, and develop an intimate familiarity with a place, and it is another to conceive of the world as an object to shape according to principles, whether innate or acquired. How we live in and interact with a world familiar to us is distinct from how we imagine the world in which we live. There is an ontological divide that separates the direct experience of space and the perception of landscape. The intersection of the two, in the colony of Algeria, is one of the central concerns of this work. Landscape is a form of idealization: we perceive and identify with the world, as opposed to merely occupying a place in it. Everyone lives in and interacts with a variety of spaces, but the term *landscape* could not be used to describe all of those. It is only when an individual applies, blindly or willfully, a subjective interpretation of the world that a space becomes a landscape. This is the most fundamental claim to make regarding the empire of landscape: in the context of nineteenth-century imperialism, landscape comes to mediate relations between humans and the world. Landscape becomes ubiquitous and functions to secure the colonizer's control over space. It masquerades as both universal (it is everywhere) and authoritative (it is impossible to deny).

In the colonial context, landscape serves an instrumental function, both political and social. Since colonialism is about control of space—literally seizing territory—its complement is the imposition of the colonizer's understanding of space onto the colonized. The French took control of El-Djezaïr and the surrounding area from Turkish rulers, so it could be argued that the residents of this part of North Africa simply exchanged one colonial power for another. Yet the nature of French control was very different and, over the course of time, the French determined to give their colony clear boundaries and eventually to privatize the spaces of the colony, replacing spaces with actual property. They were not content to control a subject people who perceived their world in a distinct manner. Previous practices of land use and engagement with urban forms were drastically altered to accommodate not just the French presence but French views of agriculture, urbanization, and transportation as well. The indigenous population of Algeria thus could not simply live under the French as they had under the Ottomans. Their own means of relating to and understanding their environment had to be adapted to French conceptions. This was a crucial aspect of the self-imposed civilizing mission of the French. Alternative conceptions of space had to be eradicated in order for French colonialism to be completely effective.[20] Further, there was an equivalent need to make the colony apprehensible to French viewers as a discrete subject in order to situate the imperialist project in the guise of contemporary society and politics. This is where landscape comes to serve a political and social function: landscape, a subjective view of the world, was deployed in order to modify both Algerian and French views about the territory of the colony.

How is it possible to explain this paradox that landscape could be at once subjective and socially mediated, or deployed in a political context? To a certain degree, this duality can be explained by virtue of the fact that landscape comes to exist through its iteration in a specific medium and perception in an environment proper to that medium. Making sense of a picture ultimately means accepting the terms it sets forth for rendering the world. Interpretations may vary, but all viewers of imagery have to agree on the basic principles proper to a medium, such as understanding that a photograph is not drawn but is instead a direct impression of light. This knowledge provides the foundation for interpreting a photograph and binds all viewers of such images together. Yet there is another means to conceive of the landscape as collective: through an analysis of historical formation.

Though a number of thinkers have investigated the logic and history of colonialism, more often studies of the unequal distribution of political and economic power over the surface of the earth in the modern world have been investigated as a function of empire. What is the difference? Does it matter? If one imagines that a single nation comes to control a large area outside of its integral boundaries (however much those may have shifted), there are two elements to the equation. One is the ideological structure that allows such a seizure of power to be conceived and rationalized—the idealization of national interests in a global context—and the other is the ability to act on that impulse, to control another territory through the military seizure of buildings, spaces, and persons. If one speaks of the Dutch trading empire beginning in the seventeenth century, the reference is to the ontological whole, the way in which a variety of corporate and national forces worked together to provide an overall system of trade and the power to maintain and regulate it. If one refers to the Dutch colonies of the seventeenth century, the discussion would hinge upon the specific plantations and networks of trading relations that developed in particular areas, from Brazil to the East Indies, that actively fed the economic engine and made certain historical figures very rich. While it is debatable whether Dutch seventeenth-century trade could be defined as an empire, properly speaking, its colonies were real enough. However, with the exception of South Africa and some areas of Indonesia, these were not lasting settler colonies of the sort that became common in the nineteenth century.

The point is that while empire is a forceful political conception, colonialism is the process of manifesting national power over foreign territory. To colonize a place is to undermine its very character, to redefine it as a means to take possession of it. Of course, this means getting rid of others who would offer up resistance to this process, or sidelining their concerns and their ability to engage in distinct activities that would threaten to undermine the seizure of the colony. Landscape helps elucidate these terms and demonstrate how they work in tandem: it is situated at the crux of creating an ideal world (its aesthetic dimension) and can literally remake the colonial map through its undeniable pictorial logic. Landscape can help viewers imagine a world in which their centrality is unquestioned and their power is unlimited, while at the same time it informs them about the particularities of a region, a climate, or a space. This study will consider images of landscapes that circulated in France and allowed viewers to imagine that distant land across the Mediterranean as part of their nation. It will also examine images that demonstrated how French settlement had definitively changed that region and marked its development. In certain cases, these two functions converge in a single landscape image.

There is a collective character implicit in landscape imagery when that vision is manifested by changes to the land itself. In the context of colonial Algeria, the French occupants and visitors did not often produce landscape imagery for indigenous Algerians and, as far as I have been able to determine, there were no indigenous inhabitants active in the visual arts during this period. However, both conquerors and subjects shared the limitations of landscape imagery that framed the relationship of an individual to the world in both a metaphorical and a very real way. There were changes to the environment put into place in Algeria that led to a totally different way of life for all the inhabitants of the colony.[21] Landscape, as a structure of perception, became a means to enforce a certain definition of territory and thus a way of legislating the relationship of self and the world. The legislation of this relationship was one of the central mechanisms of nineteenth-century colonialism—and it is also a seductive means of introducing culturally specific terms, such as individualism and property, among subject peoples.

In the period under investigation here, landscapes and images of it were produced amidst a battle over land that ultimately became a battle for cultural sovereignty in North Africa. The French won, at least for the first 130 years. Between 1830 and 1870, the most common term for France's domination of Algeria was colonialism, although between 1852 and 1870, France was officially an empire. (In 1860, Napoléon III muddied the terms even more by declaring Algeria a *royaume arabe*—an Arab kingdom—with himself as its leader.) No matter what specific term was employed, the pattern of expansion of French territory abroad continued, even accelerated, in the early part of the Third Republic.

One interpretation of this period in French history views it in isolation. While nineteenth-century versions of imperialism accelerated near the end of the nineteenth century and continued well into the twentieth, this political form of domination more or less came to an end with independence movements that developed after World War II in Africa and Indochina. The present study certainly contributes to an understanding of this semi-isolated historical process of nineteenth-century imperialism and seeks to excavate its cultural mechanisms and demonstrate their involvement in, and even contribution to, political domination in this period. Yet this historical investigation is influenced by contemporary debates as well. Contrary to the notion that historical experience of empire is an isolated phenomenon, another idea of empire has begun to gain currency in contemporary studies of politics and culture. In the book titled simply *Empire,* Michael Hardt and Antonio Negri argue for a new understanding of the term, founded on an absolute and borderless domination of the world beyond the control of any world power, such as France aspired to be in the nineteenth century.[22] Though I do not agree with their conclusions, *Empire* makes clear that the notion of empire is alive and well today despite the decolonization of the later twentieth century.

The imperialism of nineteenth-century France and the place of landscape in this development is the subject of this study. Of course, the methodology is born of our own period and cannot be divorced from landscape and empire as they are present today. There is no teleological connection—it is impossible to connect the dots—but I hope to suggest that there is a relationship between the two eras. Landscape has altered the way people interact with their environments; it continues to structure a relationship between the self and the world. The term itself is replete and imagistic. It functions not as an external force, but as a currency of interpretation. As such, landscape continues to exercise an effect on our individual and collective perceptions.

CHAPTER 1

Jean-Charles Langlois' *Panorama of Algiers* (1833) and the Prospective Colonial Landscape

Landscape is thus a way of seeing, a composition and structuring of the world so that it may be appropriated by a detached, individual spectator to whom an illusion of order and control is offered through the composition of space according to the certainties of geometry.

—Denis Cosgrove

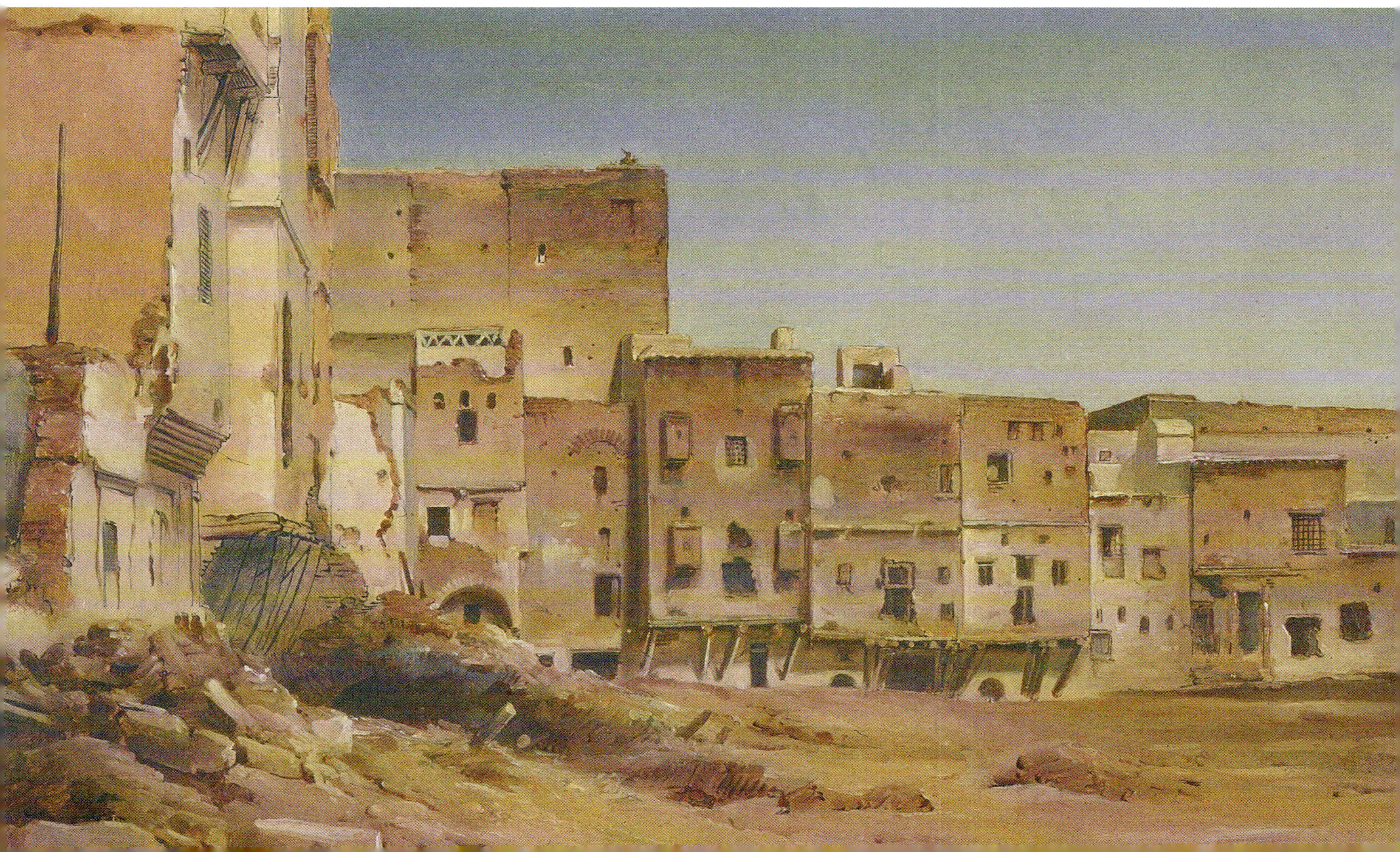

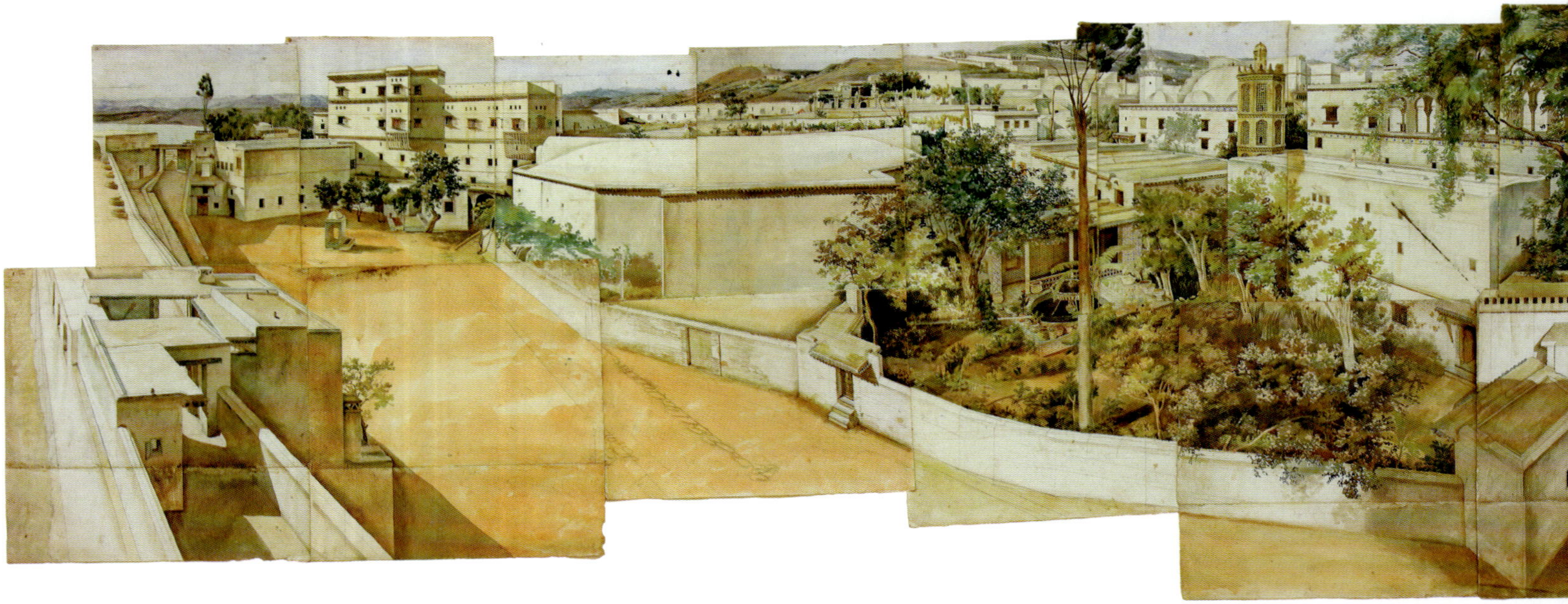

Overleaf: detail of fig. 10

Figure 1.
Jean-Charles Langlois, installation of 23 studies for the *Panorama of Algiers*, 1832. Pencil and watercolor on paper, each 48.8 × 33.5 cm. Private collection, Caen, France, and Musée Laplace, Beaumont-en-Auge, France. Photo © Musée des Beaux-Arts de Caen (Martine Seyve).

Advertisement

Have you seen the new "Panorama of Algiers" by M. Colonel Langlois? Perhaps you have experienced M. Langlois' "Panorama of the Battle of Navarin." But have you seen the "Panorama of Algiers"? You have read the accounts of the African campaign and of the glorious victory of our soldiers in Algiers, but have you seen the "Panorama of Algiers"? You have shopped at the magasins of the arcades and dined at Tortoni's, but have you seen the "Panorama of Algiers"?

Imagine sitting in a chambre turque, on the very cushions once owned by the Bey of Titeri. Imagine peering into a heavily guarded palace courtyard of the Algerian Casbah. Imagine, if you can, standing above the Casbah and looking down at the city of Algiers the very moment our victorious men-at-arms took possession of this exotic jewel. As you gaze out from this lofty perch, you will see what few Europeans have ever perceived: the spaces of this legendary pirate outpost will be unveiled for your eyes! Do you not want to let your eyes wander through France's newest acquisition? M. Langlois has created this wonder, transcribed from his own drawings made on location. In the newest and largest panorama rotunda in Paris, you too can learn the secrets of Algiers!

Rue des Marais-Saint-Martin, number 40

The Prospect

Jean-Charles (Colonel) Langlois was an officer in the French military who took part in the 1830 siege of Algiers as an artist.[1] His primary responsibility was to create images of the campaign—and his activities as a soldier/artist underline the convergence of the military conquest of Algeria and the

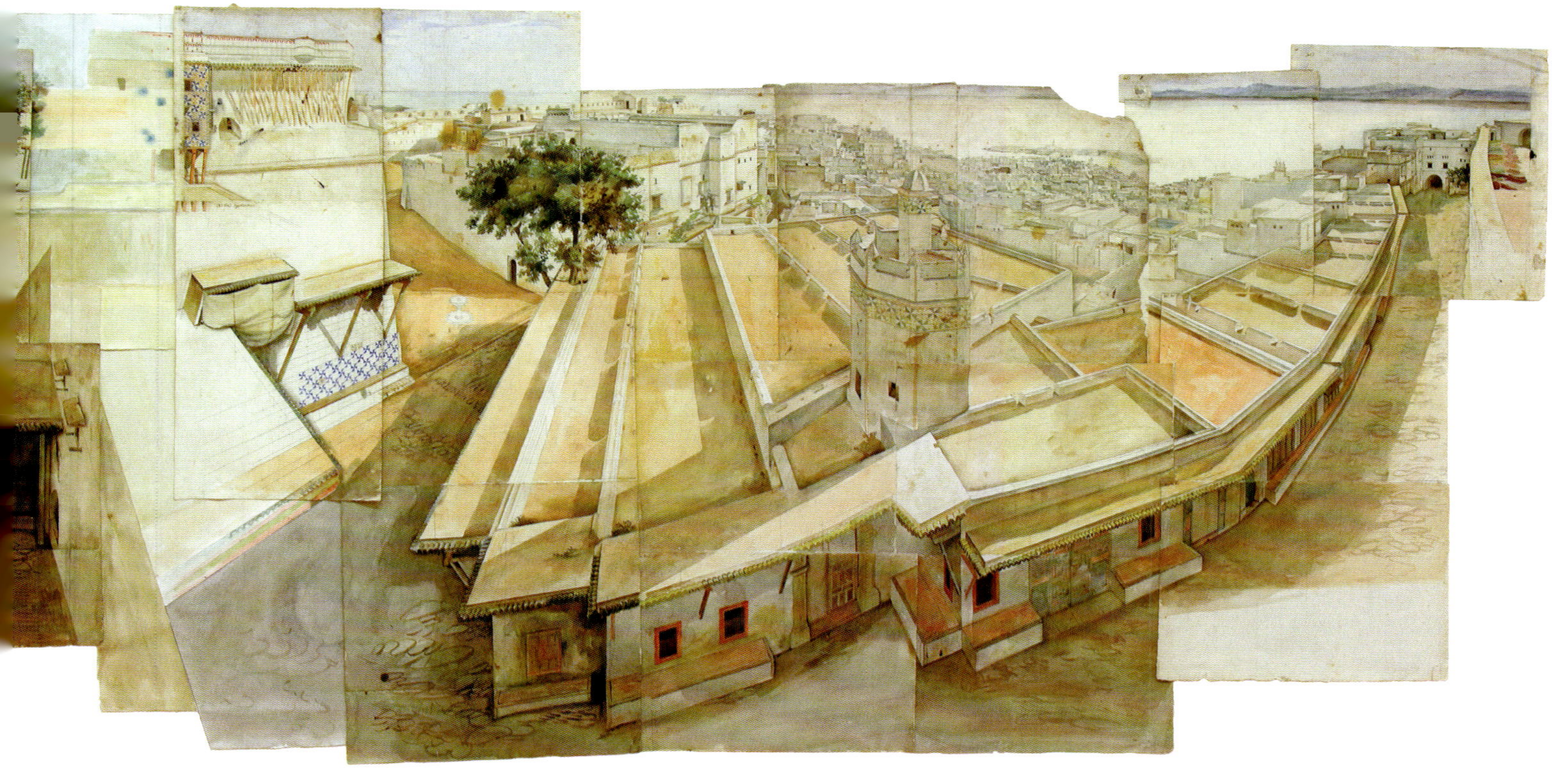

artistic representation of its spaces and inhabitants in France.[2] The French military controlled the administration of Algeria in 1833 and thus exercised a profound effect upon French artists' depictions of the colony. Only the administration could assure the safety of French artists in their travels through Algeria; moreover, military scholars produced practically all the information on the colony that was available in France. Many of the French artists in Algeria were officers, and those who were not had certainly been affected by the military's conceptions of the colony.[3]

Langlois' *Panorama of Algiers* of 1833 (fig. 1) was crucial in establishing the perceptual terms of the colonial landscape. One of the central features of panoramas, in general, is the idea of overcoming great distances (e.g., between France and Algiers) through the illusions that can be provided by the visual arts. The city of Algiers had long been considered hostile to European visitors, and its actual appearance remained mostly unknown to the French at the time of the siege. Indeed, the city's "invisibility" contributed to its legendary status as the base of the Barbary pirates.[4] While Algiers had been represented in previous imagery, both in the Turkish gouache tradition and as a site of naval battles such as Lord Exmouth's unsuccessful attack on the port in 1816, the city was always shown from the water or from the port.[5] Thus, as part of its own tradition of representation, Algiers was always seen from a distance, from the perspective of a naval invader. In contrast, Langlois' panorama provided a view of Algiers from the citadel atop the city and therefore had the theatrical charm of unveiling an exotic and unknown space to the French viewer.[6]

This spectacular effect resulted in a certain popularization of the Algerian landscape. Langlois' *Panorama of Algiers* added to the aura and exoticism of the place and helped foster an interest in the recent conquest and the continuing occupation. Since the receipts for this spectacle totaled over 68,000 francs, it clearly drew a significant crowd over the course of its exhibition (March 1833–November 1834).[7] Its purpose, originally explicated in a letter to the Minister of Commerce and Public Works requesting financial support, was the valorization of Algiers as a site of French military glory. Langlois described the seizure of Algiers as a "military expedition no less glorious to France than the naval combat of Navarin [the subject of his first panorama of 1831]."[8] The officer/artist wanted to make money with this project, but he wanted to do so by inspiring patriotic sentiment and making the city of Algiers more accessible to a Parisian audience.

A panorama claims to represent another location in its entirety, allowing the viewer to experience the place represented. This metonymy is a standard convention: a single view of a landscape can stand in for all of the territory in and around Algiers. Such a metaphorical conversion, modeled on concepts of artistic representation, organizes the divergent and discrepant aspects of a place into a seamlessly unified landscape. This was an accepted illusion in the nineteenth century, just as theatrical performances (and action films) in our own era rely upon audience members to suspend their disbelief.

Nevertheless, this particular illusion had very real consequences. The landscape presented in the *Panorama of Algiers* functioned to make that space on the other side of the Mediterranean perceptible to French viewers. Here is a double signification of the term *landscape:* the *Panorama of Algiers* invents a colonial landscape—a template for the apprehension of exotic spaces—even while it operates as a painted landscape, an artistic representation.[9] To a certain degree, this is a function of the architectural structure of panorama rotundas. The viewer is positioned on a pedestal in the center of a large cylinder, looking through darkness at an enormous screen lit by windows or gaslights. Yet the kind of relationship between metropolitan viewer and distant, exotic location offered in the *Panorama of Algiers* is one that persists among wide-ranging depictions of Algeria in various media. This analysis makes a case for the connection between visual perception, apprehension of knowledge, and the application of colonial power through the example of the *Panorama of Algiers.* Langlois' representation of Algerian territory established visual terms for the colonial expropriation of the North African landscape in the French capital. The form of visual representation he produced and the means of its consumption in the metropole allowed for a fantastical acquisition of colonial territory by Parisian viewers. Metropolitan viewers of the panorama acquired a colonial landscape, a newly defined space that was visually formulated by a soldier/artist who employed a camera obscura to create a systematic and singular representation of the divergent spaces of Algiers.[10] Deborah Cherry has discussed a similar effect in her account of the Algerian landscape, in which she relies on Gayatri Spivak's notion of "worlding" the spaces of Algeria through visual depiction. Her treatment of the representation of the Algerian landscape in this period is compelling, but the hermeneutical aspect of Spivak's theory bypasses the social process of developing a systematic and singular representation of space, which is the subject of this chapter. The central concern here is: How does such a process work in the very specific historical context of France in 1833–34, when the *Panorama of Algiers* was visible in Paris and when the French government made official a policy of colonialism in the territory that would come to be known as Algeria?

The largest colonial issue between 1830 and 1870 was the difficulty of naturalizing Algeria to France. Unlike previous colonial ventures, the ambition behind France's colonization of Algeria was an expansion of French terrain across the Mediterranean. This process of "settler colonialism" was originally analyzed in France in the nineteenth century,[11] and Algeria served as the blueprint for French settler colonies. In fact, Algeria eventually became a part of France, originally during the Second Republic and more completely in the Third Republic. Though the goal of naturalization emerged over time, the successive challenges that absorbed France's energies in Algeria during this period—conquest, colonization, settlement, and naturalization—were focused on a qualitative transformation of the exotic and faraway country into a distant homeland of the French. In the most immediate sense, the Algerian *territory* was the foundation of the entire colonial project, and the process of colonizing that territory was central to the French administration. Colonization literally means, in this case, the activity of transforming the foreign countryside into a French landscape by developing agricultural production and delimiting certain lands as private property. In this metamorphosis of North Africa's terrain, artistic conventions played a crucial role. They functioned to translate a sometimes strange-looking location, to order it according to the codes of composition and spatial recession, allowing it to be apprehended by a French viewer as a landscape. The French conception of landscape—and the French artists who made Algerian landscapes—helped the French administration literally bind the territory of Algeria, undermining all other claims on and representations of that territory. Langlois' representation allowed French individuals to see the colony of Algeria as a prospective landscape and, though his depiction featured a historical scene, the panorama projected an Algeria of the future.

The *Panorama of Algiers*

After paying 2 F 50 and receiving your explanatory booklet, you enter the largest panorama rotunda in Paris (50 feet high and 123 feet in diameter) and proceed up a staircase to the first room.[12] *In this "chambre turque," you can experience the interior spaces enjoyed by the richest of Algerian inhabitants and lose yourself in the luxury of the Oriental decor. The artist has attempted to provide a complete illusion, painting the details of all of the colorful architectural decorations and even bringing back cushions once belonging to a Turkish ruler, the Bey of Titeri. As you leave this room, you pass through a hallway that is adorned with a trompe-l'oeil painting of the "Cour du divan" of the Casbah. This elaborately detailed courtyard was where the Dey of Algiers, the supreme ruler of the region, would hold court and dispense justice. Just behind one of the crenellated doorways reposed the Dey's harem, sheltered from the sun and from view. After contemplating this spectacle for a time, you ascend another staircase and arrive on a platform, seven meters off the ground, decorated to appear as a balcony on top of the Casbah, the citadel of the Turkish rulers that stood at the highest point in the city. As you peer out through the darkness, you can make out the landscape of Algiers, both the city and the surrounding bay and hills, in 360°. Of course, you know that the city is an illusion rendered in oil paint on an enormous canvas that was painted by a team of artists overseen by M. Langlois, the author of this panorama. The painting on the canvas itself is so detailed that, from this distance, you cannot make out a single brushstroke or sign of an artist's hand.*

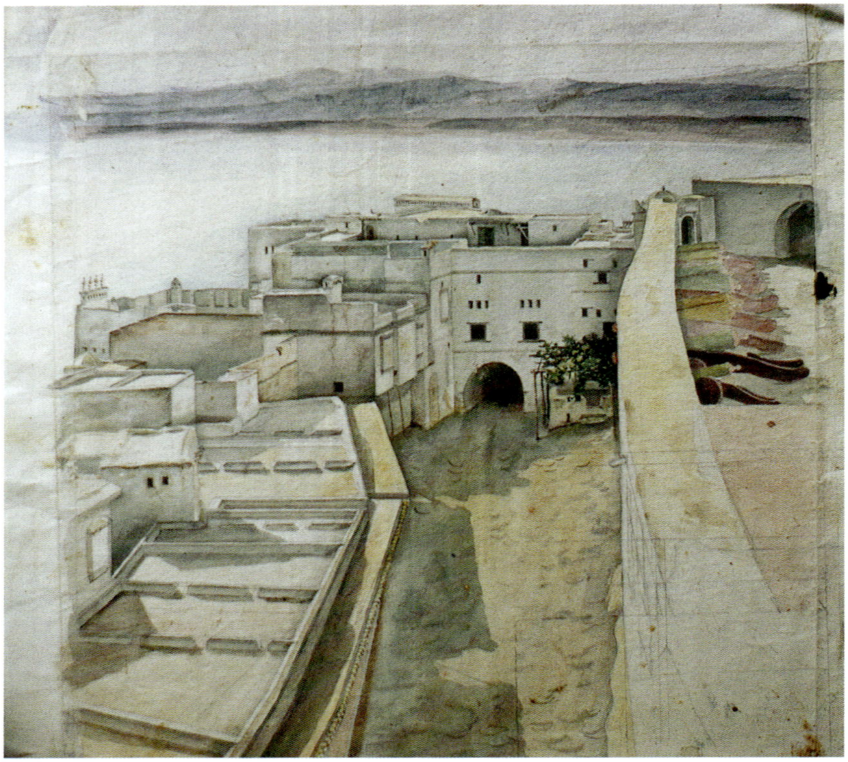

Figure 2.
Jean-Charles Langlois, untitled study for *Panorama of Algiers*, 1832. Watercolor and pencil on paper, approx. 48.8 × 33.5 cm. Collection of Dr. François Bureau, Caen, France. Photo by the author.

What is more, it is illuminated mysteriously, from above. You most likely do not know that the light is let in through a portal at the top of the rotunda and that it is refracted through a lens so that it shines equally on all parts of the canvas, but only on the canvas. The effect allows you to be duped into believing, if you stare long enough, that you are actually in Algiers. After the novelty of the illusion wears off and you begin to contemplate the image of Algiers more thoroughly, you may notice the city's complete absence of residents. You can see the traces of the French conquest—the gunboats firing from the harbor, the explosion of the Fort de l'Empereur in the distance—but that is the only sign of human activity in the image. You leave after marveling at the illusions made possible by new technology, feeling familiar at last with the city at the center of so much political debate in the last few years in France. Your eyes are fatigued and have trouble adjusting to the daylight as you walk out into Paris.

Algiers

Colonel Langlois, as he was most commonly known, was a battalion commander when he accompanied the Algerian campaign in 1830.[13] At the time, he was an aide-de-camp for Général Petit, who did not participate in the expedition, but Langlois was granted special permission to accompany the expedition and even covered his own costs to do so.[14] Having served in the army since the era of Napoléon, Langlois was a military man, but he had also received permission to study art in the studios of Gros, Girodet, and Horace Vernet during the Restoration.[15] Langlois did not have particular responsibilities in the Algerian campaign other than to make drawings representing the territory and the military events that took place in it. There is a large group of extant oil studies that Langlois made in Algeria,[16] but it is difficult to ascertain with certainty which studies were made at the time of the expedition of 1830 and which were made in 1832, when Langlois returned to Algiers specifically to prepare for his panorama project. In addition, there is a *carnet d'Alger* containing small sketches in pencil and charcoal and a couple of larger charcoal studies on brown paper in a private collection.[17] Finally, there are two sets of studies that connected to form an image of the city of Algiers in the round for the panorama (fig. 1).[18] Langlois created the studies with a camera obscura and later touched them up with watercolors (figs. 2–6). Since the *Panorama of Algiers* was destroyed in order to paint the artist's next panorama project on the same canvas,[19] these studies are the only visual materials from which to ascertain the appearance of the panorama (fig. 7).[20]

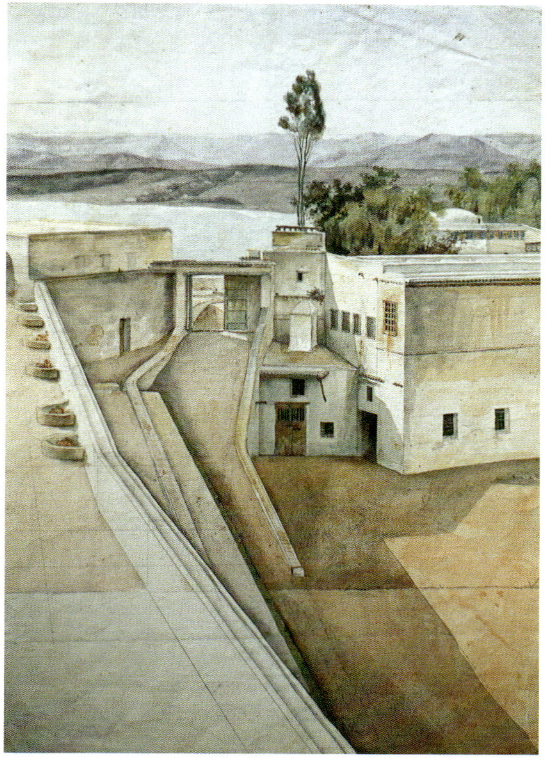

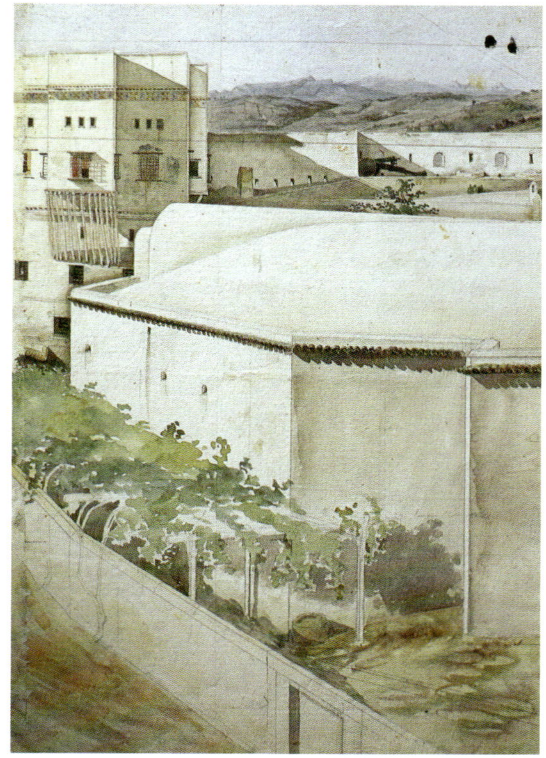

Figure 3.
Jean-Charles Langlois, untitled study for *Panorama of Algiers*, 1832. Watercolor and pencil on paper, approx. 48.8 × 33.5 cm. Collection of Dr. François Bureau, Caen, France. Photo by the author.

Figure 4.
Jean-Charles Langlois, untitled study for *Panorama of Algiers*, 1832. Watercolor and pencil on paper, approx. 48.8 × 33.5 cm. Collection of Dr. François Bureau, Caen, France. Photo by the author.

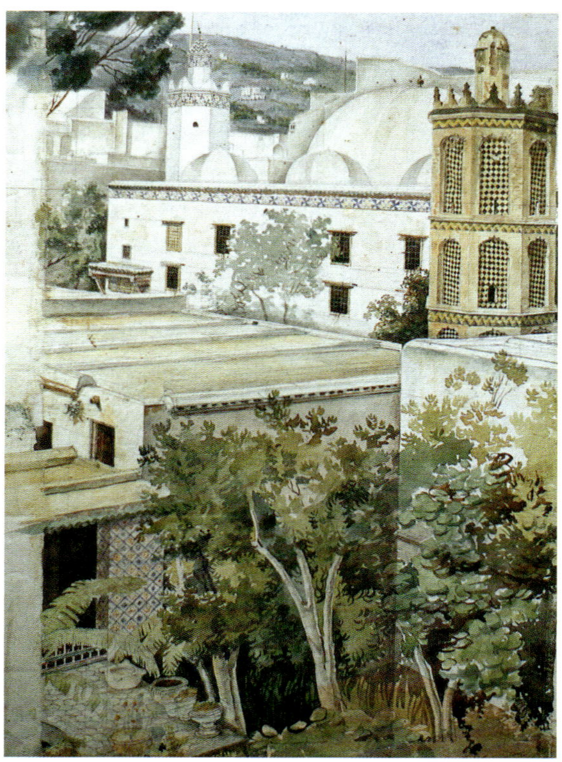

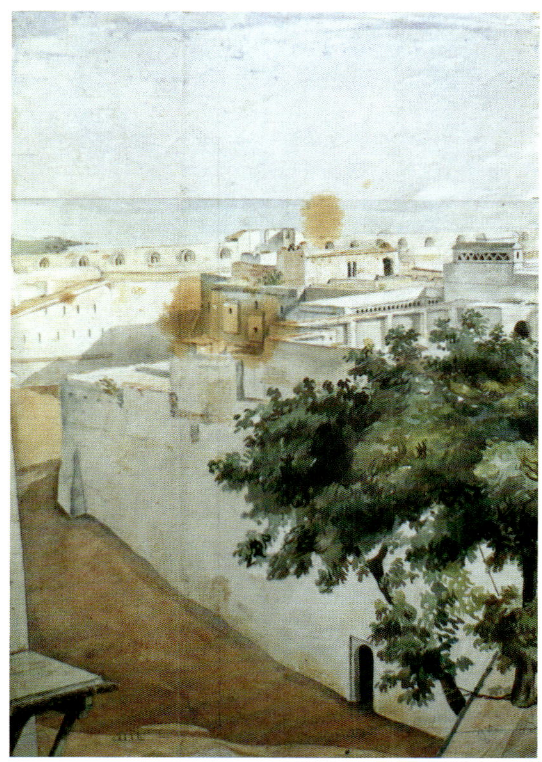

Figure 5.
Jean-Charles Langlois, untitled study for *Panorama of Algiers*, 1832. Watercolor and pencil on paper, approx. 48.8 × 33.5 cm. Collection of Dr. François Bureau, Caen, France. Photo by the author.

Figure 6.
Jean-Charles Langlois, untitled study for *Panorama of Algiers*, 1832. Watercolor and pencil on paper, approx. 48.8 × 33.5 cm. Collection of Dr. François Bureau, Caen, France. Photo by the author.

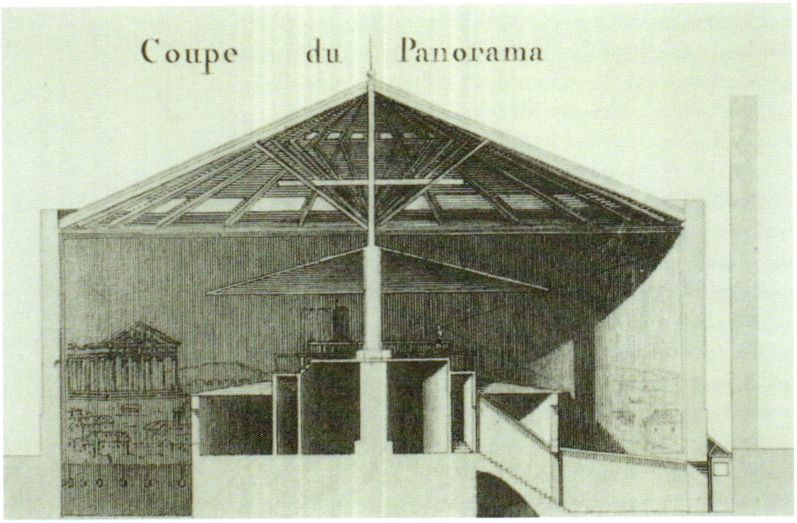

Figure 7.
Unknown artist, "Coupe du Panorama." Cross section of Pierre Provost's third panorama rotunda, built in 1816 on the Boulevard des Capucines, Paris. From A. D. Orgiazzi and J.-A. Kaufmann, *Architechtonographie des Theatres* (Paris, 1837–40).

Because there are no primary materials, such as letters or personal journals, the images the artist produced in Algeria are the only remaining evidence of his experience there. One difficulty with the Algerian sketches is that Langlois annotated only a few of them, and thus it is often difficult to tell exactly what he was rendering and when.[21] Even the *carnet d'Alger* has images pasted in it that were made on his first and second visits,[22] so the sketchbooks cannot reliably establish some coherent narrative of Langlois' journeys.

Langlois produced a number of views, both within and outside of the city, that do not correspond to any part of the panorama. These works represent a wide variety of spaces. Some views and street scenes feature genre elements (fig. 8), popular as picturesque imagery of the period. There are also meticulously studied architectural views (fig. 9) as well as rapidly executed renderings of city spaces that would soon be forever altered by the needs of the French administration (fig. 10). Moreover, the works demonstrate multiple representational methods. The picturesque imagery has a Romantic sensibility, corresponding to the landscapes of Paul Huet,[23] whereas an architectural study like *Djamaa el-Djedid, the Battery of Dey Hussein* (1830–32; fig. 9) is similar to the views of monuments featured in Baron Taylor's *Voyages pittoresques et romantiques dans l'ancienne France* (*Picturesque and Romantic Voyages in Old France*).[24] Interior scenes such as *Interior Courtyard of the Palace of the Dey in the Citadel, Algiers* (1830–32; fig. 11) are rendered with the most painstaking precision, though not precisely enough to have been made with the aid of a camera obscura. There are romantic flourishes, dappled brushstrokes, and textured surfaces here, as well as precise geometric renderings and claustrophobic linear compositions. And that is only to consider the oil studies. The artist also experimented with drawings in pencil and charcoal (fig. 12), not to mention the perspective studies rendered in pencil and then overlain with watercolor (figs. 2–6).

It is essential to differentiate between two categories of representation in Langlois' Algerian studies. Marie-Paule Petit's exhaustive analysis of Langlois' preparation for the panorama demonstrates how Langlois must have formulated his panorama studies from a variety of points of view around the Casbah, the building that crowned the city of Algiers. While beautiful, the panorama studies are produced with the aid of a visual machine and, when synthesized into a view, they present a false and formulaic completeness designed to produce an illusion of viewing a real space in the round. In brief, the studies themselves are precise and illusionistic, in the most complete sense of the term.

In the foreground of the panorama studies, one can perceive the immediate vicinity of the Casbah; just beyond, the city appears to fall away, allowing a limited view of the hills outside the city and the Bay of Algiers. On the left side, the ramparts of the city can be seen, and a large private home sits atop a hill in the distance. Further to the left, a street leads down into the city. Looking more closely at individual drawings, one can appreciate such details as a line of cannons along the ramparts, the rooftop terraces of private dwellings below, and distinctively Moorish architectural features, such as arch-covered streets. In the distant background, purple hills rise up out of the calm waters of the bay and, on the other side, the hills behind Algiers form a ring around the city. Everything is illuminated in an even, bright Mediterranean light.

The photographic precision of the line drawing is complemented by an accomplished and subtle handling of the watercolor technique. Taken as a whole, this representation transmits an authority that is wholly uncharacteristic of early Orientalist painting. The viewer does not perceive an imaginary or fantastic rendering of the space of the Orient. Instead, the view appears to be based on careful observation and has the effect of making the city appear real, despite the lack of anecdotal elements that would animate it. The image is straightforward, unified, exquisitely crafted, without an angle out of place or a clash of misplaced color. It does not represent a real space, however, but a virtual one. Its lines are too carefully measured, and the city thus appears perfect and completely still, taking on the characteristics of an exquisite object. While this communicated a sense of veracity to viewers in the nineteenth century (see below), to a contemporary observer, its appearance is more reminiscent of digital animation than historical drawing styles.

The oil studies and the charcoal sketches Langlois made in Algeria could not appear more distinct, though he sometimes achieved great precision. The painted sketches show something, as opposed to everything. In a work such as *Souk es Semarin, Azzoun Gate* (1830–32; fig. 8), Langlois made a view from outside the east gate of Algiers, usually transcribed as Porte de Bab-Azoun. The conquering French army had entered the city through this gate, a busy market area where traveling merchants sold their wares. *Souk es Semarin, Azzoun Gate* was likely painted in the open air in one or two sessions and relies on a loose, evocative style buttressed by strong contrasts of light and dark to communicate the bustling atmosphere just outside the city. The figures, who are in motion and who likely would not have posed for the artist in any case, appear as fleeting, ghostlike figures passing through an indeterminate space. In this work, Moorish architecture is less identifiable, but the strong "Oriental" light and the figures' exotic costumes echo the conventions for rendering Oriental locations—conventions that were under development at this very moment by such artists as Alexandre-Gabriel Decamps, Adrien Dauzats, and Eugène Delacroix. While the panorama studies make Algiers appear fixed and permanent, this painting registers temporality through the visible brushstrokes that

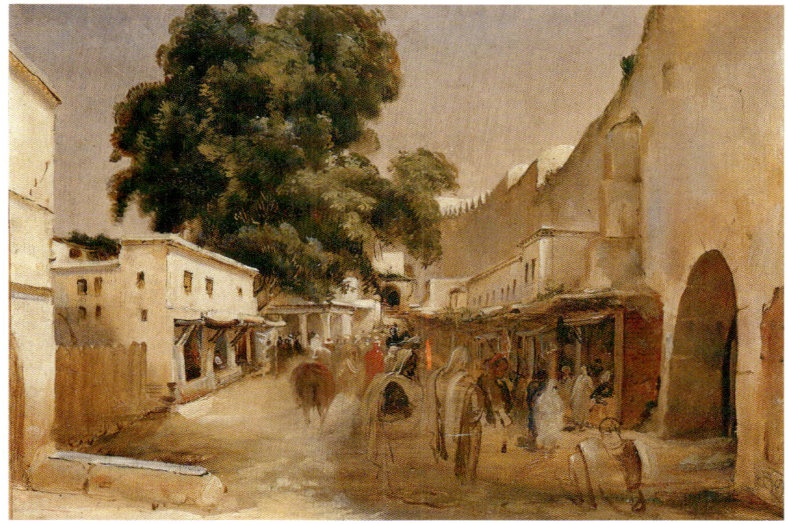

Figure 8.
Jean-Charles Langlois, *Souk es Semarin, Azzoun Gate,* 1830–32. Oil on paper mounted on canvas, 24 × 34 cm. Musée des Beaux-Arts, Caen, France (inv. 2005.1.91). Photo © Musée des Beaux-Arts de Caen (Martine Seyve).

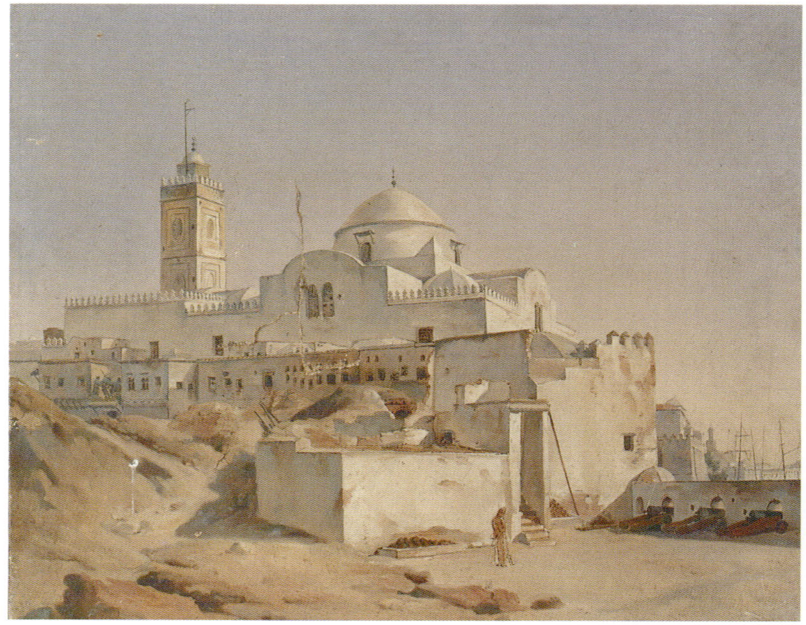

Figure 9.
Jean Charles Langlois, *Djamaa el-Djedid, the Battery of Dey Hussein,* 1830–32. Oil on paper mounted on canvas, 24 × 34 cm. Musée des Beaux-Arts, Caen, France (inv. 2005.1.97). Photo © Musée des Beaux-Arts de Caen (Martine Seyve).

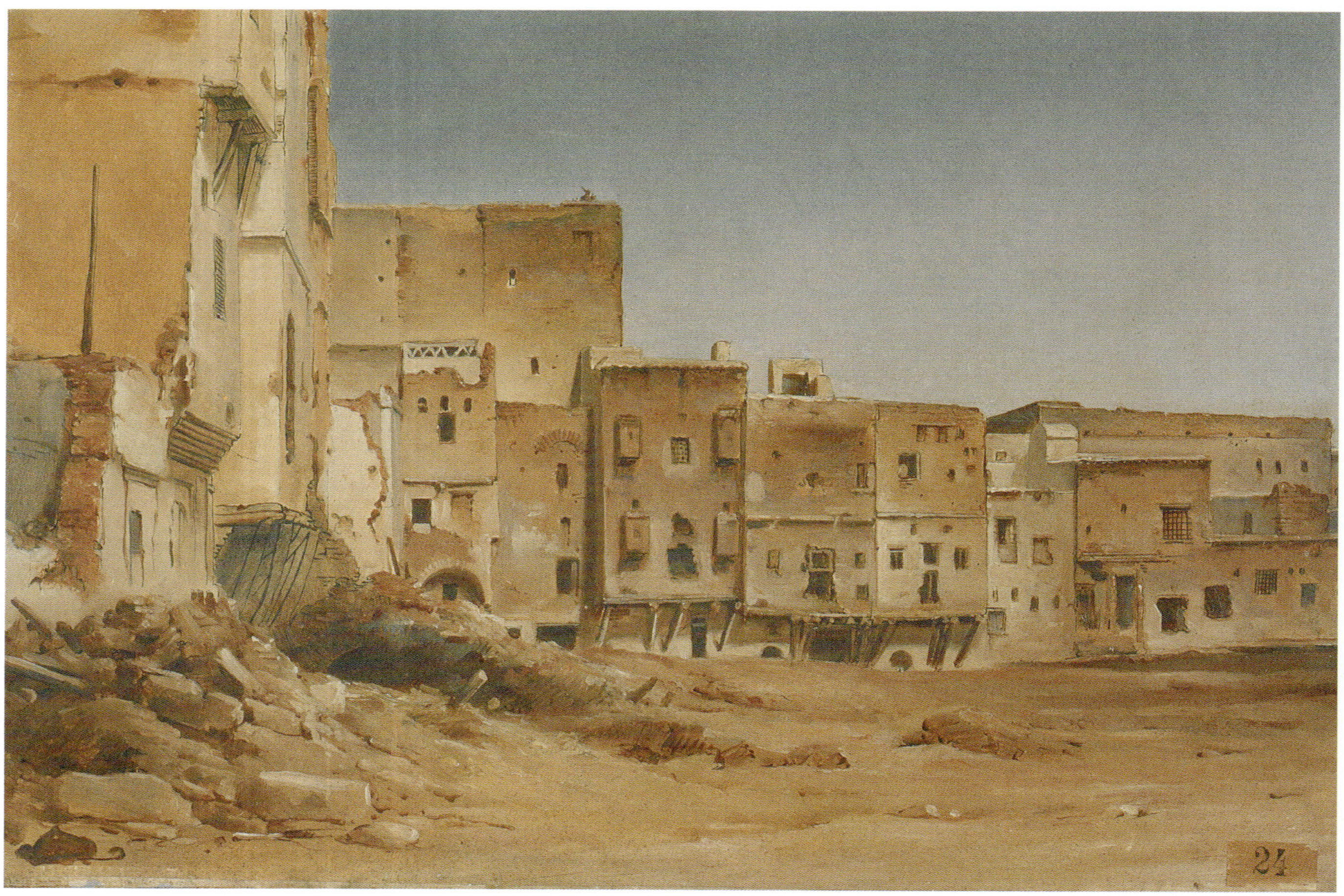

Figure 10.
Jean-Charles Langlois, *Demolitions for the Place des Armes, Algiers*, 1830. Oil on paper mounted on canvas, 35.5 × 52 cm. Musée des Beaux-Arts, Caen, France (inv. 2005.1.91). Photo © Musée des Beaux-Arts de Caen (Martine Seyve).

suggest the artist's process of making the work and through the figures' indeterminate contours, which make them appear in a state of flux.

Not only the figures were fugitive in Algiers in 1830. After the French conquest, the military began altering the city immediately to accommodate perceived administrative needs. First and foremost, streets had to be widened to allow for increased traffic and the passage of French military equipment, and many buildings were demolished in order to produce a large European-style square for the purposes of trade and large public gatherings. Langlois recorded this latter demolition with alacrity in the gritty *Demolitions for the Place des Armes, Algiers* in 1830 (fig. 10). This grey and brown study transmits in frank pictorial terms the French military's demolitions as well as the relative disrepair of this area of the city, visible in the cracked and chipped edifices of the buildings. Its stark visual terms constitute a levelheaded pictorial assessment of the French occupation and transformation of Algiers.[25]

The official destruction led even military artists to seize the opportunity to record Algiers' most significant architectural monuments. Though the picturesque tradition of illustration may have guided Langlois to these important buildings, the need to record them for posterity was a very real concern. Perhaps this concern led Langlois to produce his oil sketch of the *Interior Courtyard of the Palace of the Dey* (fig. 11) in a much more painstaking style. This painting renders the palace in almost faultless perspective and, unlike in the other two oil sketches, reading the specifics of the architectural detail is the artist's primary concern here. Gritty naturalism and pictorial immediacy give way to a process of recording a particular space. Though the palace of the Dey was ultimately spared destruction, Langlois sought to document its interior in this sharply focused and carefully detailed oil study.

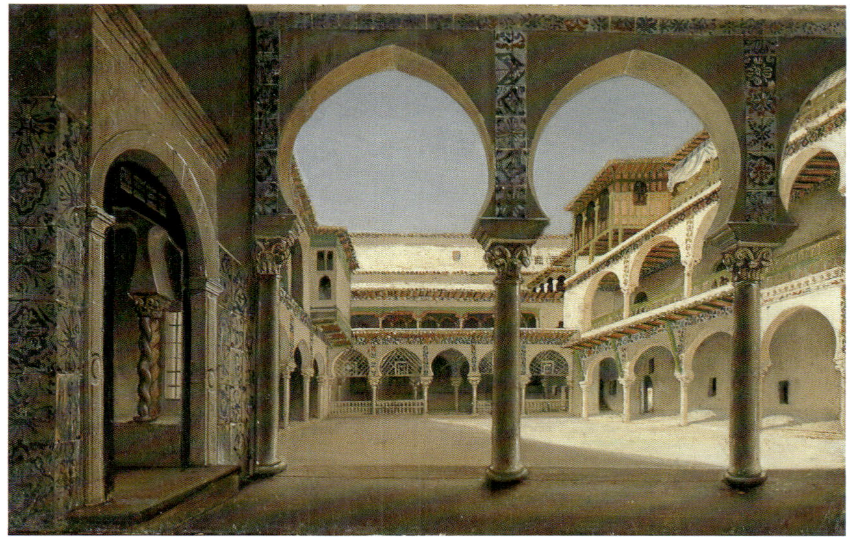

Figure 11.
Jean-Charles Langlois, *Interior Courtyard of the Palace of the Dey in the Citadel, Algiers,* 1830–32. Oil on paper mounted on canvas, 32.5 × 39 cm. Musée des Beaux-Arts, Caen, France (inv. 2005.1.94). Photo © Musée des Beaux-Arts de Caen (Martine Seyve).

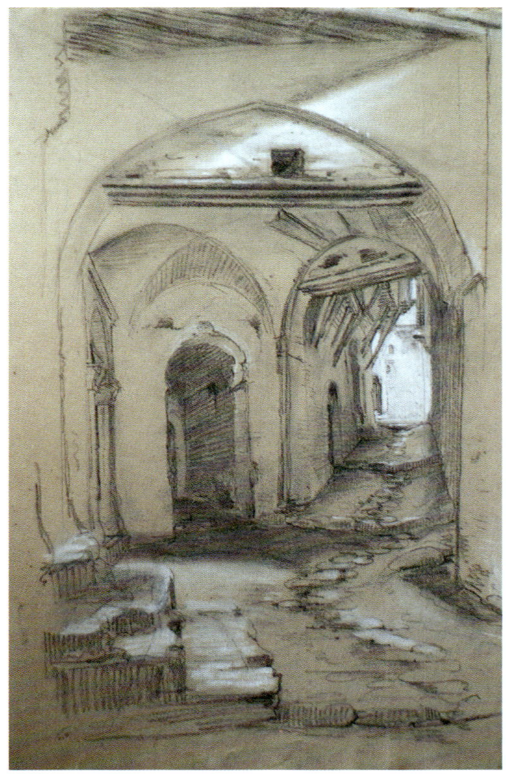

Figure 12.
Jean-Charles Langlois, untitled sketch of Algiers, 1830–32. Charcoal on paper, approx. 8 × 5 in. Collection of Dr. François Bureau, Caen, France. Photo by the author.

There is not a single way of seeing—much less a single mode of representation—that governs these works, so it seems inaccurate to describe the sketches as somehow leading to the panorama. With the exception of the studies produced with the aid of the camera obscura, the images Langlois recorded in paint, pencil, and charcoal (figs. 8–12) on his two journeys to Algiers are not studies for any particular work. Petit has described the panorama as some sort of *Gesamtkunstwerk* that drew upon all of the artist's faculties and preparatory studies, representing an extension of the artist's experiences.[26] I argue, though, that the studies must be divorced from the panorama because of the differences between the system of perception represented by the panorama studies and the ad hoc character of the others. The sketches Langlois produced in Algiers record the artist's particular experiences and artistic experimentation, whereas the panorama studies are finely crafted but ultimately programmatic.

The sketches Langlois produced in Algeria inform viewers today in ways that other forms of depiction (e.g., paintings or prints) cannot. If not fully achieved works, they are historical documents that record his shifting perceptions of an unfamiliar city. As French involvement in the region continued over the ensuing years, this space would become more familiar to Parisian viewers through repeated representations. It would be a mistake to consider Langlois' studies more sincere—or even more authentic—than depictions of Algiers achieved in France,[27] yet they demonstrate an inconsistency worth noting, especially when they are considered in relationship to the Algerian iconography generated in France in this period. Further, these studies were never reproduced or sold. They do remind the viewer that, no matter how codified and conventional the representations of Algeria that appeared in France were, the original contact this French artist had with Algiers was confusing and disjointed. Langlois' own perspective of Algiers was not formed from on high, as his panorama presented it. Rather, it resulted from his movement through a variety of divergent spaces in and around the city.

Langlois' Algerian sketches appear all the more unconventional when compared with sketches by other military artists who took part in the expedition. Granted, officers like Alexandre Genet and Ferdinand de Trelo did not have the benefit of academic training, so they would not have had an enlightened notion of the relationship of sketch to finished work of art that encouraged the imaginative use of an *étude* to compose a subject in a loose and fluid manner.[28] Further, these artists were responsible for providing accurate information to the military administration on the sites they traversed. Isabelle Bruller's work lucidly articulates the goals and successes of images produced by officers employed by the War Ministry. What may be surprising is how quotidian—not patriotic or didactic—their works appear. Works such as *View of the Bab Azoun Gate in Algiers* from 1830 (fig. 13), by Genet, or *Algiers: View from the Terrace of the Docks* from 1831 (fig. 14), by de Trelo, are direct, carefully studied pieces that allow their viewers to perceive the beauty of this distant port even while informing them of the topographical details of Algiers and its environs. More to the point, these drawings are views, offering images of landscapes that are composed and legible. They provide figures for scale, recession into depth, and open, expansive spaces. Though these artists exhibit their own personal styles, their differences are more difficult to establish than their similarities. The resulting works possess aspects of immediacy, as located, for example, in the dark-skinned figure who gazes directly at the artist in the Genet drawing or the man rowing the

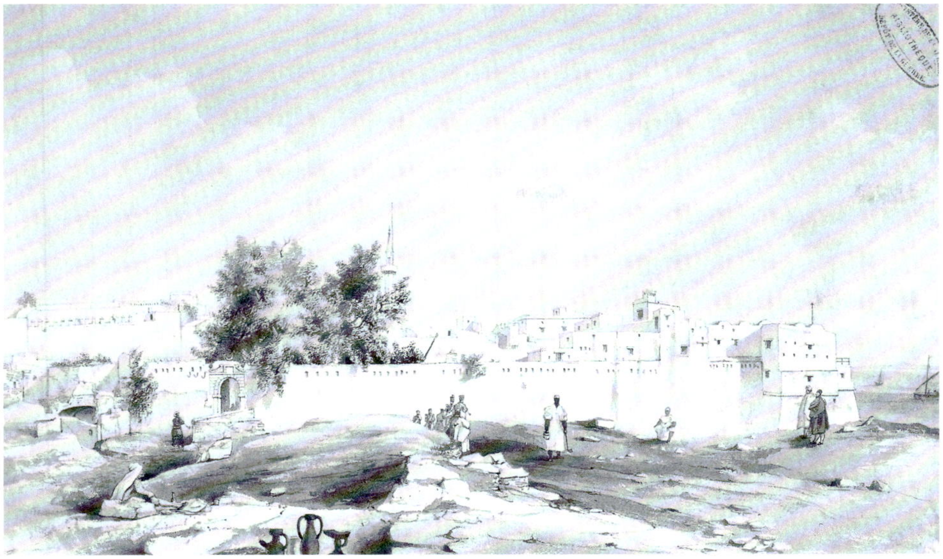

Figure 13.
Alexandre Genet, *View of the Bab Azoun Gate in Algiers,* 1830. Ink and pencil on paper, 48.5 × 29.6 cm. Dépôt de la Guerre, Service historique de l'armée de Terre, Vincennes, France (SH/D 144). © Service historique de l'armée de Terre.

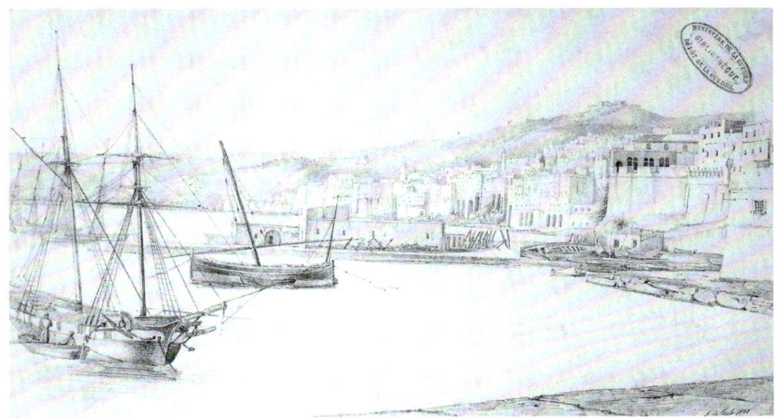

Figure 14.
Ferdinand de Trelo, *Algiers: View from the Terrace of the Docks,* 1831. Pencil on paper, 45 × 25 cm. Dépôt de la Guerre, Service historique de l'armée de Terre, Vincennes, France (SH/D 86). © Service historique de l'armée de Terre.

boat in the work by de Trelo. However, the predominant tendency in these studies is to establish the appearance of the location in a direct manner so that these images could be used as documents for the War Ministry.[29]

It is important to differentiate between the kinds of documents produced by Langlois and those produced by the officers of the État-major. Whereas Langlois recorded fleeting impressions and the transformation of the urban environment of Algiers, the ink drawings by Genet and de Trelo suggest permanence. A comparison of Langlois' *Souk es Semarin, Azzoun Gate* (fig. 8) and Genet's *View of the Bab Azoun Gate in Algiers* (fig. 13) is instructive. Both artists represented the same location, but their works feature very different aspects of that location. As discussed above, Langlois employed a pictorial vernacular of Romantic Orientalism, as is evidenced, for example, in the early work of Decamps (fig. 15). The rapidly brushed passages of paint in Langlois' rendering record the scene as well as the artist's making of it, but Genet's style tends to erase the artistic process. Langlois opted to make an image of the road into town lined with mercantile establishments, whereas Genet turned toward the water, and his picture shows just a handful of figures milling about. While Langlois provided an image of a chaotic marketplace, Genet offered a serene topographical view. It seems that the two views could not actually represent the same place. Yet the earthenware in the foreground of the Genet drawing does signify the presence of a mar-

Figure 15. Alexandre-Gabriel Decamps, *Oriental Night Scene*, c. 1836. Oil on canvas, 60.5 × 51.3 cm (23 13/16 × 20 3/16 in.). John J. Johnson Collection, Philadelphia Museum of Art, cat. 966.

ketplace, which lies mostly outside this view. In the works of Genet and de Trelo, Algiers is not a bustling city: like the Algiers of the panorama studies, it is fixed and static.

The specific documentary nature of Genet's and de Trelo's sketches would seem to result from the artists' mission and training, but another source for this imagery can be found in the *Atlas d'Alger,* an ambitious work produced by the War Ministry that was distributed to the officers participating in the expedition. The *Atlas* was actually the illustrated companion to a 216-page work on the state of Algiers that brought together all of the historical,

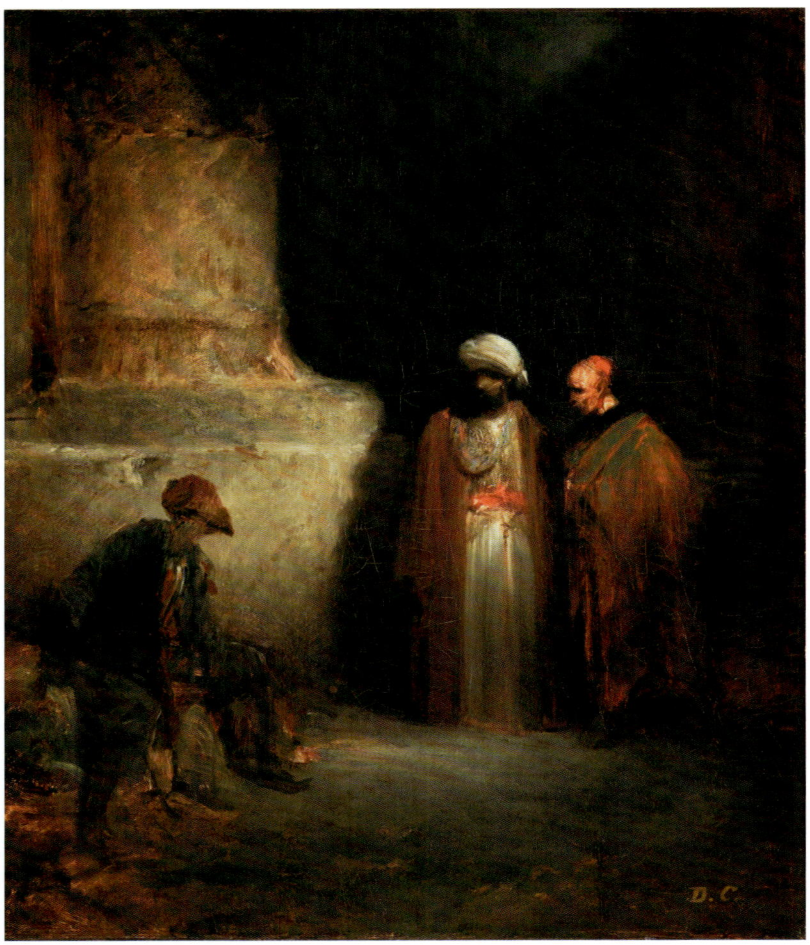

statistical, and topographical information that could be of possible use to the conquering army.[30] The *Atlas* itself comprised six maps and eleven illustrations. The maps were made from the information provided by Captain Boutin, whom Napoléon sent to study Algiers in 1808. The prints are not attributed to any artist, though the images indicate that they were printed at E. Ardit, rue Vivienne, n° 2. The text clarifies that they were provided by the Ministry of Foreign Affairs, which received them from the collection of a certain Colonel Rottiers, who was in the service of the Dutch king.[31]

The mysterious origin of these images, connected to the cloak-and-dagger world of international intelligence and foreign affairs, is titillating, but the illustrations themselves are rather humdrum. They all project a sense of lifelessness, a feeling of being outside the realm of time and the process of change. The anonymous artist clearly wanted to produce factual illustrations, not artistic compositions, though he (I must assume) did regulate his depictions according to standard artistic formulae. Two useful examples are n° 5, "View of the environs of the Fort de l'Empereur" (fig. 16) and n° 7, "Interior of a house in the vicinity of Algiers" (fig. 17). The first of these is a landscape picture stiffly modeled after an academic prototype. In the foreground, a *repoussoir* tree stands on the right, providing a vertical element to this otherwise horizontal composition; on the left, an indigenous figure carries a typical shepherd's staff. In the middle and background, two large buildings succinctly establish distance through scale. (Presumably, one is the fort.) Such a composition could be considered an exemplar of many of the techniques advocated in the era's instructional treatises on landscape representation.[32] The picture conforms to an established practice in which elements perceived in nature are systematically ordered into a comprehensible land-

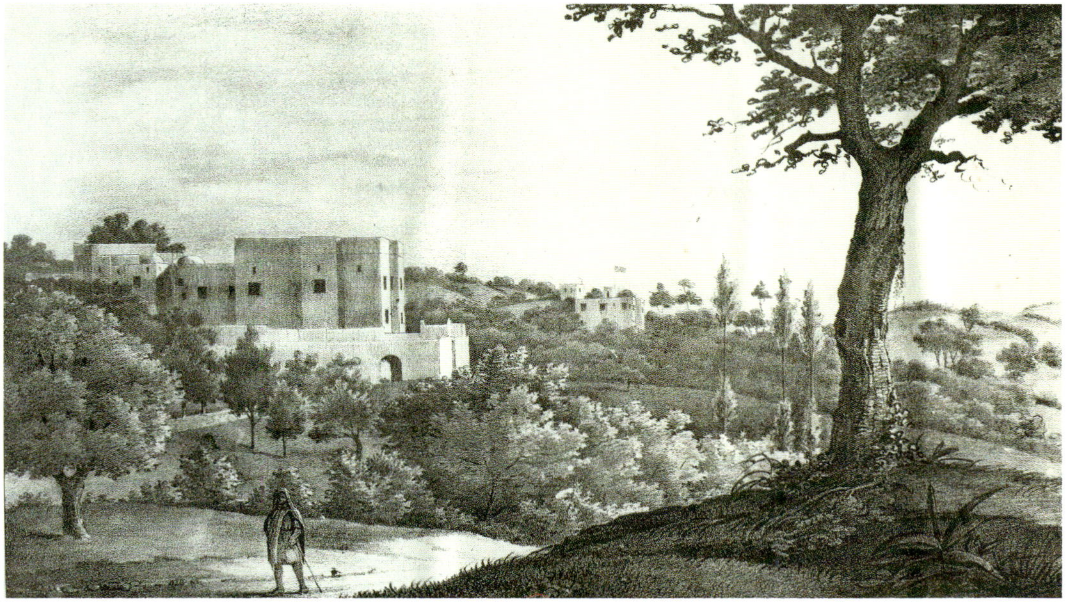

Figure 16.
Anonymous, *Atlas d'Alger*, n° 5, "View of the environs of the Fort de l'Empereur." From *Aperçu historique, statistique et topographique sur l'état d'Alger, à l'usage de l'armée expéditionnaire d'Afrique* (Paris: Ch. Piquet, 1830). Bibliothèque nationale de France, Département des Estampes et de la photographie.

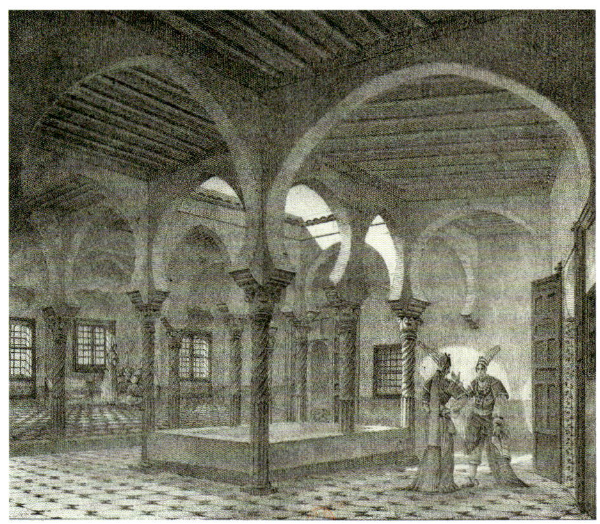

Figure 17.
Anonymous, *Atlas d'Alger*, n° 7, "Interior of a house in the vicinity of Algiers." From *Aperçu historique, statistique et topographique sur l'état d'Alger, à l'usage de l'armée expéditionnaire d'Afrique* (Paris: Ch. Piquet, 1830). Bibliothèque nationale de France, Département des Estampes et de la photographie.

scape. Similarly, the *Atlas d'Alger* divides *interior* space into geometric fragments in an attempt to make elaborate and intricately detailed architectural spaces legible for the viewer. In both cases, these stiff figures operate as props to establish the meaning of the setting through their activities—a shepherd wandering, women conversing—while they add formal compositional balance and scale to the pictures.

In fact, they provide no useful military information (such as the best approach to this fort). Contrary to later Orientalist imagery, these images normalize, rather than exoticize, the city and the surrounding landscape. The viewer thus perceives exotic architecture, costumes, and even flora, but—those differences aside—the composition of the images makes Algerian spaces appear recognizable and traversable.

The images from the *Atlas d'Alger* were supplied to the French officers in the expedition by the military administration. They are thus uniquely valuable. Providing illustrations of the territory to be conquered was not a common strategy, and these illustrations stand as an early example of the French government's projecting a very specific image of Algiers. The needs of the campaign would seem to dictate that such images should make Algiers and its environs appear different but recognizable, because the purpose of the *Atlas* was to familiarize French officers with Algiers. As such, the lithographs operate in tandem with other, more empirical representations of the place, such as maps and flow charts. The images they provide, no matter how anecdotal or artificially composed, were deemed by the author(s) of the *Aperçu historique* to be crucial evidence recorded on site. Such pictures authenticated the text, which was composed in France from secondary sources.[33] Like the lithographs in the *Atlas d'Alger,* Langlois' Algerian panorama offered viewers an illusion of intimacy and prepared them for a sustained engagement with the region.

Paris

While critics of Langlois' panorama expressed a wide variety of views concerning the politics of colonialism in Algiers,[34] they all maintained that the truth was delivered in the *Panorama of Algiers.* What they considered the truth to be is the burning question. By surveying contemporary criticism of the panorama, it is possible to connect an emergent colonial ideology in 1833–34 with the perception of landscape—and the assumptions viewers held about the experience of truth in the realm of visual experience.[35]

As Edward Said has shown, Orientalist tropes date back at least as far as Montesquieu's *Persian Letters* and were greatly reinforced by the representations of Napoléon's Egyptian campaign of 1798–99 and the *Description d'Égypte* (Description of Egypt), which was the most lasting accomplishment of that botched military adventure. Such ideas about the Orient and its inhabitants were applied to the *Panorama of Algiers,* despite its lack of figures. A contemporary reviewer of the panorama declared: "Oh! It is indeed the Orient there with its courage and its mournful resignation, impassive before the *simoun* of European civilization."[36] Despite the factual, spatial presentation of visual material it offered, the panorama was nonetheless inflected by the exoticism of the reconstructed palace interior (the *chambre turque*) and the associations that Orientalism carried with it ("courage," "mournful resignation").[37]

Contemporary remarks about the panorama also make clear that this view of Algiers dispelled facile associations with an imaginary European Orient even while it made use of them. Understanding this place to be an Oriental city would have allowed viewers access to it through the network of Orientalist texts in France. However, the *Panorama of Algiers* undermined such associations through its quasi-scientific visual rhetoric. In this case, the practice of dispelling false associations—an unveiling of the exotic city—sustained the particular illusion of visual access provided here.

Here is another critic:

> The very name of Algiers evokes a thousand distinct sentiments within us; seeing it, one sensation dominates all the others, it is surprise, astonishment. Following the descriptions of historians, of geographers, of travelers, you could have formed an idea of Algiers, created in your imagination an image of this place; before the work of M. Langlois, or rather in the city of Algiers, all these vague and imaginary creations evaporate; here, all is true, all is exact, all exists, everything lives its most real life.[38]

Note the transparency attributed to this pictorial representation as opposed to the images conjured up by texts—even firsthand accounts—that purported to represent Algiers. Even more striking is the way in which the *Panorama of Algiers* is described as vanquishing the fantasies of the city that have formed in the minds of the literate public. According to this critic, Langlois' depiction of Algiers is not even a representation; it is the presentation of exact truth, identical to the experience of the city itself.

This opinion, and others that concurred with it, demonstrates the ideological character of the image projected in the *Panorama of Algiers*. In this visual spectacle, particularities are subsumed by a totalizing, utopian view of the territory under French possession. Whereas the textual and artistic responses to Algiers had provided fragmentary images of the location (and had stressed the activities of the French military), Langlois' panorama provided a view of the entire city from the balcony of the citadel that lorded over it, a vantage point that accentuated the illusion of complete visual access. This perspective corresponds to the domination of a territory, a position uniquely available to a conquering power.[39]

The perception of truth in this context led to an idea of access—access based on visual knowledge. An anonymous critic in *L'Artiste* stated that thanks to Langlois, "we are familiar with the physiognomy of the African soil and the new French city, as if we had traversed the Mediterranean."[40] For this observer, having seen the *Panorama of Algiers* meant having access to that distant location even while in Paris, because the viewer who saw the panorama knew the lay of the North African land and the disposition of the spaces of the city.

This effect is described in one of the first writings to address panoramas, E. F. A. M. Miel's *Essai sur les beaux-arts* . . . of 1817. In this work, the author described Pierre Prévost's *Panorama of London* (*Panorama de Londres*) and remarked on its veracity and its scope. He wrote: "If I said: Whoever has seen the *Panorama of London* has been to London, I could be accused of exaggeration; but I would only be correct in saying: Whoever has seen the *Panorama of London* would be able to orient himself in London."[41] It would be an exaggeration to say that the viewer of the *Panorama of Algiers* had been to Algeria, but any viewer would be provided with an unprecedented visual access to the city and its spaces. Visual apprehension of Algiers in the metropole complements the military domination of that distant city that Langlois had witnessed and recorded.

There is an implicit transformation of African soil to French city as well. The passage from *L'Artiste* juxtaposes the two: "we are familiar with the physiognomy of the African soil and the new French city." The wording of the passage illuminates the way in which the "new" French city is laid on top of the physiognomy of the African territory, as if the French city had been planted in African soil. The material transformation of the city is echoed by a perceptual transformation of Algiers as a result of its transportation back to Paris. What was once a distant and exotic city whose appearance was left to the imagination became an accessible and traversable landscape. The perceptual transformation of Langlois' sketches into the panorama mirrors the process of bringing the conquered city back to France as a representation. The conquered city's discrete, disjunctive spaces, recorded in the sketches, were discarded and replaced by a methodically composed total vision of Algiers, made accessible in Paris for the viewer's edification and consumption. Algiers becomes French both by being brought back to France and by being represented as comprehensible for French viewers.

Critics of the *Panorama of Algiers* did analyze its artistic character, employing such notions as aerial perspective, use of shadows, and handling of materials. The praise is practically unanimous: the combination of effects added up to a verity that allowed the viewer to be transported to the distant port. The implication of a transparent representation of Algiers, when broken down into artistic terms, is the result of a careful use of pictorial techniques in order to achieve a faultless illusionism. The critic from *Le Moniteur Universel* typifies this perspective. He described Langlois' handling of materials as frank and firm and suggested that his rendering of details in the foreground left nothing to be desired. He further praised the artist's admirable resolution of the aerial perspective in this work, especially since the landscape of Africa has a drier nature, one distinct from the misty distances found in France. The anonymous critic also admired the geometric order of the work by which the viewer could make sense of distances without the presence of contrasting colors or solid shadows.[42] Evaluating these critical remarks leads to the conclusion that the conventions proper to landscape painting allowed the panorama to represent spaces to its viewers. For a viewer trained to look at landscape paintings, a panorama would need to provide similar spatial illusions in order to be read as a representation of the natural world. These conventions were undoubtedly employed to make sense of the place for the French viewer and, because Langlois had had academic training, he would have been instructed in the proper use of those conventions. While such criticism seems accurate based on the known studies for the panorama, it fails to address what is distinct about a panorama—what separates the panorama from a Salon painting both as a picture and in the way it could be perceived.[43]

However, there are two critics who help illuminate the distinct nature of panoramas. The first is Eusèbe de Salle, who made explicit comparisons between the *Panorama of Algiers* and history painting. The second, reviewing the panorama for *La France Nouvelle,* addressed the distinct problems of panoramic representation in depth.[44] Describing the *Panorama of Algiers,* Salle wrote: "It appears to me that M. Langlois has pushed the genre of the panorama, by not wanting to create a trompe-l'oeil effect exclusively. He has raised it to the rank of *grande peinture,* by idealizing and embellishing reality."[45] Salle had spent some time in Algiers. He was a translator connected to the military administration, and so it is not surprising to find that, unlike other critics, he did not take the panorama as the representation of truth based on external reality. He compared the representation with his own impressions and found that it *exceeded* the natural appearance of the city: Langlois had "embellished" and even "idealized" reality in order to achieve *grande peinture.*[46] Salle's impression of the embellishments, connected as they are to Langlois' heightened artistic ambition, led him to question the lack of action or drama that would be suitable for *grande peinture.* Pushing the limitations of his own genre, the critic specifically requests the addition of a portrait of Hussein-Pacha, looking out at the assault of the Fort de l'Empereur, surrounded by his principal officers. And Salle goes further. In this moment of crisis, would not the harem's discipline be relaxed? Why not have an odalisque or two running about half-naked?[47]

Salle takes the assumption that the panorama addresses a certain moment quite seriously. If this is the moment of the attack, then why does the city appear unpopulated? Salle's desire to temporalize the *Panorama of Algiers* introduces another issue, namely, his disappointment at the lack of anecdotal interest in the panorama. The kinds of drama Salle suggests—passive autocrats and crazed, half-naked odalisques—are intended to provide a sense of truth of the moment. If these proposals were realized, they would place Langlois' view of Algiers within the realm of Oriental constructions espoused by Salon paintings and poetic literature. From Salle's criticisms, one can derive some sense of the panorama's distinctiveness. While it purported to represent a moment, it actually presented an inert image of a place. It sacrificed a sense of the drama of the campaign but allowed for a general perception of veracity, because the lack of anecdotal detail also circumvented imaginary constructions of the Orient.

Notably, in December 1833, Langlois closed down the panorama in order to make changes. The most significant alteration he made was to populate the panorama very slightly; he inserted an image of Hussein-Pacha with his officers. (There were no odalisques added, however.) Langlois also changed the trompe-l'oeil image of an empty courtyard that viewers passed in order to reach the platform. He replaced the courtyard with a crowded representation of a market street.[48] In this way, he retained the unembellished, permanent quality of the panoramic image of the city while providing his spectators with more anecdotal flavor. These changes were meant to increase interest and revenues—this panorama was not as financially successful as his last had been[49]—but clearly Langlois wanted to retain the truth claims of the panoramic view and therefore did not add more than a handful of figures to his image of Algiers.

If Salle commented on the advisability of making the *Panorama of Algiers* more like a Salon painting, the critic in *La France Nouvelle* clearly asserted the limitations of panoramic representations, addressing the way in which panoramas diverged from paintings. He was the only critic to note, for example, that the walls of the Casbah, while rendered according to the right principle, obscured two-thirds of the city itself. And unlike other critics, he faulted the rendering of trees and plants in the foreground for bringing painting to mind (figs. 5–6). He declared that in a *tableau,* the eye searches for art and painting itself. The viewer of a panorama seeks nature—that is, a sense of reality. For this reason, the anonymous commentator asserted, panoramas are most successful when, paradoxically, they present the world as inert: "The unfortunate condition of panoramas, which fixes their limits, is that in order to give an idea of living nature, one is constrained to reduce the location to the appearance of a still-life."[50] This sleight of hand—the transformation of still life into living nature—can only be achieved in a carefully planned environment, by establishing a very particular relationship of viewer and work through the unique structure of the panorama rotunda.

The reality effect that the critics found in Langlois' representation was, then, the result of numerous characteristics. Langlois sidestepped the accepted fictions of Orientalist tropes by including exotic trappings in his panorama, but no figures. The palpable sense of truth expressed by these critics was also bound up with the presentation of a total view, a complete representation of the distant city within the terms and conventions of French landscape representation. By presenting Algiers as a landscape, the panorama conformed to French viewers' accepted means of perceiving space. This complete, systematic means of perception made the panorama convincing. However, the landscape conventions typically employed on the limited flat surface of a painting operate differently in the context of a panorama. The structure of the panorama and the view it offers are more comprehensive and captivating than a two-dimensional image could ever be.

Art critics who discussed the panorama in the terms of painting presupposed a similarity between a viewer of paintings and a viewer of panoramas, but the structure of the panorama creates a distinct kind of viewer. Seeking to imitate the effects of nature, a panorama surrounds its viewer with an image of the location it purports to represent. This image may be rendered in paint on canvas, but its enormous scale and dramatic lighting alter the conditions of the viewer's apprehension and make the image appear to exist quite apart from its architectural support. The image projected in a panorama is rendered in 360 degrees, allowing the viewer to take it all in from a central point—in this case, the platform that simulates a balcony. As François Robichon has shown, it is up to the viewer to unify the numerous partial views into a complete vision, providing the illusion of totality.[51] Petit has pointed out that the image of Algiers that Langlois projected in the *Panorama of Algiers* was itself formulated out of images rendered with a camera obscura from six different points, at three distinct levels, on the Casbah of Algiers.[52]

Yet while these characteristics seek to re-create vision in the world, the structure of the panorama actually posits an illusory centrality of the viewer in relation to that world. The panorama's recreation of Algiers was ideological, asserting French control over Algiers, because the metropolitan viewers who perceived the panorama apprehended the central position of French control as a part of the panorama's reality effect. French domination, represented by the ability of a French artist/soldier to provide this view to contemporary Parisians, was built into the means of apprehending this represented location as authentic or true. The experience of colonial domination comes home to the viewer in the *Panorama of Algiers* because it is the spectator who occupies the central position within the panorama's representational mechanism.

The viewer's primacy was based on two interlocking illusions: the fictional point of view that offered the spectator a commanding view of the territory represented, and the lifeless appearance of the city that made it appear as an object. Whereas panoramas were designed to provide a complete illusion of nature, the *Panorama of Algiers* presented an illusion of the city of Algiers outside of history and the numerous transformations that the French occupation had already brought. The illusion of space without history—and a city without inhabitants—allowed viewers to achieve a primacy in relation to Algiers, which became an empty screen for the spectator's projections.

The *Panorama of Algiers* in many ways set the stage for future representations of the Algerian landscape in France. This is not the case merely because it shared certain characteristics with landscape representation. In fact, the *Panorama of Algiers* introduced a whole new set of concerns to the depiction of the colonial landscape because of the unique ways in which it employed the conventions of landscape representation. In the panorama, we do not simply perceive the first translation of the discrete spaces of Algeria as a cohesive landscape in France. Apprehending space as landscape is raised to the level of spectacle and, as such, circumscribes the viewer as a subject even while offering the colonial space as an object for consumption and, by extension, for intimacy and for domination.

Yet it may be useful to approach the facile acceptance voiced by most critics with some skepticism. This leads to a deeper inquiry into the theme of consumption. How was the colonial landscape consumed by the viewers of the *Panorama of Algiers,* and how did it transform those viewers?

Consuming Colonial Places

As Walter Benjamin has demonstrated, the consumer culture that emerged in nineteenth-century Paris was unprecedented in scope and effect.[53] The status of the *Panorama of Algiers* in 1833–34—as a form of popular entertainment—is crucial to any analysis of its consumption. Langlois was an artist who exhibited regularly at the Salon in this period, but his panorama was literally and figuratively located in the domain of the arcades, the precursor of the modern shopping mall. Given this situation, it will be useful to explore the similarity between the viewer of a panorama and the consumer of the arcades. By considering these two historical developments in conjunction, I aim to demonstrate how both the arcades and the *Panorama of Algiers* engendered an interest in extending the self through the acquisition of desirable objects. The panorama's circuitry of representation and desire, when wired through the abstraction of landscape, produced a prospective Algerian colony and helped foster the ever-increasing acquisition of North African territory by the French in the ensuing years.

The sociologist John Urry has written, "There are complex interdependencies between consuming goods, services and places, and what links them together are the patterns of social life organised in and though particular places. Such patterns are significantly commodified but there is generally a complex mixing of both commodification and collective enthusiasm."[54] Urry's analysis of tourism in the contemporary world can help us understand the interrelations of consumption, location, and colonialism in the nineteenth century. Indeed, the "patterns of social life" in Paris in 1833 deserve to be considered in an analysis of a form of popular entertainment presented in that city. As the advertisement that begins this chapter attempts to demonstrate, the *Panorama of Algiers* was but one consumable experience to be had in Paris for those with money to spend. In Urry's language, the panorama represents one piece of a broad historical pattern of consumption of faraway lands that emerged in the early part of the nineteenth century and, as such, is a result of a mixing of "commodification and collective enthusiasm." Yet the colonial aspect of Langlois' spectacle provides a twist to this now well-rehearsed narrative of the metropolitan consumption of distant locales.

Before the *Panorama of Algiers* closed its doors in November 1834, the Chamber of Deputies had debated the fate of the French-occupied territory in North Africa, and the decree of 22 July 1834 instituted military colonization in Algiers.[55] Though the French had not known it in 1830, the occupation of Algiers they began then led to the genesis of a new colony that would soon be known as Algeria. The subsequent speculation on colonial expansion, connected to the development of overseas markets and the quest for raw materials, would lead to the largest landgrab in history, as the European powers split up the continent of Africa into shares in the 1880s. While it would be impossible to extrapolate, from this course of events, a national desire for the acquisition of colonial territory, I aim to connect the consumer desire generated by the arcades to the representational structure of panoramas just elucidated. The commodification of the colonial landscape began with the *Panorama of Algiers* but was not fully realized until 1863, when a law created private property out of the territory held by indigenous Algerian tribes. Of course, the story did not end there: France continued to expand its colonial territories in North and West Africa into the twentieth century. Nevertheless, there is a clear historical pattern of ever-increasing acquisition of North African territory by the French in the nineteenth century.

Benjamin has noted that most of the Paris arcades came into being between 1822 and 1837 and that "the first condition of their emergence was a boom in the textile trade."[56] Also important was the development of iron construction. The same methods of construction also made panorama rotundas possible. In fact, the first arcade—the Passage des Panoramas—was built between two panorama rotundas.[57] The development of the arcades in this period marked a transformation in patterns of consumption, and the *magasins de nouveauté* that lined the arcades were the first shops that stocked large quantities of luxury goods. Perhaps more important, the arcades created a space for desire and consumption. They provided a serene atmosphere, lined in marble and lit by gaslights, that gave consumers a sense of removal from the city's clatter and confusion and allowed them to exercise their desires for various commodities.

In an introduction to a volume on the consumption of culture, Ann Bermingham has argued that "one of the most extraordinary aspects of mass consumption since the seventeenth century, and perhaps the thing that distinguishes the modern period from any that preceded it, is the fact that consumption has been the primary means through which individuals have participated in culture and transformed it. Consumption should not be understood simply as a positive or a negative reality but rather as a powerful tool for social change."[58] Bermingham points to an important and often neglected aspect of consumption in a capitalist society, namely, that it is the means whereby individuals personalize the collective life of society. Consumption is not necessarily the same as commodification *per se,* and Bermingham reminds her readers that the idea that consumption somehow lessens those who engage in it is an oversimplified cliché. In fact, consumption is the only way humans can and do survive. My hope is that considering the way the colonial landscape was consumed in the *Panorama of Algiers* might illuminate how its viewers' perceptions of Algeria were shifted by it and what the implications of such a shift might be.

In theorizing "the consumption view of self," Rolland Munro has articulated a means of explaining the relations between the individual and the social that is not focused on the concept of the self as a producer, a sort of cog in the mechanism of society. His view of the self as extended through consumption is useful because it points to a way to account for the effect that the *Panorama of Algiers* had upon its spectators. If one thinks of Parisian viewers of 1833 as extending their experience of space to incorporate new and unfamiliar lands in their memory banks, Langlois' product—the colonial landscape—is nothing but a mechanism of making invisible places visible. However, Munro extends his argument by employing the formulations of the anthropologist Marilyn Strathern. Munro writes, "For her, extension is not merely a matter, say, of a surgeon adding a wooden leg. Outwardly, yes, the notion of a part depicts the mechanical, the adding of material to material. . . . Inwardly, for the subject, the notion of a part is dramatic and elicits the opportunity of another form of extension, that of *performance.* The addition of a part (object) extends the possibilities for cultural performance as a 'part' (subject). Object and subject, as effects, move hand in hand."[59] Munro's explanation of the consumption view of self is compelling in relation to the commodification of experience in the arcades. We might imagine that the consumption of goods allows the purchaser to enact a fantasy of him- or herself, and this would explain, more or less, the use of images in advertisements. Buying luxury goods, such as perfume or an imported carpet, would increase not merely the number of objects an individual has but also the number of roles s/he can play. In the context of the *Panorama of Algiers,* Munro's formulation takes on a more significant implication. By perceiving the region of Algiers for the first time in this context, the spectator does not merely add more spaces to her/his internal inventory. Rather, seeing this space as a colonial landscape from the fantasy perspective, the viewer of Langlois' panorama had the opportunity to add a part to his/her repertoire, that of the colonial conqueror. And by perceiving the region of Algiers ordered in this way, viewers consumed not merely the means to apprehend this distant site but also the means to appropriate it—by playing the new role of colonizer.

Examining the consumption of Langlois' panorama clarifies the way in which such a representation conditions a viewer's responses. While the representational mechanism of the panorama creates an illusory point of centrality for the viewer, the apprehension of this place in the panorama engenders an extension of the European viewer's capabilities both to perceive and to control. There is a technology of spectatorship in evidence here: a viewer is trained to perceive differently through a newly evolved structure of depiction. In the case of the *Panorama of Algiers,* this shift in perception is explicitly connected to the military acquisition of overseas territory and the assumption of colonial control over it.

There is a compelling link between the relation of viewer to object proposed by the *Panorama of Algiers* and that suggested by the logic of consumerism. In the arcades, viewers were offered a variety of consumable goods made for distinct purposes. The nineteenth-century consumer was constituted in relation to the panoply of objects offered for sale. On the one hand, the consumer is to be overwhelmed by the dizzying array of products, but on the other, she or he must form them into an external landscape of possibilities and options. Emerging in the realm of popular entertainment, the *Panorama of Algiers* engendered an audience in much the same way that the arcades generated consumers. By constituting a viewer and separating her or him from the object, Langlois' panorama figured both the colony and colonizer as a function of its spectacle and fixed their relations. But the concepts of extension of self and role-playing are crucial as well, for a colonizer is also one who requires external objects to be complete.[60] Just as the consumption of material goods never satiates the consumer, the recently seized landscape of Algiers, as represented in Langlois' panorama, kept the French coming back for more.

CHAPTER 2

Algeria at the Museum of French History

It is the triumph of the people written on the walls of a palace by the hand of a king!

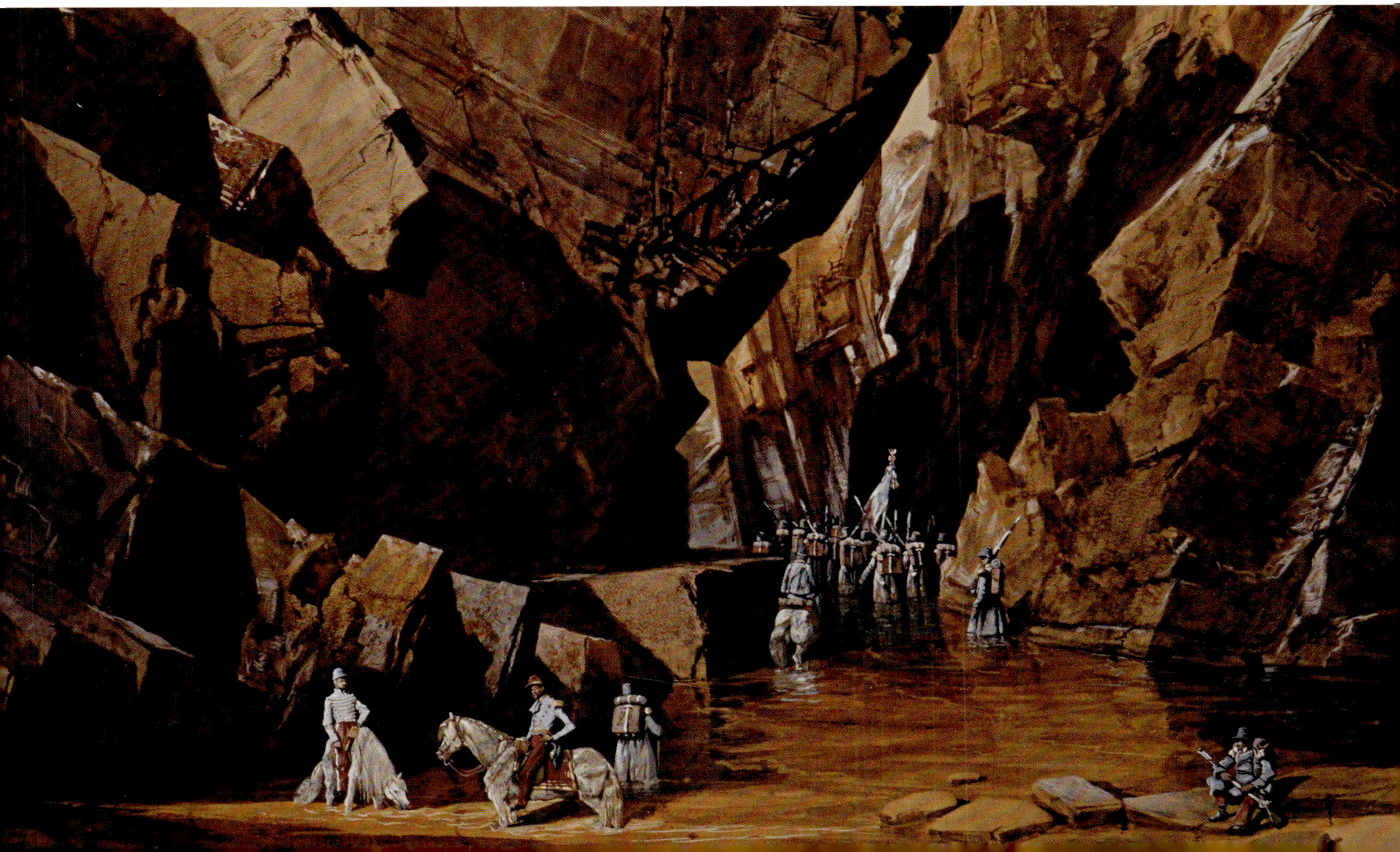

10 June 1837
Versailles—Today the King inaugurated the Museum of Versailles. With great solemnity, His Royal Highness convened 1,500 of France's most important statesmen and men of letters, representatives of the Chambre des Pairs and the Chambre des Deputés, of the Secretary of State, of the higher and lower courts, the royal court of Paris, the prefects of the Department of the Seine and of the Department of Seine-et-Oise, marshals of the Army and admirals of the Navy, the National Guard, and the five academies that compose the Institut de France.

The King and the Queen traveled at 3 o'clock from the Petit Trianon to the palace, where they ascended the marble stairs and greeted guests as they toured the newly created galleries. Their Royal Highnesses were accompanied by the King and Queen of Belgium, Monseigneur the Duke and Madame the Duchess of Orléans, Madame the Grand-Duchess of Mecklenbourg, Madame Princess Adélaïde, the Princes and Princesses of the royal family. Their Majesties were greeted by exclamations of enthusiastic devotion from the crowd of well-wishers as they examined, in the Grand Gallery of Battles, pictures of all the heights of French glory throughout the ages, from Tolbiac to Wagram. After the tour, a banquet was convened, followed by performances of Molière's "Misanthrope" and Meyerbeer's "Robert-le-Diable." After greeting ambassadors from all nations who made vivid proclamations of respect for the grandeur of this new symbol of French national honor, Their Majesties retired around 2 o'clock in the morning to the Petit Trianon.[1]

Originally conceived by Laurent-Pierre de Jussieu (son of the famous botanist) under the Restoration,[2] the Museum of French History involved the recycling of that ultimate symbol of French monarchic authority, the palace at Versailles, as a new national symbol of French military and cultural achievement. The museum was inaugurated with great fanfare in June 1837, and the newspapers in France and abroad covered this grand, if banal, event in glowing terms. Its centerpiece was the *grand galerie des batailles* in which France's most important battles—or at least the successful ones—were depicted by reigning contemporary artists. This series culminated with Napoléon's victories. In another part of the museum, visitors could find a section devoted to the crusades and, directly above that, Louis-Philippe left room for more paintings of contemporary battles fought in Algeria and elsewhere since Napoléon's reign. At least three rooms were devoted to representations of the conquest of Algeria. These Algerian works, many of them painted by Horace Vernet between 1837 and 1845,[3] were intended as monumental propaganda[4] for the cause of the Algerian conquest; the events depicted were intended to be rationalized, at least in part, by France's previous history of military success. These paintings asserted France's ability, and even its right, to expand its territorial possessions and to colonize weaker foreign enemies.

Perhaps the most active period of public debate concerning Algeria in France during the nineteenth century was in the late 1830s and the early 1840s. It was not until December 1841—eleven years after he took control of France amidst the recent seizure of Algiers—that Citizen-King Louis-Philippe addressed the contentious issue of Algeria directly, asserting that this territory would be "henceforth and forever French."[5] Until that point, he had preferred to present symbolic messages of support for the conquest and colonization of Algeria.[6] Unlike Napoléon III, as will be discussed in later chapters, the citizen-king did not issue directives, write public letters concerning Algeria, or visit the colony. Yet the wily descendant of the House of Orléans was well aware that the successful war in Algeria was achieving what his Bourbon predecessors had failed to do, namely, provide a new prototype for French glory in post-

Overleaf: detail of fig. 21

Bonaparte France. Even Napoléon had ultimately failed to conquer North Africa, but Louis-Philippe was counting a string of victories begun by Charles X. He repeatedly sent his sons to Algeria on glorious, if not strategic, missions so that his family might be written directly into the history of the African conquest, a crowning moment in France's history. To ensure that present and future generations would properly comprehend the historical import of the Algerian conquest, he commissioned a number of large-scale battle paintings for the *galeries historiques* (Museum of French History) at Versailles (figs. 18, 19).[7] These clashes were presented as the ultimate source of glory for the French nation in this period.

How strange it must have seemed to the illustrator and artist Adrien Dauzats to be invited by the crown prince, the duc d'Orléans, to accompany him on a mission to Algeria in order to record the event for posterity at the Museum of French History.[8] Unlike so many artists who had preceded him in Algeria, Dauzats had no military background and no specific experience with the French army to recommend him for the task of representing a military expedition. Moreover, unlike Horace Vernet, Dauzats was not in the habit of producing either *grandes machines* or battle paintings and had never been commissioned by the French government to represent a scene of French contemporary history.[9] Yet Dauzats was an inveterate traveler. He had accompanied Baron Taylor to Egypt, Palestine, and Syria in 1830. He had traveled throughout France producing illustrations for Taylor's *Voyages pittoresques et romantiques dans l'ancienne France* (*Picturesque and Romantic Voyages in Old France*) and also journeyed through Spain and Portugal.[10] In brief, Dauzats was a specialist in travel illustration. He worked mostly on a small scale in various media and specialized in depicting architectural monuments and general views. In light of the ongoing conquest of Algeria in 1839 and the citizen-king's preference for bombastic representations of the war, it is exceptional that an artist with no military background would be dispatched to a war zone and that the representation of an expedition led by the king's eldest son would amount to only a handful of large-scale watercolors (figs. 20–23) and an illustrated book.[11]

This period is crucial in the history of French colonialism and also in the evolution of the empire of landscape, since the Algerian landscape represented at the *galeries historiques* was a landscape of military conquest. The use of the term *landscape* may sound metaphorical in this context, but it is not meant to be. Reading battle paintings as landscapes goes against the grain of art-historical scholarship, because these pictures were considered, then and now, as history paintings. The argument for this concentration on landscape is twofold. First, it is obvious that such battles were waged over the control of territory, a fact that highlights the importance of the *field* of battle. Second, in the images that will be discussed below, the landscapes themselves were central to the narrative of the battles and therefore to the narrative implied in these "history" paintings. While these images are selective battle paintings from the period in which territory plays a significant role, they are not by any means unusual in their milieu.

This chapter analyzes the way in which two artists generated distinct visual terms to represent the French conquest of the Algerian landscape. While Vernet's room-size murals broadcasted the nationalist aspirations of both patron and artist in the representation of colonial territory conquered by the French military, Dauzats' Portes de Fer watercolors presented a landscape being won without a visible enemy to stand in the way. In Dauzats' images, the cliffs rise above both the French soldiers and their native allies like monumental architecture, and the landscape dwarfs the participants—even undermining their significance. Viewers are offered a novel visual analogy for the French conquest of Algeria in which French soldiers bravely enter a strange land, maintain their composure through the worst of it, and valiantly succeed. It is a fantasy of conquest without conflict.

Despite the fact that both representations of the French military in Algeria were commissioned for the same institution by the royal family in the same period, they forge divergent images of the colony and employ different means by which the viewer can apprehend Algeria's significance. Notably, these images bring to mind previous discussions of pictorial propaganda in nineteenth-century France, demonstrating that the state cannot control the image of the colony projected in art, even under its own patronage.[12] The relations between the colonizer and the space of the colony were constantly reformulated by artists employing various means to picture the colonial landscape. This chapter focuses only upon paintings and watercolors, but even in the narrow slice of Algerian imagery produced in France at this time, the historian can find enormous variation. Many factors could account for the differences between Vernet's and Dauzats' works, but the images reveal what kinds of representations could address the historical problem of depicting a landscape in the process of its military appropriation as a colony and how artists ruptured the limitations of traditional pictorial structures in order to respond to this emergent demand. In order to evaluate the most salient historical context for these works, we must examine in greater detail the political situation these two artists engaged.

The African Question

Despite all of the lively and multiple discussions; despite reports from two commissions, the publications of a large number of studies; despite the polemic in the press, the African question, so often broached, so often debated, so national and so current, continues to be one of those questions that occupies the public attention.

—M. P. Genty de Bussy

Even a cursory investigation of the "African question" in France in 1839 reveals an active public discourse on the future of France's territorial occupation in North Africa, both in the press and in the Chamber of Deputies. Many plans were put forward about how France ought to rule its new territory, fight the "African War," and eventually colonize this land and make it profitable. By 1839, much land speculation had already taken place, but only the very first private attempts at colonization had been made.[13] It was impossible at that point to predict the viability of colonization in a land with 2.5 million inhabitants, many of them dispossessed, hostile, and organized. Such concerns did not bother the theorists of colonization or prevent them from offering detailed and carefully defended plans based on first-hand accounts, scientific calculations, and even classical history. The detractors—among them Amédée Desjobert, a deputy representing Seine-Inférieure, and Général Duvivier, a hero of the Algerian conquest—argued that France had lost too many of its children in Africa to sustain the abstract goal of French glory and that the government should arrest the hemorrhage of resources flowing out of the capital and into this colony. In addition, while the idea of French protectorship was not questioned, some writers addressed the moral issue of whether the French had the right to govern the land of another people.[14]

The second—successful—siege of Constantine in October 1837 was a turning point in the expansion of the French conquest of Algeria. This clifftop city, the second largest in the region at the time, had successfully repelled French invasion the previous autumn. The city's geographical placement, strong fortifications, and independent populace proved to be more challenging than the French had anticipated.[15] The French defeat at Constantine was humiliating for the military, and its publicity was mostly suppressed in Paris. The subsequent success of the conquest was readily propagated by the publicists of the French military and Algerian colonization.[16] The resulting treaty transferred a large portion of the Algerian interior to the French, which had the effect of enhancing France's potential for colonial involvement. Whereas the previous colonizers of the area—the Ottoman Empire—had been content to control the coast, establishing only titular rulers in cities like Constantine and leaving smaller communities to look out for themselves,[17] the French sought control of far more territory in what would soon become Algeria. Yet the region newly ceded to the French state had been barely explored by them. The military had been so focused on conquering the regional capital of Constantine that they had sought only the most efficient and direct routes and therefore had not seriously investigated the region. As Andrew and Kanya-Forstner have argued, conquest-minded generals in the field led the French into the position of a colonial power.[18] Controlling the interior of this region would require an enormous infrastructure and a sophisticated bureaucratic mechanism, but the French military had not even traversed some of the major commercial routes in the area. The territory that composed the colony, which many in Paris were so eager to put to use, remained mostly inaccessible, and its possession by the French was by no means a *fait accompli*.

France's lack of preparation to become a colonial power in Algeria[19] was no hindrance for metropolitan theorists and scientists. In 1837, the War Ministry announced plans to set up a scientific expedition to study Algeria; it was organized in 1839.[20] Général Bugeaud, who had served as head of successful expeditions in the western part of Algeria and who negotiated the Treaty of Tafna with the native leader Abd-el-Kader in 1837,[21] first put forward his plan for military colonization in 1838.[22] It was followed by many critiques and counter-proposals penned by authors ranging from other French generals in Algeria to Père Enfantin,[23] the most strident follower of the utopian socialist Saint-Simon. In 1839, the Chamber of Deputies sent several of its members to Algeria to study the situation.[24] And in 1841 another commission, which included Alexis de Tocqueville, was dispatched to glean direct impressions.[25]

Those who published their plans for Algerian colonization were of every political stripe—and they raised a wide range of questions, such as whether a colony across the Mediterranean could be an economic success, how the French ought to treat the natives of this territory (both peaceful and hostile), how much of their culture should be preserved under French settlement, and how best to settle French workers in this distant and exotic land, if they could survive there. Politically motivated theorists who had never visited Algeria wrote a number of texts in which they assured their readers that they knew the best path toward a successful colonial society across the sea.[26] But the preponderance of authors involved in the debate had experience in Algeria. They intended to protect the interests of a particular group involved in the occupation at that moment and to extend that group's influence in the potential colony of the future.[27] Two major groups participated: the military and the civilian French settlers, the *colons,* both seeking to gain dominance in the Algeria of the future. Neither was very concerned with the rights of the natives—the former viewed them as a threat, the latter as an obstacle—and both agreed that Algeria was a source of French glory and that its conquest improved France's international reputation. The implication that England was envious of France's success in North Africa was often used as a tactic to goad the French to defend their national ability to colonize. Of course, there were a few detractors, some even in the Chamber of Deputies.[28] Their attacks on the colonial venture, expressed in terms of morality and wasted resources, were ultimately useless against the defenses of those who supported colonialism. The *colonistes* blended the rhetoric of patriotism with the promise of economic prosperity for the French in Algeria. Further, France's superiority was reinforced by the notion of a *mission civilisatrice,* through which France would bring the advantages of the modern world to supposedly backward North Africans.

Though the pro-colonial faction triumphed, the question that was most hotly debated in the early 1840s—and that plagued efforts at colonization until the Third Republic—was whether colonization in Algeria ought to be controlled by the military or by civilians. In brief, those who favored military colonization—namely, Bugeaud and his followers—maintained that first, they had ruled the occupied territories so far; second, they were needed to counter the continued threat of indigenous aggressors; and finally, only military service could provide the necessary discipline for settlers who might bring such an inhospitable and arid country to fruition. The civilian strategists of colonization were of two camps. One consisted of those who simply believed that turning colonization over to ambitious French businessmen would automatically lead to greater good (read profits) for everyone concerned. This group was led by A. G. Rozey, president of the Colonial Society of Algiers and former vice president of the Chamber of Commerce in Algiers. More scrupulous types argued for France's civilizing mission and a demonstration of French humanism and goodwill toward Algeria's natives, led by a transition to modern agriculture and, of course, to individual ownership.[29] While the long-range thinking of the latter group won out later in the century, the predominant concern for safety in a hostile land prevented many French citizens from attempting to generate a promised livelihood in Algeria at this point. Besides, if the military had ruled the occupied territory so far and would be counted on to provide infrastructure in this undeveloped land, was it not also the most organized and established bureaucratic apparatus in Algeria and thus the best guarantor of colonization's success? A plan was eventually developed for civilian colonization, administered by the military, which led to many complaints from *colons* who felt that they should have had more control if they were going to take the risks of participating in the process of colonization.[30]

This debate on colonization is instructive not only because it establishes a political and social context for interpreting imagery made for the *galeries historiques.* It also demonstrates a very active discourse in France about the practicalities of colonization. It is one thing to conquer a foreign power and another to administer a successful colony, and this array of texts on the Algerian question points to the deep level of inquiry around colonial territory—how to put it to a particular kind of use so that the entire enterprise could prove beneficial in both the administrative and the fiscal sense. The debate thoroughly explored questions of land use, distribution, and the public works that needed to be constructed to make a colonial system operative. What can be gleaned from this literature is a reconsideration of territory taking place in Paris—and no investigation of the views of Algeria's indigenous occupants. While such political writings were for the most part theoretical, it is important that these writers attended to the myriad specifics of the means not merely to extract resources from the colony but also to redistribute and settle lands seized from hostile aggressors who had been defeated and, further, to create a system of effective colonial administration. The tone of almost all of these texts was nationalistic, but the elaborate and lengthy debate on the precise terms of colonization demonstrates an extensive public knowledge of the historical situation of the French presence in Algeria as well as a determination to work out the difficulties of ruling a population abroad and putting that territory to use for France. This situation typifies the concept of colonialism (as opposed to imperialism) and clarifies the metropolitan engagement with the mechanics of colonial administration.

Vernet's Algeria in the Museum of French History

The reinvention of the royal palace at Versailles as the Museum of French History was Louis-Philippe's most important cultural project, and among the countless battle paintings that were produced for these august halls, not a few were created by Horace Vernet.[31] Vernet's canvases, the largest of which measures more than twenty-one meters in length, established his preeminence in the representation of the French conquest of Algeria, and the paintings of this subject were employed by the citizen-king with great success at the Salons and at ceremonies at the museum.[32]

In 1839, Horace Vernet's three canvases of the siege of Constantine of October 1837 were among the works featured at the Salon (figs. 18, 19). These three enormous pieces—all of them were more than five meters in height and the largest more than ten meters in length—were designed to grab the public's attention and publicize the glorious conquest. Originally commissioned as a set of seven works representing the siege of Constantine,[33] only these three were produced. Nevertheless, they were by far the most ambitious group of works depicting events in Algeria that had yet been commissioned by the state—and this set was made to serve as the cornerstone of a room in the Museum of French History almost entirely devoted to the conquest of Algeria, the Salle de Constantine.[34] Just as the citizen-king sought to bring together extremely divergent political factions into his regime, he also attempted to co-opt artists with distinct aesthetic commitments, and he tended to favor artists able to produce moralizing paintings with modern significance. He wanted *grandes machines* but also contemporary history, and though he had a weakness for bombastic flourish, he was willing to accept simple reportage if the news was good. Other art historians have addressed the development of the *juste-milieu* style under the July Monarchy in great detail.[35] For my purposes, it is enough to point out that Horace Vernet proved to be the great master of the middle-of-the-road. A man passionate about the military and the heroism of contemporary history, Vernet earned the largest and most visible commissions from Louis-Philippe's regime. Though in 1839 his fame as a painter of battles was clearly established, by the end of the citizen-king's reign he would become a national treasure, achieving the highest rank of the Légion d'honneur from the king's own hand.[36]

Vernet's canvases featuring the siege were placed in the Grand Salon and received a considerable number of responses from the press, though not so many as might have been hoped for. Most reviewers obediently observed the heroics of the duc de Nemours, another son of Louis-Philippe, who was afforded a central presence in two of the three works despite his modest age of eighteen at the time of the battle.[37] The critics were unanimous about the facility of the artist but some were not impressed by the execution of the canvases. The style was perceived as perhaps too precise, too arid. Charles Blanc was his harshest critic at the time. In seeming exasperation, he wrote, "What! You have been given fifty feet of canvas to cover, fifty feet of canvas! With this a painter can dream of something more beautiful and you have made nothing more than an official report in oil, you have simply translated a column of *Le Moniteur Parisien*!"[38] This criticism was echoed by Théophile Gautier in less strident terms, who described Vernet as a "journalist . . . he makes colored articles on the conquests of the day, he illustrates the bulletins."[39] The aforementioned critics bring attention to the central problem of contemporary history painting. In order to please the patron—the sovereign, in this case—the representation had to remain in close proximity to the official history as it was patriotically recounted in *Le Moniteur Universel,* the government's official journal. In fact, the listing of Vernet's paintings in the *livret* of the Salon of 1839 included a paragraph describing the actions in each painting in a style that could easily have been taken from an official journal.[40]

Looking at one of Vernet's paintings will clarify the problem these critics discussed. In *Episode from the Conquest of Algeria in 1837; Second Siege of Constantine by Général Damrémont; The Enemy Turned Back from the Heights of Coudiat-Ati (10 October 1837)* (1838; fig. 18), the didactic style of the work seems to inform more than to inspire viewers. In the very center of the painting stands the eighteen-year-old duc de Nemours, directing the army into battle. Along the right edge of the painting, the column of French soldiers prepares to defend itself against an approaching attack and, in the foreground, a military genre scene is presented. Here, Vernet demonstrated his highly evolved knowledge of military costume as he depicted the variety of personnel who took part in the siege, including some Spahis, indigenous Algerians dressed in military garb. This reportage is balanced by Romantic elements in the foreground. The graves and skeleton are indeed factual (the battalion built their defensive wall from tombstones), but they also reference the fateful, unsuccessful French siege of the previous year.

In light of recent writings on history painting under the reign of Napoléon put forward by Darcy Grimaldo Grigsby and David O'Brien, I should note that the central control of state-sponsored representations of contemporary history was much less explicit under Louis-Philippe then it was under Napoléon and his minister Vivant Denon.[41] The citizen-king did not select a minister to oversee the commissions but engaged the artists himself, provided the historical episodes worthy of representation, and paid them from the coffers of the royal family.[42] Implicit directives were apparent, even if he did not observe and comment upon each artistic decision. An artistic administration could propagate such an agenda without clear demands because it was in the very nature of the commission. Horace Vernet was acquainted with both the prince, the duc d'Orléans, and the king, Louis-Philippe, who had visited his studio numerous times in the years of the Restoration.[43] Further, Vernet was an enthusiast of the French military and a colonist in Algeria himself, owning a parcel of land in the Mitidja that he purchased on his first trip there in 1833.[44] Executing such enormous works for the Museum of French History would require Vernet to portray this episode in an official manner in order to ensure its glory throughout time. Vernet's Algerian battle

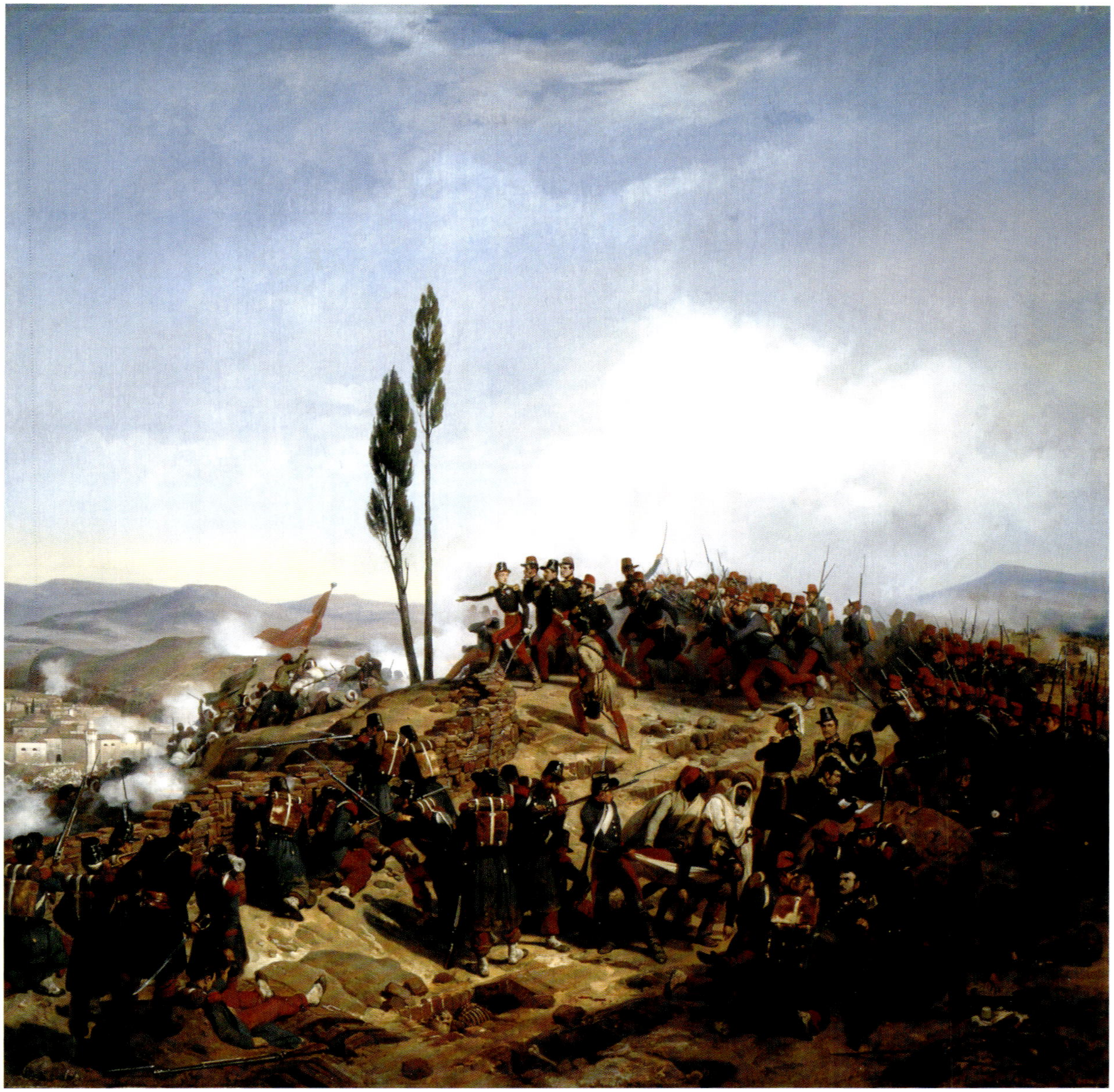

Figure 18.
Horace Vernet, *Episode from the Conquest of Algeria in 1837; Second Siege of Constantine by Général Damrémont; The Enemy Turned Back from the Heights of Coudiat-Ati (10 October 1837)*, 1838. Oil on canvas, 512 × 518 cm. Château de Versailles et de Trianon, Versailles, France. Photo: Réunion des musées nationaux/Art Resource, New York (Gérard Blot).

paintings were designed as wall decorations for a symbolic center of power, much like the halls of state decorated in sixteenth-century Rome.[45]

Wall-size canvases were a function of the museum for which they were intended, but, in any case, the works' scale was designed to attract visual attention in the Salon. Grand scales allowed the legible depiction of extended spaces and the registration of distinct activities that provide the points of interest in these compositions. Such aspects of large-scale battle paintings bring to mind the preceding discussion of Langlois' panorama of the siege of Algiers—and, in fact, Langlois was Vernet's student. He too received commissions to represent French battles for the *galeries historiques*.[46] Both artists generated artistic spectacles that shared perceptual terms and formal characteristics. Both forms of spectacle have social implications. Of course, the differences between panoramas for popular consumption and battle paintings sponsored by the king for the palace at Versailles are significant. Yet their numerous similarities invite exploration.

The manner in which Vernet and Langlois rendered their subjects sustained a visual rhetoric of truthful depiction. As established in the last chapter, this rhetoric—call it the spectacular vernacular—produces a particular relationship between the viewer and the world and negotiates the way in which the external world can be perceived. As Guy Debord has noted, "The spectacle is not a collection of images; rather it is a social relationship between people that is mediated by images."[47] While Debord's notion of the spectacle is more subtle and attenuated than the painted spectacles under consideration here, his emphasis on the ineffable characteristics of social relations, as opposed to immanent objects, is instructive. Vernet's Algerian battle paintings were designed to serve a political and social function, but how they achieve this is less a quality of the image presented—which battle? whose history?—than the means through which the image comes to function in public. As we analyze his imagery, it is important to conceive of perceptual terms and formal characteristics as mutually constitutive. They function together to suggest that the facts are simply transparent.

The presence of several spatial registers in the siege of Constantine canvases allows the viewer's eye to wander and absorb a number of discrete forms of imagery. In the largest work, *Episode from the Conquest of Algeria in 1837; Second Siege of Constantine by Général Damrémont; The Columns of Assault Are Set into Motion for the Siege of Constantine (13 October 1837)* (1838; fig. 19), the sky occupies the uppermost register, almost half of the painting. The central horizontal band is an approximation of a general view of Constantine, a scenic image of the city rendered in faded pastel colors. This register features the major monuments of the city and situates the scene in its geographical context, showing the cliffs below the city's walls. In the lowest register, the French leaders prepare to dispatch the troops against the background of their makeshift barricades. Vernet's precision in rendering military figure groups in utmost detail is highlighted in the foreground. Spahis rush into position. These troops, among the two regiments leading the charge into the city, were indigenous Algerians organized by the French military who fought alongside French troops. Vernet duly notes their participation, and he uses these soldiers' different dress to add splashes of color and exoticism that break up the monotony of uniformed French soldiers standing in rows. On the right, the feet of a corpse can be seen protruding from under a cover, a reminder of the costs of colonial conquest. These figures are all rendered in a larger scale, and their activities are most visible to the viewer.

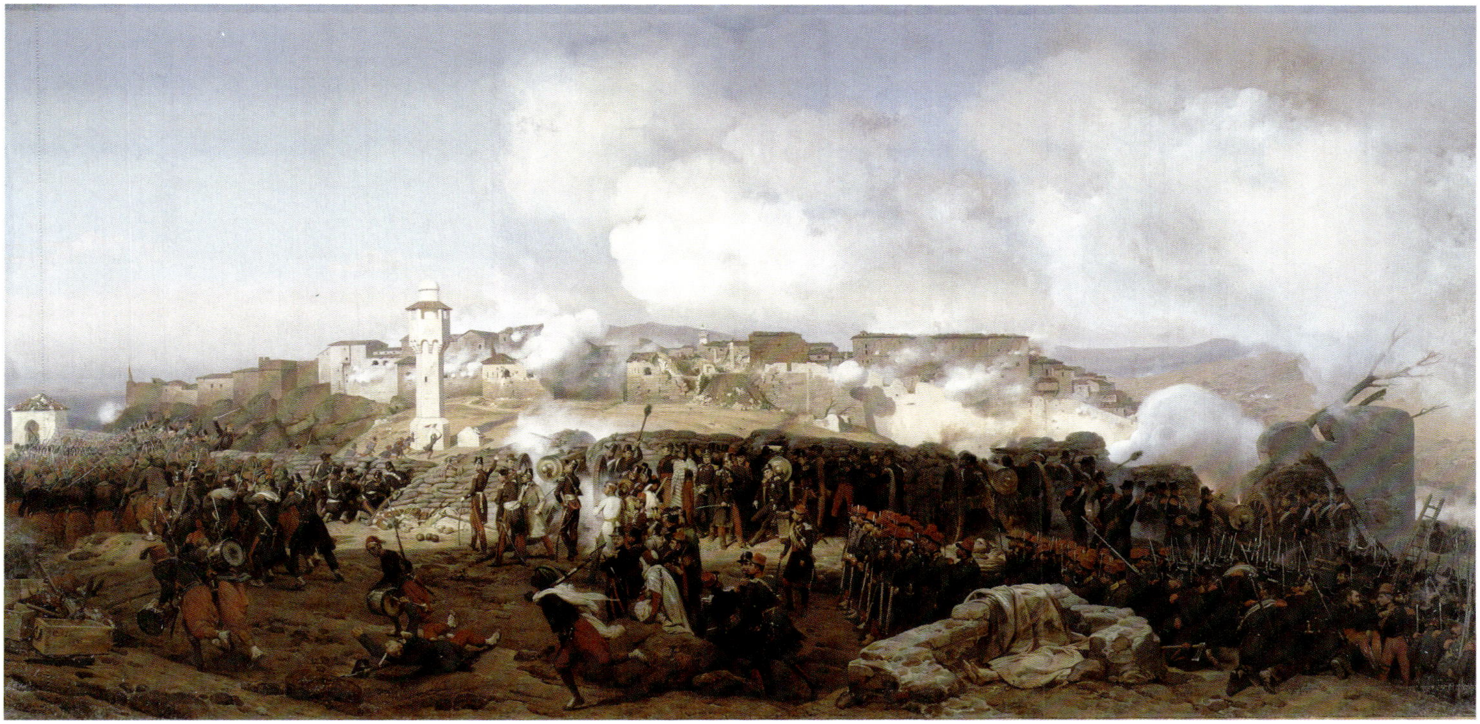

Figure 19.
Horace Vernet, *Episode from the Conquest of Algeria in 1837; Second Siege of Constantine by Général Damrémont; The Columns of Assault Are Set into Motion for the Siege of Constantine (13 October 1837),* 1838. Oil on canvas, 512 × 1039 cm. Château de Versailles et de Trianon, Versailles, France. Photo: Réunion des musées nationaux/Art Resource, New York (Gérard Blot).

This work demonstrates the lack of compositional unity that led Henry Roujon to list "piecemeal compositions" as the first in a list of the artist's evident faults,[48] but such a fractured composition is not without function. It is crucial to imagine such large works positioned above the viewer for display, as they remain today at the Museum of French History. A painting so large cannot be visually apprehended in its totality; rather, the viewer observes it relative to her or his position in the room. From a distance, it is possible to perceive the work in its general aspect. This perspective affords a picturesque view above and a battle painting below, and the viewer must unify these two realms into a visually cohesive text. Similarly, the viewer of the panorama must unify a number of discrete images into a total view. In both cases, too, the viewer must assume a particular position relative to the work. When a viewer approaches one of Vernet's battle paintings for a closer look, a sense of perspective is lost: the lowest register captivates one's perception due to the proximity to these figures, and the upper registers, seen obliquely, become a mere backdrop for the activity in the foreground.

The vernacular of panoramas is apparent here not only in the size of the works, which are designed to overwhelm and surround the viewer, but also in the restrictive use of materials. A sparse and direct handling of paint was intended to make Vernet's images appear more like windows onto the world than crafted representations. Charles Blanc dismissively referred to these works as "aquatintes," suggesting a connection between these enormous canvases and highly detailed, mass-produced etchings.[49] Yet the stereoscopic clarity, the tireless representation of every single ornament on each French uniform, gives these works a claim to truth. These prosaic images suppress the artist's handling of materials. In some sense, Vernet followed the technical conventions appropriate to *paysage historique,* the most common academic form of landscape painting. His commitment to truth telling ultimately prevented him from creating an innovative composition in these works. Though Blanc would deride Vernet for his scrupulousness in rendering every stone, such a technique possessed significance in the very year Daguerre's invention was acknowledged by the Academy of Sciences. The excessive attention to detail noted by Blanc and Gautier also alludes to the technique of producing a seemingly transparent depiction of the world through direct transfer. Of course, this is how cameras operate. (Though he was among the first to employ this apparatus,[50] Vernet did not use one to help him compose these Algerian works.)

Whether one examines Vernet's images of the siege of Constantine in relation to panoramas, daguerreotypes, or aquatints, there is one central problematic: the relationship of the copy to the original. Producing a copy has two immediate effects. The first is an assertion that the real world can be reproduced pictorially. The fundamental principle here is that the world seen by one person's eye can be re-created so that others may see the same image (and the same world), even though they have not seen the original. The second effect is that a hierarchy of verity is established, one in which the original is real and the reproduction is only a copy, deriving its value not from itself but from its relationship to the original.[51] While the first of these outcomes draws together the world and its depictions, the second separates them and establishes their relative value.

In the relationship between the real and the reproduced, a new dialectic emerges in which a copy can testify to the reality (or truth) of the original. If the activity of the image producer is not identifiable, a reproduction can be created that will be interpreted as a manifestation of reality. Therefore, if a painter subsumes his or her originality or distinctiveness, s/he can produce a work that affirms the nature of the original. If the viewer believes that the painter has succeeded in doing so, s/he is convinced of the verity of the copy *and* the nature of the original. From this dialectic is born a new convention in which artists (indeed, pictorial producers of all kinds) seek to create nonartistic renderings that, if properly executed, ensure their interpretation by others as good copies. As long as an image is rendered through a technique corresponding to direct reflection of the external world, any image the artist wishes to project will attest to the purported nature of the original. In other words, the picture will be taken as a reflection of the external world. This conclusion has far-reaching implications for photography that I will explore in Chapter 5, but it is equally relevant to Vernet's representation of the siege of Constantine and its function: to reify as history the official reports of Algerian battles.

In Chapter 1, I noted the surprising insistence of numerous commentators concerning the illusion of reality produced in the *Panorama of Algiers.* Much of the critical commentary on the panorama could have applied to any landscape depiction, since it employed formal vocabulary such as the use of aerial perspective, the convincing tones of the city's buildings, and the accurate effects of light in the landscape. These terms of criticism are conventions, for they allow viewers to perceive the image as a landscape and to make sense of what kind of landscape was rendered by the artist. In the case of landscape painting in France, a set of established techniques dating back at least to the seventeenth century allowed viewers to determine the plausibility of any visual representation of landscape—and critics eagerly applied a particular set of pictorial conventions to determine such a representation's effectiveness. For viewers who had never seen the places portrayed, these formulae, taught to students in the course of academic training and available to amateurs through instructional manuals, were the measure of the truth of the depiction.

J. B. Deperthes, a student of Pierre-Henri de Valenciennes and an author of two works on landscape painting, set out and analyzed the formal terms and conventions of landscape painting in his *Théorie du paysage* (*Theory of Landscape*) of 1818.[52] By means of categories such as these, a critic could discern the effectiveness of a visual representation. Conventions appear to operate universally and can therefore be called upon to decode any depiction of a landscape, whether it makes reference to an actual material location or is a self-conscious construction of the artist. In this sense, conventions themselves were the repositories of truth in the visual arts in this period. Paradoxically, these conventions were the result of practices repeated by artists over time, thus becoming accepted as the means to achieve a convincing landscape portrayal. As is the case with the term "conventional wisdom," artistic conventions can signify truth because they are followed by artists and reproduced in criticism.

Since conventions are founded upon tacit acceptance, new conventions can emerge from innovative artistic practices and their eventual recognition by critics. In the context of French landscape painting in this period, for example, there were two prevalent modes: the *style champêtre* and the *style historique*.[53] Both of these styles were founded on the essential importance of figures in the landscape but were differentiated based upon the effect on the viewer. A landscape painting made in the historic style was intended to elevate the viewer's imagination by projecting an idealized image of the past, but a painting in the pastoral style was intended to appeal to the viewer's love of nature and its associations with leisure or the raw beauty and power of the natural world. Deperthes did not acknowledge a concurrent tendency in landscape painting that John Barrell has termed the "georgic," referring to scenes of agricultural labor,[54] but the archetypal examples for Deperthes' text would be the historic landscapes of Nicolas Poussin and the pastoral views of Salvator Rosa. The former elevates the viewer's sensibility while the latter appeals directly to her or his senses.

The visual experience of panoramas and eventually photography had a very different effect upon the viewer, as elaborated in Chapter 1. The panorama aimed not to produce a sense of nature but a sense of truth, of information directly conveyed, and this effect is evident in Vernet's paintings of the siege of Constantine. In his review of 1839, Charles Blanc made the comparison between Vernet's paintings and the panorama explicit. He put it this way in an acerbic address to the artist: "If you have so many scruples, you should count the stones and do what M. Langlois has done with his panorama, though with a more laudable intention."[55]

In effect, Vernet traded in the hand of genius for the illusion of reality by rendering the scene as if mechanically. The landscape conventions in *The Columns of Assault* (fig. 19) guarantee that the viewer will understand the focus of this picture as a battle over a strategic location. The artist's apparent lack of creativity in rendering the scene testifies to its truthfulness. If the military looks orderly, then it must have been. If the duc de Nemours is leading the charge in the image, then he must have done so in reality. Even the sparseness of the colors was attributed to the foul weather that surrounded the expedition. In this sense, it is clear why Vernet was labeled a journalist. His intentionally matter-of-fact style makes his report convincing. But many critics were unconvinced that his methods were effective in terms of painting, and they faulted his use of color and the lack of character in his brushwork. They also pointed out the apparent monotony of rendering modern armies. As one critic observed: "One senses, on seeing the uniformity of his compositions, that the artist did not think enough before acting, that he did not sufficiently master the difficulty of art; but if he had sensed it better, we would not have these three surprising representations."[56]

Though Vernet's representations were effective spectacles, they were not remarkable as paintings, and the transparency the artist sought in his reproduction of the site ultimately damned the series as a whole. Rather than perceiving the canvases as providing a convincing illusion of reality, some critics interpreted them as presenting a convincing illusion of the official history of the battle and criticized the artist for his lack of creativity. Vernet may have failed in the terms proper to grand painting, but he did develop a modern method that figured France's seizure of Algeria in spatial terms. Vernet's battle paintings literally annexed territory into France's visual history of its own military conquests, thereby introducing an image of imperialism into the history of France.

Dauzats and the Expedition of the Portes de Fer

Rather than producing a spectacular representation of official history, Dauzats provided topographical illustrations of the colonial landscape. The military figures in his Portes de Fer watercolors (figs. 20–23) do not appear to be making history so much as dressing the landscape. Just as the artist's deployment of a new pictorial effect is crucial to an understanding of Vernet's Algerian battle paintings, Dauzats' manipulation of landscape conventions made his works both compelling and believable.

The sketches Dauzats made of the expedition while in Algeria are now mostly lost, and very few details about his perceptions of the trip or the landscape he saw there remain. All that is left now of the expedition are a couple of letters written from Algeria and a few sketches.[57] Further, few details of the commissions emanating from this trip can be ascertained.[58] The watercolors, and the paintings the artist created based upon them, were vivid and convincing despite the way they dramatically upset some conventions of French landscape painting. Dauzats produced two sets of watercolors of the Portes de Fer (also known as the Bibans). The smaller set of four is now housed at the Musée Condé in Chantilly (figs. 24–26), and the larger version, a set of five, was commissioned by the duc d'Orléans for Versailles. Only one piece of the smaller set is signed (1839), but all of the Versailles images are (1840 and 1841), which suggests that the smaller watercolors were studies for the larger ones. Moreover, the duc d'Aumale purchased the Chantilly watercolors in the sale after the artist's death,[59] so it is safe to infer that Dauzats used the smaller watercolors as the source for paintings and prints that he produced after completing the Versailles commission. Though one watercolor at Chantilly is dated 1839 (fig. 26), it would seem that these works were achieved after the expedition rather than on site, because their level of finish could not have been achieved in the few hours the prince's regiment spent in the area.

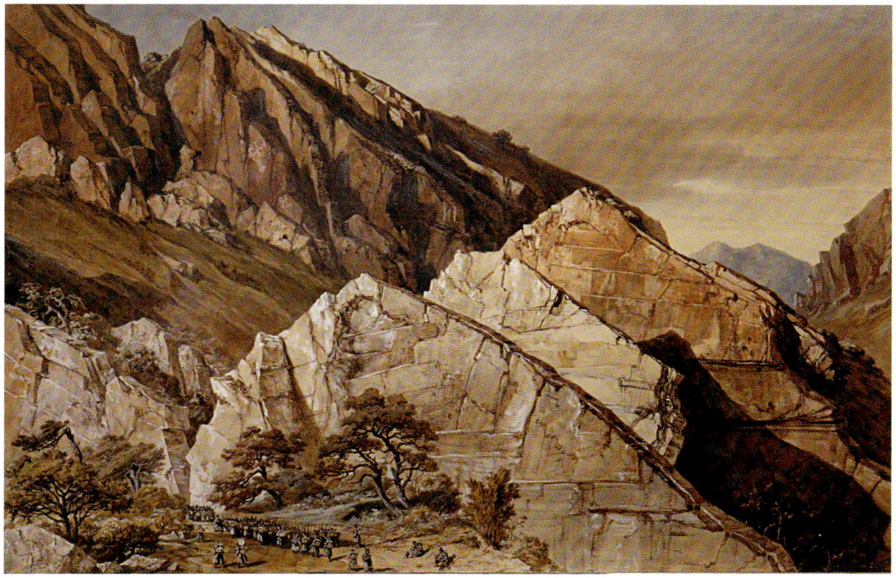

Figure 20.
Adrien Dauzats, *Second Wall of the Portes-de-Fer. Arrival of the 17th Regiment of Light Infantry (28 October 1839)*, 1840–41. Watercolor on paper mounted on canvas, 63 × 99 cm. Château de Versailles et de Trianon, Versailles, France. Photo courtesy Château de Versailles et de Trianon (Jean-Marc Manaï).

Figure 21.
Adrien Dauzats, *Third Wall of the Portes-de-Fer. The Chasseurs of the 3rd Regiment and the Soldiers of the 2nd Léger Descend into the Bed of the River (28 October 1839)*, 1840. Watercolor on paper mounted on canvas, 63 × 99 cm. Château de Versailles et de Trianon, Versailles, France. Photo courtesy Château de Versailles et de Trianon (Jean-Marc Manaï).

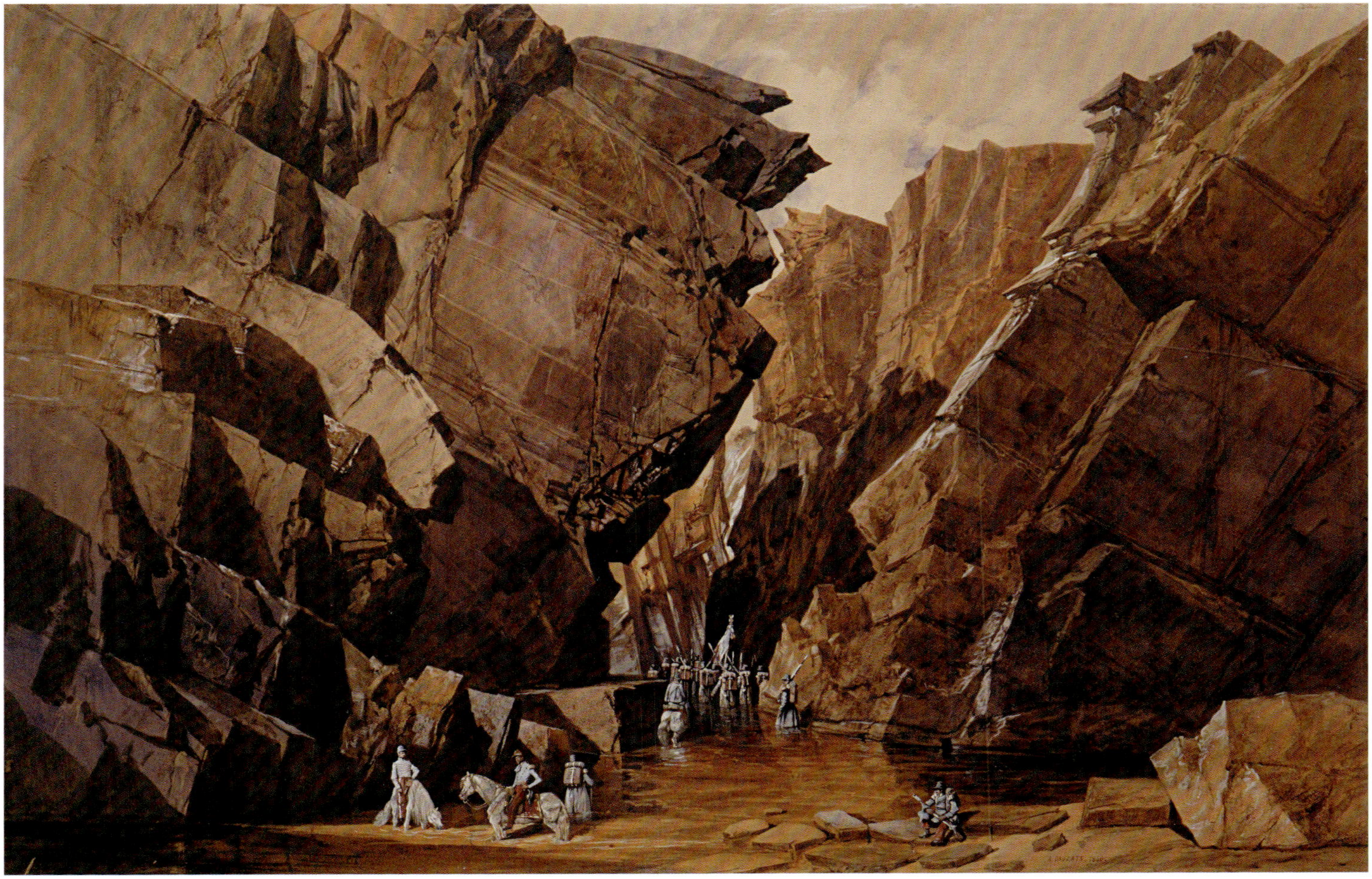

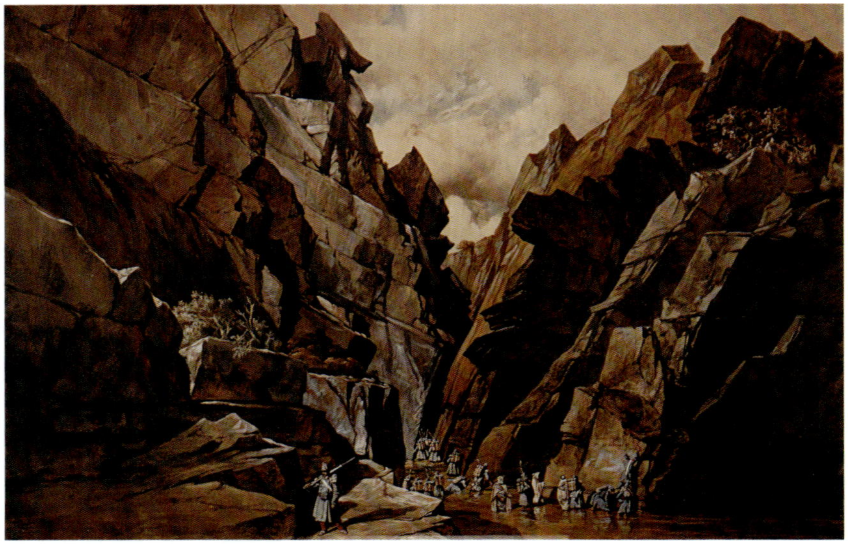

Figure 22.
Adrien Dauzats, *Third Wall of the Portes-de-Fer. The Sapeure du génie Indicates by Inscription the Date of the Passage of the Portes-de-Fer (28 October 1839)*, 1841. Watercolor on paper mounted on canvas, 63 × 99 cm. Château de Versailles et de Trianon, Versailles, France. Photo courtesy Château de Versailles et de Trianon (Jean-Marc Manaï).

The two sets of watercolors, though they represent the same sites in the same medium, are surprisingly distinct. The smaller watercolors (figs. 24–26) are approximately 24 × 30 cm, a conventional scale for watercolors. The larger ones (figs. 20–23), approximately 63 × 100 cm, are exceptional.[60] While the Chantilly watercolors are, for the most part, dense in color with a concentration of brushstrokes, the Versailles works are more open, with a looser registration of shapes and lines. The Chantilly works would appear to be the studies, but they are more finished and resolved. The Versailles watercolors have a sense of coming apart. The apparent paradox is that the massiveness of the cliffs and the overwhelming character of the landscape are better conveyed through the smaller watercolors. This effect can be explained by the artist's relative level of comfort with the material in two distinct scales. Dauzats was above all a printmaker, and his experience working on a small scale for albums of lithographs, such as the *Voyages pittoresques et romantiques dans l'ancienne France,* would have amply prepared him for the convincing registration of large spaces (*vues générales*) on a small page. The preliminary watercolors, like Dauzats' prints of earlier years, are compact, dense, and precisely composed.

There is a certain staginess to Dauzats' achievements in these works. Not only are the military figures rendered in precise detail in relation to the loose forms that surround them, but the effects of

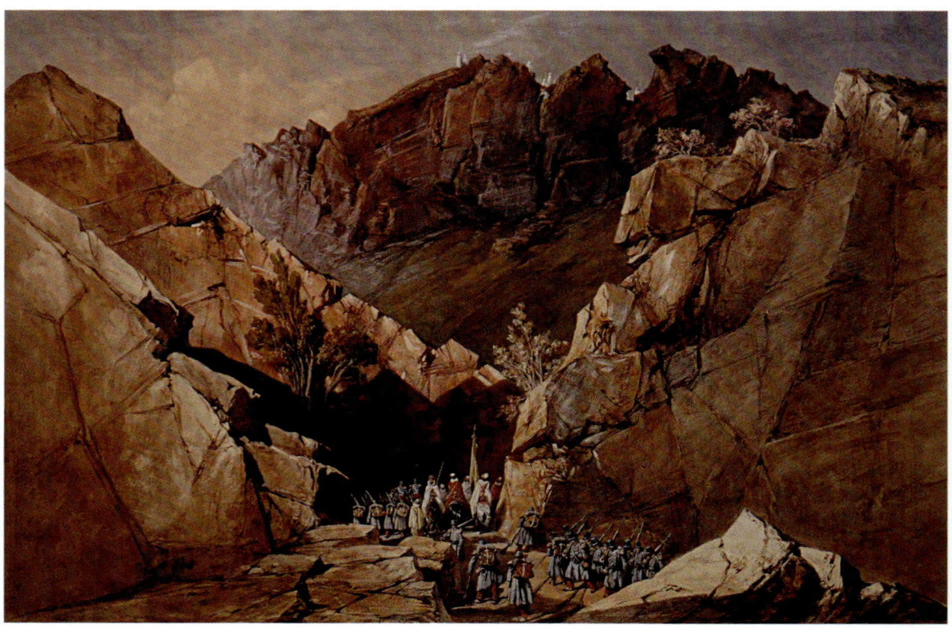

Figure 23.
Adrien Dauzats, *Departure from the Portes-de-Fer (28 October 1839)*, 1840. Watercolor on paper mounted on canvas, 63 × 99 cm. Château de Versailles et de Trianon, Versailles, France. Photo courtesy Château de Versailles et de Trianon (Jean-Marc Manaï).

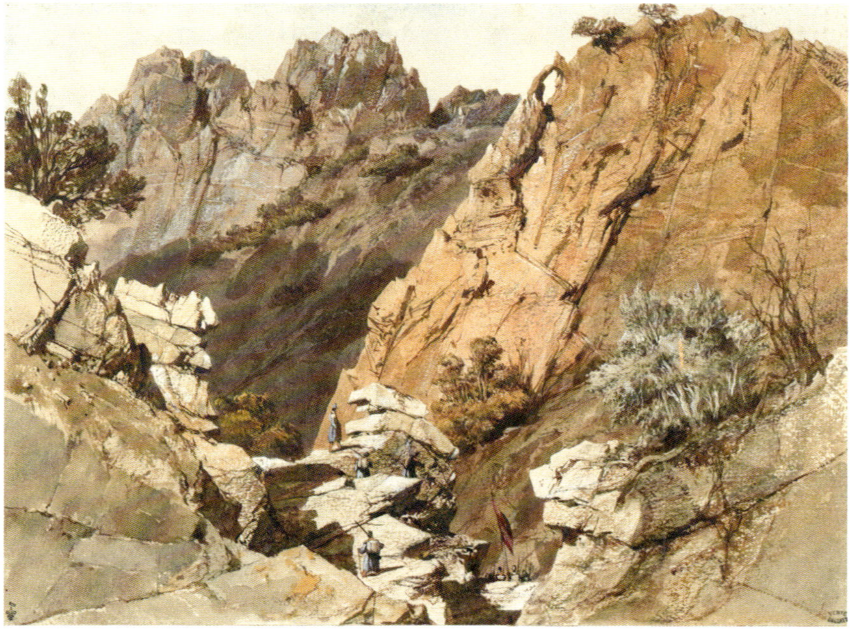

Figure 24.
Adrien Dauzats, *Passage of the Portes-de-Fer, Second Gorge*, undated. Watercolor on paper, 23.8 × 31 cm. Musée Condé, Chantilly, France (DE 694). Photo: Réunion des musées nationaux/Art Resource, New York (René-Gabriel Ojéda).

Figure 25.
Adrien Dauzats, *Passage of the Portes-de-Fer, Bottom of the Ravine*, 1839. Watercolor on paper, 23.8 × 30.3 cm. Musée Condé, Chantilly, France. © Giraudon France/The Bridgeman Art Library.

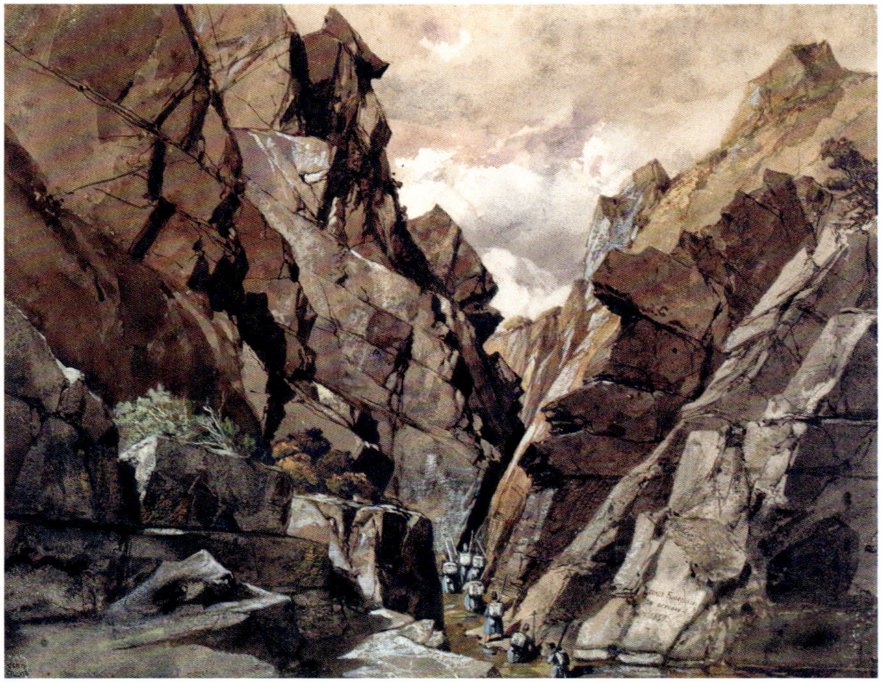

light and space are self-consciously dramatic. Whereas Langlois and Vernet sought to remove the trace of their artistic activities to produce spectacular illusions, Dauzats highlighted his activities as a draughtsman in his watercolors. Their unique appearance signals a dramatic production of imagery. There is no question that Dauzats' watercolors, seen in storage-room light, look like highly developed compositions that carefully tread the line between representation and abstraction. Yet they were designed to publicize and memorialize, and their visual language suitably addressed the metropolitan public of their day.

At the Museum of French History, these images were placed in a room reserved for watercolors in the central portion of the palace on the second floor.[61] Thus these works were set apart from the monumental battle paintings in a space where the viewer could appreciate their formal characteristics. Further, in the watercolor gallery, these images were not surrounded by other battle paintings but by a variety of scenes of French history; therefore, the martial nature of the event would have been reduced. The differences in the viewing conditions of the works were underscored by Dauzats' experimental approach in these watercolors. While working in a medium not well suited to the demands of large-scale projects, the artist seems to have cast aside the rigidity of his typical manner. This decision takes on significance when one examines the way in which the artist has chosen to represent this exceptional landscape.

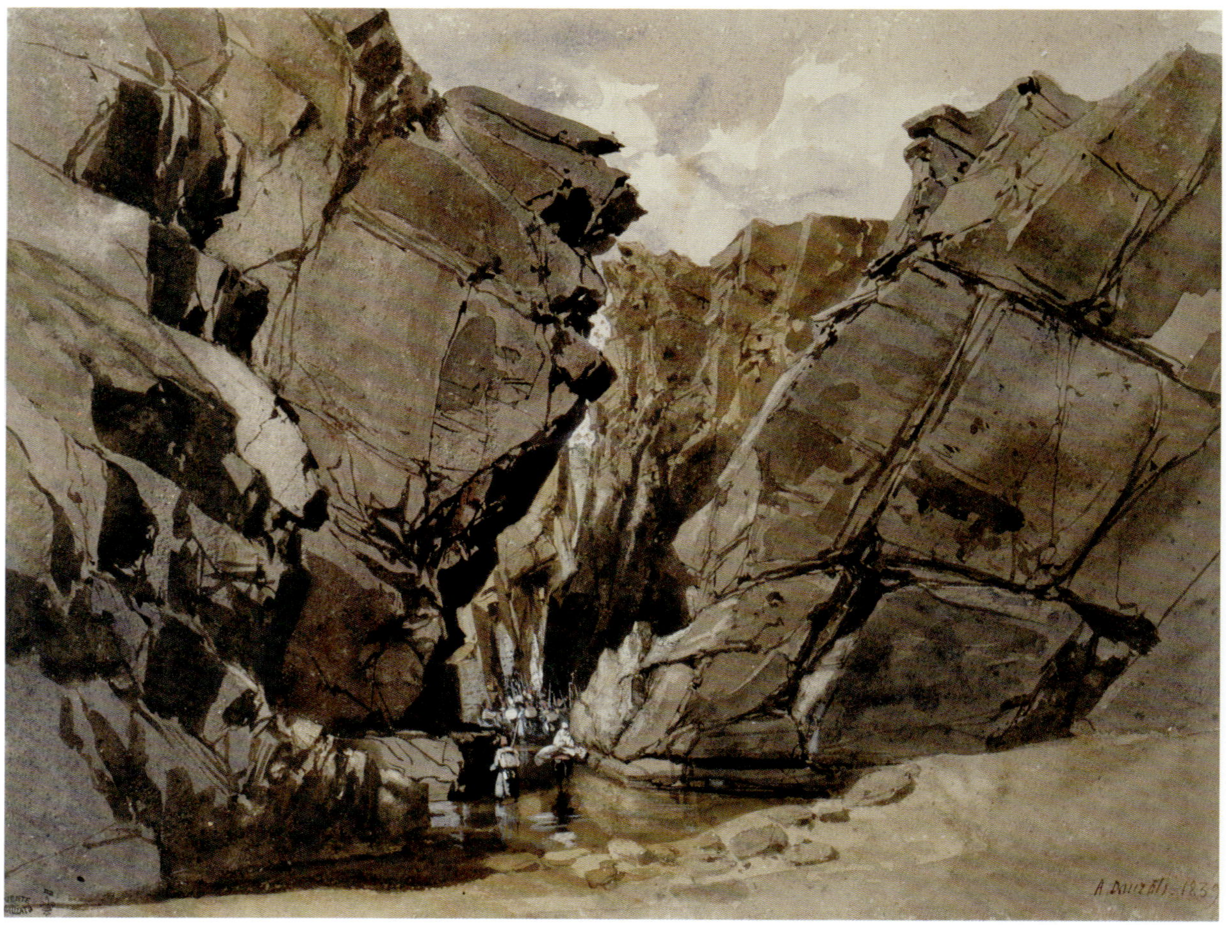

Figure 26.
Adrien Dauzats, *Passage of the Portes-de-Fer, Departure from the Last Gorge*, 1839. Watercolor on paper, 23.5 × 30.8 cm. Musée Condé, Chantilly, France (DE 696). Photo: Réunion des musées nationaux/Art Resource, New York (René-Gabriel Ojéda).

All told, Dauzats produced five compositions of the Passage des Bibans. One is a general view of huge rocky precipices seen from above (fig. 20).[62] This is the only *vue générale* of the type one might find in a *voyage pittoresque,* whether of France or Algeria.[63] The landscape looks imposing and extreme, despite the reassuring presence of traditional French landscape conventions such as trees and humans to indicate scale and the use of aerial perspective to suggest distance. However, Dauzats' arrangement of landscape forms here produces a powerful effect beyond what had been expected from landscape paintings in his era. In effect, Dauzats followed the guidelines for rendering a legible landscape as elaborated by Deperthes, but he introduced the canyon into the canon of landscape painting. Very little sky is visible; Dauzats depicted the site through the use of strong angular forms and sharp contrasts of dark and light. Even Caspar David Friedrich had never produced an image of the landscape that was so daunting. The tiny figures of the Armée d'Afrique huddled in front of the first cliff seem a meager power indeed compared to the force of nature. It is, without question, a sublime view of the world. Moreover, the artist imparted the sensation of vast distances and towering mountains with such cool precision that it produces an unprecedented sensation in the viewer.

The other four compositions are even more imposing, constraining, and extreme. In these works, the cliffs entirely dominate the images, and the soldiers appear like small ants scuttling through and over them.[64] While Dauzats went to some pains to make his soldiers more visible, important, and heroic in the Versailles versions, the viewer is mostly furnished with images of their backs as they squeeze through the narrow opening of the cliffs in a pack. The monumental architecture of the landscape towers over these tiny figures in the other four compositions, and while Dauzats' pictures produce the kinds of effect described by Deperthes in his elaboration of the *style champêtre,* he challenges many landscape conventions in them.

Because convention is based upon habit—because an idea of how a landscape painting ought to be organized is based on the appearance of prior landscape compositions—it makes a certain sense that Dauzats flouts such conventions. He was representing a landscape that had never been perceived by a French artist, and he intended to present the traversal of this landscape as heroic in itself. Why else put these images into the Museum of French History? It should not be surprising, then, that Dauzats' Portes de Fer compositions appear awesome and strange. What is surprising is that Dauzats manages to convince his audience that his representations are credible.

Dauzats sought to make his subjective response to the place visible, to demonstrate the trace of his presence in this landscape. He asserted the internal truth of the artist and he chose an avowedly subjective method of rendering the colonial landscape. This accounts for the difference in the appearance of these colonial landscapes, a heightening of their extremity. In one composition (fig. 21) the artist's vision of the landscape is translated in purely vertical terms, as opposed to the traditional horizontal nature of landscape compositions. Yet it was this image from the series that was most often reproduced throughout the artist's career.[65] Apparently, this was the most popular image of the series, since the response to this view was positive enough to generate further commissions.

Dauzats was among the first group of French artists who journeyed around 1830 to the regions known today as the Middle East and North Africa—but were then considered the Orient. The

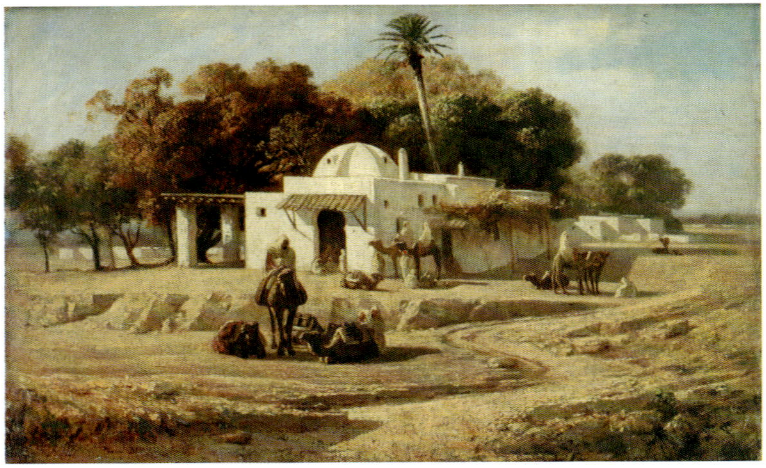

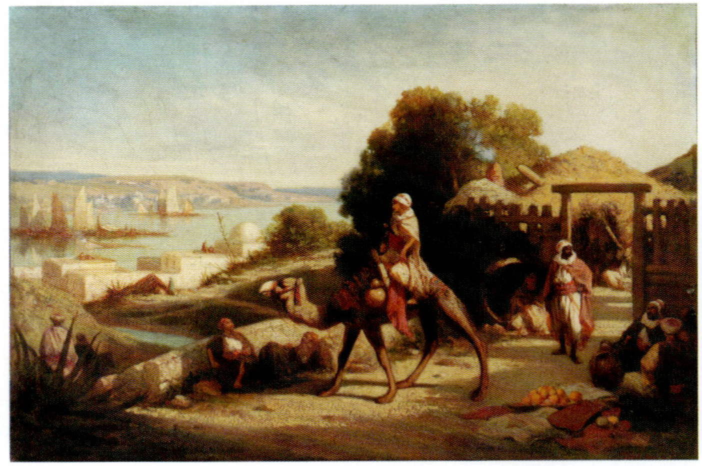

Figure 27.
Alexandre-Gabriel Decamps, *Oriental Landscape*, mid-nineteenth century. Oil on canvas, 41.3 × 59.4 cm. John J. Johnson Collection, Philadelphia Museum of Art, cat. 968.

Figure 28.
Prosper Marilhat, *Oriental Caravansery*, 1835. Oil on panel, 27.5 × 43 cm. John J. Johnson Collection, Philadelphia Museum of Art, cat. 1028.

French government helped these artists make the voyage; in addition, transportation had become relatively quick and reliable for the first time. Part of the mystique of Orientalist painting was derived from the fact that noted artists such as Alexandre-Gabriel Decamps, Prosper Marilhat, and Eugène Delacroix had seen these locales with their own eyes, made sketches there, and based their ultimate representations on firsthand information.[66] Yet these artists also needed to depict these lands as exotic.

Decamps, Dauzats, Marilhat, and Delacroix sought to offer the illusion to the French viewer that such places were beyond the familiar: take, for example, Decamps' images of Turkey, such as *Oriental Landscape* (mid-nineteenth century; fig. 27), or Marilhat's depictions of Egypt, such as *Oriental Caravansery* (1835; fig. 28), or Delacroix's portrayals of Morocco. The fantasy of a distant landscape became a fundamental part of the process of its representation: the exotic was based upon an absence of the familiar or, more specifically, the presence of the unfamiliar. In order to make their landscapes appear believable and not just wild backdrops to conventional scenes, however, the artists of this period developed a new series of conventions that allowed them to render exotic countries in recognizable terms without appearing similar to the landscapes of Italy, for example, as rendered by contemporary academic artists. Orientalist conventions, such as the use of strong tonal contrasts and bright colors, were coupled with the representation of exotic architecture and flora in order to present a cohesive image of an unfamiliar place. These practices were consistently commented upon by critics of the day and eventually became codified into a formula by the middle of the nineteenth century.

Dauzats' watercolors representing the Bibans, then, had to be singular, specific, and unique. Dauzats was the first French artist to see this territory, and his visual recording of it would be the first representation of the place offered to French citizens in the metropole. No other artist would have the authority to represent this site from firsthand observation. Yet the extremity of this landscape meant that the conventions for representing exotic locales would only be partially useful, and the artist had to improvise in order to render these scenes. As noted above, although the layout of the watercolors is horizontal, the landscapes are vertical. Further, the sky is blocked out by cliffs in all but the general view. No tropical vegetation, such as palms and aloes, that established similar scenes as exotic were present at the Algerian site, so the artist elected not to add them. Instead, he included only the scrubby bushes that clung to the rocks here and there. Thus the depicted landscapes add up to not much more than a stunning rendering of the effect of light on massive, vertical cliffs, with Dauzats focusing more upon geological fissures than subtle transitions into distance.

Although the general effect is of dark and towering masses, the cliffs themselves are very colorful. There are violets and dark reds, rich browns, and even ochre tones that are laid on top of one another to register these massive structures. The force of energy in their representation is sometimes achieved through the laying on of large patches of color and sometimes through the precise registration of narrow cracks that become linear compositional elements. The delicate balance of achieving the appearance of natural forms through abstract elements was occasionally beyond the artist's capabilities, as in the Versailles version of the *Departure* (fig. 23), in which several sections of the vertical composition—such as the rocky precipices in the left foreground—do not succeed in providing the illusion of space. Yet Dauzats was an expert at architectural renderings, and his experiences with vertical interior spaces made a believable depiction of a vertical landscape possible. Moreover, he was a skilled draughtsman, able to produce other pictorial effects that helped him achieve a sense of exotic particularity. As elucidated below, his mastery of the play of shadows and light allowed him to render effects that flout the spatial logic of perspective yet appear believable nonetheless. This naturalistic tendency—to render the natural world as perceived rather than to apply compositional formulas to it—is combined with his precise yet open handling of materials. Dauzats made landscape forms appear solid despite the gestural registration of pictorial elements.

Though the medium is listed simply as watercolor in museum documentation, the thickness of the pigment clearly indicates that the works were at least retouched, if not rendered, in gouache. Dauzats applied a thick layer of white paint on top of the dark layers to startling effect, depicting the play of light reflected from the water at the base of the canyon on the massive dark forms of the cliffs (figs. 21 and 26). This technique led Wilhelm Ténint to write: "If it is necessary to point it out, we did not expect such admirable vigor from watercolor, it seems to have survived the war."[67] Such a practice is not merely unprecedented but also surprisingly risky when employing water-based media—known to bleed when put into contact with any moisture. The crispness of the reflections is a technical tour-de-force that creates the incomparable illusion of reflected natural light illuminating a dark exterior chamber.

The artistic play of light and shadow is not merely an effect but also a structural element in the compositions, as is most readily apparent in the image of the third wall (figs. 21 and 26). A teardrop-shaped beam of light is visible between the two major cliffs that block the viewer's line of sight. In this narrow space, close to the center of the page, a light-colored distant hill and a patch of sky can be seen. This device, the only fragment of these two images that suggests distance in terms of perspective, is a mere sliver, a diamond at the center of the composition that seems to focus the energy of the bulging forms obscuring our view. This narrow opening, combined with a long triangle of sky, is the only visual release from the claustrophobic conglomeration of landscape masses. Such a concentration of pictorial energy could not be more distant from the dispersed compositions of Vernet's paintings of the siege of Constantine.

Moreover, while the strong light contrasts organize Dauzats' composition into distinct and rigid forms, the marks that constitute the landscape forms are less decisively resolved. This technique is first perfected in the Chantilly watercolors on a small scale and is intensified in the larger-scale paintings for Versailles. The latter works suggest a general loosening of the appearance of the scene, as opposed to the very precise draughtsmanship for which Dauzats was known. In both sets of watercolors, the cliffs dominate the imagery. While it is relatively easy to make cliffs appear believable from a distance, it is much harder to show how they look up close. Further, since it goes against all logic of landscape painting to render cliffs as a barrier to the composition, the artist must be very effective in order to convince his viewers that cliffs can *constitute* a landscape.

Dauzats composed his watercolors as sites of visual interest. From a distance these compositions appear clear and decisive because of the careful handling of dark and light forms, but up close, the surface and texture of the cliffs seize the viewer's eye. The layering of colors already discussed performs a push and pull in terms of depth: warm colors seem to sit on top of, or to be in front of, cold ones. Further, the linear aspects of the landscape forms—whether actual lines or edges of areas of color—enhance the dynamism of the composition. In the *Third Wall* (fig. 21), the teardrop of light is one linear element, combined with the shapes of the escarpments, that focuses the viewer's attention on the tricolor lit against the dark background of the ravine into which the soldiers advance. The vertical surface of the cliffs is a reflection of the vertical composition: the same lines and shapes that make the cliffs appear real, as composed of compressed minerals viewed in low natural light, are those that order this highly eccentric composition. These watercolors are compelling as representations of landscape, and it is significant that they represent the colony in the *galeries historiques.*

The images projected by the watercolors are immediate, perhaps too much so. If we imagine the Bibans represented by Dauzats as a metonym for the territory of Algeria, the colonial landscape takes on a formidable character. This is no grassy knoll, no verdant field to represent the possibility of French insemination of that foreign country. This landscape, replete with architectural metaphors, is a fortress, a series of imposing barriers that must be conquered one by one. Ironically, this fortress landscape is undefended, and it is rendered up to France through inscription. In two compositions (figs. 22 and 25), a soldier carves into the cliff, "ARMEE FRANÇAISE / 28 OCTOBRE / 1839." This signing of the landscape in the name of the French army is the only concrete way in which the French take possession of this landscape.[68] Despite the threat of ambush—represented as figures in white robes on top of distant cliffs, as in *Second Wall* (fig. 20)—there is no imminent danger here for our soldiers, but no comfort either. Considering the contemporary debate about the potential for colonization in Algeria, this image seems to present Algeria as a dazzling spectacle, a place of wonder and fantasy, but also of rocky shores and arid plains. It does not seem to offer an inducement for prospective colonial farmers.

By reworking the conventions of landscape, Dauzats produced another means for his viewers to come to terms with the colony as a site of interest.

These watercolors made for the *galeries historiques* do not actually depict a battle and they are not oils. Since the location is not the site of conquest, these images depart from the representations of the colonial landscape so far considered. Though Dauzats did not originate picturesque representations of Algeria, these watercolors suggest that Algeria is a place worth picturing, not just a land conquered by the French. The idea that French colonialism in Algeria is not always accompanied by the exertion of force is significant, because in these watercolors, it is possible to differentiate colonial seizure and imperial rule. The military figures featured in Dauzats' Portes de Fer images are not conquering: instead, they take possession of these spaces by passing through and by writing the name of the French army upon the wall. The mere presence of the French military signifies control over the territory, and that is what these images commemorate.

The Bibans are not actively colonized, then, and even the boosters of colonialism would be hard pressed to find a suitable use for these spaces. The French control over Algeria was here ordained by decree and by sheer ambition to know and to claim the spaces of the colony. Making this claim visible at the Museum of French History does not aggrandize the French military, as Vernet's monumental paintings do, but it reinforces the fact that the Algerian landscape, recently named and composed as such, is a territory of French history.

CHAPTER 3

Illustrated Travelogues and Imperial Tourism

The *Journal de l'expédition des Portes de Fer*

Born almost on the first day of lithographic illustration, and dying along with it, the picturesque landscape is perhaps the best symbol of it. These charming images, of an arguable exactitude, but handily crafted, light and always seductive, amused and instructed the French for half a century. Their influence on *moeurs* and ideas, literature and tourism, alone makes them worthy of study.

—Jean Adhémar

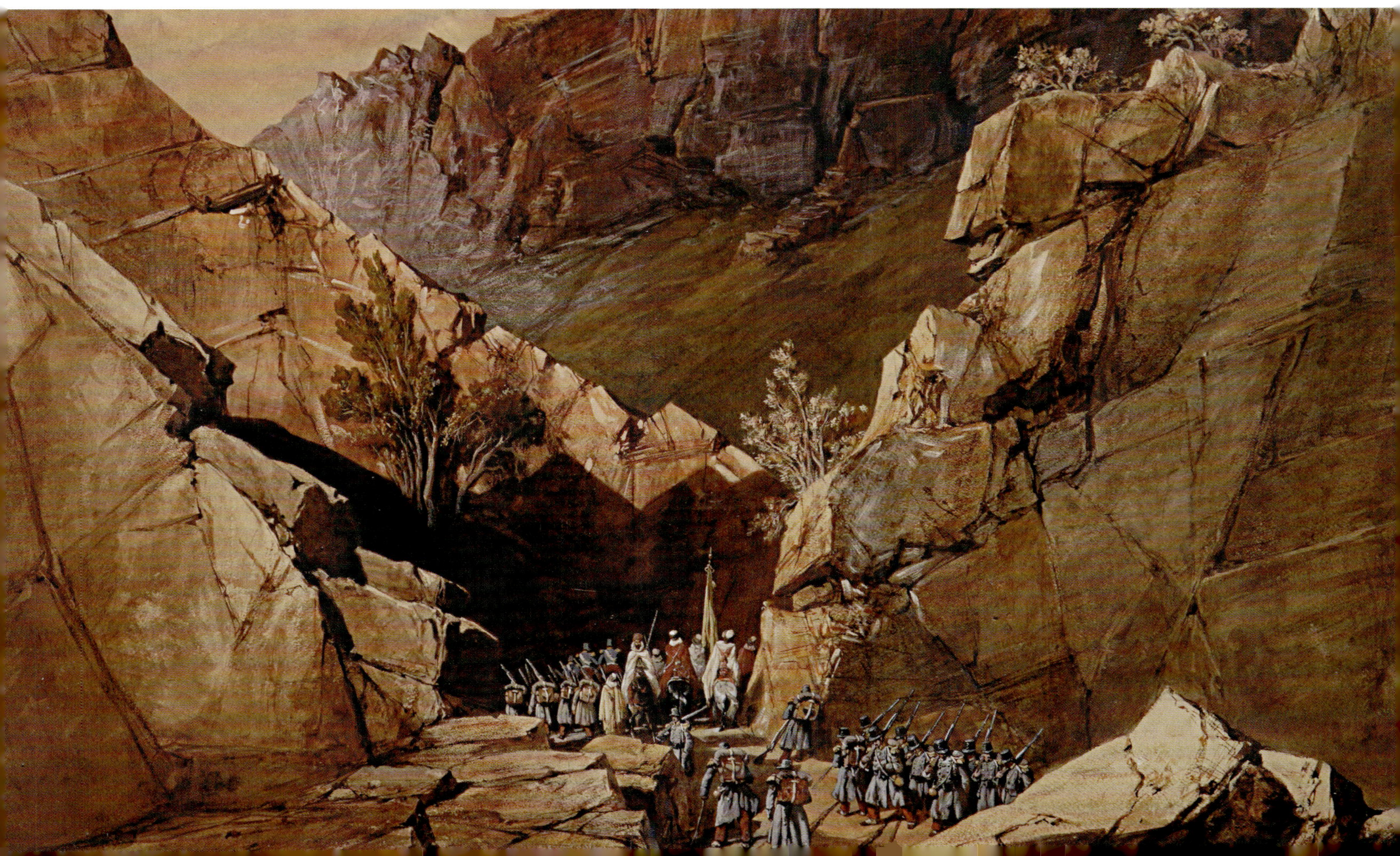

Landscape as History

The last chapter considered several manifestations of the representation of the Algerian landscape as part of the Museum of French History at Versailles, but this chapter will trace another paradigm for depicting the appropriation of colonial territory: illustration. When Adrien Dauzats created his series of watercolors for the duc d'Orléans to be placed in the *galeries historiques,* he was illustrating the expedition through a series of images. By the time he received the commission, he was already engaged in a more important project for the prince, namely, the illustrated commemorative book entitled *Journal de l'expédition des Portes de Fer* (*Journal of the Expedition of the Portes de Fer*), published in Paris in 1844. The artistic portion of this project was supervised by Dauzats, though the author is listed as Charles Nodier, who worked up the text from the duc's own notes.[1] After years of making drawings and prints for the *Voyages pittoresques et romantiques dans l'ancienne France (Picturesque and Romantic Voyages in Old France)*[2] under the supervision of Baron Taylor, Dauzats had the opportunity to orchestrate his own extravagant and high-profile illustrated book. This project was undoubtedly the highlight of Dauzats' career as an illustrator, but the illustrations and accompanying text raise many questions about what the *Journal* signifies for French history in Algeria and the representation of the colonial landscape: What is the difference between painting history and illustrating it? Can a landscape be a subject of history?

The title of the book suggests that it is an account of passing through one particular location, but in fact it records the prince's entire journey throughout Algeria. The fact that the book is called the *Journal de l'expédition des Portes de Fer* implies that the entire goal of the prince's trip was to pass through this gorge. Since there was no confrontation there, such a military expedition would not normally be worthy of commemoration, let alone a lavish 321-page illustrated book. Of course, the central actor was the crown prince—but his name is not in the title, despite the fact that the book commemorates one of his most important feats before he died tragically at age thirty-nine. Does a prince's going somewhere scenic with a huge military escort constitute history?

Overleaf: detail of fig. 23

The Portes de Fer, known today as the Bibans, were not simply scenic. As an examination of the watercolors featuring this location in the previous chapter demonstrated, it was an exceptional landscape. Indeed, the ancient Romans were turned back from this gorge without conquering it.[3] Add to this the fact that the land had recently been ceded to the French and that no military regiment had passed through it, and this passage starts to appear more like an event. Indeed, the *Journal* testifies not only to the bravery of the duc d'Orléans and his men but also to the symbolic significance of this landscape to the colony of Algeria. Further, the representation of the duc's regiment passing through this landscape in the form of an illustrated book leads to an unprecedented apprehension of the colonial landscape as a site of adventure and potential enjoyment. The Portes de Fer stimulated interest, engaged the reader, and achieved historical significance in this volume. This chapter will investigate how this landscape came to have such an effect.

After his successful campaign in Algeria, the duc d'Orléans decided to expand his earlier idea of having Dauzats make a few illustrations to commemorate the expedition.[4] He resolved to produce a book for officers and some soldiers who had served alongside him, as well as members of the royal family and foreign dignitaries.[5] This project was in addition to the other representations of the Portes de Fer that he had commissioned from Dauzats. Taken as a group, the series of watercolors for the Museum of French History at Versailles, the *Journal de l'expédition des Portes de Fer*, and an original oil painting listed in the duc's collection when exhibited in the Salon of 1840 (location unknown) amount to an extravagant multimedia depiction of the campaign sponsored solely by the duc and produced by Dauzats.

Among these representations, the book was by far the most expensive and time-consuming project, involving the collaboration of a number of artists, authors, and printmakers over a five-year period. It was a private venture with a patriotic and even diplomatic agenda—and after the prince's assassination in 1842, it became a commemorative project, as the prince's descendants decided to see the project through. Unlike most other illustrated books of its day, it was not explicitly intended to popularize a place for the public, or even to make the event available to a wider range of potential consumers. The project was a private memorial, not a market venture, and it was sent to its recipients as an entire work, not in numerous *livraisons,* or portions, over an extended period.[6]

Dauzats' illustrations of the Portes de Fer campaign in the *Journal* (figs. 29–33) bear separate examination. Illustrated book production, significantly influenced in this era by the introduction of lithography, was connected to both the development of tourism and armchair travel. Because a book is made for the appreciation of an individual in private, it offers a singular context for the reception of the imagery within it. What makes for a successful image in a book is different from that for a painting for a palace museum. Illustrated books translate the visual experience of landscape, connecting the pleasure an individual takes in appreciating landscapes to the private pleasure of interpreting a narrative that unfolds as one turns the pages. The way in which Dauzats' individual images unfold over time in the narrative signals a distinct kind of viewer, or reader, engendered by these works. The colonial landscape takes on a different guise, as both subject of a narrative and object of desire and possession. Dauzats' images, despite their reproducing an Algerian campaign for official and public use, suggest a private relationship between French viewer and Algerian landscape that progresses over time and leads to individual exploration.

Dauzats' Expedition

The previous chapter explored the political environment of the period in which the Portes de Fer campaign was executed. The campaign itself served a strategic function for the colony and created public awareness of colonial progress in France. The French saw the immediate need to establish trade routes between the newly conquered Constantine and the colonial capital, Algiers. The most direct route led through mountains and canyons, across land held by the Kabyles, also known as Berbers, the original indigenous inhabitants of this region who had survived the conquests of both the Romans and the Arabs.[7] Many of these tribes were, in theory, loyal to the French, and much of the land in the region of Constantine had been ceded to the French, but the reality of these claims had yet to be tested.[8] The military thus devised a high-profile expeditionary mission led by the duc d'Orléans, France's crown prince, to traverse a portion of this direct route. Maréchal Valée, the governor-general of Algeria at the time, decided that this expedition, peacefully concluded, would provide the perfect opportunity to lay claim to the area between Sétif and Algiers and convinced the prince to participate. The plan had the advantage of surprising any potential defenders of the region. Moreover, it

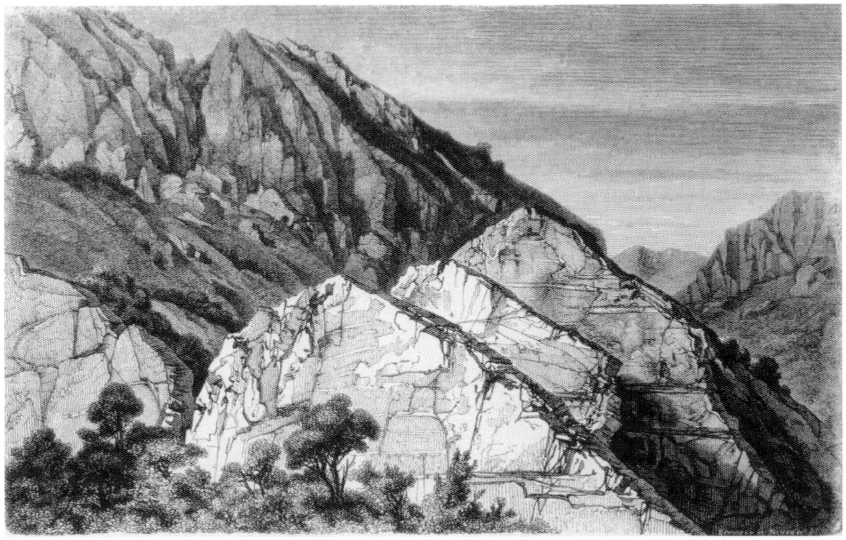

Figure 29.
Adrien Dauzats, *Portes de Fer, First Walls*. From Charles Nodier, *Journal de l'expédition des Portes de Fer* (Paris: Imprimérie royale, 1844), 260.

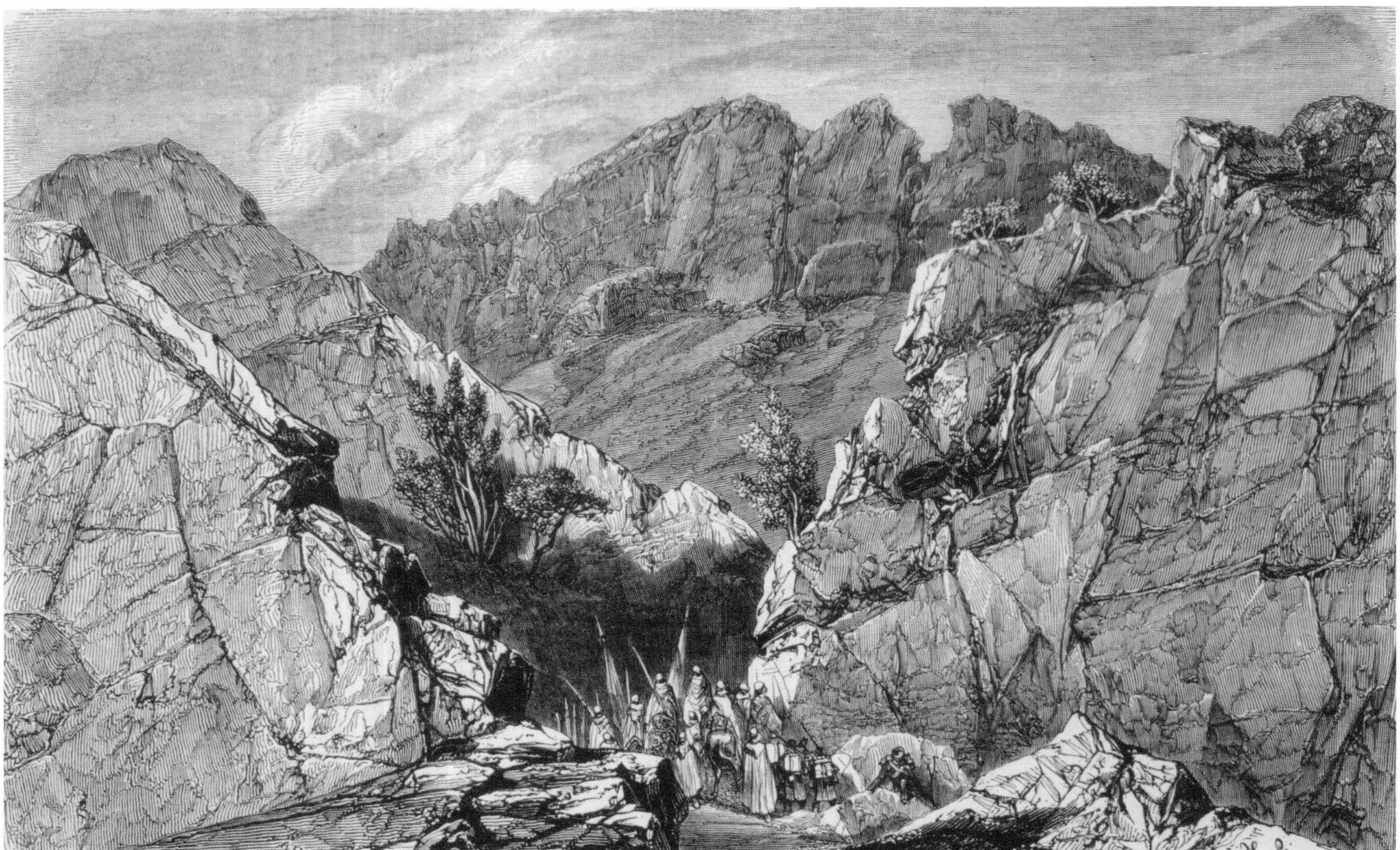

Figure 30.
Adrien Dauzats, *Portes de Fer, First Gorge*. From Charles Nodier, *Journal de l'expédition des Portes de Fer* (Paris: Imprimérie royale, 1844), 260.

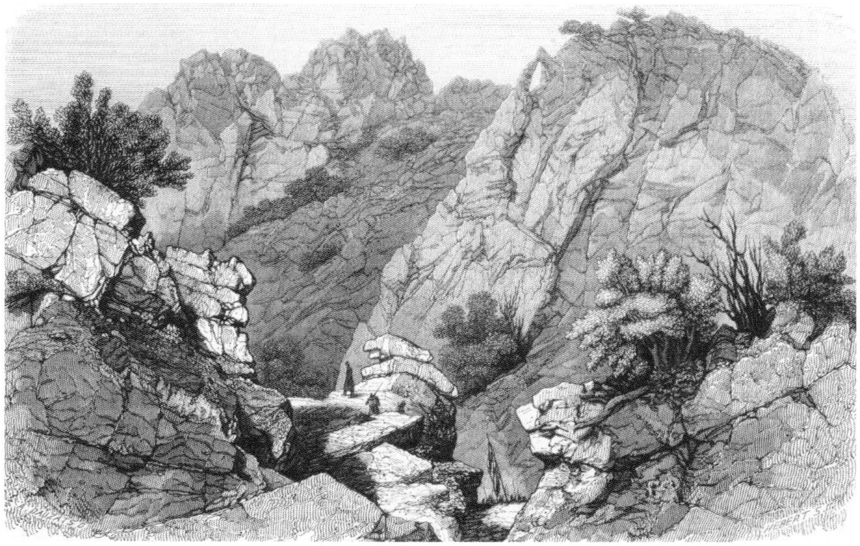

Figure 31.
Adrien Dauzats, *Portes de Fer, Second Gorge*. From Charles Nodier, *Journal de l'expédition des Portes de Fer* (Paris: Imprimérie royale, 1844), 262.

Figure 32.
Adrien Dauzats, *Portes de Fer, Bottom of the Ravine*. From Charles Nodier, *Journal de l'expédition des Portes de Fer* (Paris: Imprimérie royale, 1844), 262.

offered a way for the French to publicize the newly opened territory, since the press followed the royal family with very close attention. Having the prince lead this campaign would assure the French populace that Algeria was becoming pacified—and the risk involved in the mission was minimal. A symbolic visit from the future head of state would also reinforce the loyalty of the native Algerians of the region, particularly the members of Algeria's native aristocracy. Indigenous leaders came from throughout Algeria to shower the prince with gifts, and the prince bestowed medals to loyal chiefs in return.[9]

The company departed on 12 October and the entire expedition lasted less than a month. It traversed the Passage des Bibans without incident on 28 October, and the prince was warmly received by the local sheiks. It arrived in Algiers on 5 November and by 11 November, Maréchal Valée was delivering the news of the campaign's success and the prince's safety to the Chamber of Deputies. The French press did pick up the story, and news of the "heroic venture" was broadcast in *Le Moniteur Universel, Le Journal des Débats,* and *La Presse,* among other journals.[10] The accounts varied in their treatment, but all the journals printed the official report from Maréchal Valée. *Le Journal des Débats* sent a correspondent who issued two early reports concerning the mission from Constantine and the Sétif that were published on 23 October and 6 November, respectively. On 13 November, this journal

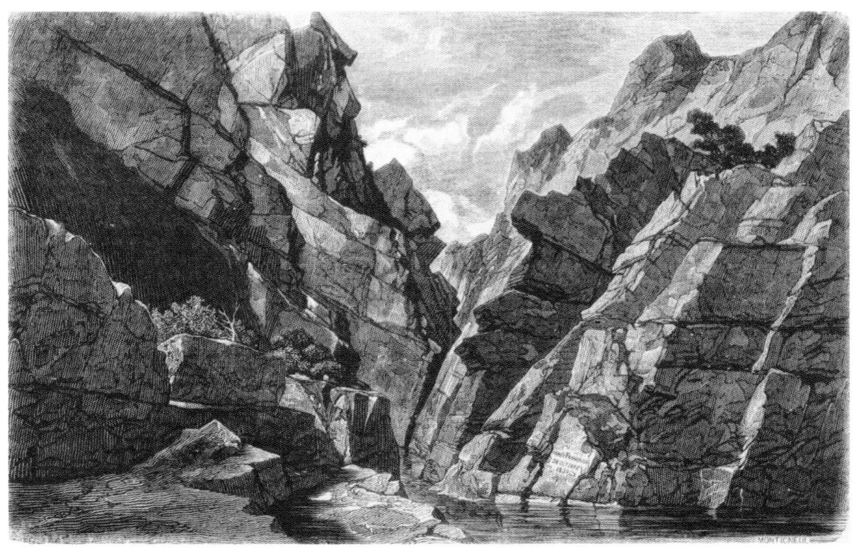

Figure 33.
Adrien Dauzats, *Portes de Fer, Departure from the Final Gorge*. From Charles Nodier, *Journal de l'expédition des Portes de Fer* (Paris: Imprimérie royale, 1844), 264.

published a day-by-day account of the campaign in addition to Valée's official report. All of the accounts focused on the enthusiastic reception that the prince had received from both colonists and natives. They all referred to the duc's heroic demeanor, his success at leading his regiment, and his desire to share the privations that the Armée d'Afrique had suffered for the glory of France. The most extensive of all reports was from *Le Moniteur Algérien,* reprinted in *Le Constitutionnel,* which provided details of the prince's triumphant return to Algiers and provided texts of the numerous speeches he gave before returning to France.[11]

No conflict was expected, yet the Portes de Fer passage did pose some risk. This was the most treacherous stretch of land between the two major cites and, in order to traverse it, the soldiers would have to pass through a very narrow and tall canyon—in some places only wide enough for a single mule to pass through, yet 600–800 feet in height—with a riverbed at the bottom. The *Journal* describes the passage in this way: "Finally, after marching for more than ten minutes in a sort of corridor formed by enormous escarpments, whose height continued to increase, and after turning right in a right angle, in the very bed of the torrent, we descend to the base of a sheer ravine dominated on all sides, where the least resistance would be impossible against the defenders of the canyon, if any presented themselves. There one finds the first door. It is an opening eight feet wide between two practically perpendicular cliffs, red above and an iron grey at their base."[12] As the *Journal* points out, this was an ideal place for an enemy ambush, and a sudden rainstorm might easily drown the entire regiment.

But what an excellent publicity opportunity for the prince! It was his good fortune that he had elected to take an artist with him to record the moment for posterity, and the choice of Dauzats tells us a few things about the nature and goals of

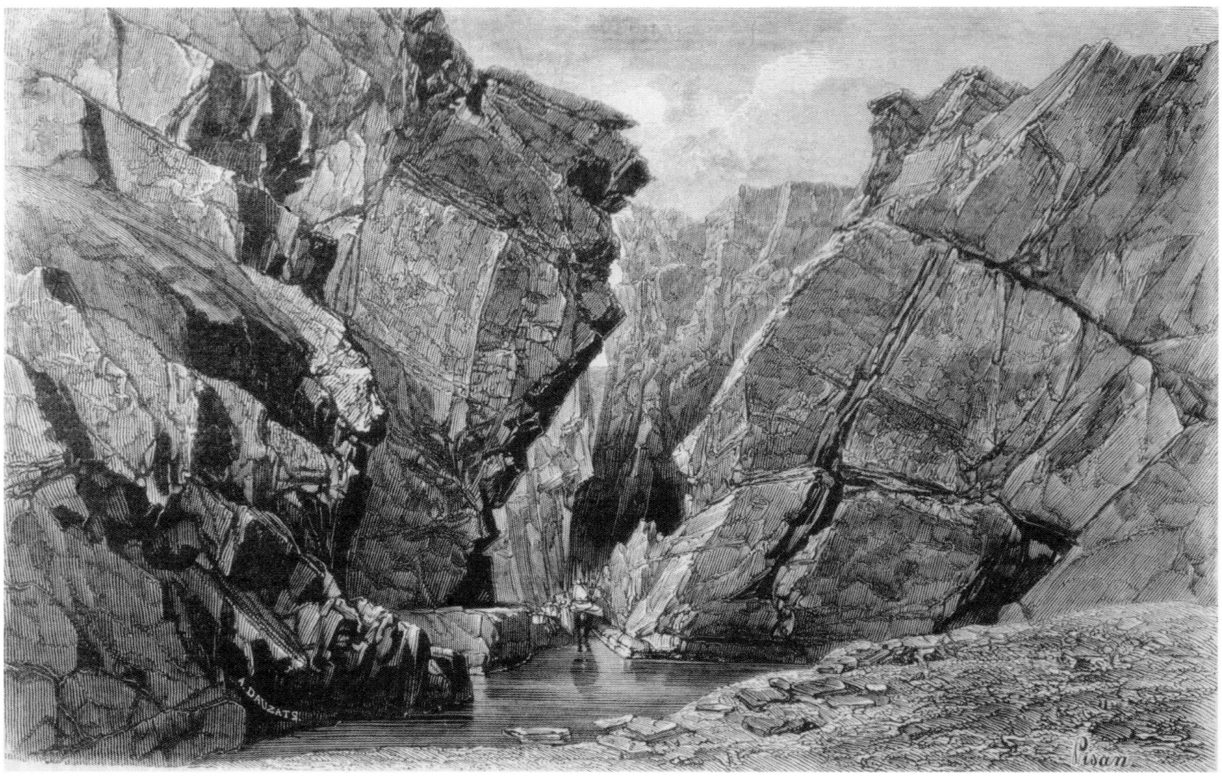

the original expedition. First, the fact that the military allowed a professional artist with no military experience or training to accompany the mission is indicative of the fact that it was considered more diplomatic than strategic. Artists had regularly accompanied diplomatic envoys in North Africa. Dauzats himself had visited Egypt in 1830 with Baron Taylor to negotiate the transfer of the Luxor Obelisk to France.[13] More famous is Delacroix's voyage to Morocco in 1831–32 with the Comte de Mornay. Also, Dauzats was known for his accurate draughtsmanship, so it seems that he would best serve a campaign mostly interested in reconnaissance, in returning to France with detailed and specific images of the region. Finally, Dauzats was an illustrator, more famous for his mass-produced lithographs than for the original works that spawned them. An artist like Dauzats could be counted on to reproduce his images and to popularize them for the largest possible audience. The diffusion of Algerian imagery throughout France would reach a pinnacle in the aftermath of the Portes de Fer expedition, and the choice of Dauzats to accompany the duc d'Orléans meant that France's ruling family would be included in the expanding sphere of colonial representations. Further, this military campaign would be commemorated through multiple reproductions that circulated more widely than the paintings of other Algerian campaigns. The implications of this practice of reproduction are significant and will be investigated later in the chapter.

Of course, it is impossible to say exactly why Dauzats was specifically selected for this mission. In a letter written from Algiers, just after the expedition was complete, he admitted that he did not know whether he had been asked to join simply to amuse the prince or to witness his reconnaissance.[14] The following year, Dauzats produced a painting of the Bibans for the Salon, now lost, which was recorded in the *livret* as belonging to the duc d'Orléans. But this painting was never part of the collection of the museum of Versailles, and the commission of watercolors for the Museum of French History did not emerge until after that.[15] It is clear, however, that Dauzats' talents were suited to the task of this particular mission.

Dauzats and the *Voyages pittoresques et romantiques dans l'ancienne France*

Adrien Dauzats began working for Baron Taylor in 1827 on the *Voyages pittoresques,* and he was a regular artistic contributor thereafter.[16] He was one of the artists sent out into the field to make site drawings. These drawings would then be remade as lithographs printed on china paper and pasted on the large thick pages (twenty inches in height) that were assembled into nineteen volumes featuring nine French provinces. This series of illustrated books was the most ambitious of any in nineteenth-century France and, though the *voyage pittoresque* form had existed since at least the eighteenth century, this particular project offered several important innovations. First of all, unlike previous *voyages pittoresques,* the locations featured in this series were French provinces. The French countryside, rather than a faraway land, became a source of research and inspiration in its own right. Like most illustrated books of its time, *Voyages pittoresques* was delivered in *livraisons* on a subscription basis and could then be collected into a volume when all the pieces had been assembled. This series was also of extraordinary size, very similar to the scale of Diderot's *Encyclopédie,* thus allowing for the large-scale lithographic prints that would become its trademark.

Beginning publication in 1819 and first collected into volumes in 1822, *Voyages pittoresques* was itself an advertisement for the possibilities of litho-

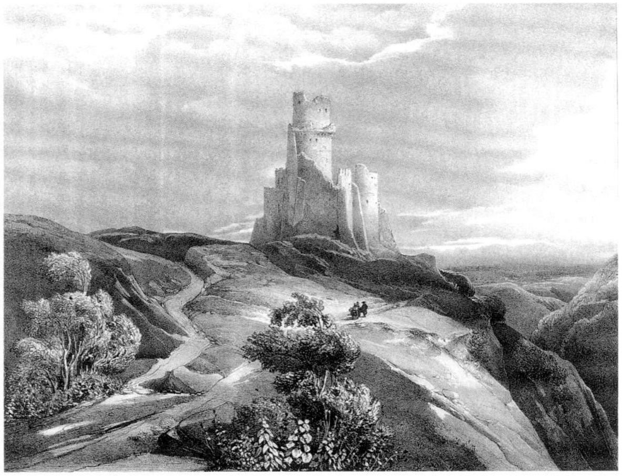

Figure 34.
J. Isadore Taylor, "Château de Tournoël: Auvergne." From *Voyages pittoresques et romantiques dans l'ancienne France: Auvergne*, vol. 1 (Paris: Bertrand, 1829), plate 21.

graphic printing. As Charles Nodier proclaimed in the introduction to the work, opinions were divided on the value of the recently developed printing technique of lithography, but the purpose of this venture was to demonstrate its advantages. He wrote: "Freer, more original, more rapid than the burin, the hardy lithographic crayon seems to have been invented in order to transcribe the free, original and rapid inspirations of the traveler who realizes his sensations."[17] Indeed, as Nodier described it, the subjective experience of the artists who made the drawings for these volumes was the key to appreciating the work: "This voyage is not then a voyage of discoveries; it is a voyage of impressions, if it is permitted to express oneself in this way."[18]

If the transmission of the subjective experience of travel through illustrations was the purpose of this publication, the reader's experience was equally essential to the project. It is not merely that the reader sees the views, sites, and monuments; rather, the reader is to appreciate them, to be affected by the beauty of these images and the experiences that are transcribed therein. Colin Campbell has discussed the importance of the viewer's empathy to Romantic art and the application of that paradigm to consumer culture. In order to explain modern consumerism, Campbell asserts that "individuals do not so much seek satisfaction from products, as pleasure from the self-illusory experiences which they construct from their associated meanings."[19] These associated meanings are exactly what the artists and authors of *Voyages pittoresques* sought, as demonstrated by Nodier's avowed interest in the emotions that these places aroused. Campbell's thesis explains how such a dynamic operates to engage the viewer through daydreaming and the production of pleasure through associations that are introduced in the imagery of the voyages. In other words, reading a travelogue offers a parallel experience to that of the traveler who went to the place and illustrated his impressions. The fact that the reader does not have to endure any of the hardships of the journey makes armchair tourism both desirable and pleasurable. What is more, since the *livraisons* came in regular installments, the reader's thirst for novelty was never exhausted but perpetually renewed.

A prime example of an image from the *Voyages pittoresques* that both translates and inspires strong feelings is "Château de Tournoël: Auvergne" (fig. 34) made by Baron Taylor in 1822 and now in the first volume on the province of Auvergne. This monument was considered so important that it received no fewer than ten illustrations in the volume. The text describes it in these terms: "About one league from Riom, a chateau rises from volcanic masses. . . . The chateau is partly dismantled but the dungeon and several towers are well-situated on the peak, braving the efforts of time, just as it has braved more than one siege and the attempts of men to destroy it."[20]

The chateau is centrally placed in this image, commanding the view of the sky over vertiginous cliffs and a valley behind. The crumbling walls of the main tower and the perimeter of the castle suggest a fortress softened by the ravages of time and men and, in this sense, the text seems to echo this image. The cliffs are mostly barren, save the two clumps of foliage in the foreground that make visible the traces of strong winds blowing across these mountains. The grey clouds above are broken by bright sunlight at the right edge that cuts across the cliffs and illuminates a group of three figures rendered in very small scale. Their proximity and their size imply not only the enormity of the distant fortress but also the puniness of humans in this grand image of the world. While the half-ruined castle dominates the landscape—indeed, its vertical appearance seems almost to be a continuation of the volcanic peaks—the figures appear as tiny creatures scurrying across the landscape. Contrasts of light and dark reinforce this sublime view of humans and the natural world. Taylor has expertly drawn on a wide range of medium grey tones to provide details in the landscape and to allow the eye of the viewer to progress from the fore to the background. Such an image is self-consciously piquant, full of sensations of nature and a feeling for this historical monument whose story is more fully elaborated in other images and in the text.

In his work on landscape imagery of this period, Nicholas Green has articulated how such images function to stimulate longing and to provide underlying meaning. Connecting landscape painting to travel literature and the development of the suburbs outside of Paris, he found that the imagery of landscape projected a sense of nature for viewers of the epoch. Attending to real estate advertisements for country houses in the period, he wrote: "The language of views and panoramas prescribed a certain visual structure to the *nature* experience. The healthiness of the site was condensed with the actual process of looking at it and moving around it with your eyes. Environmental values are here articulated in relation to visual modes of consumption that enabled the visitor simultaneously to look at 'the picture' and plunge into sensation."[21] By investigating the position of landscape and nature as ideas within the metropolitan framework of contemporary Parisian culture, Green forcefully exposes the ideological freight that landscape imagery carries. His association of a visual structure of the "nature experience" with certain forms of landscape description rings true for the *Voyages pittoresques*. The book's visual language is not borrowed from conventions for rendering landscapes that existed previously and were taught in the academy. Rather, the imagery of the *Voyages pittoresques* forms a prolepsis, forging a new relationship of image to viewer and communicating new experiences that the reader/viewer can engage both directly, by looking at the image, and indirectly, by daydreaming about the imagery.

Algeria Illustrated

The *Journal de l'expédition des Portes de Fer* is an unusually sumptuous book, but it was one of many books that illustrated the colony for French readers. Unlike more general illustrated works on Algeria, the *Journal* focused upon a single expedition. Its 321 pages of text are adorned with 193 plates. Though the book is of medium format (approximately 8 in. × 11 in.), there are a large number of full-page illustrations made in woodcut. Only one printing was ever achieved, and 1519 books were produced.[22] The text, taken from the prince's own notes, was edited by Charles Nodier, Dauzats' longtime collaborator. Dauzats was in charge of the artistic portion of the work and enlisted Auguste Raffet to execute the military portraits and Alexandre-Gabriel Decamps to produce genre pieces. Dauzats did not produce his own woodcuts, but left the engraving to a handful of specialists, including Pisan, Hébert, and Montigneul. At the time this work was produced, it was part of an efflorescence of illustrated journals and books in France. *L'Illustration*, which began production in 1843, was the first large-format illustrated journal, and illustrated *voyages pittoresques* were being produced of every imaginable destination.[23] Algeria was no exception. Further, Dauzats was himself involved in a wide variety of book projects—not only Baron Taylor's *Voyages pittoresques* but also a travel novel, without illustrations, that he produced with Alexandre Dumas[24] as well as a small illustrated book, *San Juan d'Ulùa,* that chronicled the French mission in Mexico of 1838.[25] This last work, which Dauzats helped his friend Paul Blanchard publish in 1839, was more diminutive in size and less sumptuous in terms of prints but nevertheless can be seen as the direct precursor to the *Journal de l'expédition des Portes de Fer.*

Blanchard, who had worked alongside Dauzats as an illustrator for Baron Taylor in Spain,[26] had been brought along on the French campaign in Mexico that departed on 31 August 1838. He returned with a number of sketches from the expedition, which took him across much of modern-day Mexico. France's involvement with Mexico in the nineteenth century, while not insignificant, amounted to much less contact than with Algeria. For this reason, the images Blanchard produced were the first pictures of Mexico available in France. The publisher must have counted on the novelty of these images, combined with the general French interest in their country's own military exploits, to sell the *livraisons* that appeared for 2 francs 50 each. *San Juan d'Ulùa* was the first book of its kind to bring together a lengthy account of the military expedition penned by the artist and several contextual documents—such as an *aperçu général* of Texas—with illustrations of the campaign and the landscapes traversed.[27] This work included eighteen full-page images as well as vignettes at the beginning and end of each chapter. Though the quality of the prints is greatly inferior to those in the later volume and the book was a speculative project, it is clearly the prototype for the book Dauzats developed for the prince. The prints in the *Journal* are also in woodcut, and the insertion of small images into the text itself was entirely new in book production of that period.[28] While the *Magasin Pittoresque* had juxtaposed images and text in its pages since 1833, the illustrated books that appeared in the 1830s largely kept the images separate from the text, even if the only purpose of the text was to elaborate details about monuments viewed in the prints. The integration of image and text, tentatively proposed in *San Juan d'Ulùa*, was thoroughly explored by Dauzats in the *Journal,* for which there were no concerns about production costs.

If the *Journal* followed *San Juan d'Ulùa* in terms of format and the account of a recent military expedition, it must be seen also in terms of other illustrated works featuring Algeria produced in the period. These works, seeking to acquaint French readers with the landscape, inhabitants, and customs of their emerging colony, fall into two categories. The first consists of independent, often scholarly, works on Algeria with illustrations appended to them to add interest or to give the reader a better idea of the location.[29] While the images in this kind of book were first produced as an atlas, entirely separate from the book, they eventually became incorporated into the book's format. In this category, the relationships between the illustrators and the authors varied widely. Some authors simply found artists with images of Algeria that would enhance their texts; others reprinted sketches of rank amateurs who had accompanied the author and whose sketches attempted to illustrate the scene.[30] It is not necessary to investigate this group of works in depth, because their illustrations were conceived as separate from the text. The second category of books, more relevant to an analysis of the *Journal*, was produced by professional artists. In these works, the prints serve as the focus, and the didactic text seeks to inform the reader about the importance of the represented location.[31]

As described briefly in Chapter 1, immediately after the conquest of Algiers, there was a great demand for images of this territory across the Mediterranean. This demand was initially filled by battle paintings shown at the annual Salon as well as by dioramas, panoramas, and sketches shown in other public venues. The production of travel imagery from the area around Algiers was also achieved in print. Though the first illustrated journal, *Magasin Pittoresque*, did not appear until 1833, artists began traveling to Algiers to record the appearance of the newly conquered land and, through lithography, they were able to create illustrated books from drawings made on site.

Travel literature had included print illustrations since the eighteenth century, but the flourishing of illustrated travel guides dates to after the development of lithography in France and owes much to Taylor's *Voyages pittoresques*. The format of a full-page illustration accompanied by a didactic caption became the norm. Also apparent was the developing market for armchair travel among the French public. Whereas earlier voyages of discovery had published the results of scientific studies, as in the notable examples of Bougainville's expeditions to the South Pacific and Denon's *Description d'Égypte,* the illustrated books that emerged after *Voyages pittoresques* were created to generate interest in the places represented and circulated among a wider literate population. Most important, they were structured around visual interest, describing and illustrating locations that were important monuments of views of significant sites. The illustrations in these books were designed to interest and please, not to educate.

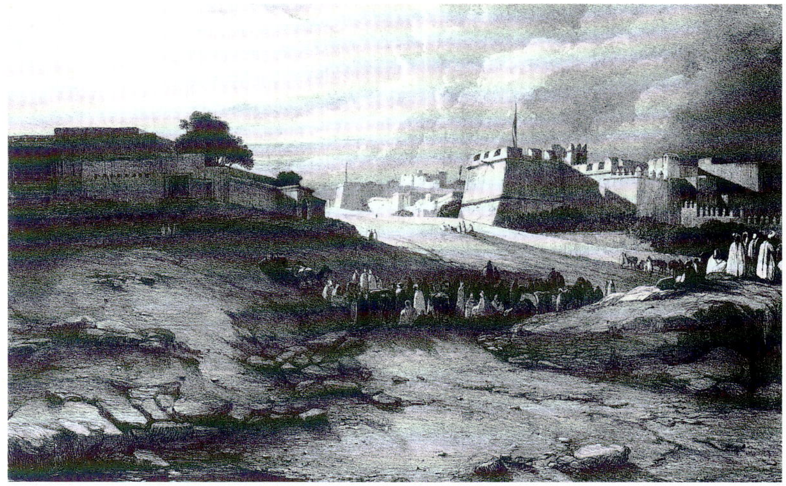

Figure 35.
E. Lessore and W. Wyld, "Ramparts of the Casbah." From *Voyages pittoresques dans la Régence d'Alger* (Paris: Charles Motte, 1835), plate 28. Bibliothèque nationale de France.

One of the first illustrated books to feature what was, at that point, still titled the Regency of Algiers was E. Lessore and W. Wyld's *Voyage pittoresque dans la Régence d'Alger* (*Picturesque Voyage in the Regency of Algiers*), published between 1833 and 1835.[32] The focus of this book was the series of fifty-one full-page illustrated scenes by Lessore and Wyld, the latter a British illustrator who made his living in Paris. Captions described the sites. In addition to the extensive captions, the book contains twenty pages of text about Algiers, its history, its geography, and so on. The images render the city of Algiers and it environs in great detail, including general views, architectural monuments, and the city's native inhabitants and the particularities of their costume. In this sense, the work is unquestionably more comprehensive in its rendering of the region than any other visual representation offered to the French public by this point. The work echoes *Voyages pittoresques* by concentrating on a single region and providing a complete representation of all of its picturesque aspects. The lithographs also echo the romantic tone of Taylor's prototype. The subjects, such as "Ramparts of the Casbah" (fig. 35), featuring a medieval-looking fortress perched on the top of a hill, are selected to generate a striking impression. Stylistically, these images follow the accepted tenets of romantic lithographic illustration, such as high contrasts of dark and light as well as a loose and sketchy handling of materials.

Despite the visual interest of Lessore and Wyld's lithographs, the book as a whole seeks to instruct its readers about the colony. Illustrated travelogues clearly intended to inform viewers about the world at large by pairing images with explanatory, educational captions. While the selection of views is well rounded in this volume, providing information about monuments, customs of the inhabitants, and the general aspect of the place, the French presence is suppressed in order to provide an anthropological tone. The result is a multilayered image of the location rendered as an exotic place that seems to have no connection to France through colonial domination or any other form of contact. This general pattern occurs in other illustrated travelogues of the period. The first illustrated travelogues in France featured places that were already of great interest to French travelers, such as Italy, Greece, and the Holy Lands, and the great impact of Taylor's project was to focus the public's interest on the regions of France, whose wonders were less known in Paris. Lessore and Wyld's volume takes the same concerns of picturesque interest and romantic style and applies them to the recently seized colony. Rather than signify the French conquest, as battle paintings and the *Panorama of Algiers* had done, *Voyage pittoresque dans la Régence d'Alger* provided an image of this region outside of recent political events as a distinct and exotic realm made available to the French viewer pictorially. Unlike so many writings on Algeria during this period, this book did not present an explicit political program for the French in the colony but instead made such changes to the region invisible. This elision of the colonizing power's presence in both images and texts has been noted by many writers on Orientalism, beginning with Said. The focus upon the picturesque aspects of the Regency of Algiers apparently involved removing the traces of the French transformation of the city that had been sketched by Langlois immediately after the siege (see Chapter 1). Langlois himself never showed these sketches or made reference to them in any finished works he showed in public. Lessore and Wyld followed this example, and their picturesque illustrations of Algiers and its immediate surroundings provided a prototype for future illustrations of the colony, but a prototype largely dependent upon previous picturesque travelogues. The sites they illustrated were visited time and again by other artists, illustrators, and writers, who, following this framework, made pictures of these same locations.

Dauzats' *Journal de l'expédition des Portes de Fer* stands apart from Lessore and Wyld's picturesque rendition of Algiers, despite the artist's deep involvement with Taylor's project.[33] It is also distinct from other predecessors because his work is not in any way an analysis or general description of Algeria, nor is the text merely a lengthy accompaniment to the plates. Nevertheless, the *Journal* can be classed with other illustrated books on Algeria because it provided a unique means for the French reader/viewer to familiarize her- or himself with the colony. The imagery in this book falls into familiar categories: general views and landscapes, figures, and genre scenes. Further, in the *Journal,* these genres were divided among the three artists who participated. Three distinct artistic styles, therefore, underline the artistic categories into which the images were parsed. This effect breaks down the cohesiveness of the narrative. As noted above, Dauzats concentrated on landscapes, Raffet

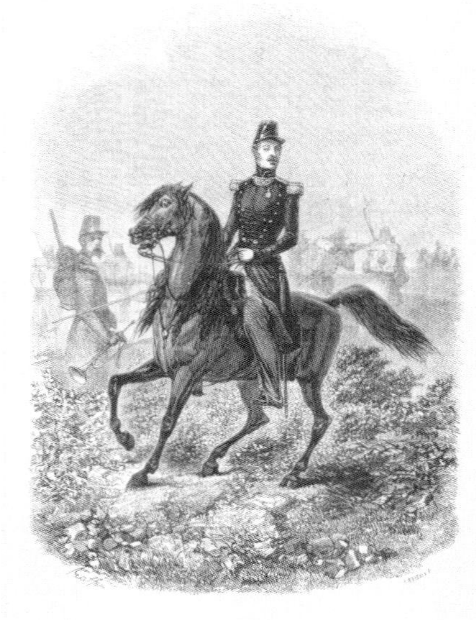

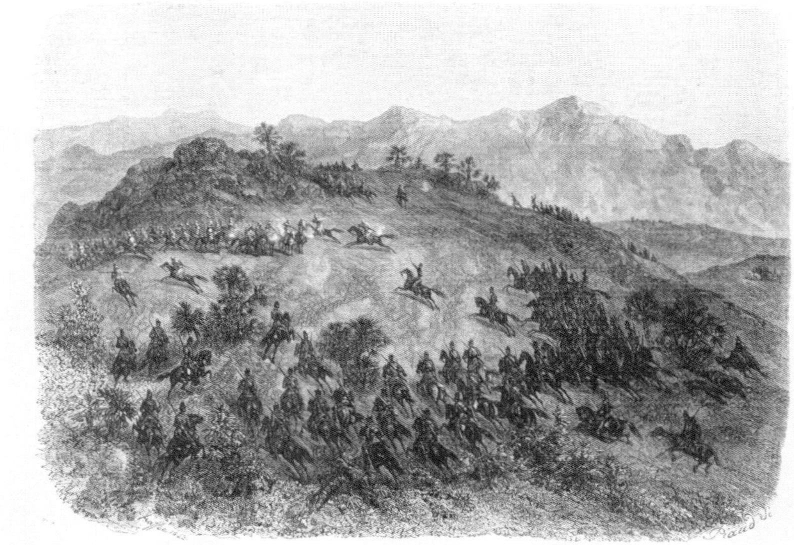

Figure 36.
Auguste Raffet, "Colonel Changarnier." From Charles Nodier, *Journal de l'expédition des Portes de Fer* (Paris: Imprimérie royale, 1844), 276.

Figure 37.
Auguste Raffet, "Circular Charge Commanded by Colonel Miltgen." From Charles Nodier, *Journal de l'expédition des Portes de Fer* (Paris: Imprimérie royale, 1844), 278.

was charged with producing portraits, and Decamps illustrated genre scenes, mostly on a smaller scale. While this division of labor played to the strengths and reputations of the three artists involved, their distinct styles led to a heterogeneous group of illustrations.

Raffet's military portraits (fig. 36) and group scenes focus on the expedition participants—mostly French officers but also Algerian natives—isolating those who took part in the campaign from the sites they traversed. In the few cases where Raffet did illustrate a background for the activities of the campaigners, such as in "Circular Charge Commanded by Colonel Miltgen" (fig. 37), he had to base his landscape depiction on the descriptions and, occasionally, drawings provided by Dauzats, since Raffet had never visited Algeria.[34] Unlike Dauzats' Portes de Fer imagery, Raffet's landscapes are backdrops for the activities of the French military, whose presence animates the settings.

Decamps' genre scenes are even further removed from the sites and activities of the expedition. Decamps never visited Algeria.[35] Moreover, he was famous for formulaic renditions of Oriental genre scenes (fig. 27), and for this volume, he was charged with illustrating Algerian natives. These Orientalist genre scenes, full of exotic atmosphere, are true to form for Decamps, who made his reputation on such material. Yet they seem at odds with the informational character of the book. Since Decamps' illustrations did not provide observed details, it seems that his works were included because of his reputation as an important Orientalist artist. The presence of such generic imagery demonstrates the continuity of Orientalist stereotypes in the context of an official narrative of a military campaign. In one of the few full-page illustrations he produced for the book, "Arabs Waiting in Ambush" (fig. 38), one sees a small group of Arabs cowering in the bushes, waiting to attack a group of hunters. This scene is totally irrelevant to the text—no ambushes occurred on this campaign, let alone by a small group of Arabs—but the image does reproduce established negative stereotypes of Arabs as devious and violent while placing

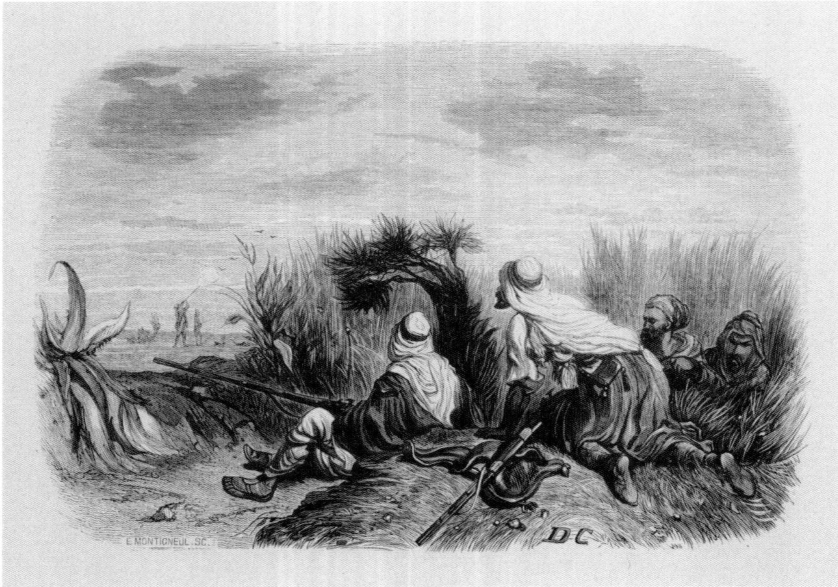

Figure 38. Alexandre-Gabriel Decamps, "Arabs Waiting in Ambush." From Charles Nodier, *Journal de l'expédition des Portes de Fer* (Paris: Imprimérie royale, 1844), 104.

them in a vaguely exotic, generalized landscape (note the strange foliage).

The woodcuts representing the Portes de Fer (figs. 29–33) were made after Dauzats' watercolors, though it appears by the disposition of figures in the compositions that they were made from the sketches now at Chantilly and not from the watercolors at Versailles. The copies are relatively faithful, but the process of wood engraving nonetheless removes many of the traces of immediacy so prevalent in the watercolors. The contours of the compositions were reproduced, but lacking are their complex color combinations as well as Dauzats' masterful draughtsmanship, which fixed linear elements of the composition while suggesting the mutability of brushstrokes. Another result of the translation from watercolor to woodcut is a systematization of shading that negates the accidental effects of light and vision in favor of a legible, comprehensible group of landscape forms. Comparing two versions of the *Second Gorge* (figs. 24 and 31) makes this distinction most evident. In Hébert's reproduction of Dauzats' watercolor, there are perhaps five tones used to depict a narrow and well-lit strip amid more obscure rock forms. These tones are divided into distinct sections registered in progressive shades of grey. In the watercolor, by contrast, the effect of shading is far more subtle. Rather than dividing the composition into discrete sections, the dark and light areas distributed throughout the composition serve to unify this landscape of angular masses. The watercolor positions the viewer in a light-filled landscape on the edge of a dark gorge, whereas the print implies that the viewer stands in a dark landscape looking at a beam of light that cuts across it. It is not merely that the subtlety is lost, but the mood, and even the meaning, of the landscape shifts.

The issue is not whether Hébert is a good copyist. Dauzats had extensive experience with illustrated books and had a royal budget to work with, so he would not have enlisted a hack. The point is that reproduction alters the appearance and the meaning of the imagery. Born as copies, book illustrations have a life different from paintings. Book illustrations are perceived under different conditions and they have a specific effect upon viewers. I want to consider further the perception and consumption of visual information through books, especially those that represent Algeria, because in book illustration it is possible to trace another modality of the empire of landscape. Travel illustrations translate Algeria into French terms, but this is achieved by reproduction and diffusion, not the merits of a particular artist. The reproductive woodcut, as deployed to illustrate the course of the expedition through this unique site, simplifies the visual experience of the place that Dauzats sought to reproduce in the Portes de Fer watercolors. The format codifies the reader's visual experience through a formulaic transcription of landscape elements. The result is a group of stunning woodcuts that form the core of the travelogue. Yet these images come into existence far from the landscape itself and can only interpret the artist's original transcription of it. The illustrations accept the transformation of space into landscape as a *fait accompli* and thereby propagate an image of the colony that corresponds to the picturesque interest that travelogues provide. While the book is exceptional, its very nature is to transmit an image of landscape to a wider audience and, in so doing, generate extensive interest in the colony and France's military campaigns there.

Looking at two other illustrated books on Algeria, produced the year before, will help elucidate the relationship of landscape imagery to the project of promoting the colony through illustrated books. Adrien Berbrugger, the director of both the Library and Museum of Algiers, oversaw the production of an enormous, four-volume tome illustrated with color lithographs and dedicated to the popularization of Algeria in France. *L'Algérie historique, pittoresque et monumentale . . . (Algeria: Historical, Picturesque and Monumental . . .)* was a comprehensive work published in 1845, identical in scale and format to Taylor's *Voyages pittoresques*. It sought to produce a comprehensive index of Algeria for its readership. The wealth of plates and historical anecdotes filling these volumes is impressive indeed, and the clear goal was to publicize and to provide precise information about Algeria. The publisher, J. Delahaye, wrote in the foreword, "In this way our readers will be made familiar at once with the regions [of Algeria] as the panorama will unravel before them in interesting pictures, being more exact since they were traced on site by men as capable as they are impartial."[36] Even if the information provided was exact and impartial, the context for consuming it was not. Berbrugger made his intentions clear in a letter to Algeria's governor-general, Maréchal Valée. In this correspondence, the author/editor connected the project of gathering views and presenting information about Algeria in Europe with presenting the "glorious events that have taken place here since France planted its flag," such as military victories and the creation of civil institutions and public works.[37] In other words, it was not merely the place that this work sought to popularize, but the French activities there as well. This is boosterism mixed with propaganda, all presented as a *voyage pittoresque,* a journey through the colony and its history. In this convoluted form, the viewer/reader consumes the visual information about Algeria transmitted as a form of landscape appreciation. The picturesque journey cuts through a colonial landscape, and the format of illustrated volumes makes it available to any individual.

Notably, Berbrugger employs the term "panorama" to describe the experience of reading a book, an experience that unfolds for the private reader over time. The reference to the panorama underlines the spectacular nature of the project and points to the goal of showing all of Algeria in an exact manner. This perspective helps explain Dauzats' illustrations in the *Journal.* When we survey his Algerian imagery in this light, there are unquestionable similarities between Dauzats' illustrated book and Langlois' *Panorama of Algiers* as a form of popular entertainment. Both mass-produced illustration and panoramas were business ventures that flowered in the first half of the nineteenth century. Both sought to profit from making imagery available to a wide public at a relatively low cost. In these specific cases, both forms of image production endeavored to popularize the colony and, in fact, their very existence depended upon the public's interest in seeing images of it. However, considering how these two forms of visual imagery were consumed clarifies the differences between them. While a panorama is something of a theatrical event, literally staged for a "run," travel illustrations are permanently available for viewing by individuals in private.[38] Further, the panorama is immediate and (apparently) complete, while illustrations, particularly when presented in a book format, are perceived serially over time. Thus, while a panorama stages a public spectacle that generates a collective desire, an illustrated book seeks a subjective reader whose desires are fueled by an interest in information mixed with visual pleasure.

Another illustrated book published in 1843, P. Clausolles' *Voyage pittoresque ou histoire de la Régence d'Alger depuis les temps les plus reculés jusqu'à nos jours . . . (Picturesque Algeria or the History of the Regency of Algiers . . .)*, demonstrates the importance of images in the presentation of history. This is a comprehensive historical work, as opposed to Berbrugger's comprehensive illustrated representation of Algeria, but the images seek to illustrate certain episodes or provide a source of pictorial interest. In this sense, Clausolles' work represents an emerging genre of this period: the popular illustrated history.[39] The book includes more than five hundred pages of two-column text, yet there are images interspersed throughout. Such a work points to a new interest in the visual apprehension of history as well as distant lands that emerged in the 1840s. Unlike Berbrugger, Clausolles did not coordinate artists and lithographers to make his history complete, but used whatever images were available. Offering visual reproductions of Algeria's sites and monuments was not the purpose of this work; rather, images were inserted when they served the historical narrative. The account of the Portes de Fer campaign, for example, includes a copy of one of Dauzats' already reproduced pictures.[40] The marginal status of images in this work and the fact that no artists were commissioned to produce drawings demonstrates that the title, *Voyage pittoresque ou histoire de la Régence d'Alger,* is playing on the popularity of illustrated travelogues. In Clausolles' volume, the reader is yet another step removed from an actual visual engagement with the spaces of Algeria, since this book reproduces prints, which are themselves reproductions. Yet it is fascinating that a serious work of historical scholarship would be published under the rubric of the picturesque. In Clausolles' work, military and political history converge with the consumption of picturesque travel. This strange hybrid employs illustrations not to demonstrate the verity of the author's arguments, but to allow the reader's eye to wander, to provide some visual interest to spice up a historical account. This mixture of military history and picturesque travel is most completely realized in the *Journal de l'expédition des Portes de Fer,* which makes most evident the implications of bringing these two genres together.

Though this is a book about a military expedition, the basic narrative is one of exploration and discovery. The work provides an account of an unknown portion of Algeria—landscapes and social groups that had not previously been encountered by the French. The landscapes Dauzats produced of the Portes de Fer (figs. 29–33) may be unconventional images, but in this work they are carefully situated in a narrative and their meaning is fixed therein. As in *Voyages pittoresques,* in the *Journal* the artist's own subjective experiences of place are the means by which to reinvent the landscape genre and to produce an effect. However, this location is in fact a site of military reconnaissance. The artist's apprehension and translation of the colony was paralleled for the reader/viewer in the *Journal* and, in the process, this Algerian territory was introduced into the French imagination. It is a site that, in its sublime grandeur, allows the viewer the opportunity to pursue daydreams and associative pleasures. Here the daydream is not merely personal but also political, because the fantasy is one of foreign conquest. What is more, this conquest takes place without apparent conflict. Not only does the viewer/reader perceive this landscape as French because the French army is taking possession of it, but the translation of that territory as a landscape makes it appear somehow apprehensible. While the images of the Portes de Fer in some ways avoid the stereotypes that reign in the Museum of French History, they nevertheless import the Algerian landscape into the history of French military expeditions abroad.

The mixture of the categories of military history and picturesque travel is striking in the *Journal*. While this work, like other illustrated tours, invites the reader to enjoy vicarious travel, it also describes important historical actors who actually made the journey and are illustrated in it. The book popularizes and politicizes the landscape of Algeria in a way similar to that of Berbrugger's work. What are the implications of bringing together history and illustrated travel when the destination is the colony of Algeria? Is it possible to think of colonialism as just a militarized form of picturesque travel?

The structure of the *Journal* allows us to think so. Here is a stunning landscape, there some friendly natives, here a famous general. The violence that is the basis of colonial conquest—that provides the threat to make the images of French soldiers at the bottom of a canyon seem somehow risky—is kept at bay. The threat of attack, which the viewer must infer, gives the images of the Passage des Bibans their *frisson*. Dauzats' images, however, do not show off the heroics of the French conquest of Algeria, as we might expect. One imagines from the book that the expedition, with three thousand soldiers and officers in tow, was something like the "promenade" of a prince that the artist has been asked to record for posterity. This landscape, belonging to the French only because of their military seizure, is stripped of its actual military and political significance. The acquisition of the territory is reduced to a simple gesture of signing the landscape in the name of the French army. Algeria is thus transformed from the field of battle represented by Vernet to a leisure destination for the prince and his henchmen.

While history achieves the level of public spectacle in the Museum of French History, in the *Journal* it becomes a tourist attraction. Just as an illustrated *voyage pittoresque* encouraged travel to see the famous sites represented, the *Journal* encouraged its readers to make an expedition to the original site of history. Indeed, in the same year the *Journal* was published, Quetin published his *Guide en Orient,* including one route (XI) in Algeria that reversed this expeditionary path and even described the sights to be enjoyed at the Passage des Bibans.[41]

CHAPTER 4

Eugène Fromentin and Laghouat

Artistic and Colonial Frontiers

But light and heat, that affect some brains with a sort of tropical folly, fills them with an unquenchable fury and pushes them to unknown dances, only elevates his [Fromentin's] soul to calm and restful contemplation. It is ecstasy rather than fanaticism. One could presume that I myself retain some form of nostalgia that directs me towards the sun; because these luminous canvases raise a heady vapor that soon condenses into desires and regrets. I am surprised to envy the sort of man who lies under blue shadows and whose eyes, neither wakeful nor sleeping, only express, if they express anything, a love of rest and a sentiment of well-being inspired by immense light.

—Charles Baudelaire

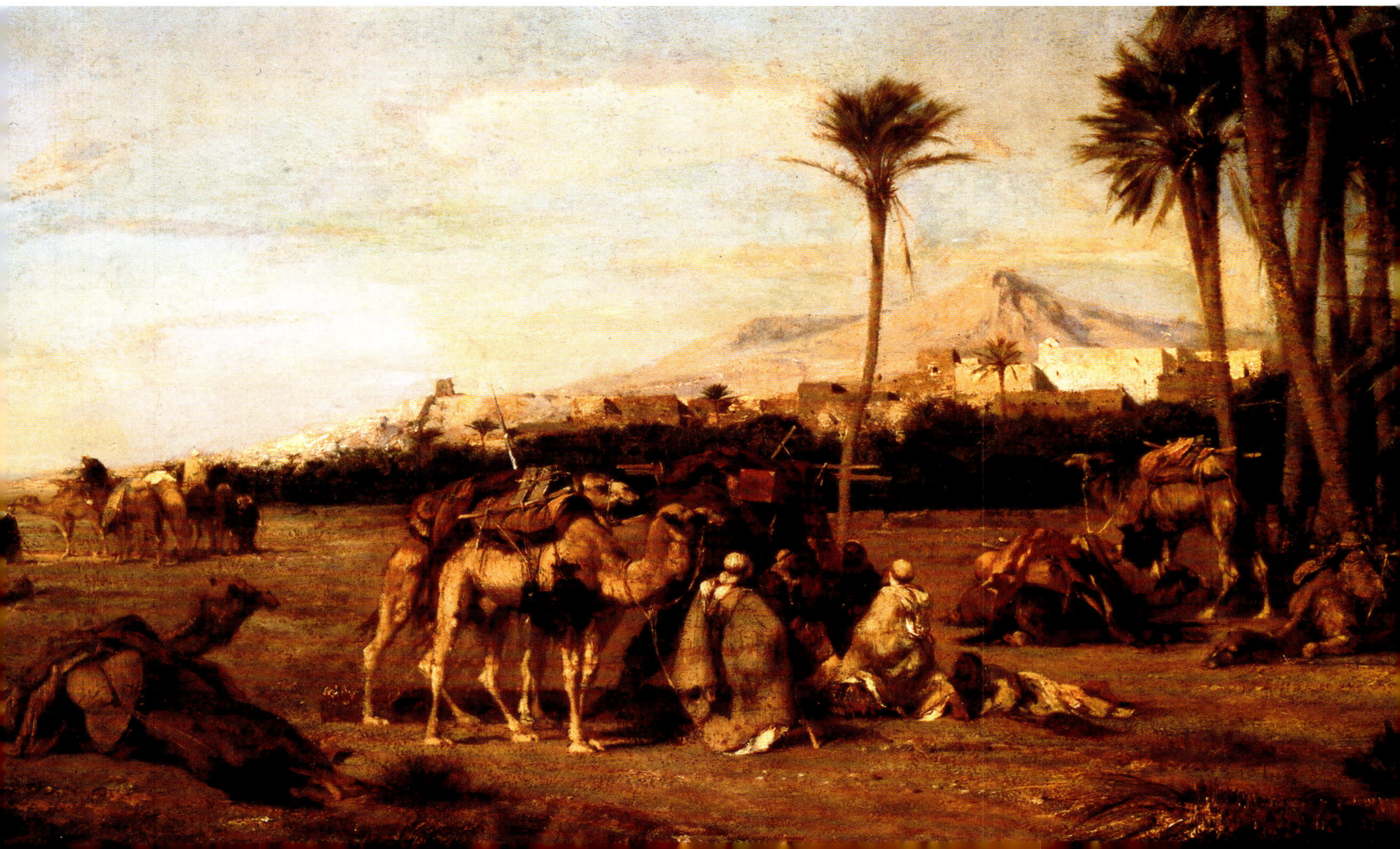

Overleaf: detail of fig. 46

Charles Baudelaire's review of Eugène Fromentin's paintings at the Salon of 1859 highlights a certain fashion for exoticism in art. Rather than seeing Fromentin's paintings for what they might tell us about the colony of Algeria, he responds to them as aesthetic statements of profound sensibility and a wealth of sensuous details. The passage above focuses on *A Street in Laghouat* (1859; fig. 39), a painting that emerges from a network of colonial relations explored below. For Baudelaire the picture takes on a personal dimension; it emits a vapor that "condenses into desires and regrets" related to faraway places of an imaginative kind. Baudelaire's fantasies run to the literary, and his interest in Fromentin's paintings is at once immediate and sensuous. His idealization of these exotic lands and their powerful character of light can be said to obscure the underlying reality of their colonial expropriation by the French government. But his sensibility, so clearly expressed in the above passage, is a key to understanding the deeper meanings in Fromentin's painting and the purpose of his journeys to Algeria. While there is evidence to suggest many reasons for Fromentin's sojourns, the sense of difference so poetically captured by Baudelaire—and the identification with that difference—was central to Fromentin's artistic self-conception. That painting, or writing, could be a journey for the viewer or reader is what inspired both of these figures. Indeed, the voyage itself—perhaps always a voyage of self-discovery—was the central theme in an aesthetic of the imagination advocated by Baudelaire and practiced by Fromentin.

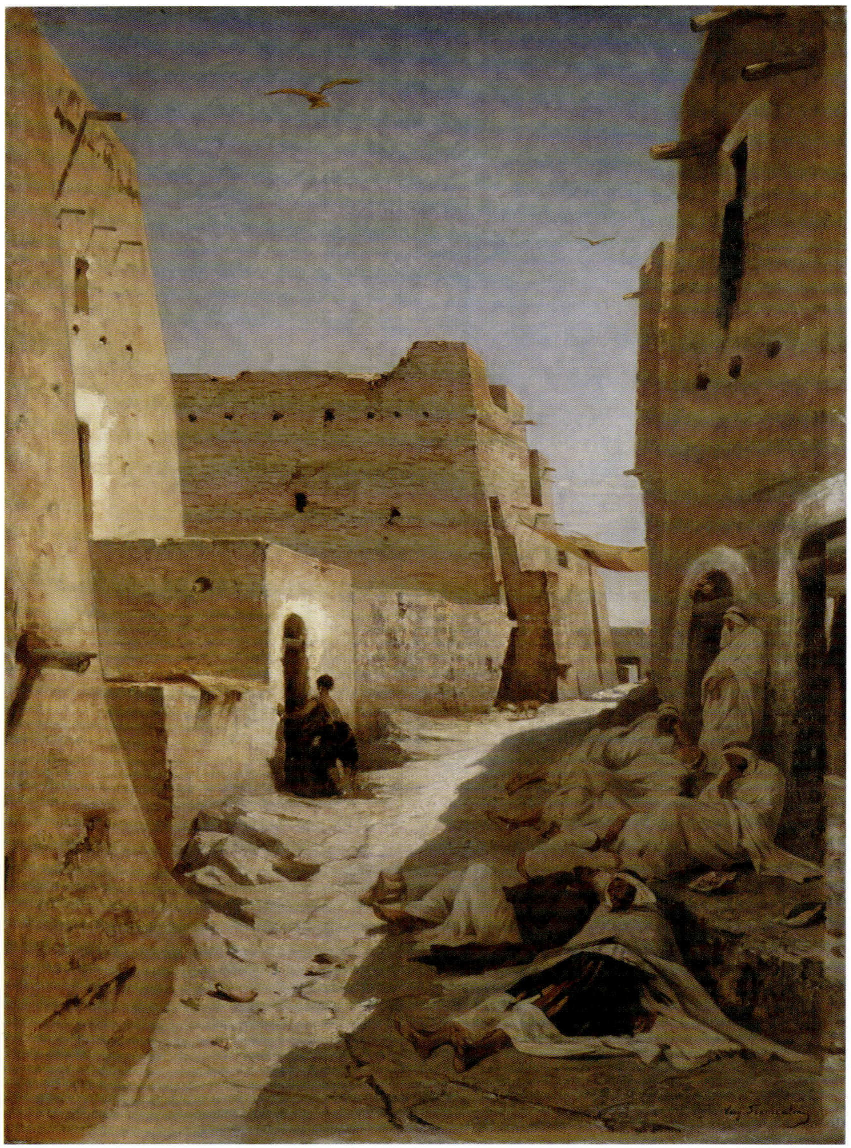

Figure 39.
Eugène Fromentin,
A Street in Laghouat, 1859.
Oil on canvas, 142 ×
102 cm. Musée de la
Chartreuse, Douai, France.
Photo: Réunion des
musées nationaux/Art
Resource, New York.

Fromentin's voyage was first presented to the public as a travel narrative, *Un Été dans le Sahara* (*A Summer in the Sahara*). There, he recorded the narrator's personal transformation as a result of his experience of the desert landscape:

> It is a sort of internal clarity that abides, after the evening has come, and continues to be reflected during my sleep. I do not stop dreaming of light; I close my eyes and I see flames, shining orbs or vague reverberations that increase, similar to the approach of dawn; in other words, I have no night. This perception of day, even in the absence of sun, this transparent repose traversed by lures like the nights of summer are crossed by meteors, this singular nightmare that accords me not a moment of obscurity, all of this closely resembles a fever.[1]

The experience described in this passage represents a metamorphosis of vision—the fundamental aspect of a visual artist's practice—and the corresponding disruption of the artist's internal processes, his ability to harmonize his life with the rhythms of the external world. The transformation of this fictive narrator takes place in the desert city of Laghouat, an outpost on the edge of France's colonial frontier, when *Un Été dans le Sahara* was published as a complete book in 1857.

This chapter, focusing on Fromentin's third voyage to Algeria in 1852–53, reverses the journey, or at least the artist/author's account of it. While *Un Été dans le Sahara* tells the tale of his expedition to Laghouat and beyond, to Tadgemont and Aïn-Mahdi, this chapter will take on the problem of Fromentin's return to France as a means to explore the gap between an artist's experience in the colonial landscape and the representation of it in the metropole. Just as the literary description of the voyage ends on the edge of the Sahara, there are also no artistic works that chronicle the artist's return to European civilization. Apparently, the account of Fromentin's voyage was to be an epic of discovery, but the central concern here is the way in which the "discovery" is translated and ultimately depicted upon the artist's return to France. Fromentin stage-managed the reception of his Salon works, publishing his two Algerian travel narratives just months before his two major Salon appearances after his return. Yet the sense of the author and artist comes through in both his texts and images: he achieved a form of intimacy with Algeria and its inhabitants that was unprecedented for a French artist. This intimacy, and the cross-referencing of paintings and novels, gave Fromentin's images of Algeria a sense of authenticity that can be perceived in the criticism of his works at the Salon. The kind of association in which Fromentin participated was, for a brief time, a model for colonial interaction between France and Algeria—a relationship in which the "mother country" would profit from the colony through engagement with the native people and respect for their customs and beliefs, as opposed to the previous and subsequent moments, in which complete domination seemed to offer the only viable model.[2] Fromentin's artistic practices manifested this broader historical development; his own brand of exotic naturalism sought a more vivid and representative image of Algeria and those who lived there.

Fromentin in Laghouat

> Laghouat is today one of the points of defense on the outer limits of the French empire, an advanced sentinel that, with Biskra and Boussâda, keeps guard of the sands of the South, just as 3,000 kilometers from there, Arras, Lille, and Metz defend the Northern frontier.
>
> —Oscar MacCarthy

This description, written by Oscar MacCarthy (whom Fromentin met in Algeria),[3] suggests the historical importance of Laghouat to France at the time of his journey. Fromentin reached this city at the edge of the Sahara at the beginning of June 1853, about six months after a particularly violent siege that resulted in the ultimate pacification of the local tribes resisting French authority.[4] Fromentin would have perceived this historical significance through his immediate sensations: the signs of the recent conquest were everywhere. The city itself was on the verge of ruin, and Fromentin describes in detail his dilapidated furnishings in one of the most intact buildings left in the city. In *Un Été dans le Sahara,* he reported witnessing traces of cannon fire and watching dogs dig up the buried limbs of French soldiers even as he arrived in Laghouat.[5] If

Un Été dans le Sahara is a narrative describing transformation, the setting of Laghouat is the crux, the location that symbolizes a turn in the artist's sensibility. Through his attempt to render this place, Fromentin developed that "certain manner of seeing, sensing and expressing"[6] that was his alone.

For Fromentin, Laghouat was the very edge of the known world, yet this city was occupied by (and thus in some sense belonged to) France. It was on the frontier of the French empire, and it had strategic and commercial significance. In Laghouat, Fromentin had gone as far as he could without leaving home. More important, he stayed there for a time. Unlike an explorer who seeks out a destination only to get crucial information and move on, Fromentin persisted in Laghouat for a month; he stayed long enough to make acquaintances and to develop habits. Further, he looked carefully, penetratingly, and attempted to record what he saw in the terms available to him as a visual artist. While the sketches the artist produced there include figure studies and images of everyday objects, the largest group of works, in both number and scale, comprises landscapes. Judging from these studies, it was not the culture and the people that most impressed the sensibility of the artist, but the site itself.

Why did Fromentin choose Laghouat? The city's recent conquest meant that its importance was known to the French public. Further, no other artist had ever visited this region of Algeria. Fromentin stood much to gain as an Orientalist artist by visiting and portraying this *terra incognita*. There is also the issue of official approbation—of no small importance to an artist of the Second Empire. From the Minister of Beaux Arts, Fromentin acquired a commission for a *paysage historique* of southern Algeria.[7] But the fact that Fromentin did not finish this work until 1856, and that it failed to represent French conquest, makes it clear that the artist accepted the commission for reasons beyond mere patriotism.[8] This commission allowed Fromentin to travel to his intended destinations with a military escort and letters of recommendation from Gouverneur-Général Randon.[9] Jean-Pierre LaFouge has pointed out that Fromentin responded to Général Daumas' suggestion that artists and writers should travel to southern Algeria in order to represent these little-known lands for the French public, and he also noted that Fromentin followed Daumas' own itinerary to the Algerian interior.[10] In their monograph, James Thompson and Barbara Wright underline the artist's own attestations to financial need and commercial prospects in his correspondence. They write that by September 1852, "he was now convinced that Algeria held the key to his originality and popularity as an artist."[11]

All of these facts suggest the artist's external motivations—the economic and political concerns of the period and the way in which Fromentin's artistic career was intertwined with them. Fromentin's official commission enabled his voyage, and his palpable sense of economic necessity led him to produce an impressive number of studies of southern Algeria, but these details only provide a frame for the artist's production abroad. In other words, there is a process of innovation that exists within the social network of colonial relations, an interaction with an external world that was made possible by colonialism but is not merely a direct result of it.[12] As a reinvention of the process of artistic travel, Fromentin's sketches operate as fundamentally conventional, reiterating the well-known discourse of travel to the Orient.[13] Through the process of sketching this place, the artist came to terms with it. He employed the formal language he knew—what else could he do?—but he recognized its limitations and sought to alter his practice to respond to what he saw. In what follows, a number of the studies created in Laghouat will be discussed, elucidating the manner in which Fromentin departed from Orientalist conventions. The process of his artistic innovation can be teased out from a careful examination of the images he generated in this distant and recently conquered colonial site.

Laghouat: Bab-el-Gharbi (1853; fig. 40) is a study of the interior of the city of Laghouat. More specifically, it is drawn from the Rue Bab-el-Gharbi, one of the main thoroughfares of the city, looking up toward the interior of a stone portal. The artist made another drawing of what appears to be the same street, looking in the opposite direction,[14] and this work also corresponds to the painting *A Street in Laghouat* (fig. 39), which features the same street and the gate in the distance. It is a large study (47.5 × 31.5 cm) made on paper that was once grey but has since turned brown.

This drawing features several figures among a configuration of architectural elements. Perhaps the most striking aspect is the work's vertical orientation. (A horizontal one was more typical for genre and landscape scenes.) This vertical orientation, combined with a tall building that occupies the right edge of the picture, provides a sense of an enclosed space from which the viewer takes in the scene. A large portion of the composition is also devoted to the sky. A single figure reclines against a building at right in the shade, and three others are visible in the distance: one who enters through the gate and two others, just perceptible, behind him. The rendering of these figures is not refined, but the two closer ones can be distinguished as natives by their costumes. Although the four figures are relatively small, they serve important functions in the composition. Their position creates a diagonal movement across the page while establishing for the viewer a sense of distance and movement over time. In other words, their presence animates what would otherwise be a static architectural study.

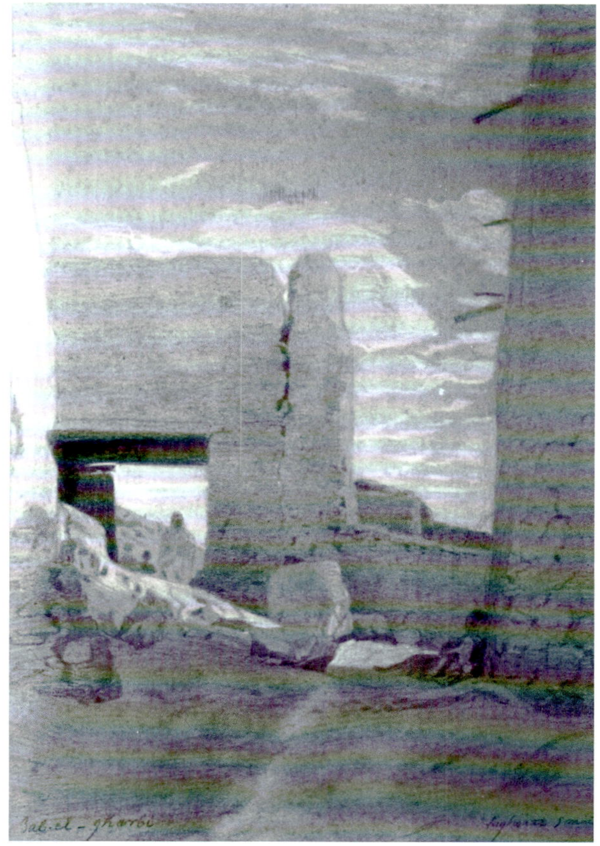

Figure 40.
Eugène Fromentin,
Laghouat: Bab-el-Gharbi,
1853. Charcoal pencil on paper, 47.5 × 31.5 cm.
Musée des Beaux-Arts, La Rochelle, France.
Photo courtesy Barbara Wright.

This drawing also departs from previous Orientalist genre depictions in its strategic deployment of light. Thompson and Wright have remarked upon Fromentin's use of grey paper, suggesting that it corresponded to the grey character of Algerian light he described on an earlier visit.[15] In this drawing, the color of the paper serves as the image's middle tone, and the artist's use of both dark and light pencil serves to establish shadows and highlights. The resulting effect is an infusion of light throughout the image as well as moments of strong contrast. This technique is distinct from the

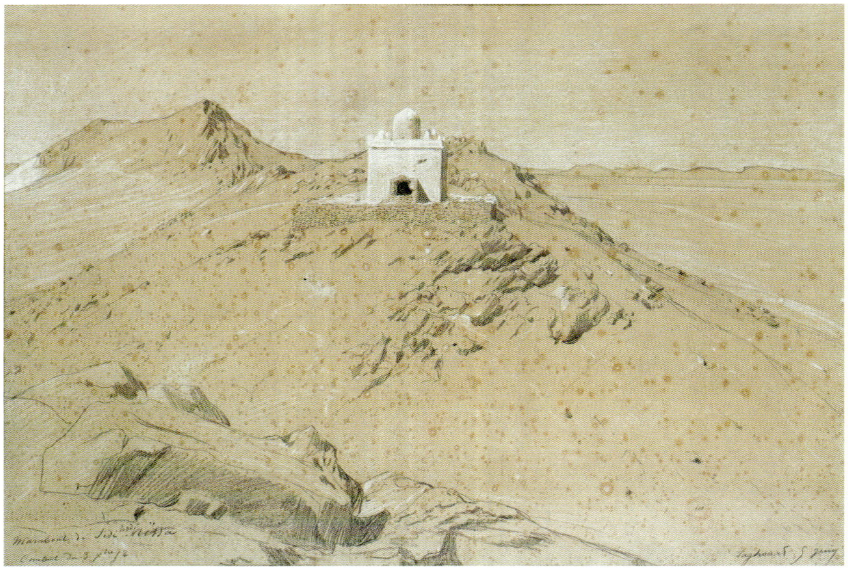

Figure 41.
Eugène Fromentin,
Marabout of Sidi-el-Aïssa (Laghouat, 5 June), 1853.
Charcoal pencil on paper, 43.5 × 62.5 cm. Private collection. Photo courtesy Barbara Wright.

light-filled landscapes of Alexandre-Gabriel Decamps or Prosper Marilhat (figs. 27, 28). The light in this sketch is particular and incidental. For example, a strip of bright white represents a portion of the ground that is lit by the sun, and the darkest point in the composition is the shaded area under the doorway. Such effects tell the viewer more about the structure of the architecture and the orientation of the buildings than about the general quality of the light in this exotic location. Further, the dark and light highlights visible through the gate draw the viewer's eye into the distance and direct attention to the figure coming through the doorway.

On the face of it, this sketch could be interpreted as just one more view of Arabs lounging among the ruins of a once-thriving civilization, a common Orientalist trope. However, if one considers the history of this city, the cracked gate and the boulder on the thoroughfare take on a different meaning. During the siege of Laghouat, this gate was near the breach opened for French troops by a bombardment. Thus the cracked buildings and rubble are the only lasting evidence of the French assault, an assault so violent and terrible that the French soldiers who traversed this street were said to have "marched in blood."[16] Fromentin has not included any clear markers of hostility in this drawing, or in any other work that he produced in Laghouat, but he did note the decay of the city that was the very condition of its occupation by the French.

In another drawing, in pencil on grey paper, the artist attempted to address the seizure of Laghouat more directly. On this landscape study, *Marabout of Sidi-el-Aïssa (Laghouat, 5 June)* (1853; fig. 41), the artist inscribed "Combat de 3 Xbre [December] 52." Perhaps Fromentin was thinking about his commission when he depicted this site of a prolonged military siege, yet one of the most remarkable aspects of this drawing is the lack of almost any mark on the landscape indicating the recent struggle, despite the author/artist's own comment that when he visited the *marabout*, every stone in sight had been marked by ammunition.[17] The distant perspective the artist chose allows such a definitive transformation of the landscape to remain invisible. How would a viewer know that the dark spot on the facade of the building was the result of cannon fire? The drawing's point of view masks the recent military alteration of this site and emphasizes another kind of visibility specific to this location. The scale of this landscape image is enormous by the standards of French painting of the period, comparable only to alpine views.[18] Here, the clarity of the landscape forms is paramount. There are no clouds or fog. Nothing obscures this view. Further, the sketch is rendered in pencil, as opposed to charcoal, the material the artist normally used for studies of this scale. Fromentin elsewhere described this distinctive light as more intense than that of Algiers.[19] The dryness of the desert air allowed the artist to view this vast expanse and render it as a landscape, an ordered and legible agglomeration of forms. In this depiction, vision itself, as a result of light and atmosphere, becomes a characteristic of this place.

The intense white of the marabout and its entrance, the darkest point of the composition, provide a centrifugal focus for the various lines that radiate from it. The architecture of the marabout is placed in such a way that it dominates the landscape, but nevertheless remains a part of it. It sits on top of a hill, but its dome appears to be equal in height to the distant mountain of the background, and the horizon line would cut through the center of the building. Marabouts are shrines of visionary saints of the Islamic faith. The power of such figures is believed to transcend corporeal existence, and the saint after whom this marabout was named was said to have predicted the conquest of the French.[20] Thus the edifice visible in this image makes reference to a spiritual practice of prophetic vision, and yet this architectural symbol was also the position from which the French bombarded the city. While Fromentin himself was aware of the interpenetration of the spiritual and historical aspects of this location, his view occludes the recent violence in favor of an image of vast space ordered by a single architectural structure. Although his travel narrative would eventually tell the public what he knew about this place, this drawing offers a view expressing what Fromentin saw.

If vision is thematized as a view in *Marabout of Sidi-el-Aïssa*, it becomes the structural principle of the oil sketches Fromentin made in and around Laghouat. Fromentin himself distinguished between vision and view in two distinct literary renderings of Laghouat he composed in *Un Été dans le Sahara*: "That is the complete view of Laghouat from the North; the first was rather a vision; this part, more extended and from which I have omitted nothing, I give to you as a view."[21] A view was meant to be complete and informative, whereas the vision of Laghouat was presented first in the narrative and reflected the author's immediate impression. Anne-Marie Christin has pointed out a direct connection between Fromentin's literary rendering of his vision of the city and a particular oil sketch, *Laghouat, 30 June, 2 o'clock* (1853; fig. 42).[22] This work is one of a group of oil sketches (figs. 42, 43) that has attracted the attention of numerous writers. The sketches' unprecedented handling of materials and radical compositional arrangements appear to defy spatial logic.[23] In Fromentin's own terms, the oil sketches seem to be visions as opposed to views, because they are direct responses to visual phenomena and not ordered compositions. There is no evidence to connect these works to the finished *tableaux* the artist produced for the Salon. Rather, the studies represent the furthest extension of the artist's faculties of depiction and stand as an unprecedented pictorial exploration of the colonial landscape.

While Christin likens *Laghouat, 30 June, 2 o'clock* to a passage in *Un Été dans le Sahara* describing the same landscape view, the painted sketch is far more muted and less defined than the corresponding literary description.[24] The language is relentlessly visual and the description full of color. While the literary description is evocative of an image, the oil sketch Fromentin made from the same point of view renders vision in a wholly distinct manner. In the painting, we see the cold greens of the oasis and the vast sun-drenched plain; the violet bar of the horizon appears at right, just barely distinguished from the tone of the sky. The sketch lacks the infusion of color and contrast that dominates the literary description. Without the knowledge that this landscape is the vision the artist saw upon his

Figure 42.
Eugène Fromentin, *Laghouat, 30 June, 2 o'clock*, 1853. Oil on canvas, 30 × 54 cm. Private collection, La Roche sur Yon, France. Photo courtesy Barbara Wright.

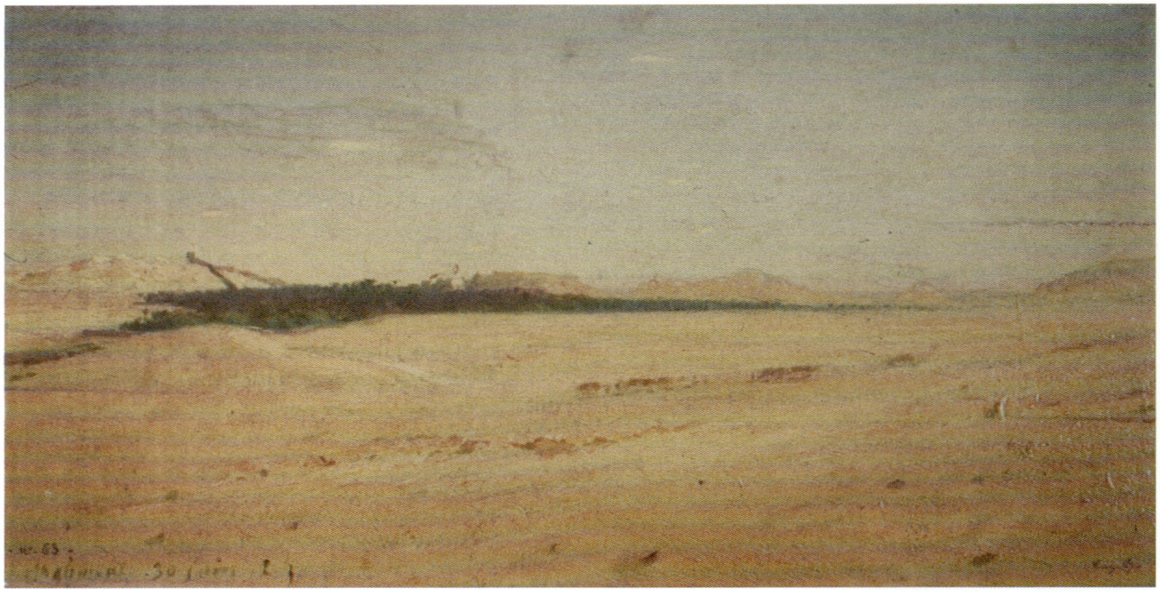

Figure 43.
Eugène Fromentin, *Laghouat, 20 June, 9 o'clock*, 1853. Oil on canvas, 18 × 25.5 cm. Private collection, La Roche sur Yon, France. Photo courtesy Barbara Wright.

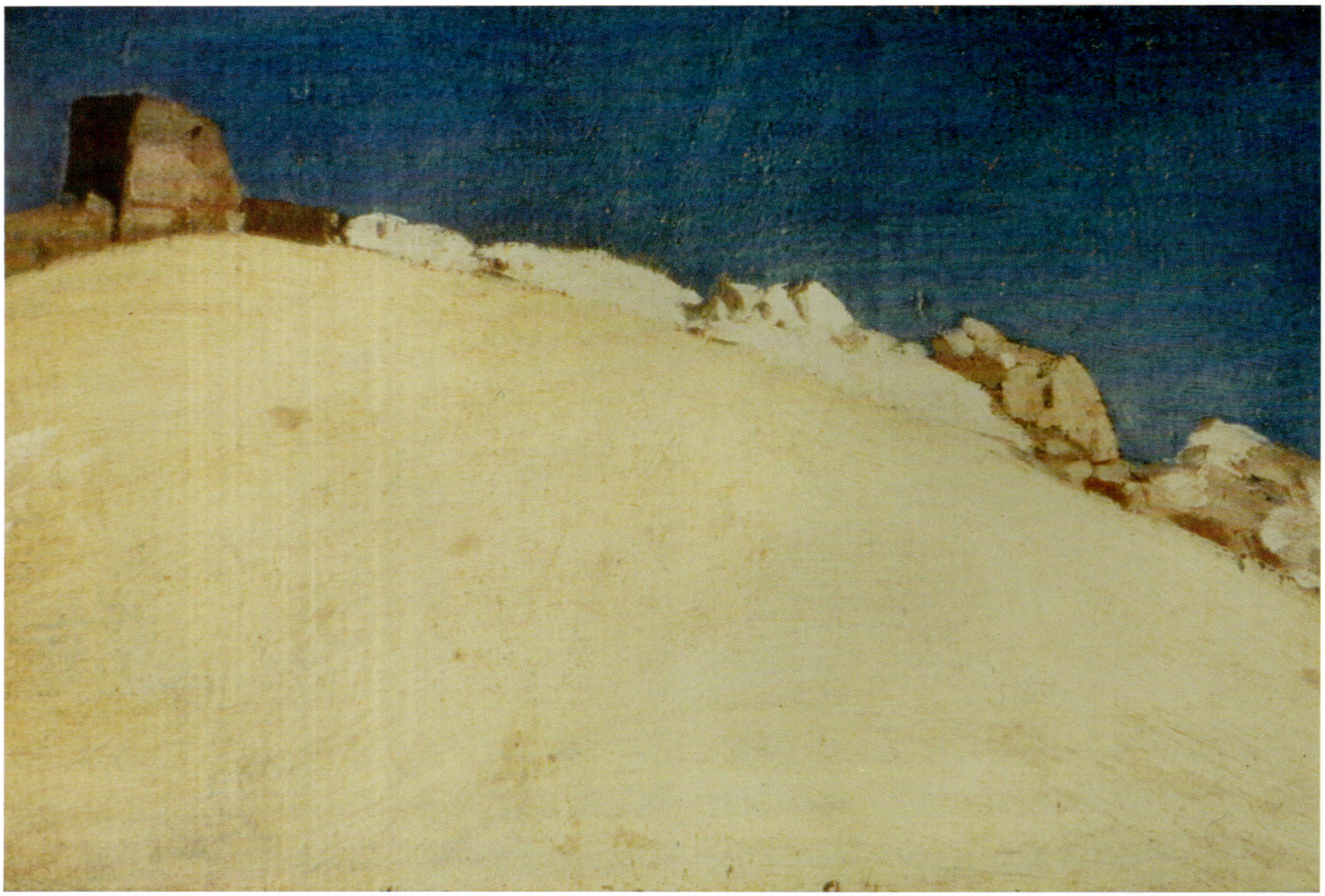

favor of a sincere attempt to render visual perceptions of this utterly unfamiliar environment.

The color in this work is muted, with the exceptions of the deep green of the oasis and the red and white rocks on the top of the hill on the left. The range of tones adds up to a group of subtle contrasts, suggesting a powerful light source that renders objects of various colors similar in appearance. The sense of emptiness is not merely evoked: the artist achieves it through delicate tonal shifts that add up to a single, bright plain. The time of day and the nature of the location are implied by such a system of rendering the landscape. This idea is also at work in the remarkable oil study *Laghouat, 20 June, 9 o'clock* (1853; fig. 43).

This view of one of the two hills behind the village of Laghouat renders bright light in a more familiar manner, by employing bright yellow paint with a blue sky in the background. These two domains of yellow hill and blue sky are separated by a narrow strip of architectural edifices and stone fragments apparently clinging to the top of the hill. While the larger areas are laid in with broad stokes, this border area is more carefully rendered, and the forms of architecture and rock outcroppings are detailed in more neutral tones. This study possesses an unprecedented directness and vigor. Its large areas of unmodulated pigment appear striking to contemporary viewers; they seem to augur a modernist moment in Fromentin's artistic development long before artists such as Henri Matisse employed such techniques for rendering the North African landscape. But the image is dated, confirming that the artist saw it as a complete study or, more correctly, an accurate trace of his impressions of the landscape at that moment.

While the forms are large and bright, there is evidence that the artist was experimenting with underpainting in order to generate particular coloristic effects and that this composition, though simpler, was as carefully developed as *30 June, 2 o'clock*. The yellow tones are brushed across the hill in broad strokes that leave traces of the hairs of the brush and allow the grey-blue underneath to remain just barely visible. This is evidence of an experimental approach to produce an effect of brightness transmitted through color. Fromentin did make this sketch with a sense of immediacy, but its visual effect was carefully devised, and the result is a powerful study of bright morning light on a desert landscape framed by a vivid and empty sky.

Fromentin evacuated landscape conventions in these studies, allowing the paintings to be filled instead with traces of his artistic activities. These oil sketches can serve as a crucial point of convergence for many of the concepts explored in this book: in this case, the landscape comes into its own as a representational modality that confers meaning both metaphorically, as inhuman, and structurally, as a means to translate vision. Christine Peltre, an author who has thoroughly explored the topic of the Orientalist landscape, offers a romanticized portrayal of an artistic interaction with such spaces: "There begins, in these expanses where the picturesque motif disappears, the essential confrontation with another space where the only thing that appears to the eye is the nudity of the terrain."[25] It is clear that picturesque motifs have been eradicated in these compositions. Yet it is not simply that in the desert the landscape has been stripped of its embellishments and is exposed for the artist to depict. The extended spaces and barren expanses of this environment must be confronted as essentially inhuman, both in their scale and in their limited availability for human habitation. This annihilation of humanity paradoxically confers an enormous power on the artist to perceive and translate the visual phenomena of the world and to fill vacant landscapes with traces of the artist's confrontation with this vision of a vast and inhuman planet.

In both of the oil studies, there are layers of pigment piled upon one another. This technique, as a manner of direct sketching, is only possible in a desert climate: only there would oil paint dry quickly enough to allow an artist to place one layer of unmixed pigment on top of another one without their blending.[26] Not only did Fromentin demonstrate his immediate responses to the site through his application of unmixed, undiluted pigment (he spent more time painting than mixing), but this sketching technique was also predicated upon the particular climate of the landscape he translated. By the time Fromentin made these studies, he had spent several weeks sketching in Laghouat, and his understanding of the limits of the materials in this location would have been clear. The aridity of the climate finds expression in the dryness of the materials, forming a dense and impacted veneer composed of spindly traces where the pigment-heavy brush glossed over an already thickly coated surface. If we remember that these paintings were each accomplished in one sitting, it is clear that the density and facture of the pigment capture an unprecedented artistic interaction in which the physical characteristics of the desert are equally evident in the appearance of the image and the means of producing it.

The various sketches so far discussed highlight the differences among the studies Fromentin realized in Laghouat, as well as their distance from the conventions for representing Oriental scenes and landscapes. Fromentin's use of specific tonal contrasts, his subtle mastery of color, his method of composing some images with only a trace of foreground or none at all, and his facture and overpainting all suggest an attentiveness to the environment, an intimacy with and responsiveness to the region of Laghouat. There are a variety of styles in evidence and a multiplicity of points of view, indicating that Fromentin's representations of this place do not form a cohesive group or follow from a single set of aesthetic or artistic concerns.

If I have considered them thoroughly as artistic works in themselves, it has been to demonstrate how the experience of travel to distant territories affects artistic production. The goal is to show that a different landscape elicits a response from the artist in the terms available to him. A confrontation with an exotic landscape does not alter the artist but, in this case, it did cause Fromentin to produce landscape imagery that looks different. There is a play of terms rather than a fixed opposition between native and exotic landscape, conventional or innovative artistic practices. The group of sketches does not stand as a fully composed text, and that is why the works are valuable. They teach us something about artistic travel and its processes. This analysis of Fromentin's Laghouat studies demonstrates that the narrow art-historical focus on major works of art and the studies made to achieve them can deprive us of a complex understanding of the process of artistic creation. Artists are not always in the process of realizing great works, but often create distinct and even incompatible representations of the world. Displacement as a result of travel, and a multiplicity of views or styles resulting from technical experimentation, leads to a certain productive disjunction. These studies demonstrate an ability to remain between the domains and genres through which we understand and define artistic practice. In Laghouat, Fromentin was able to countenance contradictions and simply depict them, rather than resolve them.

The Travel Narratives

In the preface Fromentin wrote for the Algerian travel narratives in 1874, he suggested a categorical distinction between the literary and plastic arts, asserting that his books did not repeat his painted works but instead expressed what cannot be related in painting. He described his decision to turn to writing in opaque terms but made clear that, at the time, he perceived the descriptive task of the writer to be greater than that of the artist.[27] Anne-Marie Christin was the first to suggest that the enigmas of Fromentin's studies from Laghouat could not be resolved solely on the basis of images. She has also suggested that to conjure up the image he could not make appear in painting, Fromentin was compelled to produce *Un Été dans le Sahara*.[28] Two years later, Fromentin published *Une Année dans le Sahel* (*A Year in the Sahel*), chronicling the year he spent in Algeria in 1852–53. In another article, Christin elaborated more on the particular problems painting posed for Fromentin and suggested that a literary description of the desert landscape was better suited to his aims. In "Space and Convention in Eugène Fromentin," she wrote: "The *tableau*, in his [Fromentin's] mind, is not defined just by painting . . . [it] is an ordered composition and, even more, an image defined by a *cadre* (frame, framework). . . . But how can one express the expanse of the Sahara in a tableau? Was it not in order to better express it that Fromentin set aside his brushes and, for the first time, preferred writing to painting?"[29]

Christin's argument brings to light several crucial issues concerning Fromentin's multiple depictions of Laghouat. First of all, she offers a more specific notion of limitations in the realm of pictorial representation. The structuring principles of *cadre* and *tableau* help illuminate what is lacking in the landscape sketches. Further, she reminds her readers that Fromentin's book describing his voyage to Laghouat was his first, and that this literary work represented an ambitious foray into another method of description for him. Finally, Christin's analysis makes a compelling claim for Fromentin's dependence upon the reifying structure of the tableau, despite his fragmentary travel experiences, and suggests that the narrative form was more suited to Fromentin's proclivities.

Following Christin, I propose to examine Fromentin's Algerian travel narratives in relationship to his pictorial representations of Laghouat; I will concentrate on *Un Été dans le Sahara* because that work describes his sojourn in detail. I am less interested in the texts themselves than in what they demonstrate historically, both concerning Fromentin's career and the history of the representation of Algeria. Fromentin journeyed to Algeria at the beginning of the Second Empire, the dawn of a new era in the colony's development. The literary advances in his Algerian travel narratives over previous Orientalist travel works have been well chronicled,[30] but I want to look more carefully at the conditions of their composition as well as the status Fromentin attained as a result of their publication. *Un Été dans le Sahara* conferred public recognition upon its author and qualified him as an expert on Algeria and Orientalist painting. Fromentin ultimately used the Algerian texts to promote his Salon paintings and to provide his viewers with an aesthetic defense of the images that he would eventually present at the Salon.

Un Été dans le Sahara was originally composed while Fromentin was in Algeria, and the initial conception of this work stands as a middle term between the artist's sketching of the region around Laghouat and his subsequent production of Salon paintings representing that location. Fromentin's correspondence establishes that he had finished a version of the entire work and sent it to his friend Armand du Mesnil before leaving Blidah in September.[31] Thus while the work did not result from direct interaction, as the oil sketches did, it was also not completed in France, where Fromentin would have been much more removed from his experience. In Blidah, Fromentin and his wife, Marie, lived a provisional traveler's existence during the months of August and September 1853. The lodging there was described by Fromentin as a "bivouac" with only the most rudimentary furnishings that offered no comforts.[32]

The work was produced from memory, however recent, and the concept of memory is fully explored in it. Fromentin commented on the importance of memory in his Algerian works in the preface of 1874: "The necessity to write them at a distance, after months, after years, without any other resource than memory and in the absolutely correct form of condensed memories, taught me, better than any other proof, that it is *truth* in the arts that makes nature come alive, what the latter furnishes us with is what our sensibility borrows from it."[33] This statement operates at two levels: as a compelling interpretive foil for the texts and as a historical statement of aesthetic sensibility on the part of the author.

As an evocative metaphorical text that operates through memory, *Un Été dans le Sahara* could not be more different from texts previously published in France describing the Algerian landscape, particularly those that treat the colony's interior. The prior point of reference would be the geographical texts describing the colony for the military and civilians in France. The first French geographical studies of Algeria drawn from direct observation were E. Carette's *Recherches sur la géographie et le commerce de l'Algérie méridonale* and E. Renou's *Notice géographique sur une partie de l'Afrique septentrionale*. These works appeared in the same volume of the *Exploration scientifique de l'Algérie*.[34] Both Carette and Renou were members of the Scientific Commission of Algeria, originally formed by the War Ministry in 1837, and they executed their research between 1840 and 1842.[35] While the original order for the commission was to research and compile information on Algeria that might benefit letters and arts, the fact that the expedition was organized and funded by the War Ministry suggests that the information would serve more than academic interests. Of the two studies of geography, Carette's is far more significant in length and scope. As the title suggests, his geographical study, while precise and definitive, was integrated with an analysis of the commercial activities of the region.[36] Carette's and Renou's geographical studies were the first examples of an attempt simultaneously to classify, delimit, and describe the colonial territory of Algeria. Any knowledge about routes—including how many days it would take to travel from point A to point B, what kind of terrain would be encountered, and what water sources would be available—would be useful for a military expedition. Further, information on agricultural products, indigenous trading practices, and the presence of minerals would be valuable to those attempting to establish an economic future for French colonists in Algeria.

Another geographical study that constitutes a specific point of reference for Fromentin is Eugène Daumas' *Le Sahara algérien* of 1845.[37] Unlike Carette and Renou, Daumas was an officer who had served for years in Algeria and who was the director of the *bureaux arabes* in Algeria by the time of this work's publication. In other words, he was not an imported scholar but an officer who was intimate with Algeria, one whose position in the military administration required the deepest familiarity with Algerian natives. His text, which focused on the Algerian Sahara, was far more specific than the work of Carette, as Daumas sought to detail only the remote territory that lay south of French settlement, the towns that occupied this region, and information about trade routes.

Daumas' work is not fully quantifiable and therefore not as scientific by the standards of his day. This text is ultimately more a piece of military reconnaissance than Carette's study and, at the same time, it offers more history and landscape description, making it a more readable and marketable text.[38] Daumas' study inherited a synthetic quality from the earlier work of Carette and similarly presented a wealth of information about an enormous and diverse region. Daumas' text suggests that while it is important to know details, such as which tribes inhabit and rule each town and the number of houses that can be found there, such information only accrues meaning in relation to other knowledge concerning what influence the French occupation has had on local governance and how the houses were built. The resulting text provides a synthetic description of this region of Algeria indelibly linked to the prerogatives of imperialism. This descriptive mode fuses together disparate spaces into a cohesive landscape and educates its readers.

Jean-Pierre LaFouge has connected Fromentin's Algerian travel narratives with this text by Daumas as well as with the military establishment that supported him. LaFouge has pointed out that Fromentin not only followed Daumas' own itinerary but also responded to his suggestion that painters and poets should journey to southern Algeria in order to retrieve an image of that territory for France.[39] The critic asserts that the credibility of Fromentin's account derives in large part from the work of Daumas,[40] but also notes that the artist's account is less factual, the result of "poetic transfiguration," not to mention being more empathetic toward the Arab inhabitants.[41] Besides the connections between Fromentin and Daumas uncovered by LaFouge, Fromentin's writings reveal that his native guide to southern Algeria was also Daumas' main informant about the desert.[42] In fact, Fromentin wrote directly to Daumas in March 1853 to request his aid in securing an appointment with the governor-general, a plan that successfully provided the artist with the needed letters of recommendation and military escort.[43] Not only does *Un Été dans le Sahara* discuss the military seizure of Laghouat, but this text also emerges from a militarized milieu that made Fromentin's trip possible. No matter how much this work appears to be an account of personal experiences and development, its achievements are contingent upon France's military presence in the colony.

Yet in this case, Fromentin's text forcefully denies received ideas about Algeria. After establishing the authority of his description through his intimacy with the desert landscape, Fromentin positions his text in opposition to romanticized representations of the desert as extreme or violent. His firsthand account, employing a productive slippage between author and narrator, self-consciously undermines generally held beliefs about the Algerian landscape. *Un Été dans le Sahara* offers something new in the realm of French literature, namely, a lucid and artistic description of the landscape and people of southern Algeria. In his rendering of the landscape and its inhabitants, Fromentin attempted to upset convention by calling stereotypes into question through firsthand experience.[44]

This firsthand knowledge and the success of his travelogue helped Fromentin succeed as a painter. The connection between his Algerian texts and the Salon paintings is more profound than the term "publicity" suggests. In *Un Été dans le Sahara* and *Une Année dans le Sahel*, the author primed his audience with images and with a way of interpreting and appreciating them. In the Algerian texts, it is possible to trace the emergence of an entire aesthetic philosophy that the author intended to have applied to his painted works.

Un Été dans le Sahara initially appeared serially in the *Revue de Paris* in 1854, beginning on the first of June and finishing on the first of December. Yet the book did not appear until January 1857, several months before the opening of the Salon of that year. Guy Sagnes has suggested that the reasons for this delay were beyond the control of the author,[45] a supposition that is supported in part by Fromentin's correspondence. But in a letter dated 2 September 1856 to Paul Bataillard, one of Fromentin's intimate friends and also a source of financial support, the author explains his decision to assemble the articles into a book: "It is again an attempt at another genre, to regain a little publicity, since, by my own fault or otherwise, I have totally and entirely lost any."[46] This passage expresses the pressures Fromentin perceived concerning his reputation as a painter at that point and also reveals his sense that a travel novel might aid his situation. In 1856, he had not had a major showing at the Salon since 1850–51 (with eleven paintings accepted!), having only submitted a single work from Algeria in 1853 and not having participated in the Exposition Universelle of 1855.[47] In those years, his renown had dwindled.

As noted by Thompson and Wright, Fromentin intended to employ the novel to generate publicity for his painting.[48] By all evidence, he took this project quite seriously. He had a copy of his book sent to Théophile Gautier, a prominent Orientalist writer and art critic, which was accompanied by a handwritten letter from the artist. In the letter, Fromentin acknowledged Gautier's contribution to the publication of the novel, but he further asserted that any success the work enjoyed would also be owed to Gautier, a not-so-subtle suggestion that a review of *Un Été dans le Sahara* by Gautier was its only hope of success. But that is not all. Fromentin also gave Gautier a painting in the bargain "in order to help you remember a little that I am a painter."[49] As a critic of both literature and the arts, Gautier was uniquely placed to make Fromentin's reputation, and the latter's plea was successful indeed. Gautier devoted not one but two articles to *Un Été dans le Sahara* as well as a laudatory review of Fromentin's paintings in his "Salon de 1857."[50] While Gautier was perhaps the only critic to receive a painting "in gratitude," Fromentin also worked to promote his book by sending copies to noteworthy authors of the period, including Alphonse de Lamartine and George Sand.[51] While such a practice of promoting a novel is standard, it is exceptional that Fromentin used his novel to promote his paintings.

Further, Sagnes, the editor of Fromentin's *Oeuvres complètes*, notes that the artist began his second Algerian travel narrative in February 1857,[52] even as he was busily preparing for a major Salon appearance. The fruit of these early efforts was published in *L'Artiste* in July and August 1857, while the Salon of 1857 was on exhibit.[53] The complete work, under its current title, did not appear serially until November and December 1858 and in book form in March 1859, just before the opening of another Salon. Given the well-scheduled appearance of Fromentin's literary works in relation to the Salons of 1857 and 1859, it would seem that his travel narratives were intended to promote his painterly career. This is largely demonstrated by the critical response to Fromentin's paintings at the Salons of 1857 and 1859, addressed below. Before turning to a discussion of the paintings and the critical responses to them, it is important to consider the way Fromentin employed these novels to articulate an aesthetic sensibility.

Describing his camp at D'jelfa, en route to Laghouat, Fromentin's narrator turns to aesthetic terms to articulate his travel experiences. A patch of desert grass (*alfa*) causes the narrator to ruminate on the representation of nature in art and the wisdom of *les maîtres* (the old masters): "This distant patch of alfa made me aware of the organization in this landscape. . . . She [nature] made them [the old masters] see that the goal is to express and to arrive there, the simplest means are the best. She made them see that the idea is light and needs little dressing. . . . Did I need to come so far from the Louvre in order to seek out this important exhortation to see things in a simple way in order to obtain true form?"[54] This new comprehension of the relationship of the old masters to nature takes place in an exceptional location. The narrator self-consciously points out how far he had to travel from the Louvre in order to come to terms with the works in it and the masters who created them. What does it indicate that Fromentin had to travel to a sparsely populated desert in order to appreciate the knowledge of the old masters? In southern Algeria, Fromentin finally got far enough away from French metropolitan culture and its attendant categories of artistic production (traditional versus avant-garde, Neoclassical Italy versus the Romantic Orient) that what he perceived in the North African wilderness ceased to be exotic. Rather than defining himself in opposition to this environment and thereby creating a binary of self and other, the author came to understand his own artistic practices more fully and expressed a perception of universal similarity through the idea of nature and the need to render it directly, without affectation, in order to achieve artistic truth. Surely this is what he attempted with his oil studies in Laghouat.

That said, this confrontation with nature in the interior of Algeria leaves many questions unanswered. The passage is general, fragmentary, and paradoxical. But it does underline the indirect character of the narrator's relationship to this landscape; it is mediated by past artists, despite the fact that the old masters (whoever they are) had not literally represented Algeria. Their representations of nature helped Fromentin understand how to depict this exotic-looking region. Referring back to the old masters helps the artist realize that this unfamiliar landscape, a form of the category of nature, requires simple and clear means of expression to communicate its full grandeur. As an aesthetic commentary, such a notion seeks to undermine the importance of genre and detail, particularly as they were then employed by French Orientalist artists. Though this is an early and incomplete exposition, a more thorough and detailed aesthetic analysis is explicitly made by Fromentin in *Une Année dans le Sahel*.

Near the end of this later work, in the section that takes place after the narrator's return from Laghouat, Fromentin stages an interaction of sorts between the narrator and his companion, Vandell, who has been engaged in geological research in the colony. The interaction begins with a description of Vandell's schematic drawings of "profiles of mountains, rock forms with detail multiplied within their stratifications."[55] Though the narrator points out that these plans are minutely rendered and very precise, he nevertheless continues by contesting the truth claims of such depictions. Such an iconoclastic position in an era dominated by scientific inquiry, numerical precision, and typological classification of the natural world is the beginning of a one-sided conversation that the narrator himself describes as a "dissertation." The author's aesthetic prescriptions, put here in the mouth of the narrator, give a foretaste of the positions he would eventually elaborate in a work specifically devoted to art criticism, *Les Maîtres d'autrefois* (*Old Masters of Belgium and Holland*) of 1874.[56] Guy Sagnes has even found a group of critical notes by Fromentin, conceived separately from the travel narrative, that forms the foundation of the observations elaborated by the narrator of *Une Année dans le Sahel*.[57]

Fromentin's views on Orientalist art, interpolated into this Algerian travel narrative, are exceptional because the narrator is positioned in the Orient when he addresses Orientalist art and artists. This location provides his critical comments with another order of authority. Just as artists who traveled to the Orient established the authenticity of their representations, art critics who journeyed to the Orient and wrote about Orientalist art had the authority to ascertain its relative level of authenticity. At one point the narrator refers to a "real life" scene that he and his companion pass through in order to comment upon the artistic decision to produce a genre representation. Reflecting on the scene around him, the narrator explains that in order to portray the overall sense of the place, to focus on too much detail would take the life out of the experience one was attempting to depict. In other words, Fromentin constructed a literary depiction of a genre scene in order to make disparaging comments about those artists who focused upon the details of similar scenes and to advocate against an Orientalism based on the rendering of exotic costumes, objects, and other props.[58] This passage appears to be nothing less than an intensification of the stakes for authenticity in Orientalist representations. Authenticity here comes from refuting former, no longer valid, ways of depicting the Orient. It is safe to assume that Fromentin had the best intentions and wished, above all, to establish a complexity of representational strategies that would better allow Europeans to see, understand, and appreciate a world outside their own. Yet the artist's little treatise oddly deflates this purpose, apparently operating like a game of representational one-upmanship.

Nonetheless, the "dissertation" does much to situate the artist's Algerian paintings that were offered for public consumption in France. It culminates with an analysis of three key figures, who remain unnamed in the text but whose identities would have been self-evident: Prosper Marilhat, Alexandre-Gabriel Decamps, and Eugène Delacroix. Like other critics of his era, Fromentin offered positive remarks and backhanded criticism of the three artists he addressed, but concentrated on the development of his own aesthetic posture. According to the narrator, focusing too narrowly upon details meant that the creative faculties of artists were lost, and the resulting images appeared true only in their most external form. He implies a criticism of Marilhat's handling of materials and more generally bemoans the loss of illusion and fantasy in order to render the ordinary in anecdotal terms. Marilhat's works, such as *Oriental Caravansery* (fig. 28), are very precisely rendered. They can have the quality of a crisp dream: the attention to detail is striking. Yet a sense of a larger vision beyond rendering what he saw can be entirely absent. This adulation of imagination naturally led Fromentin to praise Delacroix, who is depicted here as taking from the Orient only what suits his taste, which is informed by Venetian painting. The perfect demonstration of this is perhaps the most famous image of Algeria produced in the nineteenth century, Delacroix's *Women of Algiers in Their Apartment* (1834; fig. 44). Delacroix's well-studied masterpiece has provoked a myriad of interpretations since it was originally presented at the Salon of 1834, but it is a painting that exemplifies the artist's subjective and richly textured view of the Orient.[59] While Fromentin lauds Delacroix—indeed, even Baudelaire saw Fromentin as following in Delacroix's footsteps—he also suggests that Delacroix's understanding of landscape is limited to what it can offer in terms of color contrast. Decamps (figs. 15, 27) is praised for his success at achieving light effects through strong shadows, but is accused of sacrificing all else as a result.[60] All of these characterizations are less than fair, but they do possess more than a grain of truth—and it is important to remember that art criticism of the day, which Fromentin began writing in the 1840s, was avowedly subjective and partisan. Add to this the fact that Fromentin was trying to clear a space for himself as an Orientalist painter among his progenitors and rivals, and his comments can be seen for what they are.

While this formation of aesthetic criteria does not lead anywhere in the novel, it establishes Fromentin's interests as a painter. This extended elaboration of his aesthetic position serves to situate his painted depictions of Algeria in the minds of his readers. Appearing in March 1859, just before his most successful Salon appearance (he won a first-class medal and was made a member of the Légion d'honneur), this text explained the concerns that he was addressing in the paintings and helped establish a new and distinct position for Fromentin among other Orientalist artists. While the artist's paintings in the Salon of 1859 were addressed at length by a wide range of critics, Fromentin seized the opportunity to have the first word, to submit his defense before any accusation could be made. In this case, the travel narrative did not function as merely another descriptive modality. Rather, the author self-consciously employed this aesthetic discussion in the travel novel to buttress and explain his development as a painter and position himself in relation to other major artists depicting the Orient.

Fromentin's Portrayal of Laghouat at the Salon

In the years between 1853, when Fromentin first visited Laghouat and made his sketches, and 1857, when he first presented an image of this Algerian city to the French public, the artist produced a large number of Orientalist scenes that were exhibited in Bordeaux, Lyon, and La Rochelle and were sold through his dealer, Adolphe Beugnet.[61] Thompson and Wright have eloquently traced Fromentin's development as a pictorial artist over these years, suggesting influences of both Gustave Moreau and Eugène Delacroix. They also note a transformation in his technique, a gradual distancing from the use of thick impasto linked with the Oriental scenes of Decamps, and they argue convincingly that the works Fromentin produced in 1857 represent a stylistic break with previous paintings. My analysis will attend to the artist's newly developed techniques while retaining an (admittedly) narrow focus on his representations of Laghouat. Fromentin produced a wide array of works in the 1850s, most of which are situated in amorphous but exotic landscapes, much like the landscapes of Delacroix that he criticized. An excellent example would be *Falcon Hunting* (fig.

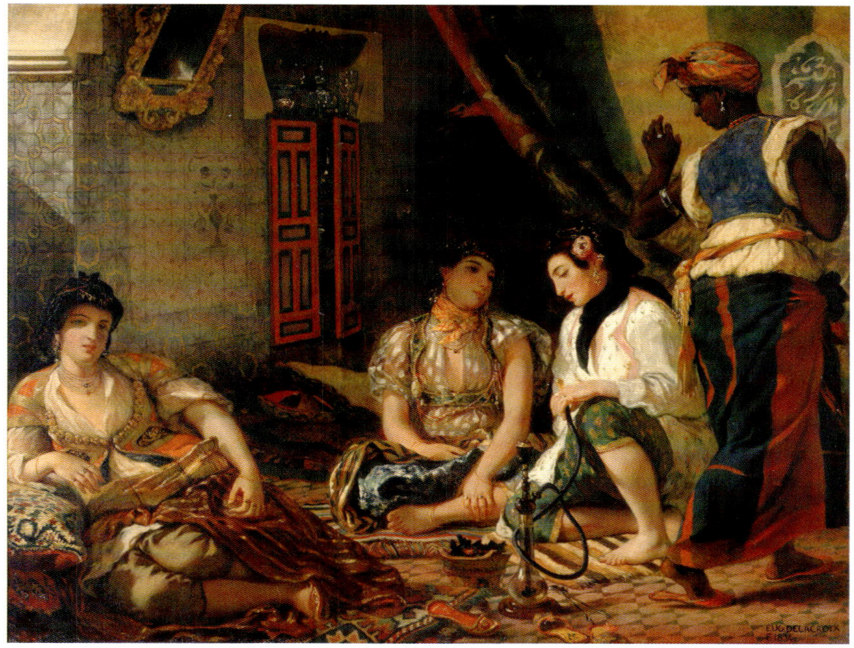

Figure 44.
Eugène Delacroix, *Women of Algiers in Their Apartment*, 1834, oil on canvas, 180 × 229 cm. Musée du Louvre, Paris, France (INV 3824). Photo: Réunion des musées nationaux/Art Resource, New York (Lemage).

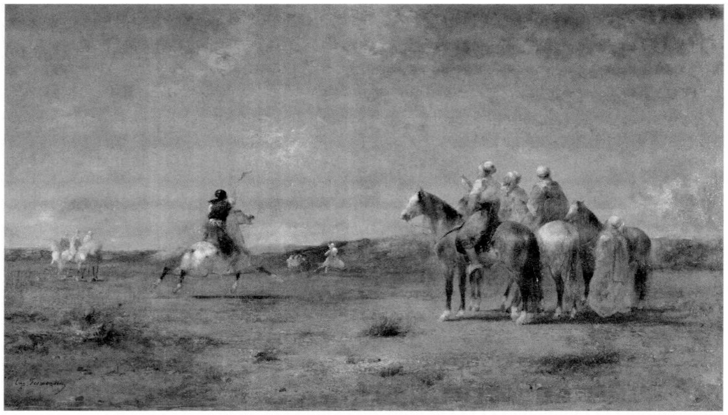

Figure 45.
Eugène Fromentin, *Falcon Hunting*, undated. Oil on canvas, 36.8 × 60.8 cm. Musée Saint-Dénis, Reims. © Musée des Beaux-Arts de la Ville de Reims (C. Devleeschauwer).

45). Like most of his paintings from this period, this work generalizes the landscape, even reducing it to the status of a colorful but vague backdrop framing conventional Orientalist figure groups.

However, two of Fromentin's most critically acclaimed works from the Salons of 1857 and 1859 are located in Laghouat. *Halt of the Merchants Before Laghouat* (1857; fig. 46) and *A Street in Laghouat* (fig. 39) are important not solely because they were highly regarded by contemporary critics, but also because they convey Fromentin's exceptional intimacy with this specific and historically significant location. Unlike the motifs of Arab caravans and regal hunters that were, without a doubt, Fromentin's bread and butter, the works representing Laghouat offer a unique view of one site of the expansion of the French colonial empire.

To begin, it is necessary to underline a central assertion, namely, that these two paintings can be productively examined as landscapes. This point requires explanation, because both pieces could be interpreted as genre scenes and are populated with numerous figures. They are not empty landscapes, like the oil sketches. Further, these works do not directly signify "nature," a representational task that goes a long way toward parsing certain paintings as landscapes in our own and past eras.[62] The point of conceiving these very different paintings as landscapes is that the subject of these two works is the place—Laghouat—and that both seek above all to communicate the artist's sense of this place. They are recreations through memory, but they nevertheless attempt to impart an impression of this region that so affected Fromentin and led to radical experimentation in his direct translations of it. *Halt of the Merchants Before Laghouat* and *A Street in Laghouat* allow an analysis of the spatial or territorial component of Orientalist painting that clarifies the territorial foundation of colonialism and its relation to Fromentin's experiences in and representations of Laghouat.

In these works it is possible to distinguish an emergent conceptual model for explaining a group's relationship to its environment, that is, the immersion of individuals into the region they inhabit. This notion would eventually emerge as regional geography, which articulated the idea that a natural region determines the social existence of its inhabitants.[63] This discipline emerged originally from an article published by Lucien Gallois in 1892.[64] In the paintings under consideration, the figures, with all their attendant baggage as cultural symbols, are folded into a new visual conception of place—a space that itself dictates a way of life for its inhabitants. By apprehending this particular space and representing it as landscape, Fromentin also produced an image of an exotic location and an Orientalist scene.

Halt of the Merchants Before Laghouat is a carefully composed, even academic landscape.[65] Many of its elements conform to a Poussinist model of landscape representation, and the work was achieved with the help of two preliminary studies, at least one of which was made on site.[66] There are repoussoir trees on one side of the composition, groups of fig-

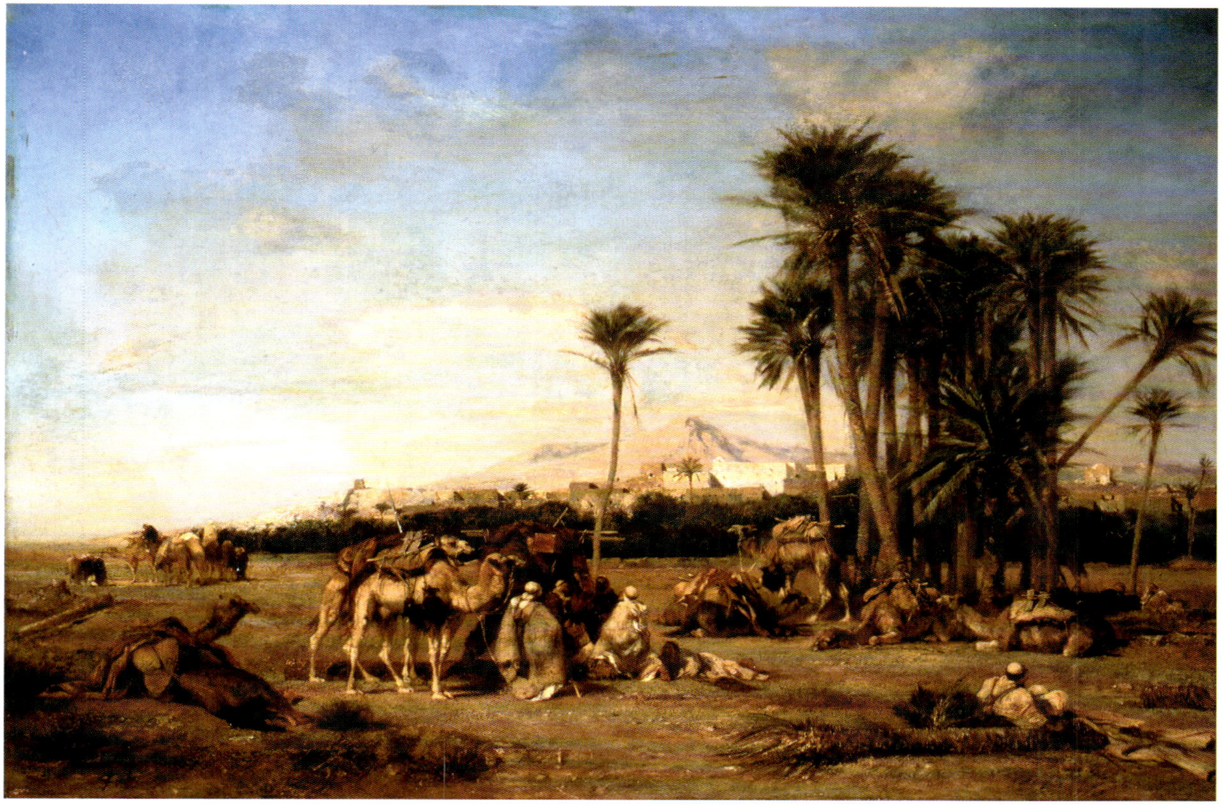

Figure 46.
Eugène Fromentin, *Halt of the Merchants Before Laghouat*, 1857. Oil on canvas, 70 × 100 cm. Private collection. Photo courtesy Christie's Images.

Figure 47.
Prosper Marilhat, *Ruins of the Mosque of Caliph El-Hakem in Cairo*, 1840. Oil on canvas, 84.5 × 130.7 cm. Musée du Louvre, Paris (RF 184). Photo: Réunion des musées nationaux/Art Resource, New York (René-Gabriel Ojéda).

ures that measure distance in the fore- and middle ground, a city in the distance, and a mountain rising behind it. The artist even guides the eye into the background through the use of aerial perspective, with cooler colors providing a sense of atmosphere between viewer and background. The work recalls the Egyptian landscapes of Marilhat, such as *Ruins of the Mosque of Caliph El-Hakem in Cairo* (1840; fig. 47), which features a group of natives and their pack animals resting in the shadows of a ruined mosque. In the tradition of both Poussin and Marilhat, Fromentin presents a clear, structured landscape composition, a view of humans in a natural environment. But the quality of that environment—its vast expanse of space, its scintillating light, and

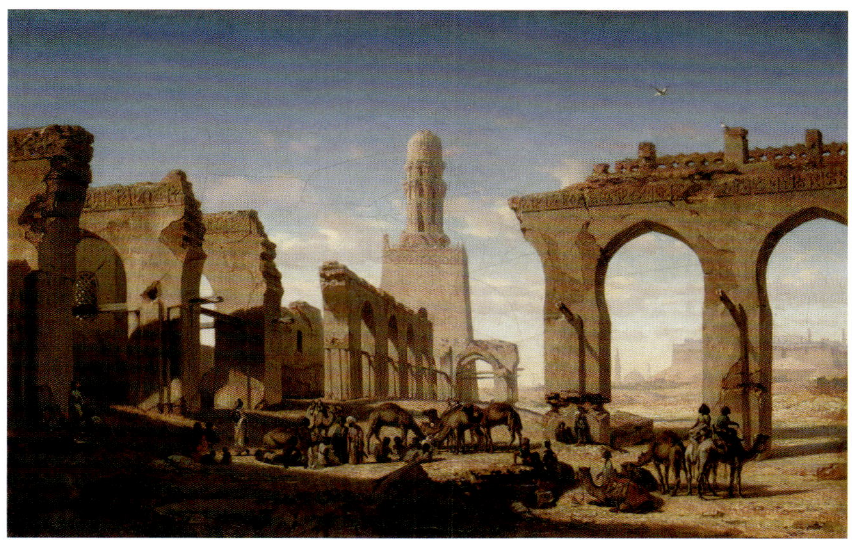

the openness of the horizon—mark this landscape as distinct. Further, the village of Laghouat in the distance is not in a state of ruin, so the meanings a viewer would read in this landscape are different. As noted by Maxime Du Camp, the means for representing this country were also distinct: "An evident lover of light and color, M. Fromentin excels at rendering both and at marrying them in extraordinarily pleasing harmonies . . . his nervous painting . . . runs lightly over the canvas like layers of air and communicates a lively and durable impression. It is indeed the Orient, the Saharan Orient with its blond nuances like honey and its immensities of horizon that no eye can plumb."[67]

The most compelling aspects of Du Camp's laudatory comments are his description of the *impression* that Fromentin's painting conveys and his assessment that this impression is linked to a specific place with certain features. From Du Camp's perspective, Fromentin's handling of materials was evocative of location.[68] Regardless of whether Fromentin actually succeeded in evoking what he saw in his oil sketches, the Salon paintings made use of the techniques he developed while making them. It is impossible to say (and it would have been impossible for Du Camp as well) whether *Halt of the Merchants* depicts Laghouat truthfully, but the ability to evoke an impression of that place was successful in this Salon painting, owing to Fromentin's expanded technical abilities resulting from his experimentation while on site.

While Du Camp referred to the Saharan Orient, armchair travel was explicitly evoked by Edmond About in his brief discussion of Fromentin in his "Salon de 1857." He wrote that Fromentin's Algerian works presented at the Salon that year "transport us commodiously to the bosom of a curious civilization."[69] This remark is echoed by Gautier's criticism of the work and is worthy of some consideration.[70]

Both About and Gautier asserted the ability of this work to take its viewer on a journey. The way the painting comes to stand for experience is compelling: it is as if by making the painting, the artist injected his own experience into the work, and the viewer enjoys access to the artist's travel experiences through the painting. This aspect of his work reflects the Romantic illustrations of Algeria discussed in the previous chapter. Fromentin's intimacy with the Saharan landscape, established by his travel narrative, allowed him to be known as an artist who overcame stereotypical depictions of the Orient in order to render the Orient as it was. This point was made in 1957 by Jean Alazard,[71] but a century earlier, Gautier, who had himself traveled to Algeria, described *Halt of the Merchants* as having neither a subject nor a drama.[72] Such a remark was meant to imply that this work was not affected or dramatized, but somehow transparent. He continued, "before this wild village that has cost our soldiers so much blood and that is now a French city, despite the fact that it possesses the air of a cemetery where no one gets buried. All of this strange and improbable nature is rendered with such a sentiment of reality, that one sees it on the canvas as if one was the painter himself opposite the scene he has represented."[73] The first sentence of the passage indicates the writer's knowledge of Laghouat's gruesome history, as it was gleaned from reading *Un Été dans le Sahara,* while the second asserts that the strangeness of this location is represented with such a realistic sentiment that the viewer feels as if s/he were the painter, standing in this "French city" her- or himself. There can be no doubt that the transparency Gautier suggests between the real location and its representation is none other than an accordance between the literary and pictorial descriptions Fromentin has offered of Laghouat. Fromentin had something of a corner on the market.

Transportation, or perhaps voyage, seems to be the theme of this painting as well as its underlying depictive strategy. The image, which features merchants at the outskirts of a city with their wares packed on camels, is self-consciously quotidian, yet it also builds a thematic connection between the artist and the subject. The figures featured in this painting may be exotic, defined in opposition to Europeans, but they share something with the artist. Like Fromentin, these men are travelers en route, not actual inhabitants of Laghouat. Like Fromentin, they have traversed great distances to reach this city in order to engage in its commerce. From merchants such as these, the artist would have bought supplies and food at the market held in the city. Fromentin was enamored of desert life and found such travelers *grand,* as opposed to the effeminate Moors who occupied the cities on the Northern coast.[74] He romanticized their peripatetic existence, but he shared it as well. Gautier asserted that Fromentin followed voyaging tribes, slept under a tent, and partook of the *diffa* (a nightly meal among desert tribes).[75] Thus these figures, despite all of their markers of exoticism, stand in as doubles for the artist. Their presence allowed Fromentin to shed his own cultural baggage and unpack his experiences of exotic travel for a French public. After all, the French artist had also traveled in this world, and a self-portrait sketch the artist made in Laghouat (fig. 48) demonstrates that, while traveling at least, the appearance he adopted would have allowed him to fit seamlessly into the exotic trappings of the painting.[76] The figures in *Halt of the Merchants* can be seen as more fantastic projections of the artist's self.

In a brief description of Laghouat published in 1854 in the *Revue de l'Orient, de l'Algérie et des colonies*, Oscar MacCarthy detailed the geographical importance of Laghouat as a trade route. Laghouat commanded one of the shortest, safest trade routes across the Sahara, and the French domination of this city would assure them control over long-range trade with the African interior. The importance of merchants in this region must have been clear to Fromentin, for three out of the seven canvases he submitted to the Salon of 1857 featured merchants.[77] In *Halt of the Merchants*, the merchants are not there merely to provide exotic trappings that contribute to a picturesque effect. They also serve to establish the importance of this site to colonial commerce. The strategic importance of this location for the French is related through the unassuming group of Arab merchants who pause to rest in it. Thus the exotic figures come to be seen within the new imperial landscape of France, one in which the colony's commerce generates a tax base that supports the colonial administration.

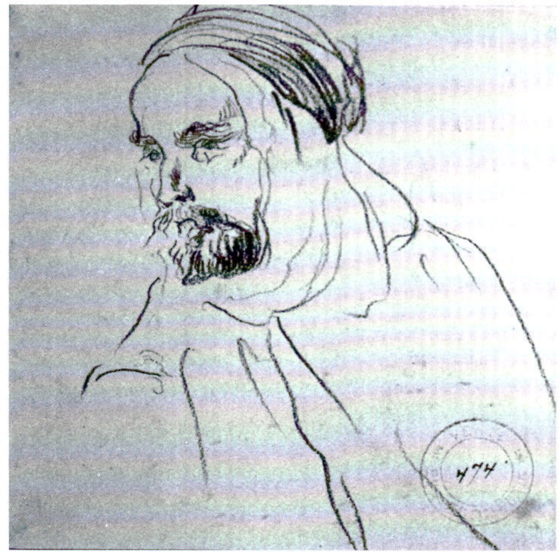

Figure 48.
Eugène Fromentin, *Self-Portrait Dressed as an Arab*, undated. Charcoal pencil on paper, 10 × 9.5 cm. Private collection, La Roche sur Yon, France. Photo courtesy Barbara Wright.

Hostilities between the French military and the native inhabitants of Algeria came to a close in 1857 with the ultimate pacification of what was known as La Grand Kabylie by the forces of Maréchal Randon.[78] Unlike Dauzats' image of a fortress landscape, Fromentin represented a recently conquered landscape in a period when trade and colonization dominated and the conquest was all but complete. Whereas the figures that populated Dauzats' landscapes were French soldiers and their indigenous collaborators, Fromentin depicted nomadic merchants. It is not that Fromentin did not see his share of French soldiers; rather, merchants accorded better with the image of Algeria that Fromentin wanted to project. The strength of this assertion is supported by the fact that Fromentin, like Dauzats, had a government commission to produce a landscape with a battle theme that never came to fruition as such.

Halt of the Merchants provides an image of landscape that charts France's imperial expansion and introduces the possibility of a worldwide French empire in pictorial terms. It would be another three years before Napoléon III, on his first visit to Algeria, would proclaim Algeria an Arab kingdom (*royaume arabe*) and name himself as its leader. In *Halt of the Merchants,* the viewer is presented an image of the "austral limits of France," an exotic landscape that is nevertheless naturalized to France, including Arab merchants whose trade will generate income for the colonizing power. The visual scheme extends French conceptions of territory and landscape so as to include other cultures within an expanded, imperial France. On a visual level, this artistic appropriation of the colonial landscape occurs by transforming the empty expanse of desert around Laghouat into a French landscape through the application of pictorial landscape conventions (Fromentin's *Poussinisme*). Moreover, the way in which Fromentin employed innovative techniques in his landscape composition to evoke this location in the metropole underscores his personal experience of travel funded, albeit indirectly, by the French government and made possible by the colonial administration. In this colonial landscape, one sees an image of France that expands its control to the Sahara and beyond, as well as the artist's role within this imperial projection.

In the next Salon, in 1859, Fromentin exhibited another landscape painting featuring Laghouat. *A Street in Laghouat* (fig. 39) was less expansive in terms of perspective and territorial ambitions, but nonetheless earned the artist a first-class medal, the cross of the Légion d'honneur, and a wealth of critical response.[79] Though this work does not depict a natural environment, it was nevertheless accepted by the Minister of Beaux-Arts as the result of Fromentin's second commission for a landscape of southern Algeria.[80] Most critics treated Fromentin as an Orientalist landscapist, while one even considered his submissions alongside those of Corot, Troyon, and Daubigny.[81] This painting is worthy of a detailed examination solely on the basis of its popularity, but it also provides a site for inquiry into the received ideas of French viewers and how Fromentin exploited such notions. Further, this work is a direct illustration of a passage from *Un Été dans le Sahara* and thus offers an exceptional example of the relationship between Fromentin's textual and pictorial productions.

Writing for the *Gazette des Beaux-Arts*, Paul Mantz referred to this phenomenon directly: "M. Fromentin appears to engage in a certain coquetry by publishing a book at the opening of each exhibition."[82] While all the critics mention Fromentin's travel narratives, Alexandre Dumas, for one, included a full-scale review of the two works alongside his ample praise for the paintings Fromentin exhibited that year.[83] Most critics referred to *A Street in Laghouat* as illustrating a scene from *Un Été dans le Sahara*, but a few reviewers even incorporated Fromentin's aesthetic discussions into their critiques of his paintings. Henri Dumesnil refers to the passage from *Un Été dans le Sahara* discussed above, in which the author describes how the desert landscape helps him understand the old masters better. After quoting a large section of that passage, the critic asserts that the artist had put into practice the method "to see things in a simple way, in order to obtain true form." In other words, Dumesnil found the qualities in Fromentin's paintings that Fromentin attributed to the old masters. By using the artist's travel narrative as a point of departure, Dumesnil asserted the importance of Fromentin the artist on the basis of the authority of Fromentin the author.[84]

Fromentin apparently did not choose to make a painting following the compositions he formulated in the previously discussed oil studies, but based his subject instead on a description of the street provided in *Un Été dans le Sahara*.[85] While the strong contrast of dark and light was a hackneyed formula to signify "Oriental light," splitting a composition into dark and light halves was a dramatic and unique gesture. In an apparent anomaly, the line running down the middle of the street, separating dark from light, does not conform to the rigid architectural forms that cast the shadow, but is a wavy, softly curving line that draws the eye into distance. The vertical composition also serves to establish a narrow, enclosed space, as opposed to the vast openness for which this region is known. The buildings on both sides block the viewer's line of sight and force an intimate confrontation with what is pictured. Further, the use of color could not be more distinct from Delacroix's famous Algerian interior, *Women of Algiers in Their Apartment* (fig. 44), which signifies the Orient through exotic paraphernalia and bright color contrasts. Delacroix also produced a street scene very soon after his return from Morocco and Algeria, *A Street in Meknes* (1832; fig. 49). Compared to Fromentin's street scene, it is a composition with a very tight focus, though it does feature a figure seated on a street outside a Moorish dwelling and another lying down in the doorway. Delacroix's street scene is smaller and less resolved than Fromentin's. In *A Street in Meknes*, Delacroix's use of color is far more restrained than in his Algerian interior, and the brushwork is much looser. Nonetheless, even Delacroix's simple portrayal of a few figures on the street is more coloristic than Fromentin's painting, which expresses the power of the sun to bleach an entire landscape. While Delacroix's figures demonstrate an array of facial expressions and appear to respond to the viewer's gaze, Fromentin's figures are mostly dozing; the standing figure in the background, about to enter a portal, has her back turned to us.

A Street in Laghouat is based on the opposition of two complementary colors, blue and gold, that provide a sense of scintillating light and graphically separate a monotone cluster of buildings from the brightness of the sky. Fromentin seems to have made only a single concession to the incidental col-

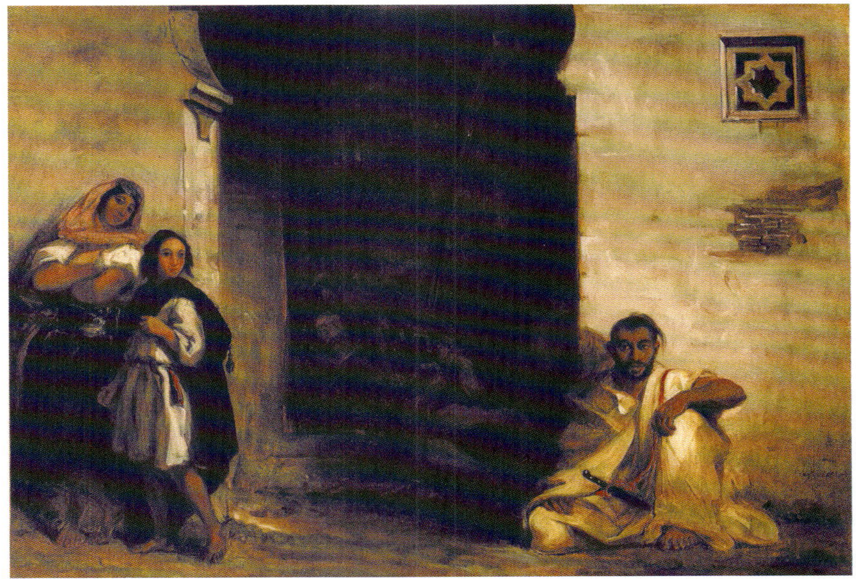

Figure 49.
Eugène Delacroix,
A Street in Meknes, 1832.
Oil on canvas, 46.3 × 64.1 cm. Albright-Knox Art Gallery, Buffalo, New York, Elizabeth H. Gates and Charles W. Goodyear Funds, 1948.

ors that characterize Orientalist scenes up to that point, namely, the open *haïk* of the figure nearest the viewer that reveals a brightly colored garment underneath. The contemporary critics made much of the careful balance of yellow light and violet shadows and also noted Fromentin's moderate use of impasto, which differentiated his work from both Marilhat's seamless washes and Decamps' reliance on facture. Fromentin pursued innovative techniques in other canvases he sent to the Salon that year as well. In *Black Performers,* Fromentin experimented with creating a sense of dynamic movement in a static, relief-like composition of figures; in *Edge of an Oasis During the "Sirocco,"* he attempted to suggest the effects of wind in a flat desert landscape. In his masterpiece of 1863, *Falcon Hunting in Algeria (La Curée)* (fig. 50), the painter created a genre scene of the hunt surrounded by a spacious landscape. Minutely rendered animals in motion are juxtaposed with loosely brushed landscape elements in order to produce a sense of immediacy.

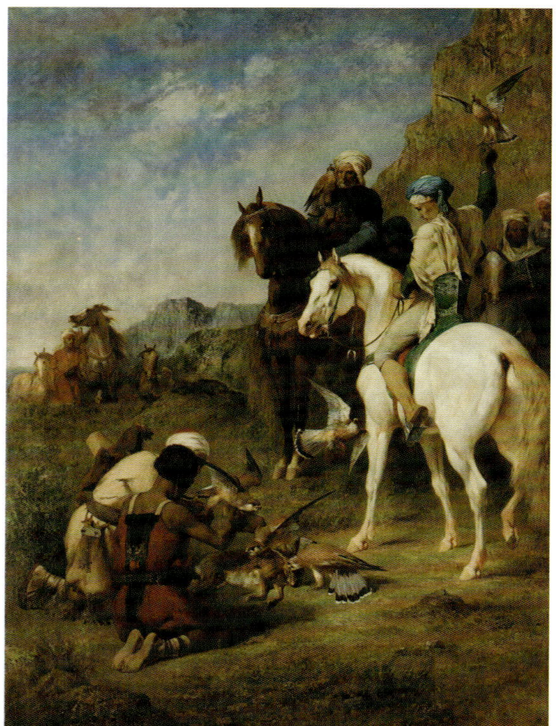

Figure 50. Eugène Fromentin, *Falcon Hunting in Algeria (La Curée),* 1863. Oil on canvas, 163 × 118 cm. Musée d'Orsay, Paris. Photo courtesy Musée d'Orsay (Patrice Schmidt).

Such innovative formal techniques should clearly establish the distance between Fromentin's Orientalist representations and those of more academically minded practitioners, such as Jean-Léon Gérôme, but Fromentin's unique landscape compositions also invite associations with Barbizon landscapists. As noted earlier, Jean Rousseau grouped Fromentin with Corot, Troyon, and Daubigny in his Salon review. He asserted that France's landscape painters of the period were achieving perhaps the highest expression in that genre ever attained, and declared that the greatest difference between earlier and modern landscapists was in execution, with new effects being achieved that had not previously been attempted.[86]

If, as Rousseau asserts, we can base claims for artistic innovation in landscape painting on the manner of execution, Fromentin demonstrates a "free and impulsive" handling of materials. *A Street in Laghouat* appears composed and solid at a distance, but upon closer inspection, the traces of the artist's hand are everywhere in evidence. Is it possible to consider Fromentin an innovator in the genre of French landscape despite the Orientalist subject of his works? Orientalist artists have traditionally been classed among the conservatives in the history of nineteenth-century French art.[87] For example, Fromentin's paintings are displayed on the right side of the Musée d'Orsay—alongside paintings by Thomas Couture and Jean-Léon Gérôme—while the landscapes of his Barbizon contemporaries are on the left, near the works of Gustave Courbet and Edouard Manet. The works of plein-air landscapists who painted in the Fôret de Fontainebleau have always been perceived as standing outside academic tradition, forecasting the developments of Impressionism and modernism—though *A Street* has been considered recently as a precursor to Impressionism.[88] In some sense, a connection between

Fromentin and Barbizon landscapists should come as no surprise: Fromentin's teacher, Nicholas Louis Cabat, was a painter closely affiliated with Barbizon. Moreover, Fromentin made sketches (currently in the possession of his descendants) that were executed in the Fôret de Fontainebleau in 1845.

Rousseau's commentary notwithstanding, there was nevertheless a reluctance to consider Fromentin's Orientalist works in the wider field of landscape painting at the time they were shown. The subject matter of the paintings, and particularly that of *A Street in Laghouat,* was what most impressed contemporary critics. No matter how much Fromentin's Algerian landscapes were formally similar to pictures representing the Fôret de Fontainebleau, it is clear that at the time, most critics considered these works in relation to Orientalist stereotypes rather than as formal advances in the realm of landscape painting. While there may yet be room for Fromentin in the history of French landscape painting, critics in 1859 judged Fromentin's success in relation to how well his works dovetailed with received ideas about the Orient in general and the colony of Algeria in particular. Yet the reception of Fromentin's Algerian landscape can inform us about the nature of the historical juncture this image illustrates.

Gautier began his discussion of this painting with an assertion that it would not please the amateurs of progress. He is referring to the dilapidated aspect of the urban environment, yet the same comment could apply to the figures.[89] They are not active, productive members of modern society, but lounge within their decrepit environment. Paul de Saint-Victor also makes a connection between the attitude of these figures and their climate, comparing them to the damned in Dante's *Inferno.*[90] His description of these figures as sorrowful souls, who can do no more then lie listlessly, demonstrates that native Algerians, considered in their cultural milieu, suffered in comparison with productive French citizens. The critics took in this scene in terms of their own experiences, fed by Orientalist art and literature. The figures in *A Street* remain figures of the imagination, occupying a fantastic place and, as such, it is hard to imagine them having views of their own, divergent perceptions of the world, or the right to contest the French authority to govern them. They are figured in contemporary criticism as little more than bodies blocking the road of colonial progress.

Gautier was more explicit in his association of artistic travel with ethnography. In the section specifically devoted to Fromentin in his "Salon de 1859," Gautier coined the term "peinture ethnographique" (ethnographic painting).[91] This tendency—explicitly tied to the development of the steamship, which made transportation cheaper and quicker—was presented as a resolution to current dilemmas of art, a next wave of artistic sensibility that followed on the heels of Romanticism. Gautier wrote: "Steam has not killed art, and perhaps it will save it by opening new horizons and by carrying it, in just a few days, to the bosom of virgin countries where the picturesque has exiled itself from civilization. . . . Today nature has replaced *le paysage historique,* and painters have perceived that there are other people besides the models of the Academy; . . . so that the Sahara sees as many landscapist umbrellas as previously seen in the Forest of Fontainebleau."[92]

For Gautier, this historical juncture, like others before it, produced an artistic movement relevant to its own epoch. Steam might be bourgeois and prosaic, but it had opened the world for artistic exploration. He asserted that the result of the new availability of distant lands would be ethnographic painting. As he articulated it, ethnographic painting would have a broad applicability, including recording the distinct appearance of distant lands. While the subsequent development of the social sciences separated the study of humans from the study of places, with the result that ethnography was classed with anthropology rather than geography, Gautier's conception of ethnographic painting brought humans and their environments together as worthy of careful study by the artist.

The passage above suggests that artists traveled in order to collect visual information, return with it, and present it to a French audience. Central here is the concept of progress, the technological developments that provide access to those picturesque refuges outside civilization. Artistic production and travel are instrumentalized in this account, because the central activity of collecting materials in the periphery and displaying them in the metropole is conceived as the natural result of technological and social transformations. In Gautier's conception of ethnographic art, both the process of translation and artistic agency are left out of the equation. Artists are transformed into functionaries responding to and serving the goals of development and, more particularly in Fromentin's case, colonial development.

Journeys such as Fromentin's were pioneering in the context of the growth of nineteenth-century capitalist culture because they guided the explorations of future tourists and even the development of railways and roads. This will be explored further in the next chapter, but I want to note here that Fromentin was driven to voyage to Laghouat not simply because of his interest in newly conquered territory but also because French colonization had already transformed more accessible locations and because artists had already been producing images of those places for almost a generation. Fromentin had to penetrate deeper into the interior to bring back a new subject.[93]

And so he did. Perhaps the most compelling aspect of *A Street in Laghouat* is the way in which it represents Fromentin's increased intimacy with Algeria as a result of more thorough penetration. The sexual metaphor of colonial conquest finds a clear realization in this composition. Fromentin himself wrote, in his 1874 preface to his Algerian travel narratives, "I have visited Algeria several times; I have just penetrated further and lived there steadily." This contact resulted in "a sort of intimate and definitive acclimation."[94] The process that the artist refers to signals the authenticity of his pictorial and literary works as well as his association with Algeria and its inhabitants. Thus Fromentin "penetrated further" into the virgin country (as Gautier reads it) of Algeria, leading to "intimate acclimation" as well as several pictorial and literary creations.

Considering the theme of penetration in relation to *A Street* allows for a unique reading of the image of Algeria it offers. Entering the colonial landscape was a central metaphor in Dauzats' Portes de Fer watercolors, but Fromentin's incursion led to a distinct image of the Algerian landscape more suited to the Algeria of the Second Empire. As in Dauzats' vertical Portes de Fer landscapes, *A Street* is an image whose spatial configuration directly suggests the metaphor of penetration. The viewer's eye moves down the slightly curved and narrow street into the distance. Instead of natural rock formations, in this image, the viewer's space is bounded by indigenous architecture, whose solid, angular, blocklike forms must have appeared entirely strange to the residents of Haussmann's Paris. Instead of active French soldiers, here we see Arabs lying on the ground. The viewer's eye does not follow anyone down this passageway, but proceeds alone. However, unlike the Portes de Fer, this is not a fortress landscape, posing a threat to those who might walk through it. It is simply a street passing through an exotic-looking village, and the artist has even left an open door at the end of the corridor to allow escape. Whereas a few sentries stood in the distance atop Dauzats' fortress, here the natives lie prone, corpselike, and the viewer must imagine walking around or even over them. In *A Street in Laghouat*, it is not only the natural world (the virgin territory) that is conquered by the French, but the inhabited one as well, the site of human residence. In this frame, colonial territory comprises natural forms as well as the inhabitants of the landscape and their dwellings.

The geographer Denis Cosgrove has written, "Landscape distances us from the world in critical ways, defining a particular relationship with nature and with those who appear in nature, and offers us the illusion of a world in which we may participate subjectively by entering the picture frame along the perspectival axis. But this is an aesthetic entrance not an active engagement with a nature or space that has its own life."[95] Looking at *A Street in Laghouat* through Cosgrove's lens, it becomes clear that the transformation of Algerian materials into European projections is not confined to the figures depicted in the painting. The space appears able to contain projections as well. While Fromentin offered an evocation of place in this work, it was structured upon the principles of landscape, a particularly European way of measuring and representing space. The viewer's eye can penetrate the city, moving along the rue Bab-el-Gharbi of Laghouat; this is an effect generated by the form of the representation. It is an "aesthetic entrance," not a literal one. While *A Street* seems to offer access to a city in southern Algeria, what it actually provides is an illusion that the viewer could move through this idealized, aesthetic space without confronting obstacles and without being reminded of the recent violent conquest.

If one shifts the focus away from the landscape depiction and concentrates on how landscape is proposed as a means to apprehend this city, the historical nature of Fromentin's representation of Laghouat becomes clear. At stake here is not just the city itself, but also the way in which the city is perceived, the way it is framed as a landscape for a European eye and, in that process, naturalized to greater (imperial) France. Offering an image of an exotic southern Algerian city as a landscape was certainly innovative, as has been shown. The power of *A Street in Laghouat* is not in its exotic trappings, but in the way the signs of exoticism are naturalized into a view of a place powerfully evoked in this work. As Théophile Gautier put it in his "Salon de 1857," "One can walk on his terrains and lean against his walls without fear . . . one feels as free in his paintings as in the desert itself."[96] This populated territory, this townscape built by Arabs and inhabited by them for hundreds of years, was now a French city. This domination was based on military force and on the ability of the French to become familiar with and to represent this place. Fromentin's intimacy with this city and its inhabitants, his very penetration of the country, allowed him to provide this illusion of landscape to his viewers. Paradoxically, by removing the traces of French conquest and occupation and presenting Laghouat as a specific place, he made this distant village a French city.

CHAPTER 5

Beyond Landscape Imagery

The Photographic Seizure of the Colonial Landscape

Mazagran, Beni-Mered, Zaatcha will no doubt disappear someday, or at least be absorbed by the intrusion of our colonization; but the thinker, the poet and the historian will be able to find them again with their original aspect in the portfolio of M. Moulin.

—Ernest Lacan

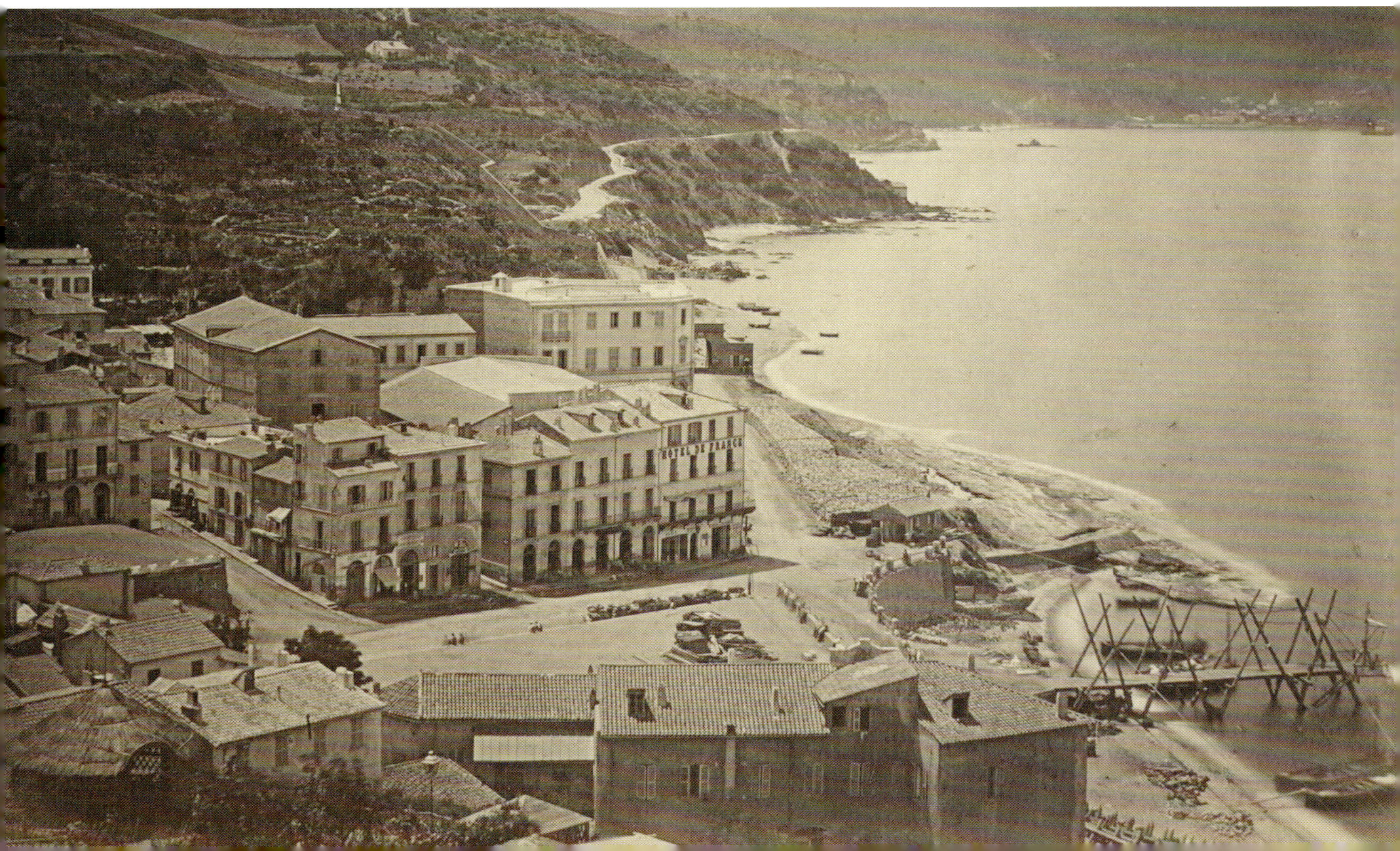

The portfolio of M. Moulin can be found today in the archives of the French military at the Château de Vincennes, outside of Paris.[1] Four very large volumes, each containing fifty photographs, most of them with extended captions, are enclosed in tidy, archival boxes. There should have been six—two volumes for each province—but only four seem to have survived, and this is the only copy known.

As a historian I had come, as Ernest Lacan knew I would, to seek the traces of Algeria known in the mid-nineteenth century. As an art historian, then in the late twentieth century, I knew that these photographs were representations, like the paintings, sketches, and prints representing the colony. Yet I could not help being overwhelmed by their documentary aspect. I felt as if I were discovering some buried treasure, some fleeting and forgotten world, with the kind of thrill I experienced on opening an illustrated magazine from an era long past. Moulin's photographs were by no means snapshots, produced as they were under the laborious conditions of early photography—yet they appeared profoundly immediate to my perception, vividly evocative of places and people mostly lost to history. Moulin's photographs presented Algeria to me in a way no other image I had examined could. Certainly, there were posed group portraits with painted backdrops and landscapes evacuated of all measure of human existence, but there were traces of presence in the banal details that often revealed themselves despite, or because of, the intentions of the photographer.

And so Lacan's prophecy was realized. For I found in these photographs a very real presence and felt the breath of history on the back of my neck. Upon reflection, I am confounded and a bit awed that even after a century and a half, these images project a sense of truth and make me feel as if I was seeing the real Algeria for the very first time.

Another Panorama

Overleaf: detail of fig. 59

Félix-Jacques-Antoine Moulin's *Panorama of Constantine* (1856–57; fig. 51), from the artist's album *L'Algérie photographiée*, is a singularly meaningful image of a colonial landscape, even if it is somewhat uncharacteristic of Moulin's production.[2] This photograph can be read for its historical import because it depicts a site of particular symbolic significance in the history of France in Algeria—and it represents a development of the empire of landscape. Looking at previous images of this city, it is clear that the photograph introduces a new dimension into the history of French depictions of the Algerian landscape. What is achieved in the panorama mirrors the French transformation of Algeria. While the French administrators planned and redesigned the multiple and fragmentary spaces of Algeria into a singular and cohesive representation of a colony in space, Moulin replaced earlier romantic and historical associations with the exotic Algerian landscape previously available in France. This panoramic photograph mirrors the French ministrations to North African territory, consolidating the power of technological transformations—represented by the photographic mechanism—to usher in a new era in the perception of the colonial landscape. This constitutes an evolution in the technology of spectatorship, in which the viewer's ability to apprehend the colony's spaces is reconditioned by the newly developed medium that represents them.

In Moulin's photograph, perception and image have become fully intertwined in the ideological production of the real through the technological development of the means to perceive it.[3] By showing the material transformations of Constantine as a result of the French colonial occupation, the *Panorama of Constantine* reinvents the multiple spaces of Constantine as a singular colonial city and, in the process, reifies France's claim on this region of Africa, presenting the visual evidence of its authenticity.

This reification is possible because of photography's special status as a representational tool.

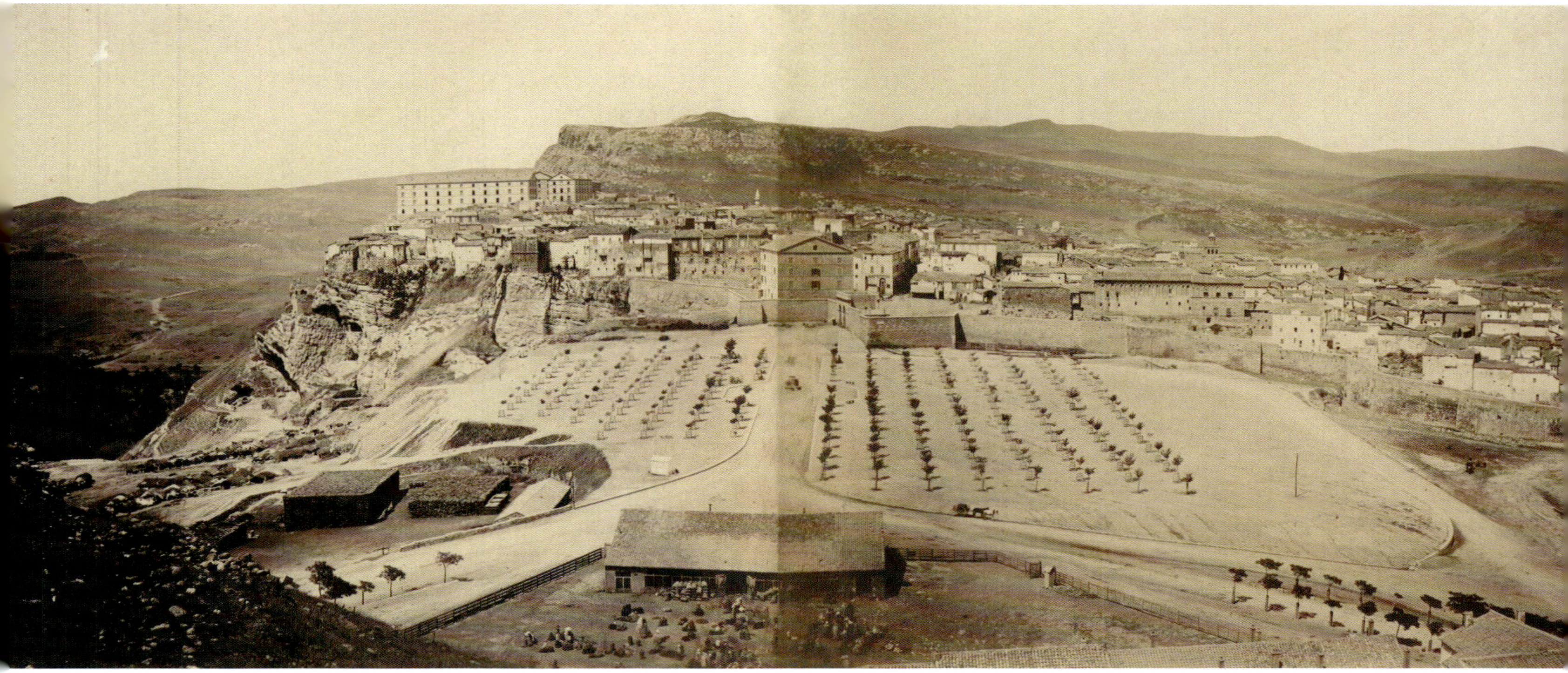

While the character of photographs was perceived differently in Moulin's period than in our own, the distinction between photographs and other artistic works was just as salient then as it is now. Joel Snyder has claimed that "by the mid-to-late 1850s, photography came to be separated in conceptual terms from the other depictive arts, and this separation was described increasingly not in terms of the differences between media but in ontological terms. Painting and the graphic arts were conceived as representing the realm of the imaginative, cognitive, and the ideal, while photography was, depending on the interest of the writer, consigned or elevated to the realm of the factual, the material, the physically real."[4] To back up his argument, he quotes Baudelaire's "The Modern Public and Photography," a section of his *Salon de 1859*. Baudelaire's ideas on photography were, of course, inflected by his conception of its commodification, an issue that this chapter will address below. In order to demonstrate the ubiquity of this ontological distinction, Snyder also quotes Oliver Wendell Holmes, who wrote, in 1863: "It is well enough for some Baron Gros or Horace Vernet to please an imperial master with fanciful portraits of what they are supposed to be. But the honest sunshine [i.e., photographic mechanism] is nature's sternest painter, yet the best, for always true."[5] Holmes' remark is a clear manifestation of the perception that photography presented the world truthfully. This statement is particularly compelling in the context of Moulin's *Panorama of Constantine,* because the location from which

Figure 51.
Félix Moulin, *Panorama of Constantine*, 1856–57. Albumin photograph, 19 × 46 cm. From F. Moulin, *L'Algérie photographiée* (Paris: Goubaud, 1860). Service historique de la Défense, Vincennes, France.

Moulin took this image was represented previously by none other than Horace Vernet. Vernet's depiction of Constantine was not made for Napoléon, or even Napoléon III, France's "imperial master" at the moment of Holmes' article. It was, however, produced as French propaganda for Louis-Philippe's museum at Versailles.[6]

Moulin's *Panorama of Constantine* is an image taken from the heights of Koudiat-Aty, the very point from which the duc de Nemours reportedly led the second, heroic siege of Constantine in 1837. In Vernet's painting, *The Enemy Turned Back from the Heights of Coudiat-Ati* (fig. 18), the French army is the predominant source of pictorial interest. The soldiers are defending their barricade of stolen gravestones, and the city of Constantine is just visible behind the army of native insurgents clambering up the opposite side of the hill. Vernet did not compose a landscape image, looking down across the contested territory from its highest point. Rather, by focusing on the activities of the French military in the foreground, he commemorated this location as a site of French history worthy of being placed in France's newest and most elaborate museum. This site—Koudiat-Aty—was brought back to France to become part of the French landscape of heroic military victories compiled in the museum at Versailles.

Building upon the significance of this site for the French colonial project in Algeria, Moulin returned to this location in 1856 to make a view of Constantine. What was obscured in Vernet's representation—the view from the heights—becomes the subject of Moulin's image. We can now see what was visible only to the duc de Nemours in Vernet's work: a magnificent clifftop city and the landscape behind. As with other panoramic images featured in his album *L'Algérie photographiée*, Moulin has taken two separate photographs and merged them into this almost seamless elongated view. Here, the domination of the landscape viewed from above is coupled with the power of colonial conquest, previously depicted in Vernet's siege of Constantine series.

Here is the ancient walled city of Constantine, a fortress of stone perched on the edge of a cliff. Here is the city that the French failed to conquer the first time they attempted it in 1836 because they had underestimated both the intractability of its inhabitants and its strategic placement in the landscape. Here is the city that inspired countless romantic and picturesque images during the July Monarchy, continuing in Moulin's own period, featuring torrential waterfalls and rudimentary clifftop dwellings made of stone. What the viewer takes in from this angle is a large plaza that has been cleared just in front of a gate to the city. This is the same portal that was created when the French army opened a breach in the defensive wall and poured into the streets of Constantine during the successful siege of 1837.[7]

To contemporary viewers of this photograph, this makeshift public space appears provisional at best. The tiny trees, planted in perfect rows like military columns, provide no shelter from the sun and appear as last-minute additions to a rather unimaginative escapade in urban planning.[8] The city behind is somewhat flattened from this perspective, and the fact that it is dramatically surrounded by a cliff on the other three sides is hardly noticeable. We do not get a sense of the traditional architecture or spatial design of this timeless city. Rather, the most notable architectural edifice on view is a five-story French military hospital perched on the edge of an invisible abyss at the upper left. This image is prosaic, to say the least, contributing to its perceived documentary value. It is not difficult to determine what separates Vernet's composition from Moulin's photographic panorama. Considering their subjects alone—a battle painting versus a panoramic topographical view—leads to clear distinctions of the kind supposed by Holmes. More interesting are the conjunctions between these two works—and the fact that Moulin went to the heights of Koudiat-Aty in order to capture a panoramic image of Constantine.

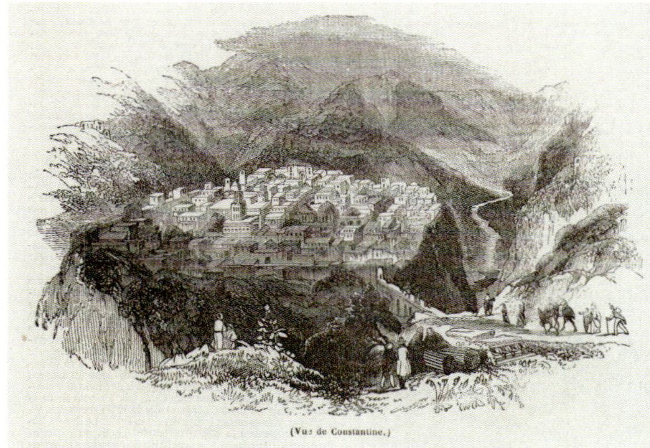

Figure 52.
Anonymous, *View of Constantine*. From "Algérie: Description géographique," *L'Illustration* 2, no. 47 (1844): 332.

Pictures of Constantine

In Moulin's photograph, one perceives an image of a landscape frozen in time. Yet the landscape we see demonstrates the material transformations of that place, the city of Constantine, as a result of the French colonial presence in 1856, when the photograph was taken. This work takes on a documentary quality because as time passed and the spaces of the city were further transformed, this picture of Constantine remained the same. If one can perceive in Moulin's image the material transformation French colonialism effected on Constantine as of 1856, the ability to comprehend this change is a function of photography, which is itself a result of a material transformation in French society.[9] Like all other social transformations, the technological development of photography is not neutral. As André Rouillé has shown, the social transformations of the Second Empire conferred a political dimension on photography.[10] In an era of great transformation in France, the idea of truth held profound appeal, and photography conferred a palpable sense of reality to social progress (and the French nation) in a variety of ways.

Moulin's photograph complicates and overwhelms both the form and the associations of previous landscape depictions of Constantine. The *Panorama of Constantine* can be paired with two other images of the city that had previously circulated in France: a print from an 1844 edition of *L'Illustration, View of Constantine* (fig. 52), and a watercolor by Théodore Jung, *First Attack on Constantine in the Night, 23 and 24 November 1836* (1838; fig. 53).[11] In these two works, which date to the early years of colonialism in Algeria, the viewer perceives a dramatic, even romantic, landscape. The first image, an anonymous woodcut, is radically simplified and stylized, but the unique placement of the city within this landscape is highlighted through its position in the very center of the composition, surrounded by

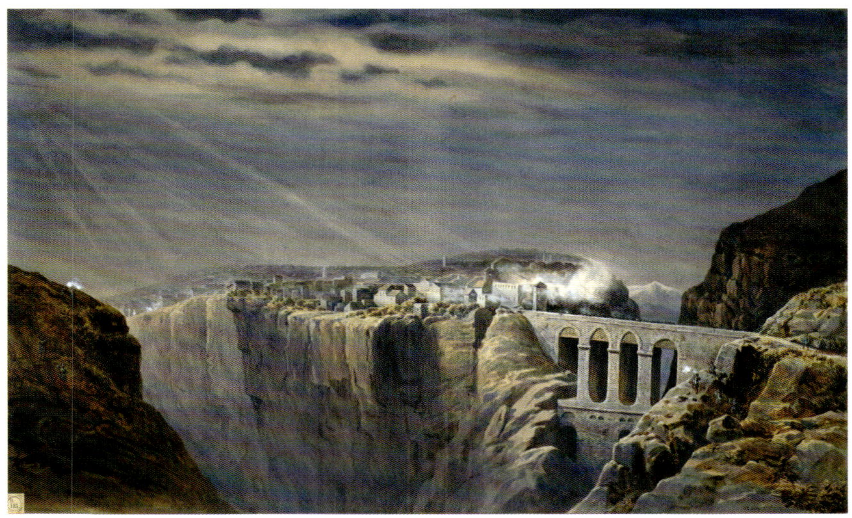

Figure 53.
Thédore Jung, *First Attack on Constantine in the Night, 23 and 24 November 1836*, 1838. Watercolor on paper, 91 × 68 cm. Dépôt de la Guerre, Service historique de l'armée de Terre, Vincennes, France.

steep ravines and sheer precipices. In Jung's print, the city's centrality is, if anything, even more pronounced. The foreground is composed almost entirely of cliff faces, and the city looms above the unplumbed and obscure depths below. The painting further conveys a mood of desolation through the blue tones pierced by a few isolated steaks of yellow light. Jung undoubtedly accentuated the perilous aspect of Constantine's geographical placement as part of his effort to represent the unsuccessful French siege of the city in 1836[12]—not painted, of course, until it could be paired with an image of the city after the French had conquered it in 1837. In any case, both the print and the watercolor show Constantine as a self-contained entity, a landlocked island—a portrayal likely influenced by the difficulty the French had in conquering it, but nevertheless reinforcing the idea that this city was cut off from outside influence.

Conversely, Moulin's *Panorama of Constantine* illustrates the city's interaction with both the surrounding landscape and French culture. The boulevard leading into the city structures the composition of the image, splitting to form an elongated triangle at the bottom of the picture. Moreover, the city does not appear severed from its environs, and the topographical drama of the cliffs is softened from this perspective. The French military hospital provides the most dominant architectural edifice in the city, representing French authority in and settlement of this area. The road in the foreground demonstrates the integration of this urban space into the region, a notion seconded by the granary in the foreground, where indigenous laborers lounge among sacks of grain harvested in the surrounding countryside. Even the amazing artificiality of the plaza is ultimately the result of an attempt to create a transition between the developing urban space of Constantine and its natural surroundings. The lines of trees signify French urban planning and the goal of restructuring this space along French conceptions, such as the opposition of nature and civilization. A large public space split by a boulevard and opening onto a view of the surrounding landscape is a vivid example of French spatial planning in action.

The question remains, however, about how Moulin's contemporaries viewed his works. Due to the fact that Moulin's album is so rare today—only one copy seems to exist, and that is not complete[13]—it is hard to imagine that it was read by many of Moulin's contemporaries. Only three reviews of the album appeared, and their tone conveys a sense that Moulin provided a great service by making the colony fully visible through photography, "capturing the facts of nature and reproducing them with the most minute exactitude."[14] The anonymous reviewer in *Revue Photographique* discussed technique the most, and his manner of critiquing the images is to provide a litany of all of their evident qualities and their lack of evident faults: "everything is firm, picturesque, full of originality, everything is relaxed, easy, charming, hardy, delicate, gracious, true, natural."[15] In all the reviews, a more practical (as opposed to aesthetic) approach dominates. Though photographs are today considered works of art and appreciated for their aesthetic merit, there is evidence to suggest that the viewers of Moulin's images of Algeria interpreted them as if nonfiction had just been invented, as if they were seeing real pictures of the colony for the first time. For the historian, the task of interpreting such imagery rests upon decoding visual information in the photographs, and the choices the photographer made seem clear indeed.

The previous schematic renderings of Constantine's architecture in the print and the watercolor are replaced, in the panorama, by an apparently factual account of the city's urban fabric and its transformation since the French conquest. The activity of producing architectural or urban documents held a deep significance for Moulin, because it was the *raison d'être* of his representational enterprise, as the epigraph by Lacan explains. As will be shown, Moulin took his share of picturesque landscape views modeled on the imagery from illustrated books like Baron Taylor's *Voyages pittoresques et romantiques dans l'ancienne France* and Nodier's *Journal de l'expédition des Portes de Fer*.[16] Yet the *Panorama of Constantine* gives tangible form to the idea that photography could produce the kinds of rational, factual documents that were impossible to contest because they were not the result of individual initiative but were literally drawn by nature, to use Fox Talbot's phrase.[17] It was precisely Moulin's intention to make photography do what it claimed—to represent nature truthfully—that led him to make this prosaic photograph that illustrated the French transformation of North African spaces even while it displaced the reigning French conception that the Algerian landscape was somehow distinct or exotic.

Denis Cosgrove has argued that claims of realism in the landscape (meaning here the definition of a region or space as a landscape) are inherently ideological because they assert real, particular relations between viewer and land.[18] In a more historically specific context, André Rouillé has pointed out that photography constituted the material basis of positivism, a central aspect of bourgeois ideology in Second Empire France. In his view, the period's widely accepted notion that photography reflects the natural world conferred upon photography an enormous power to manipulate information while obscuring the fact that photographic images are representations.[19] Moulin's photograph of Constantine, implying a direct reflection of space, recasts the empire of landscape—not merely as an image but also a way of perceiving the space of colonial relations—because the landscape was itself formulated through pictorial and social conventions. The apparent lack of pictorial conventions in this landscape picture expresses both the ideology of Moulin's image (what it avers about the nature of colonial Constantine) and the proof of its accuracy. The city pictured here is no exotic location or imaginative construction. It is real and it is French. This ideological assertion of realism and Frenchness replaces previous artistic/imaginary reconstructions and their associations, such as exoticism and peril.

The effect of such images on the viewer is distinct from the effect of a painting or even an illustration. Rather than an image that provokes fantasy or daydreaming through romantic or picturesque imagery, the viewer's sense of reality is reinforced by the facts the photograph seems to transmit. An affective convention—being moved by views of the Algerian landscape—is replaced by the transmission of information. For metropolitan viewers, the colonial landscape is altered in the process of its photographic reproduction; what was once an Orientalist fantasy is now a colonial reality. Nature, beauty, and aesthetics are not suitable terms to deploy when confronted with the *Panorama of Constantine*. There is something entirely raw about the landscape projected here. It is not merely that the huge, ordered plaza is empty, or that the new colonial buildings dwarf the traditional dwellings. Moulin elided the beautiful and mystical interpretations of previous landscape imagery, and the landscape that takes shape here seems rather like a sad fact.

In addition to its irrepressible status as a document, this image suggests an emergent conception of landscape based on the eradication of the previous character of this place. What counts most in representations of landscape, such as pleasing agglomerations of forms and the associations they engender, are sublimated in Moulin's picture. Constantine's prior urban form and the spaces that characterized it are re-placed, through photography, with spaces that come to exist as a result of the newly developed activities of imperialism, such as urban planning, trade, and agriculture (note the grain storage shed in foreground). In his study of photographs resulting from British geographical expeditions in the same period, James Ryan articulated this concept in broad terms: "The photographs made on these expeditions then are not visual witnesses to the discovery of unknown regions. Rather, they are a part of the projection of the imagined landscapes of an expansionist Britain."[20] Thus the fantasy of exoticism is replaced by the fantasy of progress.

Moulin did not present Constantine as a point of interest or as a romantic evocation of that place based on structures in the French imaginary. What he provided instead was the image of the colonial city. This new city differs from its previous incarnation in ways that exceed the aesthetic differences between photograph and picturesque landscape. Moulin's photograph represses the distinctness of the locality and offers instead a barren space, populated by anemic deciduous trees like those found in every other colonial town or city in Algeria.[21] It is a space of commerce, a space of exchange, a space of domination—and the only way we can perceive this transformation is through the medium of photography. Ironically, it is photography's very illusion of reflecting the world directly that makes it possible for us to appreciate how much the image of the city is mediated through colonial ideology. The *Panorama of Constantine* is a cipher for the spatial logic of colonialism and the social relations embedded within it.

Moulin was not the only French photographer to visit Constantine. Other photographs of this place do not yield the same result but provide more angles from which to investigate the relations between photography and imperialism. Gustave de Beaucorps produced *View of the Right Side of the Rhumel, Constantine* (1859; fig. 54), an image that is in many ways antithetical to Moulin's panoramic view.[22] The viewer sees only a fraction of the city in this image, which appears indeterminately cropped. Upon further examination, however, the composition is carefully broken into three roughly equivalent horizontal bands of rock, city, and sky. This observation points to the photographer's rather definitive and artful composition, further indicated by the tower hovering above the horizontal band of city just off the center of the image. The view is partial, but it is meant to communicate a sense of the entire city through extension.

In fact, everything about this image seems to mean more than is immediately visible. Here is a city hanging onto a sheer cliff with a clear sky above. This tightly focused composition, combined with perfect depth of field—allowing the entire picture to be in focus and removing the illusion of distance—forces the meaning of its forms to the surface. The play of shadows, for example, creates a divide between the complex, interweaving patterns of the eroded cliffs and the foliage below and the angular shadows of the architecture. In this image, the French presence, symbolized by the larger and more regulated architectural structure on the right side,[23] is placed among and interacts with the indigenous architecture of Constantine. In the tripartite schema established through the formal properties—rock, city, sky—the French building is integrated into the urban framework, despite its narrow windows and lack of porches. In effect, the French presence is here naturalized by positioning its representative building among one of the three elements on view. Civilization may be French and it

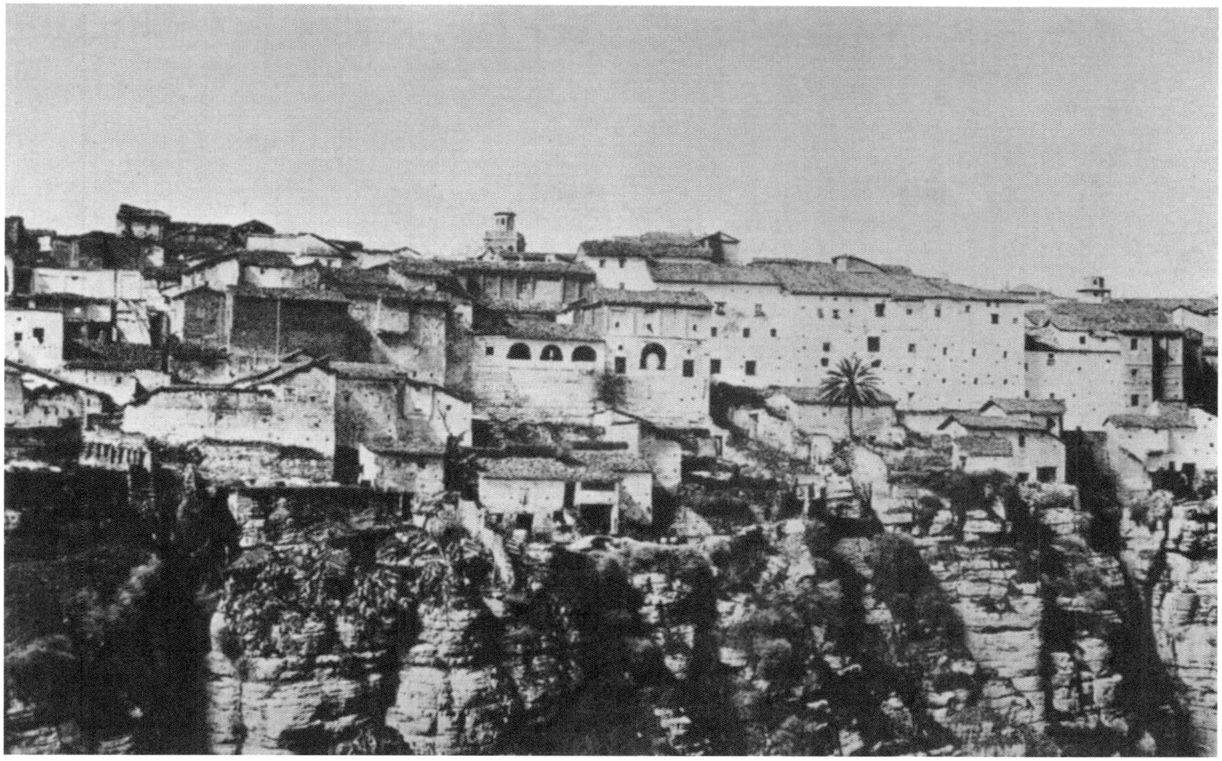

Figure 54.
Gustave de Beaucorps, *View of the Right Side of the Rhumel, Constantine*, 1859. Albumin photograph, 26.8 × 37.8 cm. Private collection.

may be North African, but it is no more than a few buildings clinging to a cliff under an open sky. In de Beaucorps' view of Constantine, the social context is subordinated to the natural order of the universe.[24]

Edouard-Dénis Baldus' *The Bridge of El-Kantara* (1864; fig. 55) presents a very different pictorial conception of the external world.[25] The bridge Moulin photographed outside of Constantine, *View of the Rhumel* (1856–57; fig. 56), was originally built by the Ancient Romans. It collapsed, coincidentally, while Moulin was in Algeria taking photographs in April 1857. As Estelle Fredet has pointed out, this event did not pique Moulin's interest, and it appears that he did not return to the area to photograph the collapsed bridge, because no images of the disaster are extant.[26] Baldus' photograph, however, portrays the building of a new bridge on top of the remaining Roman base. The technological advance of this structure, built upon the foundation of the bridge laid by the last European colonists of North Africa, was a clear visual symbol of modern colonialism and the progress bestowed by it. The French engineers' sheer audacity in restoring the bridge was a sign of the power of (European) technology to overcome the forces of nature as well as to supersede the last European power that administered the entire region.

Baldus' photograph of the bridge highlights this feat of engineering as a monument to French domination even while he ignores the city the bridge was built to connect to the outside world. In this image, technology itself is monumentalized, without reference to those whose lives it is supposed to benefit.

Figure 55.
Edouard-Dénis Baldus, *The Bridge of El-Kantara*, 1864. Albumin photograph, 44 × 32.5 cm. Bibliothèque nationale de France, Département des Estampes et de la photographie.

Figure 56.
Félix Moulin, *View of the Rhumel*, 1856–57. Albumin photograph, 25 × 19 cm. From F. Moulin, *L'Algérie photographiée* (Paris: Goubaud, 1860). Service historique de la Défense, Vincennes, France.

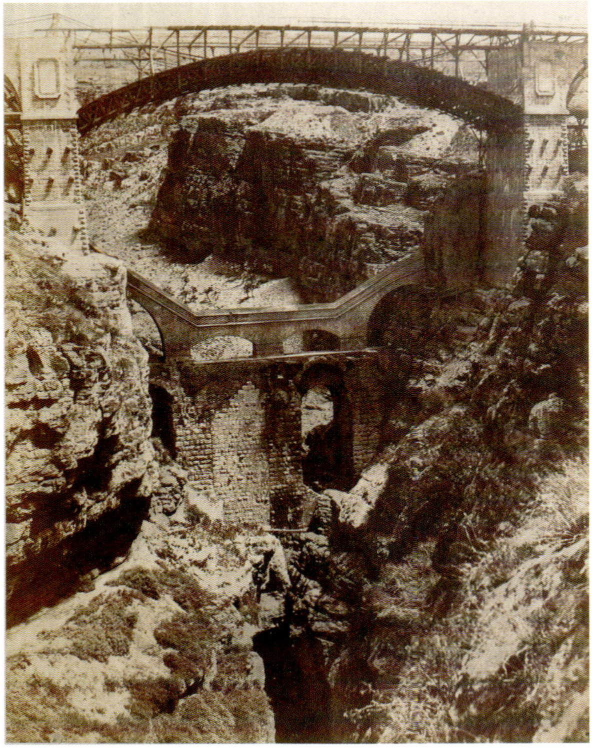

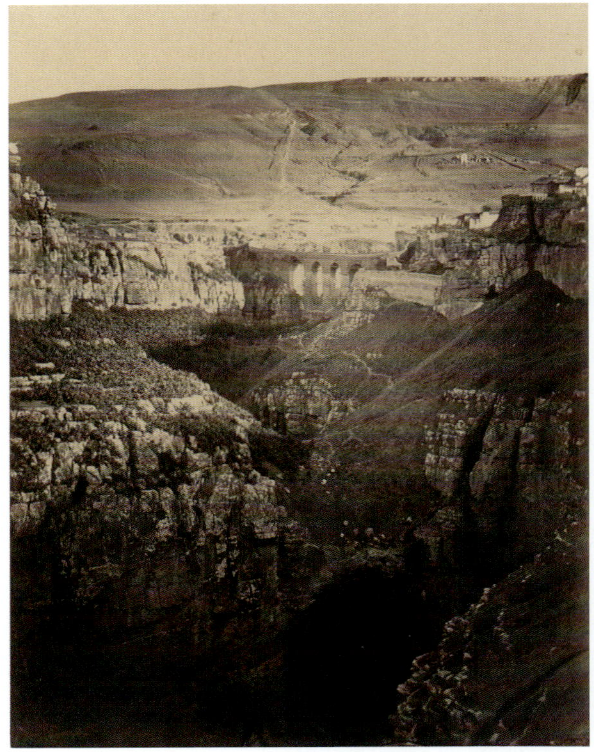

Baldus earned his renown early in the Second Empire through official commissions, such as his photographing the progress of the Louvre expansion in 1857.[27] His large-format images demonstrate a formal mastery of the medium and court a direct style uniquely suited to the grandiosity of monuments. *The Bridge of El-Kantara* appears as a monument in this photograph, not a mere engineering project allowing for improved transportation. The bridge is not finished, though, and this fact invests the resulting image with the significance of a historical document, representing a moment in the French colonial development of Algeria.

Here is technological development crystallized into a real form. Space, in this image, exists to be spanned and even mastered by the French colonizers. This picture signals this notion indirectly by not showing the two sides connected by the bridge, but also by placing the bridge in the middle distance, between the cliff on which the photographer stood and the road along the bottom of the ravine in the distance. Baldus' photograph monumentalized French colonial development through a celebratory image suggesting French domination of the spaces of Algeria through technology—both the technology to build this bridge and the technology to reproduce it and to signify this moment of French colonial progress for posterity.

The photographic image of Constantine presented by these three photographers appears utterly discrepant. The distinct appearance of the city in these works testifies to the divergent modes of representation available to practitioners of photography. The images reflect differing and competing conceptions regarding the city's appearance and the French presence within it. Since none of these images of the city can be declared true, the historian needs to look more carefully in order to uncover what sort of visual fidelity photography offers and how photographs make viewers believe in their veracity. It may be tempting to explain distinctions between these three photographic images of Constantine as the result of the distinct artistic temperaments of their producers. To a certain extent, this explanation may account for these pictorial differences, but photographers have a very different relationship to the world from that of artists, because of the indirect method of picturing (opening the shutter) and the indirect method of rendering (developing the negative and positive through chemical processes).

If it were not for the invention of the camera and the perfection of the chemical processes for developing both negative and positive images—that is, photographs on paper—photographers would have nothing to show us. Their skills are based on the effective manipulation of these new technologies, as opposed to the age-old methods of rendering with the pencil, charcoal, or brush. Through technological means, artistic images can be mass produced (as in illustrated books, for example), but with photography, the creative process itself is bound up with technological developments, and thus photographs suggest a distinct social process around the production of the work. In effect, the image is now produced, not created. Walter Benjamin has written, "It is the peculiarity of *technological* forms of production (as opposed to art forms) that their progress and their success are proportionate to the *transparency* of their social content."[28] With this statement in mind, it will be more valuable to dwell on the similarities between these images and the means they develop for the elaboration of the colonial landscape.

Having already described what these images of Constantine show us, it seems appropriate to consider what they do not. The first point to make is that none of them present landscapes as the term would have been understood at that time. Though all three images replace traditional landscape conventions in distinct ways, the visual organization of space into a legible order is supplanted by a direct recapitulation of the visible aspects of the world. This is one aspect of photography's transparency.

The indexical nature of these images is also important. De Beaucorps' unpopulated landscape fragment is one of series of such fragments that he made while he traveled in Algeria. Another image he made on this trip, *Biskra, Arab Tents and Negro Village* (1857–59; fig. 57), featuring an oasis on the edge of the desert, is no more animated. In all of de Beaucorps' Algerian landscape photographs, abstract spatial forms and fragmented elements establish the pictorial terms. In the case of Baldus, the bridge he photographed is most directly related to the railroad bridges throughout France the emperor commissioned him to represent in the 1850s and 1860s.[29] Though the bridge of El-Kantara is a unique structure that carries singular significance,

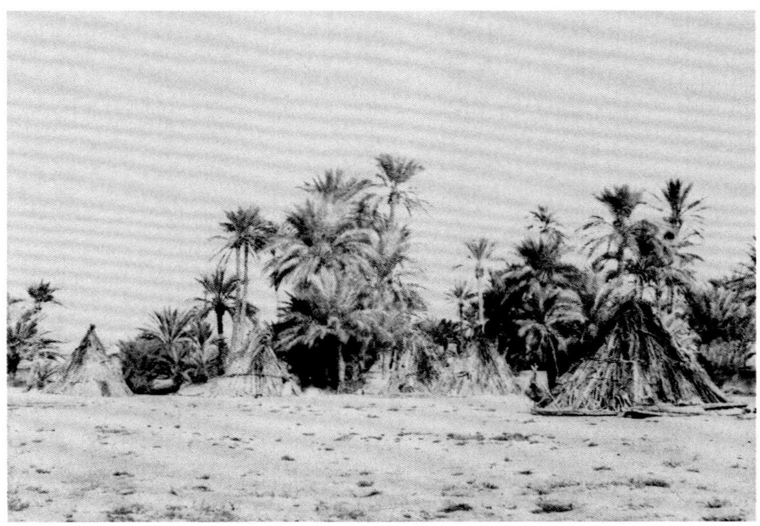

Figure 57.
Gustave de Beaucorps, *Biskra, Arab Tents and Negro Village*, 1857–59. Waxed paper negative, 29 × 39 cm. Musée d'Orsay, Paris, France (Pho1991-22-2). Photo: Réunion des musées nationaux/Art Resource, New York (Franck Raux).

it is one of a series of bridges pictured by Baldus, seemingly independent of the landscape surrounding it. As for Moulin, his image is just one (actually two, because two separate pictures form the image) of the three hundred he intended to produce for his album *L'Algérie photographiée*. Though these pictures run the gamut from portraits to genre studies to territorial photographs, the *Panorama of Constantine* is one view among many, a single aspect of Algeria as it was photographed and then graphically compiled by Moulin.

Creating an index through photography is another social dimension of this picturing practice. Since a single image is part of a series, what it shows is dependent upon outside information regarding the practitioners' activities. There is social content, as Benjamin terms it, in a voyage across Algeria recorded through a series of photographs, as in the case of de Beaucorps, just as there is in a series of photographs of newly constructed bridges. The social content of Moulin's album was to publicize Algeria, which brings us to another aspect of photography's success at making its social content transparent.

The most significant commonality among these three images of Constantine is their shared function in the popularization and vulgarization[30] of the Algerian landscape in France. All of these photographers participated in a project that was begun with France's conquest of Algiers and was prominently demonstrated in Langlois' *Panorama of Algiers*, namely, the diffusion of images of Algerian territory in France as a source of interest, entertainment, and edification. As demonstrated in Chapter 1, the popularization of Algeria's landscape was accompanied by a means of perceiving it that can only be described as ideological. In order for an individual to perceive Algeria's landscape in France in 1833, that landscape must have already been ordered in a manner to make it apprehensible to a French viewer. This process necessarily involved destroying, or at least disregarding, divergent methods for seeing and comprehending the spaces of North Africa.

Vulgarization, meaning here the diffusion of this ideological projection into an ever-wider circle of the French population, may have begun with the colonial landscape as a form of popular entertainment in the *Panorama of Algiers*. In the context of photography, however, vulgarization reached a new level, because the mechanical means of reproducing imagery led to a greater profusion of images within French society as a whole. Further, the process of reproduction is the very structure of photographic depiction. Like other works analyzed in this study, these three photographs were intended for display at public exhibitions. Unlike paintings, watercolors, and even illustrations in books, the process of vulgarization is part of the representational character of photographs.[31] Their reproducibility, even more than the mechanistic nature of their production, confers upon them a status of "duplicate" that doubles as a form of visual equalization. In order to examine Moulin's case more fully, it will be useful to examine the context of *L'Algérie photographiée* and its goal to popularize Algeria through the medium of photography.

Algeria Photographed

What was Moulin's mission in Algeria? Unlike Auguste Salzmann, Timothy O' Sullivan, and other early pioneers of topographical photography, there was no scientific mission attached to Moulin's Algerian sojourn. According to the title page of *L'Algérie photographiée*, Moulin received a letter of recommendation from the War Ministry (who coordinated the activities in all the colonies) as well as the approbation of the governor-general of Algeria, who was just then completely at odds with the War Ministry. No trace of any official commission exists, however, and it is clear that Moulin did not receive any official financing for the eighteen-month trip. We are left with the ambition of the title and one minor comment about the intended purpose of the six-volume album, which was appended to the title and therefore probably penned by the publisher, Goubaud: "National Publication, under the auspices of His Excellency the Minister of War. . . . This publication, destined to publicize Algeria, has been welcomed with favor by His Majesty Napoléon III, who has indicated it by receiving the dedication; it includes the principal cities, Roman ruins, and the most interesting picturesque sites, oases and Arab villages of the three provinces."[32] Whether this dedication of sorts was composed by Moulin or Goubaud hardly matters, because the point is that the ultimate product of Moulin's extensive journeys throughout Algeria was this six-volume photographic album so enthusiastically received by otherwise contentious government officials. The crucial phrase here is "destined to popularize Algeria," though it is unclear whether this was the photographer's mission or the intention of the publisher to make a lot of money through extensive sales of the work. The support Moulin apparently received from the uppermost echelons of the imperial government could be read as official support for Moulin's popularization of Algeria in France—or as an obligatory gesture toward a figure who sought to profit from his access to government officials.[33]

The exhibition history of these images does not help us gauge the context in which Moulin's Algerian images were put before the public. His studio sent two images to an "Exposition photographique" in Brussels in 1856, while Moulin was still in Algeria.[34] In 1859, forty of his Algerian images were shown at the exhibition sponsored by the Société française de photographie in 1859 at the Palais des Champs Elysées, and in 1864 Moulin exhibited views from Algeria at another show sponsored by the same organization. In the meantime, he sent some of his views and Algerian types to be exhibited in the photographic section of London's World's Fair of 1862.[35] Such exhibitions featured a wide variety of photographic works made for utterly distinct purposes, and thus Moulin's participation in them does not establish a particular context for the diffusion of his images. It is clear that he exhibited his Algerian topographical views on numerous occasions but, despite the "industrial" rubric of photographic exhibits at World's Fairs in the nineteenth century, the audience for the images remains nebulous. Since critical commentary on Moulin's contributions to these exhibitions is lacking,[36] one can only surmise that his works must have been successful, because he continued to exhibit them. Unfortunately, it is impossible to establish on what grounds they were found interesting, or by whom.

Both intent and context, it turns out, are far from clear in Moulin's case, but commercial concerns cannot be left out of the equation.[37] An aesthetic evolution occurred in photography during the Second Empire, one in which beauty and use-value were brought into a more intimate rapport—hence vulgarization. In Moulin's landscape images, there are a number of conventional views modeled on artistic landscape depiction, and considering some of these will demonstrate the presence (and perhaps even the guidance) of commercial prerogatives in Moulin's work. And looking beyond the commercial concerns of professional photographers, it will be useful to consider similar topographical photographs made by another photographer, the marquis de Courcival, because he never sought to publish, exhibit, or offer for sale any of his photographic compositions. Analyzing the topographical photographs of Moulin and de Courcival in tandem will lead to a more nuanced articulation of commercialism and vulgarization in the production of images of the Algerian colonial landscape. Further, it will allow us to consider how the photographic image of the colonial landscape lent itself to another practice of consumption linked to the social production of space—namely, the development of tourism.

Two Photographic Voyages in Algeria

Moulin's *L'Algérie photographiée* brings together a diverse collection of images in an attempt to reproduce Algeria. There are figures and views, ancient monuments and modern French buildings, vast deserts and condensed urban spaces, industry and agriculture, white people and black people and every tone in between. How else to reproduce an entire colony? If the photographer were capturing images simply for the sake of compiling a compendium of how a place (a colony, a country, whatever) looks, or looked, the more the better. Moulin had this spirit and produced as much as possible for the level of technological development he possessed. His goal of 300 photos was considerable in 1856–57,[38] and Moulin spent a full eighteen months traveling in Algeria with 1,100 kilograms of baggage.[39] In effect, he produced as complete an archive—Estelle Fredet counts 297 extant prints of Algeria[40]—as he could have. Nevertheless, the necessity of limiting the number of images he could make in Algeria led Moulin to determine what was crucial to reproduce: the most important sites and the most significant people. It was also important to create a diverse image of the entire colony. His plan was to produce two volumes of each province,[41] thus guaranteeing a balance of landscapes, figures, and the like from each region of Algeria. He did not succeed in producing six volumes, however. In fact, he generated two of the province of Constantine and only one each of Algiers and Oran.

Moulin was such a dedicated studio photographer that he elected to carry his studio around with him, in addition to the other burdensome necessities of photographic production in this early period. Judging by the reviews of Moulin's works before he left for Algeria in 1856, studio photographs dominated his oeuvre. Ernest Lacan, Moulin's most frequent reviewer and the editor of France's first serial devoted to photography, *La Lumière,* categorized his photographic production as "genre photography." After perusing the photographs Moulin made in Paris before his departure, now at the Bibliothèque nationale, Département d'Estampes, it is clear that most of Moulin's photographic imagery emerged from the studio, though he did generate some images of monuments in Paris. Yet almost half of the Algerian photographs now extant are topographical views,[42] demonstrating a transition in Moulin's production when he traveled in Algeria. Apparently, as he was forced to choose how to represent the colony, he considered Algeria's external spaces crucial.

Moulin's *Panorama of the Port of Algiers* (1856–57; fig. 58) is a view from the port, located at the bottom of the hill on which the city was built. Yet the photographer's view from below the city is actually a view from above, as the viewer is entitled to the perspective available from the tower above the port. Here one takes in the city as a form, covering a hill at the upper right with a humplike mass of white buildings. Below, on the left, and in the middle ground, along the quay, it is possible to perceive the French additions to and reconstructions of the

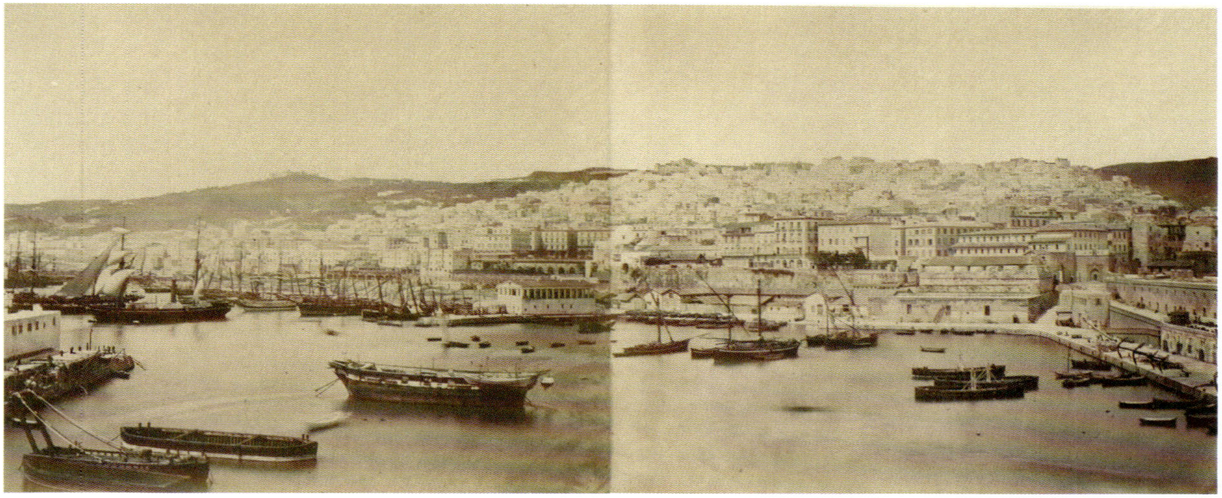

Figure 58.
Félix Moulin, *Panorama of the Port of Algiers*, 1856–57. Albumin photograph, 19 × 46 cm. From F. Moulin, *L'Algérie photographiée* (Paris: Goubaud, 1860). Service historique de la Défense, Vincennes, France.

city of Algiers, respectively.[43] The regularized, rectangular forms of these buildings provide a barrier to the landscape beyond, but their clear definition structures the composition and provides a sense of order, making possible the measurement of distance. Despite the lengthy exposure necessary to produce the glass negative, there are figures visible here, in boats and along the quays. These presences provide the image with some minimal sense of activity and register a passage of time that was denied in Langlois' *Panorama of Algiers*. Unlike the earlier panorama, there are no buildings in the foreground blocking our view of the city and, though the viewer can take in a wide expanse, the city of Algiers all but fills it and even seems to be growing out toward the boundaries of the image. In the background on the left, clusters of tiny white buildings are visible in more distant stretches of the territory, providing the eye with a way to gauge distance in the landscape image. These outlying settlements demonstrate that in the years between the creation of these two panoramas of Algiers, the prospective landscape outside of the city had in fact been claimed by European colonists.

Compare to this image another view from the same album, *Philippeville and Stora: View from the Military Library* (1856–57; fig. 59).[44] Moulin once again provides a view from above. Unlike Algiers, this town is nestled into the coastal topography and appears utterly French. It is, in fact. Philippeville was created in 1838 from scratch. It was the first entirely French town in Algeria, built at some distance from Stora, an indigenous town nestled in the landscape visible in the distance.[45] This portrait of two towns, separated by a rugged coastline and a body of water, visually elaborates the implantation of French social structures in Algeria. Rather than expanding the preexisting site, the governor-general at the time made the decision to build a new town on the site of an ancient Roman port. Such a move demonstrates the executive character of France's military colonial administration as well as its interest in aligning itself with ancient Rome. Moulin's "topographical" view recoups the power of France's colonial hierarchy by presenting a view of the area from a perch in the military library. From this lofty perspective, one can see a miniature France—a bastardized provincial town across the

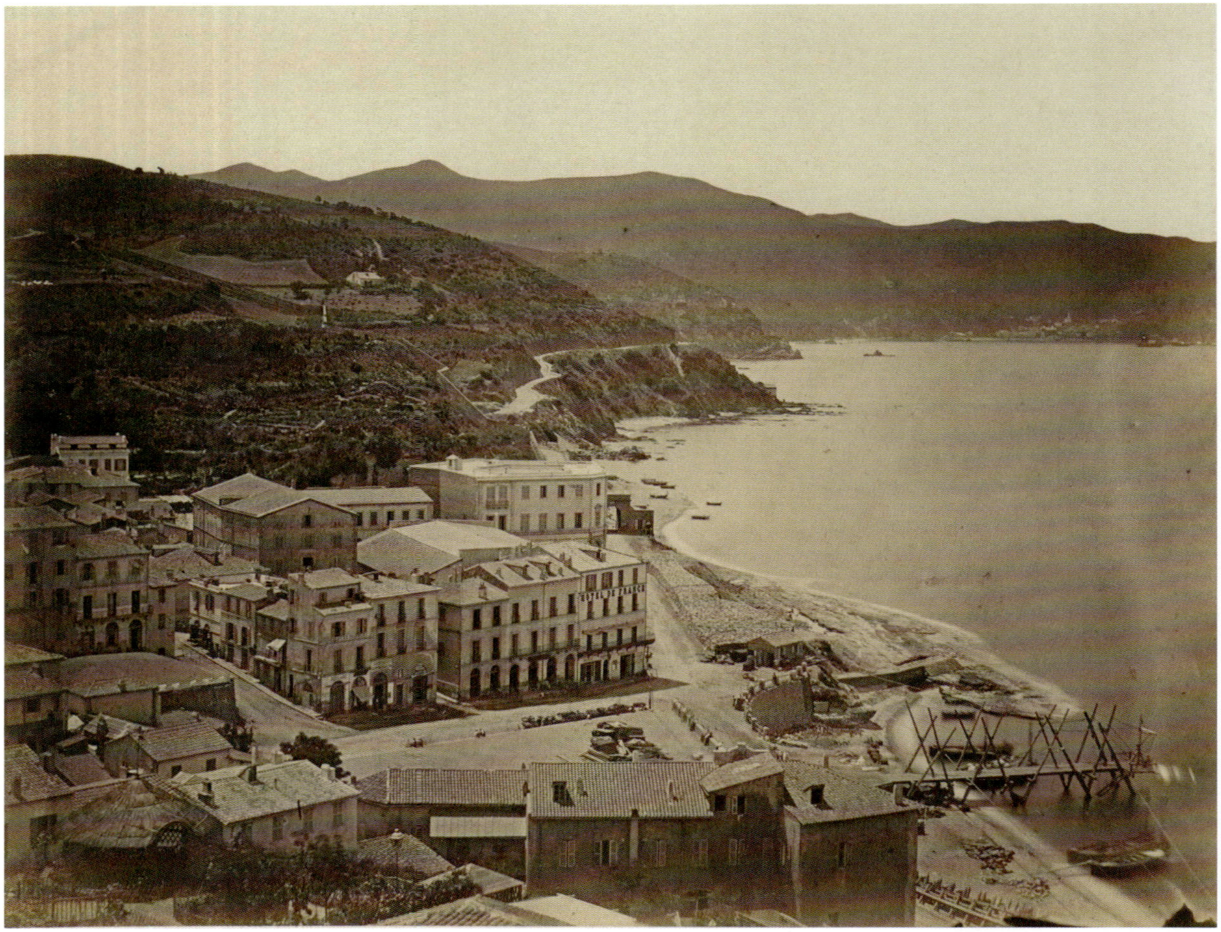

Figure 59.
Félix Moulin, *Philippeville and Stora: View from the Military Library*, 1856–57. Albumin photograph, 19 × 24.5 cm. From F. Moulin, *L'Algérie photographiée* (Paris: Goubaud, 1860). Service historique de la Défense, Vincennes, France.

Mediterranean, complete with its Hôtel de France on the edge of an open plaza.

Whereas the panoramic view of the port of Algiers pictured colonial urban planning as an expansive phenomenon, here, the French city is a sanctuary in the landscape, protected by a stone wall (an aqueduct, actually, but the visual metaphor is operative) ascending the hill in the background. In both of these images, Moulin has established a certain harmony of forms, a balance between habitations and environment. In *Panorama of the Port of Algiers*, the city is compact and white, but its form is traced by a delicate serpentine line, and the nearly empty basin of water in the foreground balances the density of architectural forms. In *Philippeville and Stora*, the prematurely dingy buildings are carefully tucked into a niche of rugged but nonetheless aesthetically pleasing coastal hills. French colonialism has clearly marked these regions but has not destroyed them as landscapes, sources of visual pleasure for the French viewer. The image *Philippeville and Stora* suggests that one might have seen a wild frontier along the north coast of Africa before, but now that these regions have been devel-

oped by the French, they can offer picturesque pleasures to their viewers and the viewers of these photographs.

In light of this aestheticization of French settlements along the Algerian coast, it is significant that Achille Fillias, in his *Nouveau Guide général du voyageur en Algérie* (*New General Guide for the Voyager in Algeria*) of 1865, reproduced this photograph along with his description of Philippeville (fig. 60).[46] Significantly, Fillias has removed the distant village of Stora from both the picture and the title, not to mention the aqueduct that functions like a wall. The effect of these erasures is to make Philippeville appear as an isolated French town in a bucolic coastal landscape. Both the natives and the threat they represent are removed from the landscape. As the guidebook explains: "The environs of Philippeville are productive, picturesque and frequented by strollers."[47] Fillias' image and description clearly function as a distortion, an erasure of the impact of the previous inhabitants of this region on the landscape.

While this analysis sets up Moulin's photograph as a point of contrast that provides the reality effect (actually, there is a wall around the town and a city in the distance), it is justifiable to inquire whether Moulin's image of these villages and this stretch of coastline establishes the terms for Fillias' elision. As previously stated, this landscape image is fully aestheticized by the photographer along French conceptions of pictorial imagery. Further, this picture was taken from a point of view that emphasizes French colonial immersion in the area. Finally, Moulin had already removed from this image any reference to the indigenous inhabitants of Algeria. Yes, Stora is visible in the distance, but it is a mere collection of minute patches of light that provides no details, let alone figures. The caption explaining Moulin's image, recuperated as the landscape description in Fillias' guide, explains the genesis of the city on a Roman ruin and further explains that Philippeville cannot accommodate a port, even though it was the site of the French customs house. Travelers and goods would have had to disembark at Stora and make the four-kilometer journey over land to Philippeville. This system must have been amazingly inefficient, but such incompetent planning is obscured by the strategic deployment of Orientalist tropes. The caption also claims: "We [the French] did not find even the smallest indigenous village."[48] In this location, the French found Roman ruins but not a trace of native Algerians. This site of ancient glory, then, entirely neglected by the indigenous inhabitants, was reclaimed by the French.

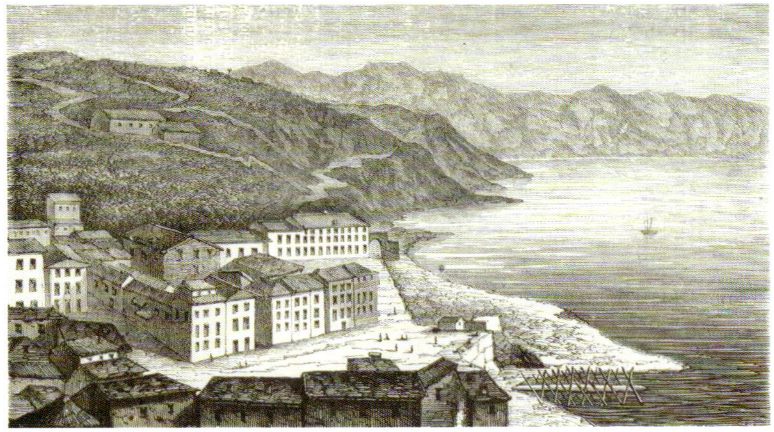

Figure 60.
After Félix Moulin, from Achille Fillias, *Nouveau Guide général du voyageur en Algérie* (Paris: Garnier frères, 1865), 190.

Though this was a conventional stereotype of Muslims in nineteenth-century Orientalist texts, Moulin's photograph seems to demonstrate this faulty conception in colonial Algeria. *Philippeville and Stora* justifies the French prejudice against the natives of Algeria, accusing them of lacking industry rather than applauding their adaptability for not trying to maintain a port city that could no longer sustain a port. The resulting message is an endorsement of France's goal of rehabilitating this land of ancient wonders through the process of colonization. Further, such a conception is married to a picturesque view of the landscape: the lack of a port provides the village of Philippeville with a surprisingly premodern appearance. Despite the visible contemporary buildings, the absence of industrial machinery, warehouses, and the like provides a sense of retreat from the industrial world—an idyllic French colonial retreat. Above all, Moulin provided a pleasing vista for the viewer to examine. Here the ideological power of photography to make false assumptions appear true is combined with the visual pleasure of perceiving a landscape. The social content of this photograph is indeed transparent.

By contrast, the marquis de Courcival did not take any pictures on the coast.[49] This cavalry officer began his photographic journey well inland at the French military encampment of Sétif, originally captured by the duc d'Orléans in 1839 and celebrated in Dauzats' painting *Seizure of Sétif* (1844, Musée des Beaux-Arts, Orléans). The result of de Courcival's journey is a series of 110 images arranged into a single album, now in the collection of the Archives de la Société de géographie.[50] In one of the first images in this album, the viewer can perceive a similar, if less artful, marriage of French settlement and Algerian landscape. The eleventh picture in the album, *Sétif: The Gardens to the West of the City* (1861–62; fig. 61), is an image of a hillside covered with parceled agricultural lots and French farm buildings beneath a village on the upper right. Both the countryside and the town look as though they could be in France, emphasizing the French transformation of this stretch of North African territory. The parallel lots separated by willows and other deciduous trees native to France are aligned along straight roads leading into an agglomeration of multiple-story, rectangular structures in the distance. While this landscape image could not be described as picturesque in the same manner that Moulin's photograph *Philippeville and Stora* clearly can, there is a sense of pictorial order achieved by balancing the distant city with these well-maintained farms that support it. While de Courcival was not as talented a technician as his professional counterpart and could not produce an image with as many middle tones, for example, he shared an interest in demonstrating the way in which the French settlers had re-created the Algerian landscape. To a contemporary eye, this lack of visual complexity is the best way to guarantee the fidelity of the visual record. This landscape image appears uncomposed and gives the viewer a sense that it could have been taken anywhere. In other words, this point of view seems randomly chosen and, therefore, one infers that the photographer could have pictured the same level of French settlement regardless of where he chose to aim his camera.

A similar effect is created by the next image in the album, taken from the inside of the city: *Sétif* (1861–62; fig. 62). This photograph would have been a shocking composition to contemporary viewers, because of its unprecedented focus on the modern architectural structures in the foreground.[51] There is just enough visual information provided on the left side of the image for the viewer to perceive that the interior of the town looks as French as the gardens to the west of the city. One cannot today ascertain clearly how the space of this village has been arranged, though it is clear that it had been laid along some kind of grid. Any viewer would be left confused as to her/his orientation within the space pictured, because the geometric forms upset normative conceptions of pictorial space in Moulin's era and in our own. Referring to this image as a topographical photograph, as opposed to a landscape picture, does not help matters, because there is no topography to

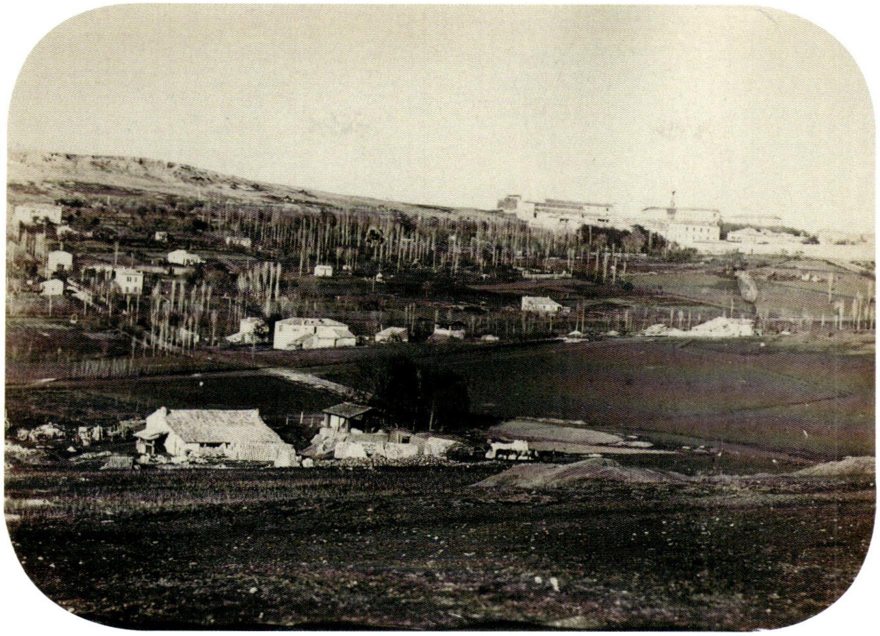

Figure 61.
Le marquis de Courcival, *Sétif: The Gardens to the West of the City*, 1861–62. Albumin photograph, approx. 15 × 20 cm. Bibliothèque nationale de France, Département des Cartes et plans, collection of the Société de géographie (We 25).

Figure 62.
Le marquis de Courcival, *Sétif*, 1861–62. Albumin photograph, approx. 15 × 20 cm. Bibliothèque nationale de France, Département des Cartes et plans, collection of the Société de géographie (We 25).

be made out. Even as a document, this image provides precious little information about the topography of the region, the size of the town, or the intentions of the photographer.

But Sétif does look modern and French, and since one might guess that these buildings are barracks, there seems to be a lot of room for military personnel. The only reference point that fixes this image in Algeria is the top of a minaret that extends above the horizon on the left. This kind of image would not have had any commercial value, and it certainly would not have induced tourists to visit the area. Its spatial ambivalence and visual confusion act as a counterpoint to Moulin's composed and picturesque image of French Algeria, *Philippeville and Stora*. Unlike Moulin's *Panorama of Constantine*, this photograph does not record how

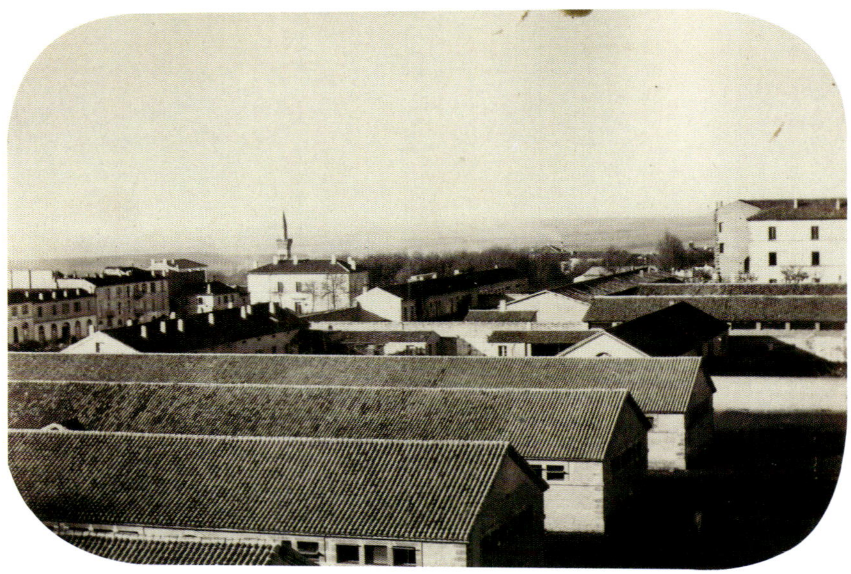

the place was changed by the French administration of urban space. This photograph merely shows the French town and does not provide much visual information to help the viewer interpret anything about the location. De Courcival's *Sétif* properly functions within another context, however—namely, as the starting point in his photographic chronicle of a journey into the desert of southern Algeria. Although this is not the first image in the album,[52] Sétif is the first location featured in it, and this eponymous image is de Courcival's only attempt to picture the entire town. These jarring geometric forms provide the entry into a visual narrative, one that begins in this last vestige of French civilization and takes its viewer on a journey into the wilderness of the Algerian desert.

As noted earlier, de Courcival was an officer in the French military. He spent four years of his professional life in Algeria, between 1861 and 1865, as a cavalry officer in the Régiment des chasseurs. His photographs from Algeria were all taken on a single expedition. The expeditionary *colonne du Souf* departed from Algiers in September 1861 for the Saharan city of Touggourt, which they reached in January 1862.[53] For reasons unknown, de Courcival did not begin making photographic images of the expedition until he reached Sétif. The album is thus a visual record of a one-way journey into Algeria made by an army officer over the course of the military expedition. Like the previous chronicles of Dauzats (prints as illustrations for a book) and Fromentin (a travel novel), de Courcival's album is a voyage of discovery of the colony transmitted to a French viewer. The two primary differences between de Courcival's album and the works of Dauzats and Fromentin are that de Courcival was not trained as an artist and that his album, as far as I know, never reached the public until it entered the Archives de la Société de géographie. In effect, de Courcival was an early amateur who narrated his journey in Algeria through images. The album he eventually produced was made for a particular private audience, a certain Captain Bernard, who donated the album to the archives. While Moulin traveled widely throughout the colony in order to create a comprehensive view of it, de Courcival's photographic record was limited to five months of the four years he spent in the country and illustrates a single, cohesive expedition. More important, Moulin's professionalism and his desire to profit economically from the Algerian imagery he created contrasts with de Courcival's status as a career officer and aristocrat who had no interest in a commercial photographic enterprise and had no previous photographic experience, as far as anyone can tell.[54]

Given these major differences, it is all the more striking to see strong similarities between certain images made by these two practitioners. Moulin explored a portion of the route de Courcival's expedition later followed, so some sites are represented by both photographers. A direct comparison of corresponding images captured by Moulin and de Courcival allows for a detailed analysis of the differences in their photographic records. Further, the similarities that emerge point not only to the way photography responded to previous pictorial representations of Algeria, but also to the ways in which both photographers diverged from them. Moulin's topographical images of Algeria sought to popularize the landscape and served the purpose of stimulating trade in Algeria and France by spurring tourism and diffusing the image of the colony throughout France. By contrast, de Courcival's private album functioned (and continues to function) as a historical document in the archive of one of the most prominent scientific societies of the period.

Though many of the topographical works of Moulin and de Courcival are similar, there is only one place represented by both of them in more or less identical images: the Gorge of El-Kantara. Photographers did, in fact, produce landscape images, and such images functioned differently from other topographical images. The fact that both Moulin and de Courcival photographed this place demonstrates that it was a location of some significance. The bridge shown in both pictures was built by the ancient Romans, but that was hardly unique in Algeria. Rather, the significance of this site was its status as a natural wonder. The Gorge of El-Kantara, as it was pictured by Moulin in *Gorge of El Kantara and the Roman Bridge: Entry to the Desert.—View on Arrival from Bathna* (1856–57; fig. 63) and by de Courcival in *Route from Batna to Biskra: Gorge of El-Kantara* (1861–62; fig. 64), was the point of entry into the Sahara. The mouth of this canyon, opening onto an oasis on the edge of a desert—signified

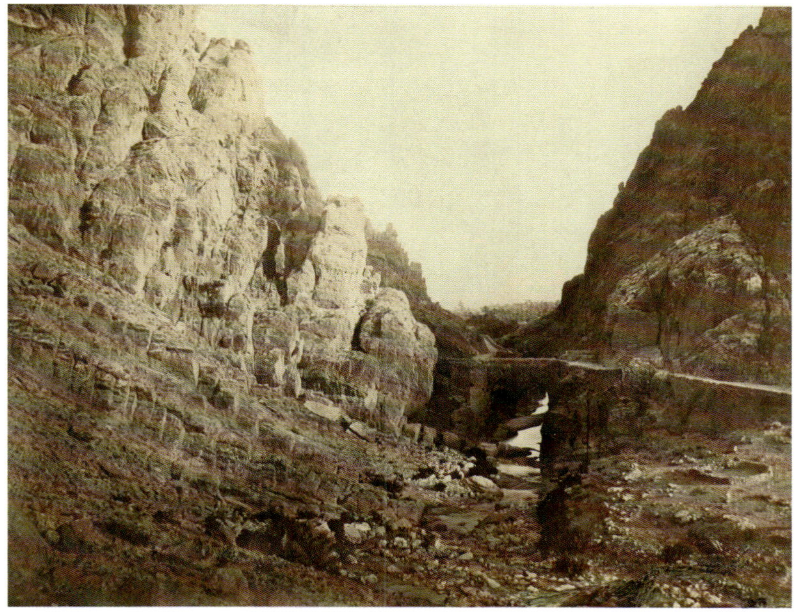

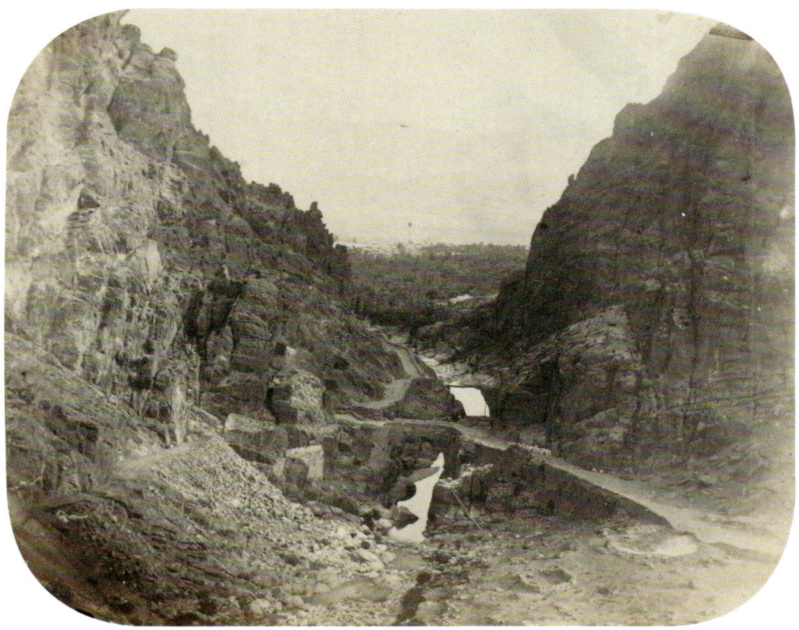

Figure 63.
Félix Moulin, *Gorge of El Kantara and the Roman Bridge: Entry to the Desert.—View on Arrival from Bathna*, 1856–57. Albumin photograph, 16 × 20 cm. From F. Moulin, *L'Algérie photographiée* (Paris: Goubaud, 1860). Service historique de la Défense, Vincennes, France.

Figure 64.
Le marquis de Courcival, *Route from Batna to Biskra: Gorge of El-Kantara*, 1861–62. Albumin photograph, approx. 15 × 20 cm. Bibliothèque nationale de France, Département des Cartes et plans, collection of the Société de géographie (We 25).

here by a triangle of palm trees in the distance—was a natural barrier between the two distinct geographical regions of Algeria, the arable lands to the north and the desert to the south. A more metaphorical interpretation would be that these images depict the threshold dividing the Mediterranean basin from Africa.

The significance of the location was marked by Fromentin, who described this location as a door of gold opening onto the Orient.[55] The terms of his description signify a personal experience in which this place has been imbued with meaning as a passage into another world, opening up new perspectives for the author/artist. By contrast, the extensive caption provided in Moulin's album explains the significance of the site in more prosaic terms. The sense of wonder upon traversing this threshold is registered nonetheless.[56] The picture that accompanies this caption is focused more on the visual boundary separating the viewer from the "terrestrial paradise" that lies beyond. Since the image has been carefully vacated of any figures, it would be difficult indeed to perceive the different people and their *moeurs* that Moulin describes. Instead, the mouth of the canyon provides a visual analogy for the concept of threshold. The division of the composition between light and dark, the way the cliff walls almost block our view, and the road that winds through the composition connecting the foreground with the oasis in the distance all register this passage between two worlds in visual terms. De Courcival's picture, taken from a slightly higher vantage point at almost the same time of day, provides an identical association, but without an accompanying caption.

James Ryan has written that "as well as shaping images of indigenous people, [imperial] photography tended to rationalize the landscape aesthetic as a rational, distanced way of viewing and organizing space."[57] By deploying traditional conventions of pictorial landscape representation, the topography visible in these photographs acquires a symbolic significance and proposes a meaning for this place. This effect has the double function of signifying the distinct character of this natural site and naturalizing its exotic appearance as landscape, a self-enclosed system for making sense of the spaces of the world. In other words, both images fit well into the problematic of the empire of landscape.

The landscape forms naturalized by Moulin and de Courcival bear a striking resemblance to the Portes de Fer compositions Dauzats produced between 1839 and 1844, such as the watercolor *Third Wall of the Portes-de-Fer* (fig. 22). Here again is the canyon with enormous escarpments, the narrow passage overbrimming with symbolic significance, and the bright highlights that throw the stony forms into relief. In Chapter 2, I argued that Dauzats recomposed the landscape conventions of his era in order to produce an image of an exotic landscape that would be nevertheless believable to a French audience. Moulin and de Courcival built upon this visual prototype, as well as on Fromentin's textual description, so their photographic landscapes appear both natural and meaningful. They even evacuated the image of figures, such as the people with whom they traveled, in order to make the resulting landscape appear unaffected by their European presence—a technique employed effectively by Langlois in order to convince his audience of the veracity of his representation.

This instance of framing the spaces of Algeria as colonial landscapes through photography demonstrates that topographical photographs, even when created by two practitioners with differing intentions, were not necessarily distinct from landscape paintings produced in previous generations. Moulin's and Courcival's images of the Gorge of

El-Kantara do not conform to traditional landscape representations any more than Dauzats' paintings do. Yet the images draw on previous references to Algerian landscapes in order to communicate their meanings. These images document how preexisting depictions of the Algerian landscape were recuperated even through dissimilar technological mechanisms. The image of Algeria is given a new life in these works, despite the fact that the automatic nature of photographic representation was thought to have dispensed with such self-conscious constructions. Even as reflected in the mechanical eye of the camera, the spaces of the colony could be persistently organized through the conventions of landscape painting.

It is useful to compare the way in which Dauzats' illustrations of the Portes de Fer contrast with Moulin's photographs of colonial spaces in terms of their mutual popularization and diffusion of the Algerian landscape in France. Dauzats' five illustrations of the Bibans were originally created as paintings for the Museum of French History at Versailles and later were incorporated into a book that chronicled the campaign for a private, though extended, audience.[58] The views of Algeria offered by Moulin, who traveled through Algeria with Quetin *fils*—son of the famous guidebook author—were also produced with the intention of distributing them to a wider public. Though Moulin's photographic album does not seem to have circulated widely—and I cannot find evidence that it was ever completed—some of his images found their way into other publications as well, such as *L'Illustration* and Achille Fillias' *Nouveau Guide général*.[59]

Perhaps it would be impossible to say for whom Moulin's and de Courcival's photographs were made, and that is exactly the point. These images were not made for any particular audience, but for a speculative one. It is important to delineate the difference between the two kinds of speculative audiences relevant here—commercial and private—because they have distinct characters. Nevertheless, what the photographic images of the Gorge of El-Kantara share is that they were produced for a potential (French) audience rather than for particular individuals or institutions (though the image made by de Courcival did end up in an album he gave to a fellow officer). As such, they can be understood to be directed at a prospective viewer, if you will. These practitioners first produced the view and then went looking for someone who might want to possess it. Unlike Salon paintings—also produced on spec—there was no clearly identifiable group, such as Salon judges or art critics, to whom these works might be pitched. They were made for anyone who might be interested. And who might be interested? Moulin suggests a particular readership on the title page of *L'Algérie photographiée*: "for they who have lived [in Algeria] and for those who are avid for information about this country so little known and so worthy of being known."[60] In other words, it was made as a memento for those who had lived in Algeria—namely, military officers—and as an informational guide for armchair travelers. Basically, Moulin's album was an expensive coffee-table book, and de Courcival's was more like a personal photo album that you might give to a friend with whom you traveled.

These two albums thus play a part in a developing economic practice that has recently become one of the largest sectors of the global economy: tourism.[61] The travelers' tales told by the two photographs of the Gorge of El-Kantara operate within the network of a nascent international tourist industry, one made possible by other technological developments, such as the steamship and the railroad. The Gorge of El-Kantara was not a tourist destination in 1858, nor would it be anytime soon after.

The significance of these images in the context of tourism is that the aestheticized exotic landscape of Algeria is projected to an unspecified European viewer. The two cases of Moulin and de Courcival are indeed distinct because of the intended audiences of their two albums. Of the two, Moulin's pictures are more readily interpolated into the development of tourism, because his work sought a public audience and its purpose was to diffuse Algerian imagery throughout French society.[62] This beautiful and symbolic image of a faraway land was exactly the kind of material that was (and still is) used to goad well-off metropolitans to leave their comfortable boudoirs and travel to distant locales.

John Urry's concept of the tourist gaze helps clarify the relations between images of an exotic landscape and tourism. He notes, "Places are chosen to be gazed upon because there is an anticipation, especially through daydreaming or fantasy, of intense pleasures, either on a different scale or involving different pleasures from those customarily encountered. Such anticipation is constructed and sustained through a variety of non-tourist practices, such as film, TV, literature, magazines, records and videos, which construct and reinforce the gaze."[63] Urry's notion of daydreaming and fantasy is derived in part from Colin Campbell's analysis of consumption,[64] but for my purposes, the crucial element in the passage is the way anticipation is "constructed and sustained" by other practices, most of which involve the projection of images. While Urry, as a sociologist, is primarily concerned with the social relations embedded in tourism today, I want to argue that the process of image projection, linking a metropolitan audience to faraway locations, was crucial to the development of tourism in the nineteenth century.

Moulin was not a photographer directly involved in the tourist industry. Unlike Alary and Geiser in Algiers or the Maison Bonfils in Lebanon, for example, his photographic practices were not determined by the tourist industry in those locations.[65] Nonetheless, his production of imagery fed into the developing practices of tourism by reproducing the spaces of Algeria as distinct and significant landscapes. While it is beyond this analysis to present all of Moulin's topographical photographs of Algeria featured in *L'Algérie photographiée*, a number of them follow his *Bridge of El-Kantara* by distinguishing sites of interest for the potential tourist. The best example of such a site is the *Hammam Meskoutin (bains maudits),* or *Baths of the Damned* (1856–57; fig. 65). This fantastic site led Moulin to devote three separate images to rendering its awesome strangeness. In the caption provided beneath one of the photographs, the author even suggests improving this area so that it could be transformed into a spa, where "bathers will find paths to scenic sites, distractions and all things necessary for life."[66]

Photography and the Image of Colonial History

In the epigraph to this chapter, Ernest Lacan made reference to landscapes that had already acquired significance in the French imagination as sites of notorious battles. The implication is that these places will have already been altered by the French presence so thoroughly as to be unrecognizable by later tourists. In fact, Lacan comments on the striking transformations the French have already undertaken.[67] Another comment by the anonymous reviewer in *Revue Photographique* is relevant here: "It is history—living history—that the practitioner of whom we speak [Moulin] has caught in the act in this Algeria which, destined to become a new France, need no longer keep any secrets from the mother country."[68] Leaving aside the reference to Algeria's destiny as well as the possibility of surveil-

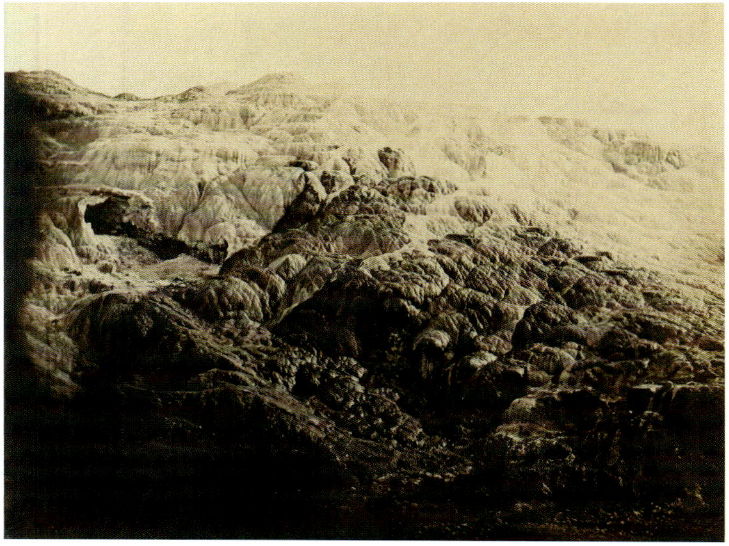

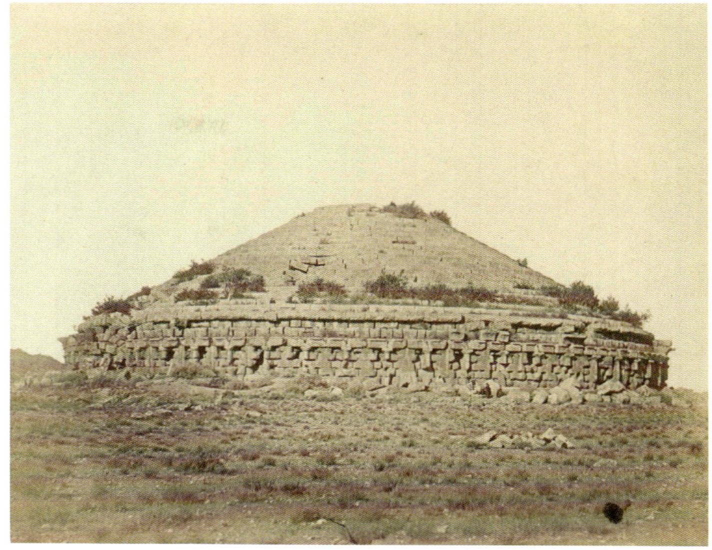

lance that this reviewer perceives in Moulin's album, the idea of "catching history in the act" is a fascinating proposal. As we can infer from the title of the album, Moulin intended to produce a complete catalogue of colonial life for viewers in the metropole and, in this sense, the final product was self-consciously historical. With his camera, he framed not only Algeria of the present, but of the past and of the future as well. The past comes through in views of ancient monuments and crumbling villages, e.g., *Tomb of the Christian* (1856; fig. 66), while the future can be traced in signs of emergent colonization, such as newly planted trees in rows and areas of development where French buildings overflow former urban boundaries, e.g., the *Panorama of Constantine*. Thus, the history that surfaces when we regard the album today is not simply the present of 1856–57, but what was then the past and future. If it is history Moulin has caught in the act, it is the moment of history between the past and future—literally, the instant of history. Though ubiquitous, such a history is obscure until the instant a photograph is taken. This immediate seizure makes the present visible through the unique technology of photography.

The instant of history is there in Moulin's *Panorama of Constantine* (fig. 51) and also in two other images by de Courcival, *Hodna-Bou-Saâda, Panorama of the City from the Door of the Fort* (1861–62; fig. 67) and *Route from Batna to Biskra: Plain of Ksour and the Camp of the Spahis at Aïn-Touta* (1861–62; fig. 68). While reflecting upon the French alteration of the landscape of Algeria, it is important to address the perceptual transformation that these images of Algeria foist upon the viewer.

Courcival's *Hodna-Bou-Saâda* shares many characteristics with Moulin's *Panorama of Constantine*. Prominent are the anemic deciduous trees recently planted to line the road in the foreground. As a point of contrast, the viewer can perceive behind the town a prodigious grouping of palms, indigenous greenery that stretches the entire length of the

Figure 65.
Félix Moulin, *Baths of the Damned*, 1856–57. Albumin photograph, 19 × 23 cm. From F. Moulin, *L'Algérie photographiée* (Paris: Goubaud, 1860). Service historique de la Défense, Vincennes, France.

Figure 66.
Félix Moulin, *Tomb of the Christian*, 1856. Albumin photograph, 19 × 25.5 cm. From F. Moulin, *L'Algérie photographiée* (Paris: Goubaud, 1860). Service historique de la Défense, Vincennes, France.

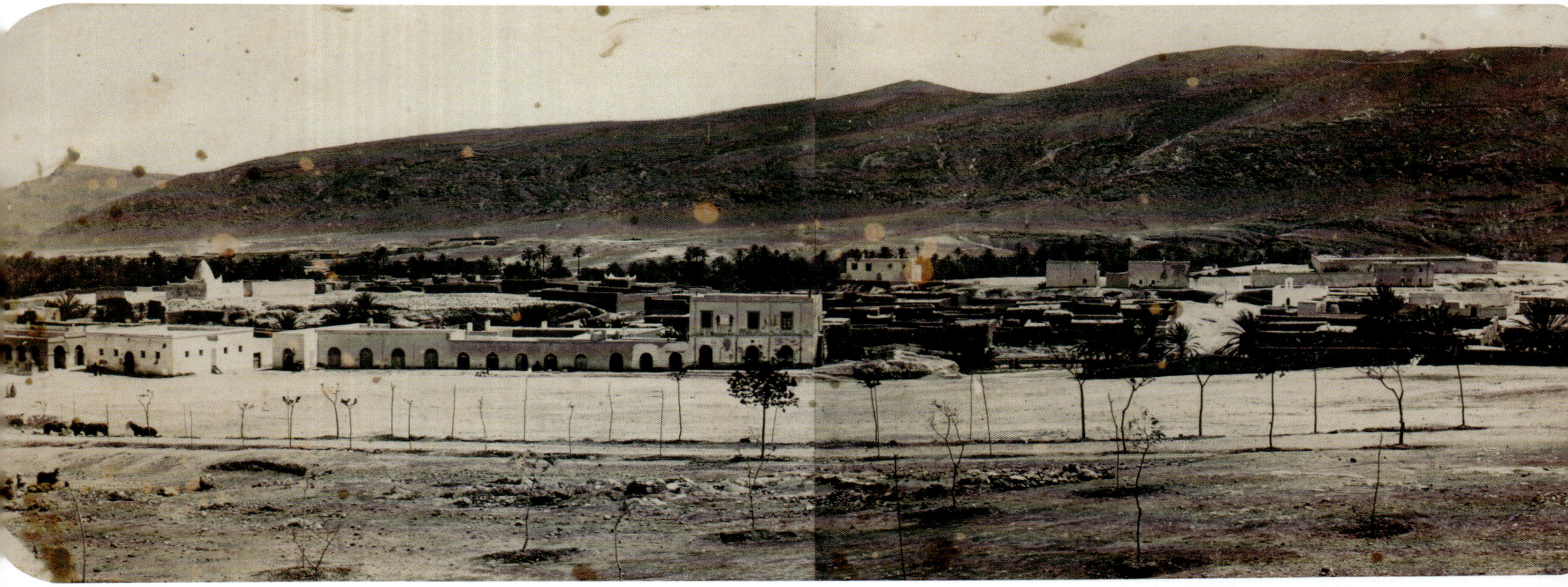

Figure 67.
Le marquis de Courcival, *Hodna-Bou-Saâda, Panorama of the City from the Door of the Fort*, 1861–62. Albumin photograph, approx. 15 × 40 cm. Bibliothèque nationale de France, Département des Cartes et plans, collection of the Société de géographie (We 25).

two-part image. The town itself, on the opposite side of this wide plaza in the foreground, is a curious blend of indigenous and recent French buildings, and signs of French cultivation are visible on the distant hill. Further, both of these images feature figures in the foreground indicating that the spaces are occupied, unlike the idealized landscapes of the Gorge of El-Kantara that appear timeless.[69] Both panoramas are complete views of cities made by carefully composing two photographs that would link up to create a single, elongated view.

Yet there are also significant differences. Moulin's panorama features a prominent historical site in the French conquest of Algeria, whereas de Courcival's picture illustrates what might be called a frontier town, a distant if significant oasis in the Sahara that was a source of interest for explorers but was certainly not a noteworthy site of French conquest.[70] Another point of contrast is the complexity of Moulin's composition, organized by diagonal elements and stacked landscape forms, as opposed to the stagnant horizontal format of de Courcival's image. Finally, the quality of the images is significantly different. While the two photographs that make up Moulin's panorama are equivalent in terms of their exposures and free of spots, de Courcival's panorama demonstrates his status as an amateur. The image on the right is significantly darker than that on the left and the pictures themselves are badly spotted and discolored, demonstrating improper rinsing of chemicals in the process of producing negative or a print.[71]

These technical errors in de Courcival's photograph mark his production of this landscape view as a technological process that is, in some crucial respects, out of the control of the practitioner.

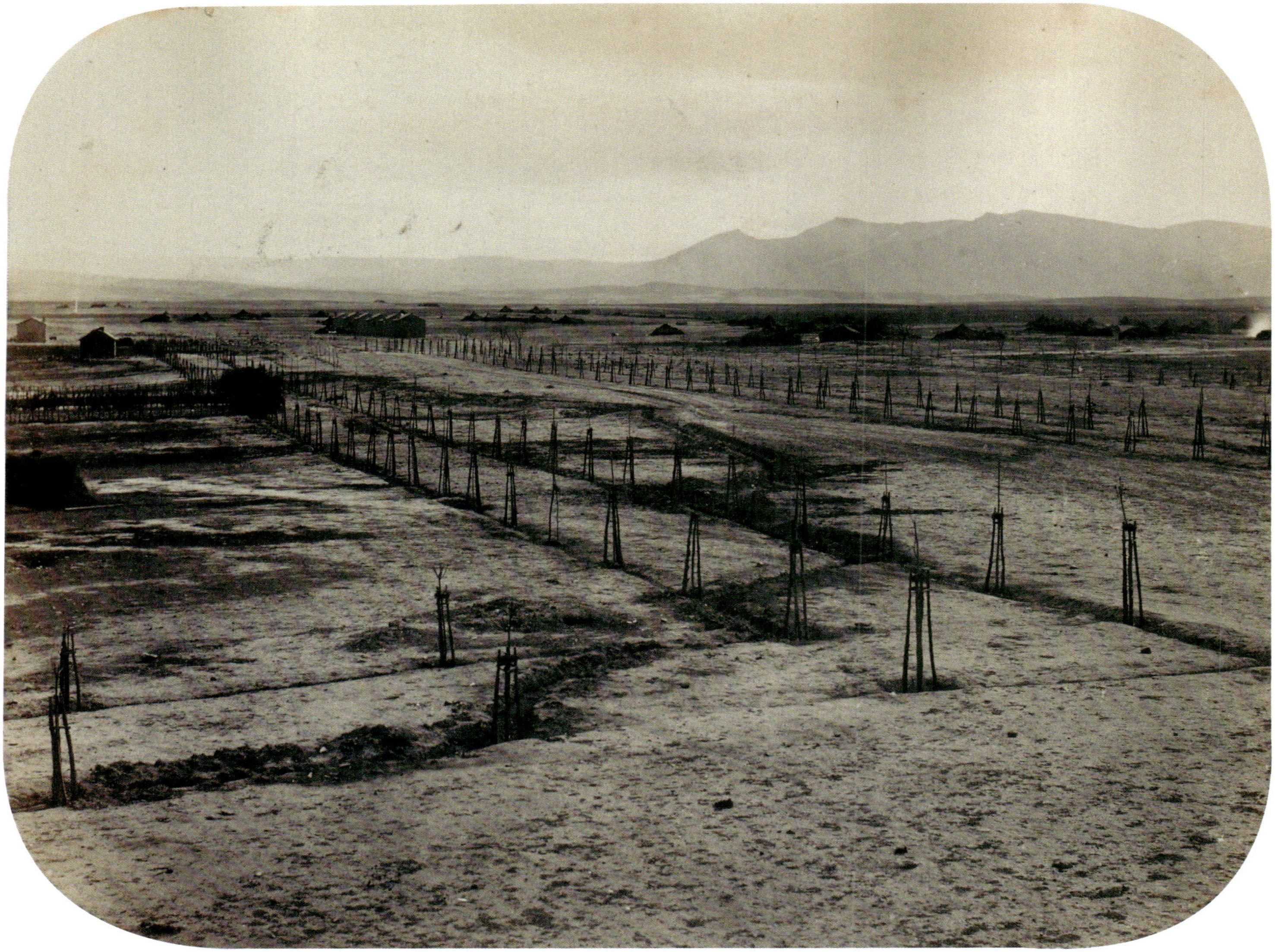

Figure 68.
Le marquis de Courcival, *Route from Batna to Biskra: Plain of Ksour and the Camp of the Spahis at Aïn-Touta,* 1861–62. Albumin photograph, 15 × 23 cm. Bibliothèque nationale de France, Département des Cartes et plans, collection of the Société de géographie (We 25).

Thus the flawed landscape view offered in *Hodna-Bou-Saâda* is an image of photographic production as much as it is an image of the French production of space in this distant colonial city. Through the discolorations and spots, we can perceive the mis-shapen chestnut trees that were put there to line this dusty expanse that will, one day, become a flourishing plaza. Despite the fact that one half of this landscape looks darker than the other, the viewer can make out the way in which the French have expanded the city toward the heights and can imagine what the city will look like as the French presence continues to grow. This is only perceptible through a technological process that has already adapted this landscape image to its means. If we can see in de Courcival's Bou-Saâda a destruction of the idealized colonial landscape depicted by previous artists and by himself at other points in his album, this is perceptible as a result of photography's power to structure an image through a mechanical apparatus linked with a technological form of production. Because de Courcival understood the interaction between chemicals and light, we can now see what Bou-Saâda looked like in 1861. As with the *Panorama of Constantine*, one sees a colonial urban landscape and a process of producing it in a single image. Are we not, as viewers, constituted by this social form of production through our ability to perceive this image as transparent, as providing a direct reflection of the world?

On the subject of Second Empire photography, Eugenia Parry Janis has written: "In the search for the proper place to stand, the proper distance between camera and subject, the establishment of the frame, a photographer was not only making a photographic picture, he was literally collaborating with his instrument to invent a new language."[72] I want to extend this compelling argument further and suggest that photographers did not only produce a new language in collaboration with their cameras and their processes of development. They altered the way visual reality could be perceived by demanding from their viewers a new understanding of the relationship of the world to the image. Our ability to perceive the city Bou-Saâda in de Courcival's photographic image represents an evolution in the technology of spectatorship. In this photograph, as in Langlois' panorama, a viewer's perceptions are dictated by the form in which an image is presented. In Chapter 1, it was argued that the viewer's position was structured by the representational form of the panorama, which made possible an unprecedented manner of viewing space while determining the way in which a spectator could perceive the landscape of Algiers. The photographic image of the colonial landscape is another instance of image conditioning reception, but without the external spatial structure of a panorama.

When a viewer looks at an image such as de Courcival's *Plain of Ksour* (fig. 68), it is impossible to make out a landscape as such in the image, which pictures little more than a broad and desolate space. Here is a barren plain planted with rows of trees that lead to two puny buildings in the distance and a cluster of tents. Even if one considers this photograph as one piece in a collection that portrays a long journey through distinct topographical regions, it is difficult to perceive why the photographer chose to picture this particularly bleak view on a hazy day. The lack of a strong light source denies even clear definition to the forms that appear within the frame.[73]

A contemporary viewer of de Courcival's *Plain of Ksour* would be similarly befuddled by the kind of landscape image proffered here. The vastness of the space seems to defy pictorial definition, and one cannot imagine that a viewer of the 1860s would have derived any aesthetic pleasure from such an image. Yet the clear markings of the French presence on this landscape were intended to demonstrate French settlers' ability to inhabit and even to order this mind-numbing environment—and this blind hope in the progress of colonial development is visible today. The question that remains is whether such images engendered beliefs in colonial progress or whether they would have seemed as ridiculous to viewers of the period as they do today. It is impossible to know, since there are no historical responses to this image. The reviews of Moulin's album are relevant here, though, particularly the references to disappearing indigenous villages and history caught in the act. What one can see in de Courcival's images of Bou-Saâda and the Plain of Ksour is a history of the future caught in the act. The attempt to project a French landscape onto this faraway territory, through the planting of trees and other escapades in spatial planning, confirms the intention to redefine and order even the most remote spaces in Algeria. The photographs do not only record those efforts but also confirm them, making them manifest as an image that can be transported back to France. The wild optimism that must have motivated these French Spahis—indigenous Algerians who fought with the French army—to make an *allée* in the middle of nowhere is the result of the same belief in progress that fueled the hopes for colonial development and led Moulin and de Courcival to take pictures of Algeria in the first place. In this instance, the empire of landscape is a form of image production in which the force of technology sustains the illusion that progress is a definitive result of colonial development.

Whether their topographical photographs recorded precolonial spaces in the course of their disappearance or projected a titillating image of an exotic landscape to lure viewers abroad, the images produced by Moulin and de Courcival made the social processes of colonialism transparent even as they exposed photography's involvement with those processes. Though photographs offer viewers a more direct translation of Algerian topography, these images of a colonial landscape are produced as aesthetic objects through chemical processes. The representations of the Algerian landscape these practitioners returned to the metropole reinvented the activity of viewing landscapes, just as they made visible the French reinvention of Algerian spaces. As a result, the viewer's activity was, and remains, intertwined with the transformation of the object viewed—the material production of a colony in space.

CHAPTER 6

Abstracting Space

Remaking the Landscape of Colonial Algeria in Second Empire France

The world of images and signs exercises a fascination, skirts or submerges problems, and diverts attention from the "real"—i.e., from the possible. While occupying space, it also signifies space, substituting a mental and therefore abstract space for spatial practice.

—Henri Lefebvre

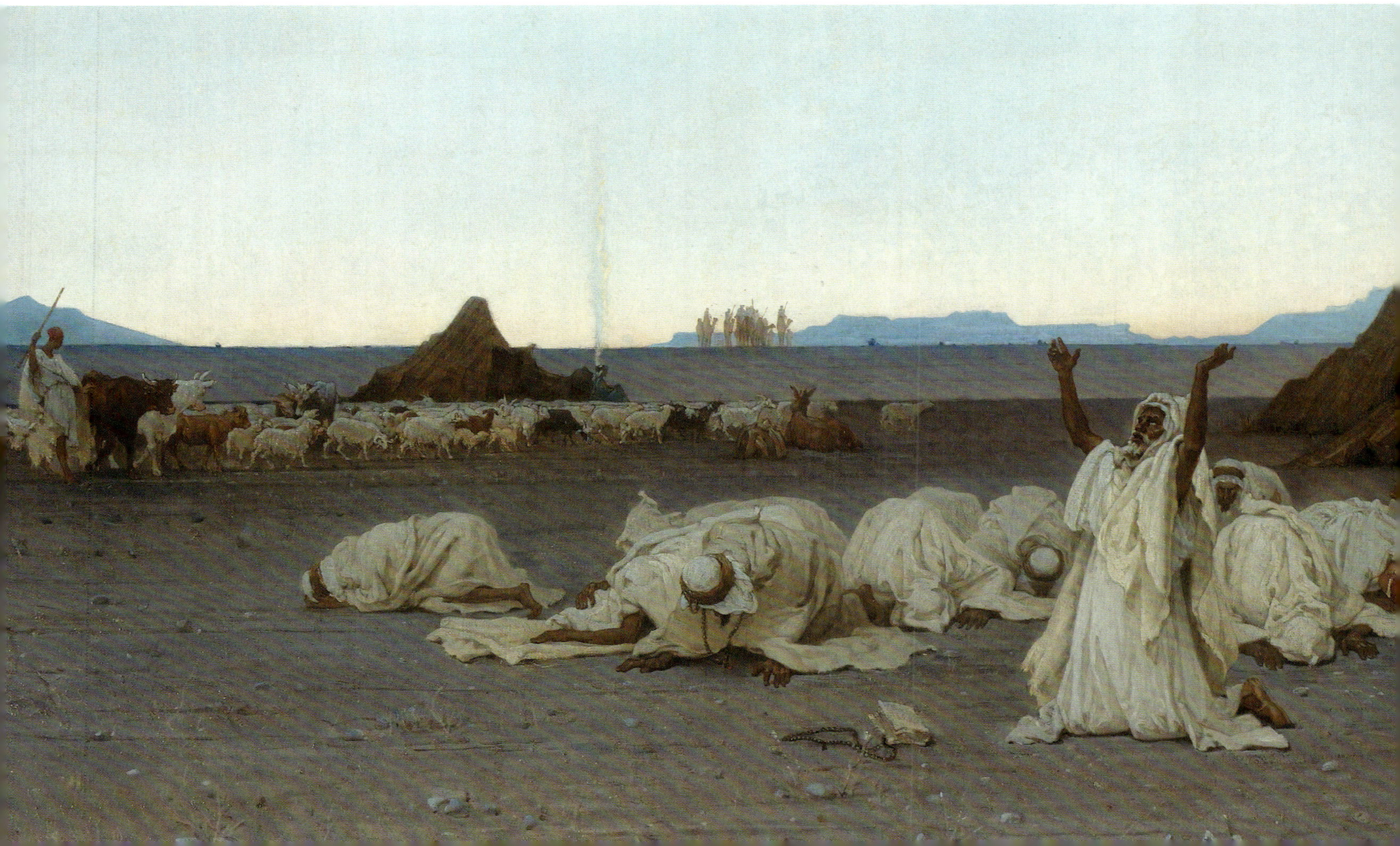

This chapter takes as its subject the negotiation of spatial and individual boundaries in the colonial context of Algeria under France's Second Empire. My subject involves the representation of the most distant and wild of Algeria's landscapes, the desert. The paintings I consider are more experimental in their technique than other Orientalist paintings produced at this moment in France. Nevertheless, such a limit case illuminates one recurring theme in the history of artistic and colonial exploration: while works of art enhance a viewer's understanding of a world beyond view, they reflect and articulate a particular set of conceptions, an interpretation of the world. Such an interpretation exists in dialogue with other representations, but the terms of representation manifest and represent an existing set of values. In the case of landscape painting, it is space that is ordered into a pictorial language, which is a manifestation of both artistic conventions and the individualized technical practices of the artist. Landscape paintings represent the world in a more or less subjective way, and one of the keys to understanding the development of French art in the latter half of the nineteenth century is the way in which landscape painting became more individualized and less conventional. The effect that landscape paintings had upon viewers changed during this period as new forms of representation—*plein air* painting, Impressionism—required a more direct engagement with the artists' process than earlier academic landscapes, or *paysages historiques*, had.

Landscapists generally began to provide specific characteristics in their paintings that evoked the place represented, aiding the viewer's engagement with the site depicted and allowing the artist to signify his or her particular way of representing it. Curiously, the desert landscapes discussed here actually deny the specific characteristics of the place that they purport to represent, offering instead a seemingly abstract space. This practice allowed nineteenth-century viewers (and contemporary historians) to erase or obscure alternative or competing interpretations of the spaces in which people lived and continue to live. In other words, the potential power of landscape paintings to enact a form of possession for the artist and viewer, when realized in representations of Algeria in the Second Empire, replaced the spaces of human activity with the space of pictorial representation. This imperial act is consistent with the colonial domination of the era: this form of possession takes place in the realm of projected ideas and marks a new manifestation of the empire of landscape. As will be shown below, this representation of the Algerian desert paralleled the development of new paradigms of landscape description in colonial geography. Territory, that raw material of colonialism, is paradoxically also the product of colonial practices, the implementation of a certain imperial view of the world *upon* the world and those who inhabit it.

Here, I want to trace a certain historical shift in spatial representations of the colony. This transformation had a visual character as well as social and political dimensions in the French colonization of Algeria that occurred in the last years of the Second Empire, between 1863 and 1870. The space of France's colonial desert, the Algerian Sahara, was the very limit of its empire in the 1860s and, as such, it represented a liminal terrain both in material terms and as a symbol of French national landscape when depicted in works of art. In order to describe the metamorphosis of representations of colonial space in the last half of the Second Empire, it will be necessary to compare legislative and geographical representations of Algeria with a handful of artistic ones created by Gustave Guillaumet and Eugène Fromentin.

In brief, a self-consciously colonial posture arose among many of the writers who addressed

Overleaf: detail of fig. 70

the issue of France's political problems in Algeria in the 1860s. The future of colonialism in Algeria had been a pressing political issue in France between 1839 and 1844, but in the 1860s, ethical concerns and practical problems that might complicate the unrestrained exploitation of the colony's resources were brushed aside. In the early 1840s, the opposition criticized the colonial administration for its ineptitude and its unjust treatment of Algeria's indigenous population. In the 1860s, the opposition criticized the colonial administration for its ineptitude and its overly generous treatment of Algeria's native population. Although the conquest was complete and the military administrators of Algeria were not entirely consistent, there is ample evidence that they continued to undermine native social and religious institutions during the Second Empire.[1] It was the political rhetoric that shifted—partly as a result of the increased organization of the colonists, which allowed them to voice their sense of entitlement.

While interesting in themselves, such political debates gloss over the deeper changes that constitute the foundation of the rhetorical arguments from this period of Algerian colonialism. Such a transformation of conceptions is very difficult to pinpoint, but here it will be useful to turn to a French theorist of society and space, Henri Lefebvre. Central to my argument is his concept of abstract space: "Homogenous in appearance (and appearance is its strength), abstract space is by no means simple. In the first place, there are its constitutive dualities. For it is both result and container, both produced and productive. . . . For, while abstract space remains an arena of practical action, it is also an ensemble of images, signs and symbols. It is at once lived and represented, at once the expression and foundation of a practice, at once stimulating and constraining, and so on."[2] The basis of Lefebvre's notion is that lived space and the means of perceiving it through vision are intimately connected by representation. Abstract space is an order into which human activities are placed, but it is ultimately a conception of space that shifts practices. It constitutes a way of perceiving the world that changes what the world is and what happens there.[3] For this analysis, the visual aspect of abstract space is crucial and, as will be shown, a landscape painting can represent an abstract space even though it is a figurative painting.

In Lefebvre's terms, any landscape painting would be an abstract space, but the issue here is how such a thing might come to be represented. At this point in history, our sense of abstraction is perhaps as various and nuanced as our sense of nature (which is a strong reason for investigating it more fully). Here, I will examine how representation—in whatever form—can serve to denature a subject, in this case a colony, a desert, and a landscape.

Social Dimensions of Desert Imagery

The Second Empire is particularly significant for the colony because, at this point, France initiated the legal and administrative process of fracturing Algerian terrain into units in an effort to spur colonialism and to engender an understanding of private property among the native inhabitants. The metropole thereby promulgated an abstraction of the colonial landscape. This process of rupturing the country of Algeria in the service of its French expropriation corresponds, in many ways, to depictions of denuded, empty landscapes. It is not simply that the desert, once described as "the negation of Europe,"[4] represented the outer reaches of a colony that had been little explored and still retained an element of distant romanticism. Rather, the desert functioned as a powerful symbol, as analyzed by the

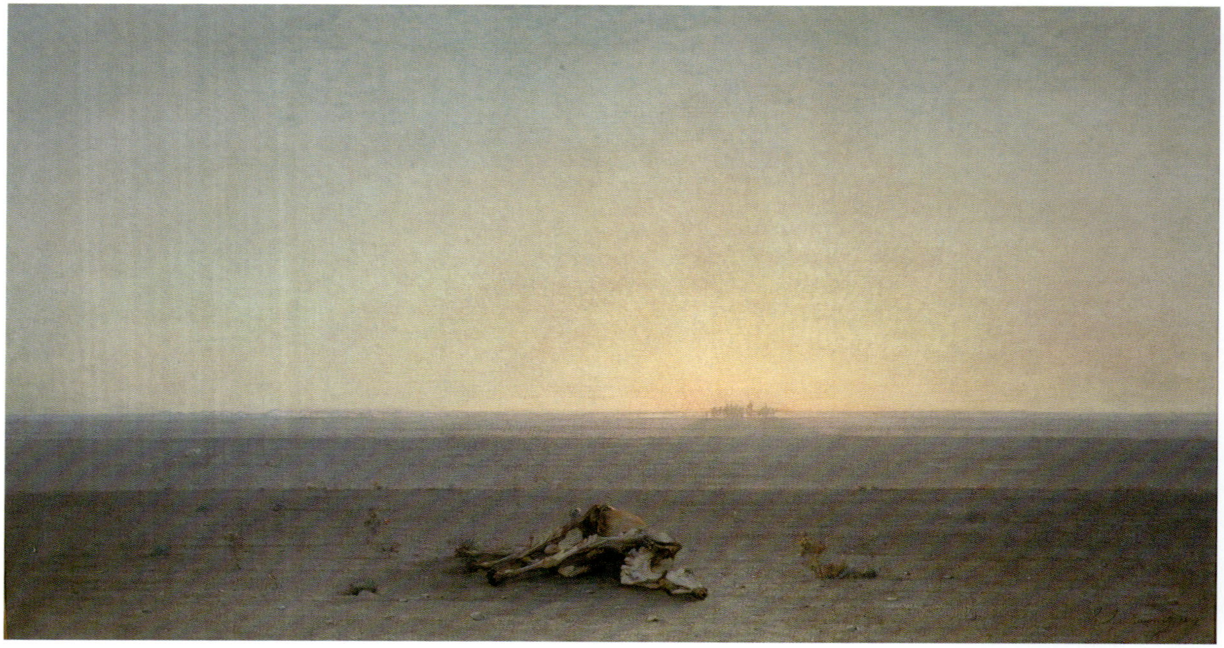

Figure 69.
Gustave Guillaumet, *The Desert* (or *The Sahara*), 1867. Oil on canvas, 110 × 200 cm. Musée d'Orsay, Paris. Photo courtesy Musée d'Orsay (Patrice Schmidt).

geographer Michael Heffernan. In his article "The Desert in French Orientalist Painting During the Nineteenth Century," he argued for the desert's double signification: it was the land of "desolation and infertility," yet the desert also implied the power of (European) society and progress to restore it to a mythical former time of prosperity. Such an opposition of meanings, according to Heffernan, led to an ambiguity that, "instead of breeding confusion and vacillation, became a source of imperial power. Europeans could, and did, profess admiration for a separate and distinctive Orient while at the same time promoting the necessity of a transforming and beneficial European imperial presence in the Orient."[5]

This ambiguity will play a role in my analysis of Guillaumet's desert landscape, *The Desert* (1867; fig. 69), also known as *The Sahara*, but it is crucial to make the point at the outset that the desert existed as a symbolic construction of a land outside of time (history) and outside of civilization (society/progress). In terms of European conceptions of space, it was an empty landscape in the sense that it was, by definition, uninhabited—an oasis being within, though not part of, the desert—and therefore an open screen for the projection of whatever meaning a viewer might perceive in it.[6] In this case, the idea of a "pure landscape"[7] possesses historical piquancy, because a landscape image that features a denuded space is open—both to interpretation and to potential settlement. Private property and pure landscapes are ideas that are constituted in relation to an atomized individual who functions as the locus of legal and visual representations of space. Further, pure landscapes, like private property, are an accepted fiction. Just as deeds function to secure private ownership of territory, a painting of the desert secures the notion that the colonial landscape is, in fact, empty, open to European settlement. Of course, this landscape does not look ripe for settlement, but its lack of apparent landscape characteristics functions in much the same way as an empty room would, allowing the free play of the viewer's imagination without providing any sense of inhabitants who might have marked this space in any particular way.

Guillaumet's *The Desert* could be described as a pure landscape: there are no traces of human presence here, and the space is rendered in a direct, uncomposed manner. More important, it delivers a sense of space that overrides any anecdotal interest, providing a view of a remote corner of the world as a landscape. This is a radical proposal for what can constitute a landscape, and even what can constitute a landscape painting, but it serves as a limit case whose pictorial language illustrates the denaturalization of the colonial landscape in this period.

This painting has received more attention in the last thirty years than in its own epoch, but the descriptions of it provided by contemporary historians are, for the most part, anachronistic. Donald Rosenthal has described *The Desert* as "surreal" and drawn a comparison between this work and the "fantasy academicism" of Dali.[8] Philippe Jullian stated that Guillaumet's landscapes "might have achieved an abstract quality if he had not given too much emphasis to some of the details in order to convey the desolation."[9] Perhaps the most compelling observation comes from Robert Rosenblum: "Throwing aside any notion of perspective as useless in this context, he deploys a limitless space, half-way between documentary reportage and a nightmarish mirage."[10] These comments all share a notion of abstraction common to twentieth-century viewers that would have been lacking in 1867. Only Rosenblum's remark details the way in which the artist ignored the conventions of perspective to achieve his effect. Rosenblum reminds us that the artist elected to deny perspective in order to achieve a sense of limitless space as well as the dreamlike quality of the work that makes it appear surreal. Théophile Gautier's "Salon de 1868" provides a contemporary indication of the artist's ability to evoke a limitless expanse of space without contrivance: "Never has the infinity of the desert been painted in a simpler, more grandiose or more moving way."[11]

The effects Guillaumet achieved in this work are, in some ways, obvious to twenty-first-century viewers steeped in Impressionist and Post-Impressionist art. Through a denial of perspective and recognizable land masses, the artist has reduced the terms of this landscape depiction to the point that the viewer becomes aware of sensations of light and atmosphere. These effects are achieved through the artist's technique, such as the scumbling of paint in the sky and the use of light strokes of dry paint laid horizontally over darker, grey-green tones to achieve the illusion of light on a horizontal plane. The pastel tones inform the viewer that it must be either dawn or dusk. Traces of yellow pigment on the blue surface of the sky suggest dust hovering above the ground and surrounding the viewer with light. The desiccated camel in the foreground provides a decisive form that contrasts with the evanescence produced by sand and sky. The image is also completely static. The lack of movement only enhances the perception of a moment frozen in time, despite the traces of the artist's hand that indicate the time it took to make the painting.

This composition constitutes an interruption in Guillaumet's pictorial production. While he did, in other works, evoke this kind of vast space, it was always populated by exotic figures and trappings and therefore was more conventional as well as more appealing to the state. Looking at an earlier work, *Evening Prayer in the Sahara* (Salon of 1863; fig. 70), it is apparent that Guillaumet's career of official

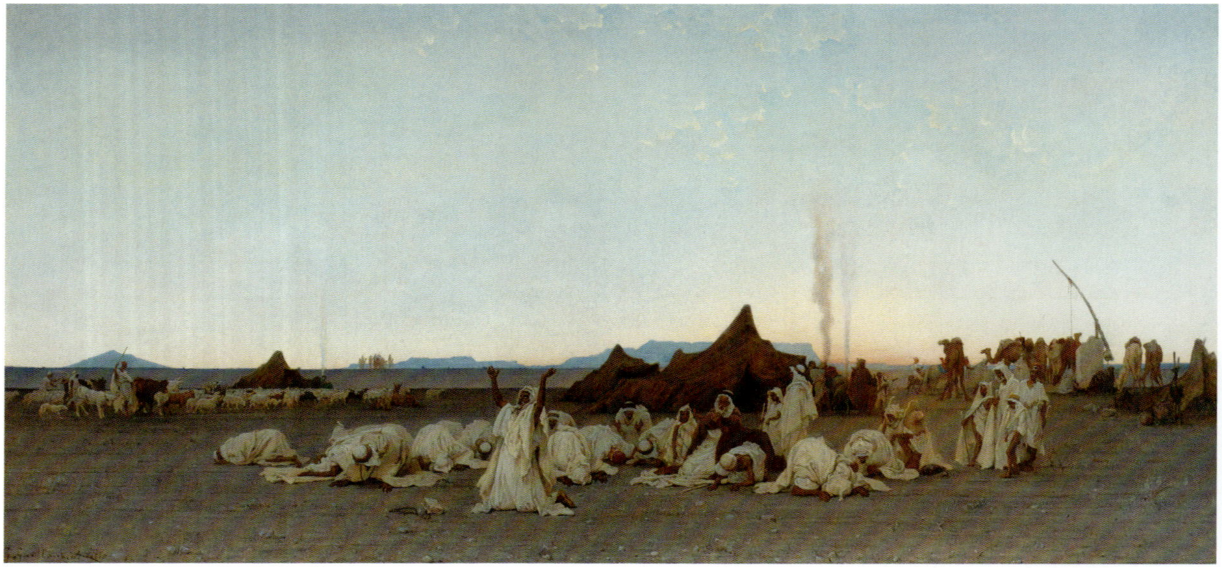

Figure 70.
Gustave Guillaumet, *Evening Prayer in the Sahara* (Salon of 1863). Oil on canvas, 137 × 285 cm. Musée d'Orsay, Paris. Photo courtesy Musée d'Orsay (Patrice Schmidt).

success began with a more standard Orientalist genre scene, albeit one that evokes a real place in southern Algeria that the artist had traveled to and seen for himself.[12] While this earlier work was rewarded with a Salon medal and a state purchase for the young artist, *The Desert* was mostly ignored by the press and the Salon judges in 1868; the work entered the national collection only after the death of the artist in 1887. The question of what led the academically trained Guillaumet to produce such a radically simplified composition is compelling, perhaps because it is inherently impossible to answer with any certainty. Yet the painting itself and its symbolic references continue to inform viewers about the depiction of the outer reaches of the French empire in the 1860s. The emptiness of this landscape, its most profound pictorial legacy, is the aspect of the picture that demands interpretation. This emptiness is not only meaningful in itself, but it produces meaning as well. It is a representation of Algeria that pictures it as a stretch of naked earth, a landscape with no inherent character, a placeless space full of light and extending forever. The means through which *The Desert* makes the colonial landscape available for the viewer's apprehension and interpretation are also worthy of exploration. Therein lie the mystery and power of this picture. After an investigation of colonial land policy in Algeria at this moment, the significance of this emptiness will be clearer.

Colonial Land Policy and the Political Economy of Landscape

The *sénatus-consulte* of 22 April 1863 appears, on the surface, to be a piece of legislation enacted by the French government for the benefit of the Arab population of Algeria.[13] It begins, after all, by declaring the tribes of Algeria the rightful proprietors of all "permanent and traditional" lands occupied by them. Considering the fact that this law put an end to the practice of *cantonnement*, or the direct expropriation of a portion of tribal territories by the French administration for the purposes of French settlement and colonization, it was indeed a step in the right direction for the indigenous inhabitants of Algeria. Further, in light of received ideas in France about Arabs in general and Algerians in particular,[14] the *sénatus-consulte* was an enormous improvement in the French conception of Arabs. This law formalized their status as individuals in the French Empire, granting them the rights to hold property and, further, to own the lands from which they generated their livelihood—something French peasants had enjoyed since the Revolution. This law was followed in 1865 by another *sénatus-consulte* granting the native inhabitants of Algeria full French citizenship under certain conditions. This law was later expanded in 1873. In other words, the law of 1863 was one in a string of legislative concessions to indigenous Algerians. It was the kind of metropolitan domination of colonial affairs that infuriated both the colonists and the military administration in Algeria. In the eyes of critics, such laws guaranteed the rights of the Arabs over and above those of the French settlers.[15]

In fact, the *sénatus-consulte* was not created in the interests of Algerian natives at all. It was designed to allow for the future expropriation of tribal lands for French settlement, newly legitimated by the process of granting the natives private property, which could, of course, be bought and sold. As an added benefit to the French administration, it sought through legal means to fix the *douars*—the social groupings of Algeria's rural indigenous population—in place, replacing their nomadic existence with a sedentary one. This process had a history in the efforts of the *bureaux arabes* up to this point. As Patricia Lorcin explains: "In the period up to 1858 a concerted attempt was made to sedentarize the nomadic population through the construction of houses and public utilities, such as fountains, wells, public baths and markets (but not mosques or Koranic schools), and the development of a more sophisticated agrarian economy through the introduction of new crops and agricultural methods."[16] The *sénatus-consulte* was an ambitious attempt to transform the life of Algeria's native rural population completely, but it was not without precedent. Through it, the French government sought to complete the process of replacing traditional lifestyles and indigenous agrarian practices so that the French could guide the Arabs to a greater degree of civilization. Though he welcomed the application of the *sénatus-consulte* and later, in 1873, was the author of a law bearing his name that extended its effects in Algeria, Dr. Auguste Warnier was frank about its effects on the Arab population and its possibility of failure: "When the time comes that an imperial decree orders the creation of private property among the Arab tribes, a complete social revolution will be decreed and it is not at all certain that the tribespeople accustomed to the yoke of their tribal leaders . . . will not themselves repudiate the benefits of private property, in order to preserve the communism of collective ownership more in harmony with their nomadic lifestyle."[17]

This is an excellent example of colonial paternalism mixed with revulsion at the foundations of the nomadic practices of many indigenous Algerians. Warnier was, in fact, one of the most prominent publicists of Algeria during the period. A colonist himself, he ceaselessly defended the rights of the settlers, which, he felt, were neglected by Napoléon III's colonial administration. In his view, the interests of the colonists were sacrificed to those of the traditional Arab aristocracy, a group whose interests were to maintain their feudal control over the native population at the expense of the progress of colonialism. He stopped at nothing to besmirch the *indigènes*. In the passage above, he insinuates that their way of life is a form of communism, and elsewhere he supposedly provided mathematical proof, based on official figures, that a colonist was worth ten natives.[18] The fact that such a proof rests on agricultural production and paid taxes explains much about the colonial interests of the settlers and the French government. The ideal colonial citizen, whether native or settler, grew a wealth of crops and paid his share of taxes, assuring the prosperity of the colony. Such a view is as simple as it is universal. It is founded on conceptions of production and society that, the author admits, were fundamentally foreign to at least a portion of the indigenous population. These notions are polemical and, when accompanied by the mathematical *proof* of the superiority of one group over another, potentially dangerous.

Warnier's text reveals the intractable biases of a French settler who arrived in Algeria early enough to have lived through many years of battle with the native population, but it further points to some of the fundamental ideas about the colonial project that emerged in this era in France. Progress and colonial prosperity were central, but these notions were tied to French ideas of production and economic success. Further, there was a tendency to assess these factors numerically, as evidenced by Warnier's reduction of cultural difference to an abstract equation (1:10) that can be *factually* established.[19] Through these means, he establishes the predominance of the colonizer and represents the colonized as a fraction. Such thinking demonstrates the use of abstractions to explain the difficult problems that colonialism faced at this juncture. Rather than considering how best to integrate the two distinct populations with different practices of agriculture and patterns of land use, Warnier instead sought a means to quantify the difference between settlers and natives. His equation may seem ridiculous to us now, but in the political debates of the era, Warnier's ability to produce quantifiable evidence for his position was significant. It allowed him to make demands on behalf of colonists like himself, demands based on statistically verifiable information.

In this light, Napoléon III's interest in preserving the cultural autonomy of the native population seems progressive indeed. However, describing Algeria as an Arab kingdom (*royaume arabe*)[20] and granting tribes the ownership of their lands were two manifestations of a paternalistic posture, concealing the fact that the application of the *sénatus-consulte* would aid the colonial administration in its efforts to maintain a higher level of surveillance of the *douars* and prevent revolutionary or other allegiances from developing among tribes whose lands would be formally separated. In this sense, the effects of the *sénatus-consulte* would have been similar to those of the Haussmannization of Paris that occurred in the same period. The method for achieving this increased control of indigenous Algerians based upon spatial fragmentation—the distribution of private property to *douars* and individuals—was intended to inspire a respect for European (read civilized) values among Algeria's native population.[21] However, the attempt to delimit and attribute parcels of land to individuals or families who had always understood themselves as part of a collective and who may have never farmed the same stretch of land two years consecutively must have seemed incomprehensible to the members of the *douars*.

Three types of property existed in Algeria among rural populations, both Arabs and Kabyles: *Beylick*, or the domain of a *douar* or a tribe; *arch*, or collective property; and *melk*, something like private property in the sense that it belonged to a family and could be passed from generation to generation. This third category was most common in Kabyle societies, which was one reason this group was favored by French intellectuals over the more nomadic Arab tribes.[22] In the texts of the *sénatus-consulte* and the instructions for its application, only the *Beylick* and *melk* forms of property are mentioned, with a single notable exception. Such an omission constitutes turning a blind eye to one of the fundamental tenets of Arab culture, and worse. The "Instructions générales pour l'éxecution du Sénatus-consulte du 22 avril 1863 et du règlement de l'administration publique du 23 mai suivant" clarify the intentions of this legislation. The constitution of individual property "consists in putting an end to indivision in the colony by determining the respective rights of families that are property holders."[23] It continues: "This substitution of individual rights not commutable to the collective right of the *douar* on a portion of the *douar's* own territory is a true revolution to set in motion in terms of the status of property laws among the Arabs; it is, in effect, the abrogation of the obscure Muslim property rights concerning land called *arch* or *sabega*."[24] This honest admission of the French government's attempt to supplant Islamic law fully on the issue of collective property demonstrates that, far from aiding the Arabs in their quest for self-determination, this piece of "Arab-friendly" legislation actually sought to undermine the legal codes and cultural practices of the Arabs native to the colony.[25] The need to "stop indivision" through the administration of the *sénatus-consulte* had a double purpose for French colonialism in Algeria. On one hand, the law sought to make members of *douars* or tribes into atomized individuals who would protect their own interests. This is nothing less than attempting to foist liberalism and individualism on traditional collectives by singling out individuals to make into landowners. Once an individual owns his own tract of land (only males need apply), he will naturally protect his interests over and above those of the collective. This pursuit is one that I cannot hope fully to analyze here, but it hinges upon France's self-imposed civilizing mission and demonstrates the Second Empire's obsessive fear of collectivization in any form. It was this sentiment that found expression in the text by Warnier analyzed above.

On the other hand, the advantage of making tribal lands into individual parcels was that it opened them up for French settlement. While the previous law of 1851 had held tribal lands apart from the market, the *sénatus-consulte* intended to distribute parcels to individuals who would then, acting in their own interests, sell the parcels to French colonists who sought to expand the colonial empire. In retrospect, this does not seem like a foolproof plan, since it assumed that the indigenous population of Algeria would immediately reproduce the individualistic interests of French entrepreneurs. Before analyzing the process of delimitation, it seems prudent to investigate in greater detail the basis for the perceived need for territorial expansion. As the social scientists who also acted as publicists for Algerian colonization assured their readers, making more land available for settlement was central to France's ability to expand the economic vitality of Algeria.[26] The way in which they arrived at such opinions, however—by figuring the number of inhabitants per hectare—betrays an increasing quantification in the French analysis of social processes, such as colonial settlement, as well as in their approach to territory.

In the geographical writings of the 1860s pertaining to Algeria, the character of the colonial landscape was altered, leading to a conception of space as value. Whereas the earlier French geographers set out to classify, delimit, and thus synthesize the variegated territory of Algeria into comprehensible units, the works of Jules Duval sought to integrate such findings into the sphere of political economy. It was Duval who began his analysis of Algeria from the perspective of political economy and who eventually attempted to marry the information provided by geography to the systems of political economy in his theoretical work of 1863, *Des rapports entre le géographie et l'économie politique (On the Relations Between Geography and Political Economy)*.[27] Duval was something of a one-man intellectual force, serving as both the secretary of the Société de la géographie and as the director of *L'Économiste Français,* and he also was one of the most prominent authorities on and boosters for Algeria. His essay "French Colonial Politics, Algeria," appeared in the *Revue des Deux Mondes* in 1859 and advocated what became Napoléon III's two central policy initiatives in Algeria in the 1860s: the privatization of tribal lands and the naturalization of native Algerians to France.[28] In brief, he was a uniquely significant figure for Algerian policy in Second Empire France who also articulated a theoretical application of geographical knowledge to economic issues.

Like Warnier, Duval was a *colon* who promoted the interests of the settlers in the French press, and in 1869 he collaborated on a book with Warnier.[29] Yet Duval's writings are, for the most part, less polemical. Duval was the first to articulate fully the colonial tactic of assimilation and to spell out what forms it would take in Algeria.[30] In *Des rapports*, he made an argument about the geographical determination of economic factors: "Whether one discusses continents, portions of the world or less expansive regions, the contour exercises an influence that manifests itself in the destiny of its inhabitants: based upon whether it is whole or broken, angular or rounded, based on the respective proportion of these diverse traits, the political and economic effects will themselves be quite diverse."[31] The use of the term "contour" is self-consciously general and abstract, and therefore universally applicable. It is possible to divine that he refers to "natural separations," such as bodies of water and chains of mountains, that were elaborated in previous geographical works on Algeria by authors such as Carette, Renou, and Daumas.[32] Of course, the notion that innate geographical characteristics could affect the development of economics and politics would seem to belie the universalist claims of Duval's observation: an argument for attending to distinctions between places ("diverse traits") when analyzing their economic and political development could undermine the undifferentiated formulas of political economy. Duval resolved this apparent contradiction, though, by pointing to exchange as *the* universal condition of humans: "In effect, exchange is the supreme sign of sociability in the material world. Certain animals work, only man exchanges and engages in commerce." He continued,

> Society, in its turn, has instituted the diverse rules of exchange between the metropole and the colony, between people united by certain traits, etc.
>
> In this alliance of human forces, geography indicates the exchanges, commerce executes them and political economy discovers the laws.[33]

While distinctions between countries exist and are the topic of geographical inquiry, exchange is the fundamental principle that connects these regions to one another. In Duval's view, commerce functions to assure relations through exchange; the role of political economy is to study this process and establish laws of exchange. While I am in no position to evaluate the universal validity of political economy as it is articulated here, it is necessary to point out the way in which spatial configurations are deprived of meaning in this schema. Even a relatively meaningless abstraction of space, such as contours (of the earth? the earth as a body?), ceases to have importance in a world that is regulated by exchange that only political economy can properly understand. The "laws" of political economy, since they express the patterns of commercial exchange, regulate the meaning of space because they cut across it. Regional distinctions are unified into a global economic picture in this framework and, more important, distinct places and cultures lose their meaning in the face of the laws of economic exchange. They become nothing more than the spaces that commerce must traverse in order to achieve the goal of exchange. This line of reasoning is emblematic of abstract representations of space.

Such a system begins to have meaning in the context of Algerian colonization when, in a later work, Duval applies some of the laws of political economy to the colonial project. In 1866, he wrote, "Between the surface expanse of a nation and the forces necessary to exploit it, there is a natural relation." He added, "It can be said that, to a great degree, the amount of budgetary expenses is proportional to the extent of spaces in all civilized countries."[34] These two observations lead the author to insist upon the necessity for more settlers in Algeria, who then need to be granted more land, so that the territory can be more densely populated and thus produce more revenue. The concern is not so much with the policies articulated as with the way the territory of Algeria is rendered in such formulae. The idea that a natural relationship exists between the size of a country and the forces necessary to exploit it reduces the landscape to a measurement of space and reconfigures it as an abstract element (x) in a system governed by questions of productivity. In this equation, Algeria's spaces become fixed and quantifiable, a bounded terrain. Though people live in this space and are crucial in determining its value through the payment of taxes, the formula necessarily negates their presence and their practices in order to maintain its universal validity. The second proposition informs us that because the spaces involved are large, it is also expensive for the colony's governing body, because this expansive space must be covered with public works, such as roads, artesian wells, and the like. The formula articulated here is as follows: the more densely populated a space, the greater the return on expenditure, since more people will contribute to its tax base. Though Duval actually employs the term "spaces" here, indicating that there are differences between them that force the writer to use the plural form, these spaces are so fully abstracted that they form one part of a mathematical equation.

These principles of political economy are new to the discourse of the colonial landscape. The reduction of the spaces of the colony to an abstract, quantifiable signifier was a significant step in the dematerialization of Algeria's terrain. Though this transformation occurred within the realm of the social sciences, it evidences a social metamorphosis in French culture, namely, the ability to denature a terrain completely, emptying it of any other meaning than its quantifiable numerical equivalent (14 million hectares). Based on this number, Duval advocated the adoption of particular policies in Algeria. The equations he employed allowed him to perceive the inhabitants of Algeria as distinct from the lands they occupied; he was able to render the terrain separate from those who resided on it. In essence, this was the task of the *sénatus-consulte*. Though this legislation offered tribal lands to the tribes and individuals within them, the real process of delimitation was to make formal the separation

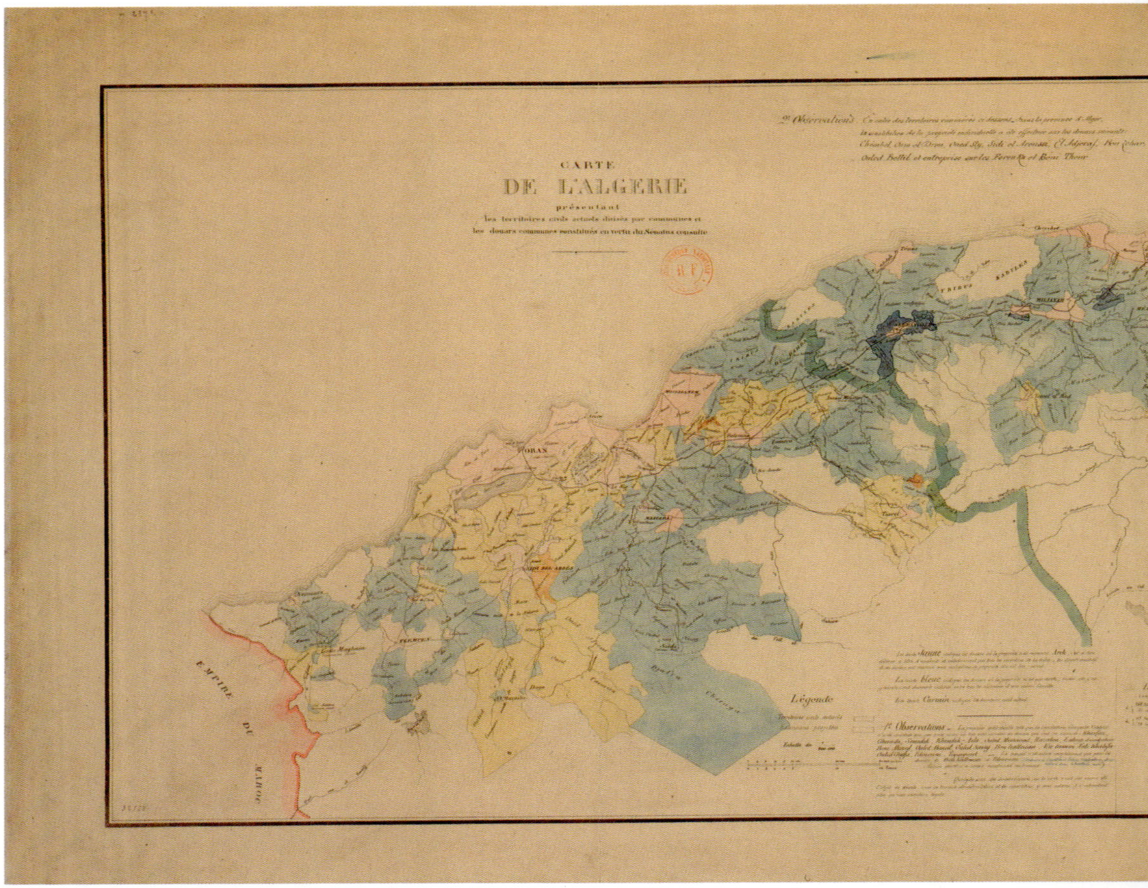

Figure 71.
"Map of Algeria presenting current civil territory divided by *communes* and *douars* constituted by virtue of the *sénatus-consulte*," 1870. Bibliothèque nationale de France, Département des Cartes et plans, Ge D. 4167.

of each landholder from the piece of property whose deed he held.

The process of delimiting territory was the central administrative task of the *sénatus-consulte* and, in the context of the representation of the colonial landscape of Algeria, the most ambitious project for reconfiguring the space of the colony. For the purposes of this inquiry, the application of the *sénatus-consulte* was significant because it remade the map of the colony, both literally and metaphorically. Even more pressing is the way in which it attempted to replace traditional indigenous conceptions of place with the abstract concepts of both private ownership and parcels of land. The former was represented as a deed of title—words on paper—and the latter was delimited mathematically through surveying. Leaving aside the issue of whether the native population was able to understand the nature of such abstractions or whether they might have been hostile to such a transparent attempt by French authorities to undermine their way of life, it is clear that the administration of the law would lead to French domination in at least two ways. First, the second set of instructions guided the subcommissions to study the tribes whose rights they were adjudicating with great care. In

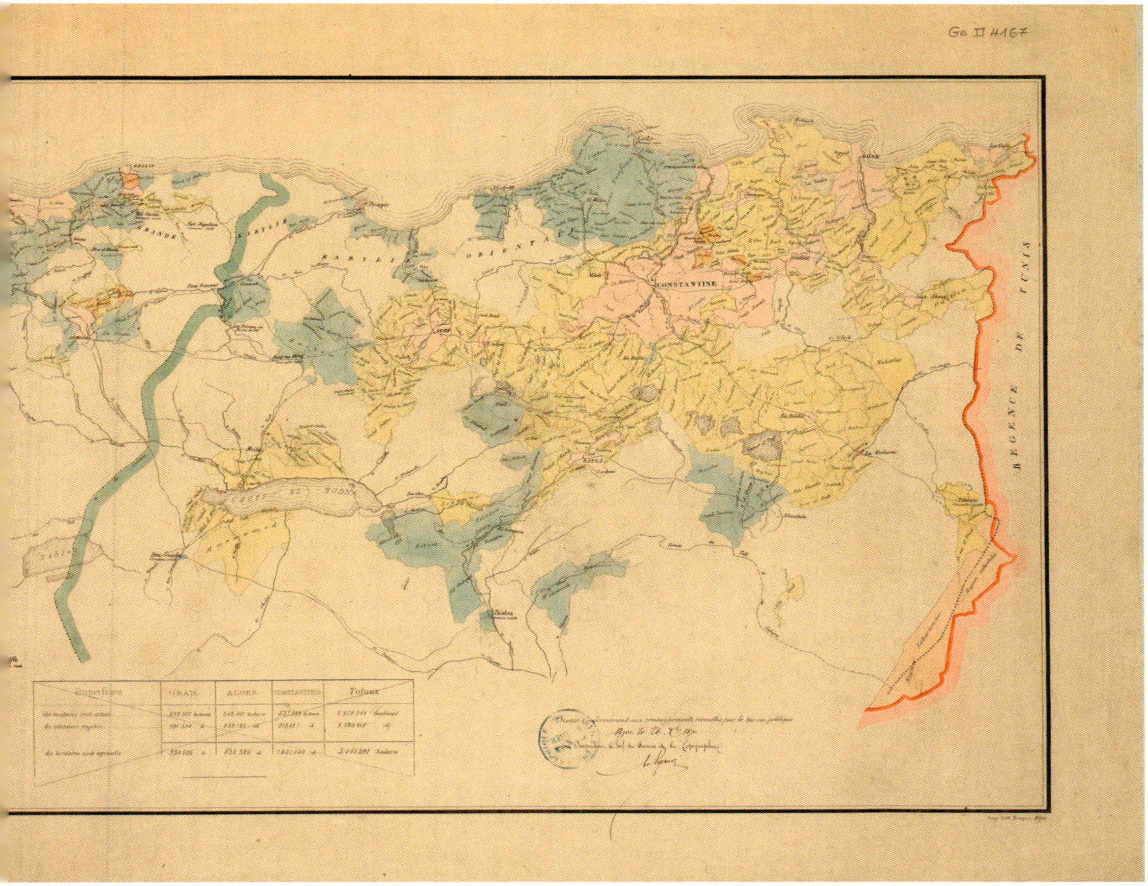

order to safeguard the interests of all, a full inquiry would have to be made about each tribe or *douar* whose property was to be delimited.[35] Of course, information gleaned from the surveillance of tribes would lead to a greater degree of control over those tribes. Further, the delimitation of territory, literally fixing the area of each tribe or *douar* and parceling it into pieces, represents the official triumph of French cartography and pictorial conventions for the depiction of landscape. Obviously, the division of collective land requires a clear and decisive map so that the boundaries forged by the *sénatus-consulte* can be accurately traced and positively fixed. This map—called the "Map of Algeria presenting current civil territory divided by *communes* and *douars* constituted by virtue of the *sénatus-consulte*" (fig. 71)—was finally produced in 1870, at the very end of the Second Empire.

The map shows that by the time the Second Empire fell, the administration had actually accomplished precious little in terms of privatizing tribal lands and opening them up for settlement. This map of Algeria is divided into three sections: civil territory—pink (the only region available for colonial settlement); the *douars* in which property had been recognized as collective—yellow—known as *arch* in the native dialect; and the *douars* where property was not *arch*, but remained generally undivided—blue. Looking at the map, it is clear that the colony is dominated by the second two categories. Inscriptions on the map spell out what these categories suggest. Out of hundreds of *douars* delimited, the inscriptions explain that the lands of only two have become part of civil territory (i.e., become open to settlement), and private property has been established on only twenty-two others. Tribal autonomy appears to have been sustained in the last years of the Second Empire, despite the French government's attempt to impose the status of "individuals" onto the native inhabitants of Algeria. Yet the patchwork of shapes in this depiction reveals that the process of delimitation had proceeded successfully in Algerian territory.

Following earlier French maps of colonial Algeria, the map of the *sénatus-consulte* speaks volumes about this legislation's clear administrative division of territory. Maps are designed to organize information and to present it visually in an immediately legible way. This map arranges the colony into abstract visual units whose labels explain their significance. In some sense, the *sénatus-consulte* was intended to make possible just such a representation of the colony, because it sought to transform the tribes into administrative units, each occupying a specific territory. Michel de Certeau has discussed the way maps present information graphically in a way that erases the processes involved in their creation: "The map thus collates on the same plane heterogeneous places, some *received* from a tradition [geometry] and others *produced* by observation. . . . The map, a totalizing stage on which elements of diverse origin are brought together to form a tableau of a 'state' of geographical knowledge, pushes away into prehistory or into its posterity, as if into the wings, the operations of which it is the result or the necessary condition. It remains alone on the stage. The tour describers have disappeared."[36] While the *sénatus-consulte* did not lead to the intended privatization of indigenous lands, the map demonstrates that it did effectively redefine the colonial territory in abstract terms. In this representation, Algeria takes on the characteristics of a well-ordered colony, and the activities that made it that way—the painstaking trouble of delimitation, the negation of indigenous conceptions of land and space—have been eliminated from the representation. This is the very visual representation of the abstraction of space achieved by the *sénatus-consulte* and theorized by Duval and Warnier. The map frames Algeria as French. Its proliferation of administrative divisions demonstrates the predominance of French methods of perceiving and organizing space on the surface of this territory.

Abstract Space as Landscape Painting

Turning to the pictorial representations of Algeria during this period, it is noteworthy that the desert is the focus of landscape painting for the first time in history. As previously discussed, Heffernan has considered the symbolic aspects of the desert in the nineteenth century, which he has interpreted in the pictorial works of Guillaumet and those of Eugène Fromentin, the first artist to make an artistic subject of the Algerian Sahara.[37] Heffernan described the symbolism of the desert in the nineteenth century as two-sided. On the one hand, the desert was the place of ultimate desolation; on the other, it represented the possibility that civilization and progress would reclaim this barren land and put it to productive use. Further, there is symbolic ambivalence in the figures just visible on the horizon. As a viewer, one wonders if it is sunrise or sunset, if these figures are moving toward or away from the viewer, bringing salvation or abandoning

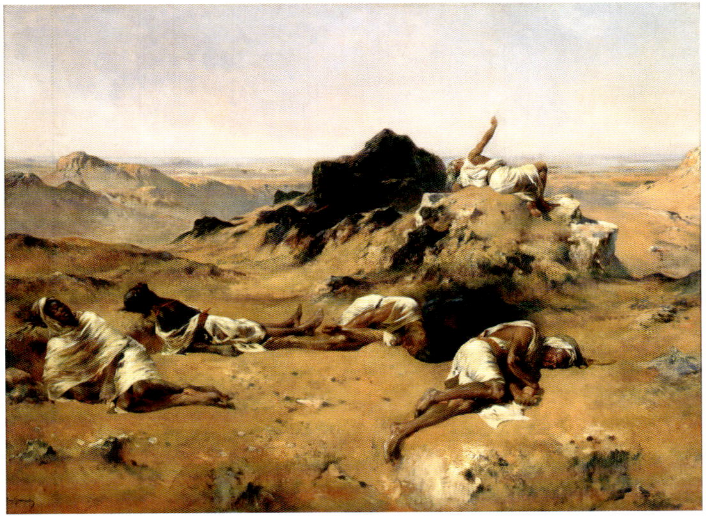

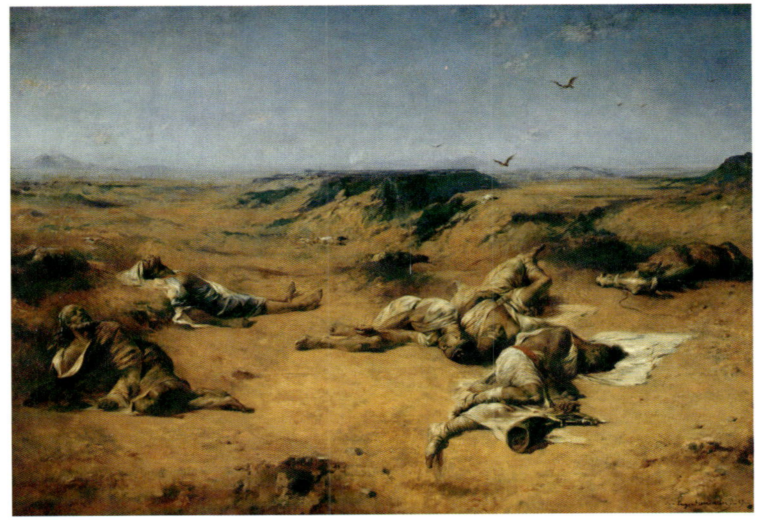

Figure 72.
Eugène Fromentin,
The Land of Thirst,
undated. Oil on canvas,
103 × 143.2 cm. Musée
d'Orsay, Paris. Photo
courtesy Musée d'Orsay
(Patrice Schmidt).

Figure 73.
Eugène Fromentin,
The Land of Thirst, 1869.
Oil on canvas, 103.5 ×
144 cm. © Royal
Museum of Fine Arts of
Belgium, Brussels (inv.
3424). Photo: Cussac.

the viewer to desolation. It is even more difficult to read the symbolic message in a work that is nearly without figures. The skeleton of the camel in the foreground is a one-liner, but its presence in the center foreground of this composition makes it difficult to get beyond.

If one considers *The Desert* in relation to other paintings of the Algerian Sahara produced by Fromentin in the same period, it is possible to derive a sense of the work's unique power. There are a number of desert images in Fromentin's oeuvre, dating back to his first trip to Laghouat in 1853, but the most pertinent comparison is between Guillaumet's *Sahara* and Fromentin's two versions of *The Land of Thirst* (figs. 72, 73). In the latter compositions, made in the last years of the Second Empire (only the second is dated, in 1869), it is possible to compare an anecdotal representation of the desert to Guillaumet's extreme simplicity. Like so many of his famous works, Fromentin's composition is based on a story from one of his novels—in this case, a story at the end of *Un Été dans le Sahara*, originally published in 1857. These figures, abandoned in the desert, are literally expiring in our midst; the desert itself, as a powerful force of nature, is paramount in this representation. While the figures add an element of human interest, Fromentin has provided them with realistic (as opposed to fantastic) dress, perhaps in order to make more forceful the actual tragedy the viewer witnesses. In the earlier composition (fig. 72), the central figure reaches for the sky, in a gesture remarkably similar to that of Géricault's *Raft of the Medusa*.[38] In the second composition (fig. 73), the artist has replaced this dramatic gesture with a number of vultures above the horizon. In both works, the placement of the figures is meant to appear natural, but is in fact rather artfully composed.

There is a landscape here of sorts, a place full of geographical features that provide the eye with a terrain to explore. There may not be any vegetation in sight, nor any sign of human civilization, but the landscape itself has a clear structure, a set of rises and valleys that communicates its rugged character and gives these pictures a sense of particularity. There is legible symbolism, but the story a viewer can impute to these paintings involves a certain kind of place and the nomadic people who inhabit it. This specificity allows a viewer to put an interpretive framework in place and to read this picture as a narrative. Whether it reflects the artist's view of imperial ideology, as Heffernan has suggested,[39] or whether it reflects his response to the catastrophic drought that was raging in Algeria at this historical moment, the paintings convey a message through the landscape and the figures that populate it and provide a legible drama, a tableau of balanced pictorial elements—both figures and landscape forms—for the viewers to interpret.

Unlike Fromentin's two versions of *The Land of Thirst*, *The Desert* cannot be described as a tableau. This composition is not ordered, balanced, or self-conscious. Guillaumet, who was otherwise a successful academic painter, turned his back on landscape conventions when he created this piece. Whereas other French painters of Algeria made use of landscape conventions in order to present the exotic terrain of Algeria as recognizable to a French audience, Guillaumet excerpted the desert in such a way that it appears abstract. *The Desert* cuts off the Sahara arbitrarily, cleaving its apparent limitlessness into a comprehensible fraction. Further, the manner in which Guillaumet rendered this plot of land is loose and evocative. The sensations of light and atmosphere, which are the painting's most tenable subject, lead the viewer to a more intimate and personal experience of this territory. The landscape here needs to be translated by each individual who perceives it. In the process, this piece of desert comes to mean something and to belong to the viewer.

Perhaps the most relevant symbolic evocation of the desert to emerge in Guillaumet's *Sahara* is the sense of unlimited space. In this sense, *The Desert* departs most significantly from other contemporary manifestations of landscape painting in France. The recognizable traces in the composition—the camel, the distant caravan, the few plants—do not measure space with the conventions of landscape paintings. There are no trees or figures to establish relative distances, and though a sense of atmosphere is palpable, a systematic use of aerial perspective is also absent. In the terms of landscape painting, *The Sahara* is unmeasured. Beyond the absence of pictorial devices to measure space is the utter lack of any sign of human habitation or cultivation. The desert evoked is the place where human interaction with the terrain, in the form of agriculture, is impossible due to the nature of the place. It is literally a land without masters, because humans could not squeeze an existence out of such a landscape. There is no hope of occupation, let alone agriculture, so the place is necessarily beyond the control of any individual or government.

Following this line of argument, the archetypal desert rendered by Guillaumet is a romanticization sharing little with the historical development of colonization traced earlier. In line with recent scholarship on Orientalism and the fantasies it conjures, one might be tempted to consider *The Desert* as a mystification. Though Guillaumet traveled repeatedly to Algeria and had experiences with the various landscapes and settlements on the edges of the desert, one could argue that he represented the desert as an Orientalist fantasy of landscape. Just as Linda Nochlin has asserted that Gérôme's religious ethnographic art generated the appearance of an unthreatening Islam that diverged from historical reality,[40] one could argue that Guillaumet's archetypal desert distracts its viewers from the very real transformations the French government was effecting in the Algerian landscape. *The Desert* could be read as the very opposite of the map of 1870: it provides a fantasy of a limitless space in the face of the application of the *sénatus-consulte*.

Yet I am not certain that the landscape painting is fundamentally different from the map. Despite the evocation of limitless space it appears to proffer, the frame of the painting actually provides a boundary for the desert. Guillaumet delimited an enormous expanse of space in this work: he squeezed the entire Sahara into a frame of 110 × 200 cm! In *The Desert*, we see a synechdochic substitution. The painting renders this stretch of the Sahara and thereby lays claim to representing all of it. When a viewer perceives this painting, he or she does not see this fragment of the Algerian Sahara. Rather, the painting evokes the desert as an archetype. It acts as a magnet for received ideas because there are no particularities to dispel them. Nevertheless, if one thinks more literally of the frame and its function, the metaphorical conversion of part into whole takes on a different meaning.

Another result produced by this sort of painting is that the location represented is similarly supplanted by the effect of it. The Sahara is what we might call a geographical fact. It is a desert in North Africa and it is big. In Guillaumet's painting, the Sahara is less the subject than the way it looks to a viewer perceiving it. In other words, if one considers the pictorial representation as a signifier and the Sahara as the signified, what becomes clear in this case is that when a viewer confronts this painting, the signifier does not necessarily direct attention to the signified. Rather, the viewer is able to seize upon the effects captured by the artist, to be immersed in the impression conveyed by the painting without considering it as a representation of any place in particular. Through a newly developed pictorial language, this place is transfigured into an abstract space that can be both measured and divided but only in the viewer's imagination. For what kind of fool would ever attempt to take possession of a desert? How can an artist make a landscape out of a limitless vacuity?

Guillaumet's *Sahara* frames the unlimited spaces at the edge of France's Algeria while conveying the effects of the desert in terms that can only be construed through an individual's perceptual faculties. This artist's flight from landscape conventions ultimately leads to an illustration of the colonial landscape whose terms are analogous to those of the French social scientists and legislators of his epoch. *The Desert* does possess symbolic meanings, but more forceful is the lingua franca it intones, which denudes the colonial landscape of its character and allows for its possession by metropolitan viewers. By making the desert appear abstract yet accessible through the terms of landscape painting, Guillaumet succeeded in framing the Sahara, France's empty Algerian frontier. Summing up Guillaumet's career after his death in 1887, one critic wrote: "As a picturesque description, as a graphic philosophy, dare I say of this once barbarous country today become a new France, the work of Guillaumet is a second conquest of Algeria, the conquest of art after the conquest of war."[41]

Epilogue

The Recurrence of Empire and Landscape

By the time of France's Third Republic (1871–1940), the country's career as a self-described empire was behind it. Yet in this period France's imperial ambitions and conquests accelerated, along with those of other European powers, to a level previously inconceivable. To attribute such changes to landscape artists would be sheer folly, yet as the spaces of the globe were conquered, they needed to be seen. Tour books multiplied; artists continued to visit colonial spaces and translate them as landscapes. Photography came to prominence as the preferred method for rendering the archive of the world's places. This was largely due to technological developments that made hand-held cameras available in the 1880s, but alongside this expanded photographic universe, new means to represent were developed based on personal perception and apprehension.

The rise of avant-garde painting in France—the invention of pictorial modernism—in the years of the Third Republic was the result of a self-conscious proposal, among artists, to focus upon the process of translation inherent in painting. Avant-garde artists seized the means to represent the world in individualized terms. Needless to say, landscape was a central part of these developments, and the way that artists mediated the world became a highly subjective affair. Many art historians have demonstrated how this was fundamentally a social development—modernism rising as a means to confront modernity—and have explained that the key to understanding these new changes is an awareness of their process of figuration, the ability of the artist to make a subjective impulse into an objective image.

The value of works by French artists who came to Algeria and Morocco during these years, such as Pierre-Auguste Renoir and Henri Matisse, is not determined by the level of objective truth or conventional narrative offered. Rather, the formal qualities of the works themselves—the results of the artists' pictorial experimentation—count most. Such individuated responses to North Africa would seem to undermine the idea that pictures negotiate colonial relations, or engage in a second "conquest of art," as the paintings of Guillaumet were thought to do. The paintings of North Africa made by avant-garde artists spell out a new language for the empire of landscape that can serve as a bridge to connect the imagery of Algeria's early years as a colony to the experience of empire that persists today. Simply put, as the government of France passed off the responsibility for colonial development on individuals (*colonistes*), the artists who represented the colony translated its spaces in pictorial terms tangible to individual perception. The artist's role in the propagation of colonial ideology was entirely distinct.

Looking at Pierre-Auguste Renoir's *Arab Festival, Algiers* (1881; fig. 74), one perceives more than

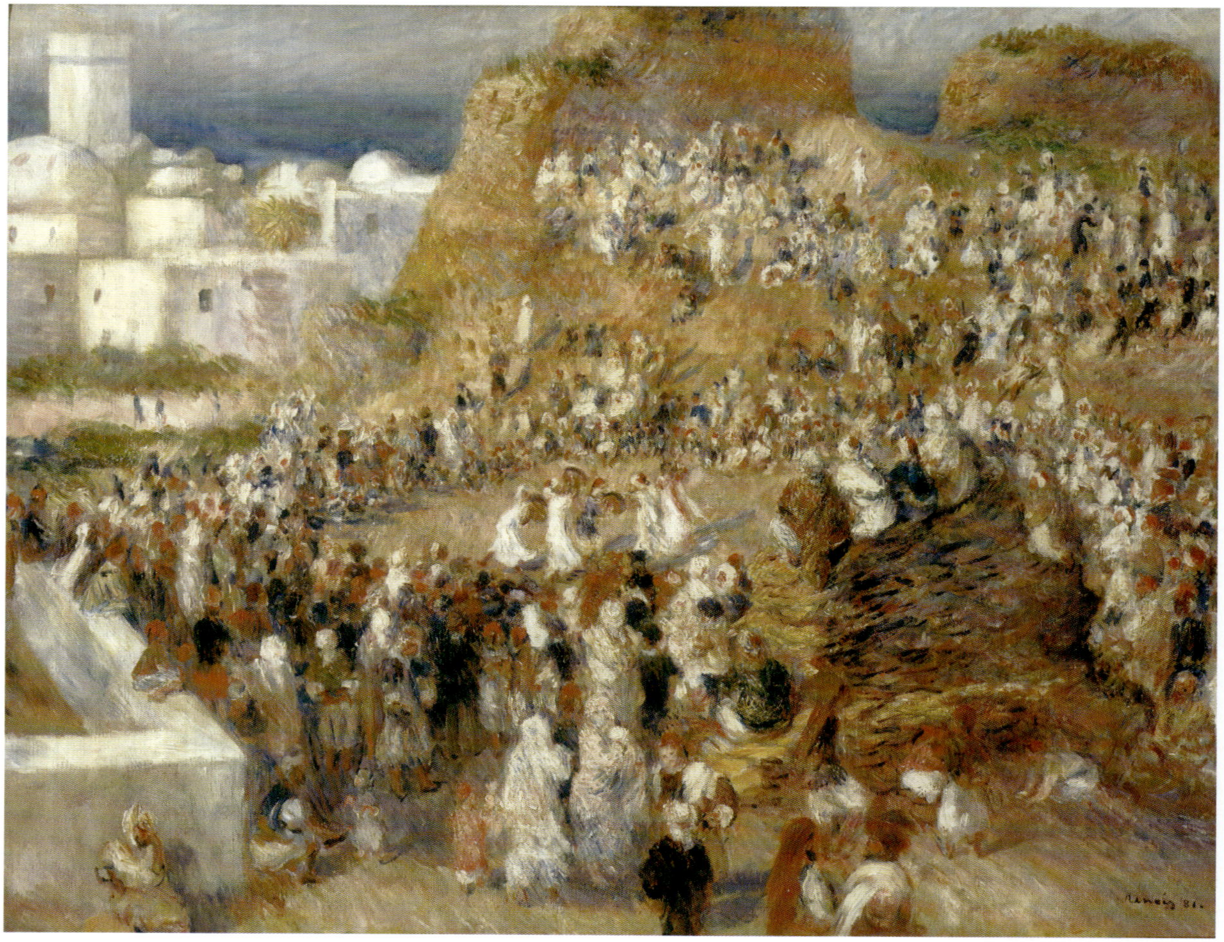

Figure 74.
Pierre-Auguste Renoir, *Arab Festival, Algiers*, 1881. Oil on canvas, 73.5 × 92 cm. Musée d'Orsay, Paris (RF 1957-8). Photo: Réunion des musées nationaux/Art Resource, New York (Hervé Landowski).

an ethnographic study of the activities of indigenous North Africans in a scenic locale. Reminiscent of Delacroix's images of festivals in Morocco, Renoir's treatment of this public spectacle in Algiers is full of motion and color. While the activity of the crowds in the foreground and the performing musicians they watch are unquestionably the focus of the picture, the painting features a site that is significant in the history of the colony—the Casbah—and the surrounding landscape. Langlois' *Panorama of Algiers* featured the view from the Casbah, but Renoir chose instead to offer a more immediate image of the area just behind the crumbling ramparts of the city. (This painting features the same site represented by William Wyld in a lithograph of 1833; see fig. 35.)

Many studies of Impressionism have explored the innovative techniques of artists like Renoir who made their immediate visual impressions apparent through strokes of raw pigment that would blend into a harmonious picture only in the eye of the viewer. The staccato rhythm of the brush in this picture is intense, perhaps responding to the musicians and dancers who are the ostensible subject.

Like other earlier Impressionist pictures by the artist, this painting represents a scene of modern life, albeit in an exotic locale. The variety of costumes signals distinct ethnic groups indigenous to Algeria as well as European viewers among the crowd, demonstrating a blending of social types. But this scene owes more to the influence of Delacroix than to Manet. The powerful color and light are reminiscent of Romantic painting, and the Oriental location is clearly marked by the glimpse of the Casbah visible in the upper left of the painting. What results when the methods of Impressionism are applied to an Orientalist subject in the depiction of France's newest province?[1]

The Impressionist technique signaled an immediacy of perception and a heightened awareness of individuality for both artist and viewer, because the images were visibly subjective translations of the world, and they proposed to their viewers the opportunity to translate the confusing array of blotches and jabs of color in order to make sense out of the picture. The significance of perception in Impressionist pictures brings to light an apparent aporia in the modern world. As developments in technology shifted the activities and experiences of those who lived in the urban centers of Europe, the traditional means to connect the present to the past dissolved, jeopardizing the sense of continuity among categories such as individual, family, and community. Temporality was broken into smaller increments. In effect, Modernism attempted to figure these changes through artistic means. Renoir made such indeterminacy visible by making a painting that is, after all, an object and not a window on the world. Thus paintings became a sort of theater for an artistic performance whose meaning was left for the viewer to establish. By perceiving an image of the world composed out of visible strokes of pigment, a viewer becomes aware of the artist's trying to make sense of discordant visual perceptions and comprehends the need to fuse these daubs of color into a seamless whole.

But each artist's, and each viewer's, perceptions are distinct, and so the spaces of the world, represented through avant-garde painting, emerge as wholly individuated despite their social context. Renoir's image of the Arab festival in Algiers is not a collective spectacle, like Langlois' panorama or Vernet's battle paintings, but it is similarly spectacular in that it mediates social relations through image. Rather than projecting an image of the city that posited a position of control, or an image of a conquered and now colonial possession, Renoir's image of Algiers continues in the tradition of Dauzats. It is both picturesque and made for subjective appropriation. By breaking down the visible world into strokes of pigment that divide and coalesce according to the perception of the viewer, this painting signals that the visual spectacle of colonial space and imperial domination is a shifting field, one that can be seized privately and momentarily but that cannot be reified by the state or controlled by its military apparatus. Renoir's image is characterized by a free flow of visual information and a pleasurable agglomeration of stimuli. It is joyful, bright, musical, and confusing.

Henri Matisse, another avant-garde painter who traveled in North Africa, went to Algeria in 1906 and, more famously, journeyed to Morocco in 1912 and 1913—the latter being the year Morocco became a French protectorate. His imagery forms a kind of end point for this study of the evolving terms of the empire of landscape. The Moroccan landscapes he made in and around Tangiers translate the world as a sort of sensual feast through bravura techniques that, in understated terms, allow the viewer to perceive painting as an act of beautification. For Matisse in Morocco, painting landscapes was a means to create a

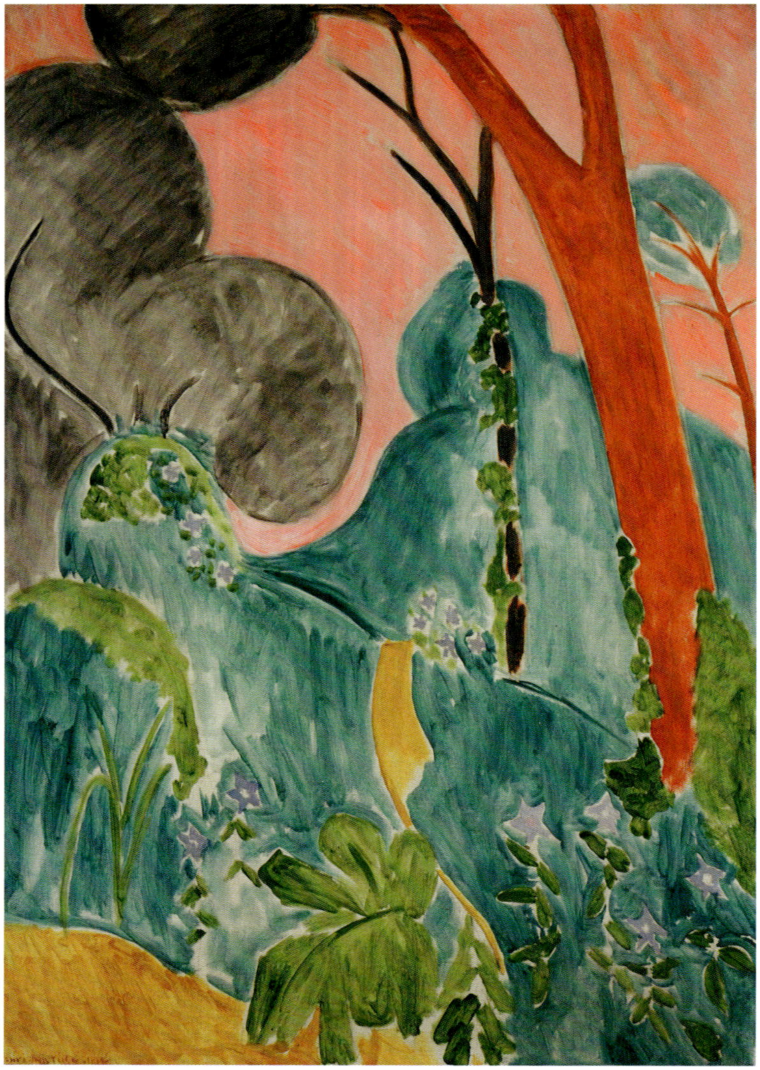

more beautiful world that bore little relation to the frenetic and destructive pace of Europe on the eve of the First World War.

To cite but a single example—*Periwinkles, Moroccan Garden* (1912; fig. 75)—Matisse's rendition of the landscape suggests the artful composition of a master landscape gardener. The arabesques of succulent colors generate an image so full of harmony and charm that one does not want to leave it. Unlike *Arab Festival, Periwinkles* is an image of a well-ordered and beautiful natural environment that self-consciously reflects the patterning of North African decorative arts, which the French were particularly interest in trying to salvage despite their modernization of the region.[2] The process of painting is even more self-consciously registered here, but the appearance of the final work is more composed, divided into areas of color like a stained-glass window. Of course, such a delightful arrangement of forms is designed to provide pleasure, as more traditional landscapes would. Yet Matisse's studied artificiality, like so many landscape images produced in the nineteenth century, transcends reference to an actual place. Figured here is an imagined world that corresponds to the fantasy the artist wished to project and share with his viewers, one made possible by colonialism and inflected by imperialist ideology.

In Matisse's painting, French colonial territory in North Africa is rendered through such a personal aesthetic that it ceases to refer to the territory at all. Matisse's brand of avant-gardism subsumes the materiality of the place and suggests its meanings through visual metaphor. Without the title, it is clear that this is a landscape of fancy—a lovely retreat from the uncomfortable realities of modernity, yet rendered in a modern pictorial idiom. The playfulness of the colors and forms, the way that the artist has left visible his brushstrokes and even allowed the primed canvas to show through where some of the colors meet, bespeaks a simplicity and directness and suggests a landscape of personal accommodation. Leaving aside the stereotypical attributes of the Orient that could be read out of this image, the image is innately subjective. Viewers see not Morocco, but the artist's Morocco.

While landscape continues to mediate relations between viewers and the world, in the works of Renoir and Matisse the colonial landscape becomes so subjectively rendered that the artists transmute the nature of the territory into the stuff of dreams and fantasies. It is not that these colonial spaces, or the power relations proper to their governance, had become any less real, but these landscapes make colonial locations more personal, subjective, and immediate. The territory—the very grounding of colonialism—comes to belong to viewers not through deed or title but through imagination. Such is the power of artistic projection. By seizing the means to translate the world through landscape imagery, by referencing the practice of picture making in equal terms to the subject of landscape, Renoir and Matisse demonstrated how realms of imperial power could be transmogrified into lovely, vibrant images. This may be the most insidious pictorial form of colonial ideology surveyed here, but the subjectification of colonial imagery allows for an unprecedented engagement by the viewer in the empire of landscape.

These two landscape paintings are not falsifications, or even obfuscations. Rather, *Festival of Algiers* and *Periwinkles* make visible a real transformation of the world. The Maghreb portrayed by these artists is one of their own making, but this subjectivity was itself wrought from generations of imperialism abroad. These images are not negations of previous ideas of place, as was the case with the map of 1870. Instead, they reflect how those places—indeed, all places—have become subject to redefinition despite their natural characteristics and often disputed histories. Artistic representation is but one form of image production, one way for a space to be redefined. The empire of landscape is finally personal, something we all carry around within us and apply to the world as the need arises. Our task and our responsibility, even, is to remake it—through image and through imagination—and thereby come to participate in it not as passive spectators but as active viewers.

Figure 75.
Henri Matisse, *Periwinkles, Moroccan Garden*, 1912. Oil, pencil, and charcoal on canvas, 116.8 × 82.5 cm. The Museum of Modern Art, New York. Gift of Florence M. Shoenborn (341.1985). © Succession H. Matisse, Paris/ARS, New York. Photo © The Museum of Modern Art, licensed by Scala/Art Resource, New York.

Notes

Introduction

1. Edward Said, *Orientalism: Western Representations of the Orient* (New York: Vintage, 1978).

2. Donald A. Rosenthal, *Orientalism: The Near East in French Painting, 1800–1900* (Rochester, N.Y.: Memorial Art Gallery, 1982); Lynne Thornton, *Les Orientalistes: Artistes-Voyageurs, 1828–1908* (Paris: ACR Éditions, 1983); MaryAnne Stevens, *The Orientalists: Delacroix to Matisse; European Painters in North Africa and the Near East* (London: Royal Academy of Arts, 1984); and Roger Benjamin, *Orientalism: Delacroix to Klee* (Melbourne: Art Gallery of New South Wales, 1997).

3. Three examples would be Todd Porterfield, *The Allure of Empire: Art in the Service of French Imperialism, 1798–1836* (Princeton: Princeton University Press, 1998); Darcy Grimaldo Grigsby, *Extremities: Painting Empire in Post-Revolutionary France* (New Haven: Yale University Press, 2002); and Roger Benjamin, *Orientalist Aesthetics: Art, Colonialism, and French North Africa (1880–1930)* (Berkeley and Los Angeles: University of California Press, 2003).

4. Dominque Bernasconi, "L'Image de l'Algérie dans l'iconographie française (1830–1871)" (mémoire de maîtrise, L'Institut d'Études Politiques de l'Université de Paris, 1970).

5. Abigail Solomon-Godeau, "A Photographer in Jerusalem, 1855: Auguste Salzmann and His Times," *October* 18 (Fall 1981): 91–107; James R. Ryan, *Picturing Empire: Photography and the Visualization of the British Empire* (Chicago: University of Chicago Press, 1997); James R. Ryan and Joan Schwartz, *Picturing Place: Photography and the Geographical Imagination* (London: I. B. Tauris, 2003); *Photographes en Algérie au XIXe siècle* (Paris: Musée-Galerie de la Seita, 1999); Zeynep Çelik, "Framing the Colony: Houses of Algeria Photographed," *Art History* 27, no. 4 (2004): 616–26.

6. Homi Bhabha, *The Location of Culture* (London: Routledge, 1994); Deborah Cherry, "Algeria In and Out of the Frame: Visuality and Cultural Tourism in the Nineteenth Century," in *Visual Culture and Tourism*, ed. David Crouch and Nina Lübbren (Oxford: Berg, 2003), 41–58.

7. Jill H. Casid, *Sowing Empire: Landscape and Colonialism* (Minneapolis: University of Minnesota Press, 2005). In this important work on the topic of landscape and colonialism, Casid points out some of the limitations of Bhabha's model of hybridization.

8. Said confronts this problematic in his later work. Edward Said, *Culture and Imperialism* (New York: Vintage, 1993), 31–35.

9. The catalogue *De Delacroix à Renoir: L'Algérie des peintres* provides an important step forward in terms of analyzing the imagery produced in France depicting Algeria in a wide range of media. The team of scholars that takes up this topic brings to light much new material as well as new perspectives from which to understand it. *De Delacroix à Renoir: L'Algérie des peintres* (Paris: Institut du Monde Arabe, 2003). See also Peter Benson Miller, "Théodore Chassériau and the French Colonial Project in Algeria" (Ph.D. diss., New York University, 2003), and Miller, "By the Sword and the Plow: Théodore Chassériau's Cour des Comptes Murals and Algeria," *Art Bulletin* 87, no. 4 (2005): 690–718.

10. An exception here would be the work of Christine Peltre. See Peltre's *Atelier du voyage: Les Peintres en Orient au XIXe siècle* (Paris: Gallimard, 1995) and *Orientalism in Art,* trans. John Goodman (New York: Abbeville, 1998).

11. This is less the case in the study of American painting, where numerous scholarly books and catalogues have contributed to a better understanding of the significance of landscape to the United States in the nineteenth century. John Davis's *Landscape of Belief: Encountering the Holy Land in Nineteenth-Century American Art and Culture* (Princeton: Princeton University Press, 1996) is particularly relevant to this study, but Barbara Novak's *Nature and Culture: American Landscape Painting, 1825–1875* (Oxford: Oxford University Press, 1980), is definitely a touchstone in the study of landscape and is currently in its third edition. See also Edward S. Casey, *Representing Place: Landscape Painting and Maps* (Minneapolis: University of Minnesota Press, 2002).

12. Two pioneering works, one recent and the other less so, on the category of landscape in nineteenth-century France are Nicholas Green, *The Spectacle of Nature: Landscape and Bourgeois Culture in Nineteenth-Century France* (Manchester: Manchester University Press, 1990), and Greg M. Thomas, *Art and Ecology in Nineteenth-Century France: The Landscapes of Théodore*

Rousseau (Princeton: Princeton University Press, 2000).

13. Various essays on this topic are featured in Denis Cosgrove and Stephen Daniels, eds., *The Iconography of Landscape: Essays on the Symbolic Representation, Design, and Use of Past Environments* (Cambridge: Cambridge University Press, 1988). See also Denis Cosgrove, *Social Formation and Symbolic Landscape* (London: Croom Helm, 1984); W. J. T. Mitchell, ed., *Landscape and Power* (Chicago: University of Chicago Press, 1994); and Martin Warnke, *Political Landscape: The Art History of Nature* (London: Reaktion Books, 1994).

14. Exceptions include Robert Herbert, *Monet on the Normandy Coast* (New Haven: Yale University Press, 1994), and Renzo Dubbini, *Geography of the Gaze: Urban and Rural Vision in Early Modern Europe,* trans. Lydia G. Cochrane (Chicago: University of Chicago Press, 2002).

15. Anthony Pagden, *Lords of All the World: Ideologies of Empire in Spain, Britain, and France, c. 1500–c. 1800* (New Haven: Yale University Press, 1995), 2.

16. Pierre-Paul LeRoy-Beaulieu, *De la colonization chez les peuples modernes* (Paris: Plon, 1874).

17. According to the Oxford English Dictionary, the term *landscape* was first used in 1599 to describe pictures of the world, but it is compelling to think of the term arising from the combination of the Dutch terms *land* and *schappen*, meaning literally "to create land," as in to reclaim it from the sea. My thanks to Robert Herbert for pointing out this derivation.

18. Stephen Daniels and Denis Cosgrove, "Introduction: Iconography and Landscape," in Cosgrove and Daniels, *The Iconography of Landscape*, 1.

19. A number of authors have informed my thinking on this topic. Among them are Henri Lefebvre, *The Production of Space*, trans. Donald Nicholson-Smith (Oxford: Blackwell, 1991); Timothy Mitchell, *Colonizing Egypt* (Berkeley and Los Angeles: University of California Press, 1991); and Derek Gregory, *Geographical Imaginations* (Oxford: Blackwell, 1994).

20. On the colonial spatial order in Algeria, see Frantz Fanon, *The Wretched of the Earth*, trans. Constance Farrington (New York: Grove Press, 1967), and Zeynep Çelik, *Urban Forms and Colonial Confrontations: Algiers Under French Rule* (Berkeley and Los Angeles: University of California Press, 1997).

21. These questions are productively examined in William Cronon, *Changes in the Land: Indians, Settlers, and the Ecology of New England* (New York: Hill and Wang, 1983).

22. Michael Hardt and Antonio Negri, *Empire* (Cambridge: Harvard University Press, 2000). Countless books and articles have emerged to challenge the claims of this work.

Chapter 1

The epigraph to this chapter is drawn from Denis Cosgrove, "Prospect, Perspective, and the Evolution of the Landscape Idea," *Transactions of the Institute of British Geographers* 10 (1985): 45–62.

1. Langlois (1789–1870) has recently received a retrospective exhibition at the Musée des Beaux-Arts, Caen; see François Robichon et al., *Jean-Charles Langlois (1789–1870): Le Spectacle de l'histoire* (Caen: Musée des Beaux-Arts, 2005). John Zarobell, "Fragments of a Dream (History)," review of *Jean-Charles Langlois (1789–1870): Spectacle de l'histoire, Nineteenth-Century Art Worldwide* 5, no. 1 (2006). See also Marie-Paule Petit, "L'Oeuvre algérois de Jean-Charles Langlois," 3 vols. (thèse de troisième cycle, Université de Paris I, [ca. 1983]); E. Charles Bourseul, *Biographie du Colonel Langlois, fondateur et auteur des panoramas militaires* (Paris: Dupont, 1874); and Stephan Oettermann, *The Panorama: History of a Mass Medium*, trans. Deborah Lucas-Schneider (New York: Zone Books, 1997), 158–64.

2. Napoléon's expedition to Egypt (1798–1800) was the prototype for the convergence of military conquest and the gathering of information and images. Though this venture turned out to be a military failure, the material compiled by artists and scholars who traveled to Egypt was published in the twenty-two-volume *Description d'Égypte* between 1809 and 1822. The *Description* and the Egyptian campaign have been analyzed by Said in *Orientalism*, 80–87, and, more recently, by Anne Godlewska, "Map, Text, and Image: The Mentality of the Enlightened Conquerors; A New Look at the *Description de l'Egypte,*" *Transactions* 20, no. 1 (1995): 5–28. Paintings representing the campaign have been addressed by Darcy Grimaldo Grigsby, "Rumor, Contagion, and Colonization in Gros's *Plague-Stricken of Jaffa* (1804)," *Representations* 51 (Fall 1995): 1–46; Todd Porterfield, *The Allure of Empire: Art in the Service of French Imperialism, 1798–1836* (Princeton: Princeton University Press, 1998), 43–80; Darcy Grimaldo Grigsby, *Extremities: Painting Empire in Post-Revolutionary France* (New Haven: Yale University Press, 2002); and David O'Brien, *After the Revolution: Antoine-Jean Gros, Painting, and Propaganda Under Napoleon* (University Park: Penn State University Press, 2006). One distinction between this earlier expedition and the conquest of Algiers

is that, in the era of the École Polytechnique, the military officers also performed the tasks of scholars and artists. This is the case with Langlois, who attended the École Polytechnique in 1806.

3. This study relies on primary sources wherever possible, but comprehensive histories can be very useful: see Charles-André Julien, *Histoire de l'Algérie contemporaine,* vol. 1, *La Conquête et les débuts de la colonisation (1827–1871)* (Paris: Presses Universitaires de France, 1964). The classic analysis of the way the French military commissioned and influenced visual representations appears in Gabriel Esquer, *Iconographie historique de l'Algérie jusqu'à 1871* (Paris: Plon, 1929), 1:I–XXXVII. Another helpful work is Dominique Bernasconi, "L'Image de l'Algérie dans l'iconographie française (1830–1871)" (mémoire de maîtrise, L'Institut d'Études Politiques de l'Université de Paris, 1970).

4. Almost all of the works published in France concerning Algiers at the time listed piracy as one of the central reasons for the conquest: "Ainsi, en vingt jours, cette armée avait vengé le pavillon français, détruit la piraterie, et enfin accompli les voeux qui formaient depuis trois siècles les hommes généreux et éclairés de toutes les nations." See Pierre-Paul Denniée, *Précis historique et administratif de la campagne d'Afrique* (Paris: Fain, 1830), 91.

5. See Esquer, *Iconographie historique,* vol. 1, and the recent work of Marion Vidal-Bué, *Alger et ses peintres, 1830–1960* (Paris: Hazan, 2000). Théodore Gudin's battle picture from the Salon of 1831 (#2966), *Attaque d'Alger par mer, prise des hauteurs qui dominent cette ville* (Versailles, Musée nationale du château), is taken from above but does not feature the city itself.

6. Of course, it was not the first image of Algiers that had been seen in Paris. Three artists submitted works featuring the Algerian campaign to the Salon of 1831: Julien Gilbert, Théodore Gudin, and Tancrède de Labouère. Esquer, *Iconographie historique,* 1:x. A group of six works by Eugène Isabey, entitled *Panorama du camp du Sidi-Ferruch (16–18 juin 1830),* may or may not have ever been executed, but a group of lithos, simply titled *Campagne d'Afrique,* remains. Atherton Curtis, *Catalogue de l'oeuvre lithographié d'Eugène Isabey* (Paris: Paul Prouté, n.d.). More commercial are the gouaches and aquarelles that were shown in 1830 at Le Cosmorama de l'abbé Gazzera, in the Passage Vivienne, and the panoramic views in oil, also shown in 1830, at the Musée Cosmopolite de Mazzara on the rue de Provence. Petit, "L'Oeuvre algérois," 1:178.

7. The price of 2 F 50, however, insured that only a bourgeois audience could afford such forms of "popular" entertainment.

8. "Fait des armes non moins glorieux pour la France que le combat naval de Navarin," Archives Nationales, Paris (CARAN), F21 8.

9. Deborah Cherry has discussed this historical development in her article "Earth into World, Land into Landscape: The Worlding of Algeria in Nineteenth-Century British Feminism," in *Orientalism's Interlocutors: Painting, Architecture, Photography,* ed. Jill Beaulieu and Mary Roberts (Durham: Duke University Press, 2002), 103–30.

10. Langlois' use of the camera obscura was first documented by Marie-Paule Petit. Petit, "L'Oeuvre algérois," 1:52.

11. Pierre-Paul Leroy-Beaulieu, *De la colonization chez les peuples modernes* (Paris: Plon, 1874).

12. I offer this reconstruction of the *Panorama d'Alger* in order to allow the reader a complete idea of the experience of this panorama. The facts provided in this description are culled from Jal's explanatory booklet, from contemporary critical responses to the panorama, and from Oettermann, *The Panorama,* 159.

13. My sources on the conquest of Algiers include A. M. Perrot, *La Conquête d'Alger, ou Relation de la campagne d'Afrique* (Paris: H. Langlois, 1830); Denniée, *Précis historique;* Auguste Théodore Hilaire Barchou de Penhoën, *Mémoires d'un officier d'état-majeur, expédition d'Afrique* (Paris: Charpentier, 1835); and, more recently, Julien, *Histoire de l'Algérie contemporaine,* 1:21–63, and Amar Hamdani, *La Vérité sur l'expédition d'Alger* (Paris: Balland, 1985).

14. Service historique de l'armée de Terre, Vincennes, Dossier Personnel, Colonel Jean-Charles Langlois.

15. École Polytechnique, *Livre du centenaire, 1794–1894* (Paris: Gauthier Villars et fils, 1897), 3:432–33. The authors note that Langlois received a second-class medal at his Salon debut in 1822 for his *Bataille de Sédiman.* See also Robichon et al., *Jean-Charles Langlois.*

16. Now housed in the Musée des Beaux-Arts, Caen.

17. The collection of Dr. François Bureau, Caen.

18. One of these is in the collection of Dr. Bureau, and the other is at the Musée Laplace, Beaumont en Auge, France.

19. Petit, "L'Oeuvre algérois," 1:45.

20. Fig. 1 is a compilation of numerous individual studies; figs. 2–6 are examples of these studies. Fig. 7 represents Pierre Prévost's third panorama rotunda, built in 1816 and different from that of Langlois in several ways. Nonetheless,

it should provide a visual sense of the basic structure of a panorama.

21. The painted sketches on paper from the collection of the Musée Langlois, Caen—now housed in the Musée des Beaux-Arts, Caen—were first annotated by François Robichon, who proposed dates for some of the works based upon when the architectural edifices featured were destroyed in the course of the French occupation. Yet even these dates are slippery, because Langlois seems to have produced some reconstructions of sites already destroyed. Documentation, Musée des Beaux-Arts, Caen, fichier Langlois.

22. One drawing in pencil is inscribed "Staoaely–19 juin," corresponding to the dates of the military encampment there that preceded the siege of 1830, while another small pencil sketch is labeled "ferme modèle," which was the first French attempt at agriculture in Algeria and did not exist before 1832.

23. Isabelle Bruller has argued that the representations of Algeria generated by the artists attached to the War Ministry between 1830 and 1837, such as Alexandre Genet and Gaspard Gobaut, possess a Romantic sensibility due to the artists' efforts to render the mystery of Algerian culture for the French viewer. Isabelle Bruller, *L'Algérie romantique des officiers de l'armée française, 1830–1837* (Vincennes: Service historique de l'armée de Terre, 1994). Though Langlois was not one of these officers, he would have worked alongside these men in the campaign of 1830.

24. This series began with Baron Taylor, *Voyages pittoresques dans l'ancienne France: Normandie* (Paris: Firmin Didot, 1819).

25. One contemporary commentator wrote, concerning the mosques of Algiers, "there are a few with quite remarkable interiors; one of these was demolished because it stood in the area that the French authorities wanted for a large public square; another has just been consecrated to the Catholic faith." D.-J. Montagne, *Physiologie morale et physique d'Alger, 1833* (Marseille: Camoin, 1834), 14.

26. Petit, "L'Oeuvre algérois," 1:245.

27. However, Langlois' personal experiences in Algiers certainly mattered to his contemporaries and supported the truth claims of his panoramic representation.

28. See Albert Boime, *The Academy and French Painting in the Nineteenth Century* (London: Phaidon, 1971), 150–55.

29. Apart from other, more informative purposes, the sketches sent back by artists like Genet and de Trelo were employed by notable artists working for the War Ministry to produce imagery for both the Salons and the ministerial collection. Artists such as Théodore Gudin, Théodore Jung, and Siméon Fort were charged with producing works to popularize the conquest in France and to provide a visual account of the military victory. See Bruller, *L'Algérie romantique,* and Esquer, *Iconographie historique,* 1:x–xiii.

30. *Aperçu historique, statistique et topographique sur l'état d'Alger, à l'usage de l'armée expéditionnaire d'Afrique* (Paris: Ch. Piquet, 1830).

31. Ibid., vi–viii.

32. Jean Adhémar provides a bibliography of lithographic illustrated books between 1817 and 1854, including a large number of instructional treatises on landscape representation. Two of those are A.-E. Michallon, *Cahier de quatre paysages animés, d'après nature* (Paris: Lasteyrie, 1817), and J.-A. Rousseau, *Élémens de paysage* (Paris, 1819). Jean Adhémar, *Les Lithographies de paysage en France à l'époque romantique* (Paris: Armand Colin, 1938), 284–366. Another instructional work to consider, particularly in relation to the officers of the État-major who were charged with recording information for maps, is L. N. Laspinasse, *Traité du lavis des plans, appliqué principalement aux reconnaissances militaires* (Paris: chez Magimel, Anselin et Pochard, 1818). This text includes instructions for mapmaking and landscape depiction.

33. While much information compiled in these volumes could have been provided by the Foreign Ministry, it is likely that they relied upon the most complete study of Algiers produced to that date, namely, Shaw's *Voyage in the Regency of Algiers*, which was translated and published in France as Shaw, *Voyage dans le Régence d'Alger* (Paris: Marlin, 1830). Shaw's work was the basis for later geographical explorations of Algeria, most notably by E. Carette and E. Renou.

34. Not surprisingly, the critic(s) who wrote in the official mouthpiece of the government, *Le Moniteur Universel,* and the one who wrote for the opposition paper, *Le Temps*, held different views of how the French military was handling the occupation. See below.

35. In *Techniques of the Observer*, Jonathan Crary has explored in depth the relationship between perception, perceptual models, and the visual arts in this period. This inquiry is laudable for its intellectual ambitions and its groundbreaking interdisciplinary research but Crary's intellectual history of modern perception detaches subjective perception from the object perceived. My interest is to inquire into the way that the subject comes into existence in

relation to a particular object, a colonial landscape. In this way, one can observe how perceptual techniques are conditioned by representational forms. Jonathan Crary, *Techniques of the Observer: On Vision and Modernity in the Nineteenth Century* (Cambridge: MIT Press, 1990). More relevant to my understanding of exhibition and visual truth are the analyses offered in Timothy Mitchell, *Colonizing Egypt* (Berkeley and Los Angeles: University of California Press, 1991); Derek Gregory, *Geographical Imaginations* (Oxford: Blackwell, 1994); and Roger Benjamin, *Orientalist Aesthetics: Art, Colonialism, and French North Africa (1880–1930)* (Berkeley and Los Angeles: University of California Press, 2003).

36. "C'est bien là l'Orient avec son courage et sa résignation morne, impassible devant le simoun de la civilisation Européenne!" Ch. L., "Panorama d'Alger: Peint par M. Ch. Langlois," *Le Cabinet de Lecture*, no. 259 (9 May 1833), 13–14.

37. In *Orientalism*, Said refers to latent and manifest Orientalism, a distinction that applies here.

38. "Le nom seul d'Alger éveille en nous mille sentiments divers; à sa vue, une sensation domine toutes les autres, c'est la surprise, l'étonnement. D'après les récits des historiens, des géographes, des voyageurs, vous avez pu vous faire une idée d'Alger, créer dans votre imagination une image de ce pays; devant le tableau de M. Langlois, ou plutôt dans la ville d'Alger, toutes ces créations vagues et imaginaires disparaîssent; ici tout est vrai, tout est exact, tout existe, tout vit de la vie la plus réelle." Al. C., "Beaux-Arts: *Panorama d'Alger*," *Le Moniteur Universel*, no. 121 (1 May 1834): 1696.

39. The Casbah was, in fact, the view of those who controlled the city. This palace was constructed in the sixteenth century, but it was Hussein Dey's predecessor who took refuge there in 1816 in order to avoid assassination and to be able to survey the entire region. Julien, *Histoire de l'Algérie contemporaine,* 1:2. While the rooftops of Algiers visible in the panorama would, of course, have offered visual access to the city, they would not have provided the complete view from the top. The Casbah palace was immediately occupied by the conquering general, Berthezène, after the capitulation of the Dey.

40. "Nous connaissons la physionomie du sol africain et de la nouvelle cité française, comme si nous avions traversée la Méditerranée." Anon., "Panorama d'Alger, par M. Langlois," *L'Artiste*, 1st ser., vol. 5 (1833): 45.

41. "Si je disais: Qui a vu le panorama de Londres est allé à Londres, je pourrais être taxé d'exagération; mais je ne serais que vrai en disant: Qui a vu le panorama de Londres sera en état de s'orienter dans Londres." E. F. A. M. Miel, *Essai sur les beaux-arts, et particulièrement sur le Salon de 1817, ou examen critique des principaux ouvrages d'art exposés dans le cours de cette année* (Paris: Didot le jeune, 1817–18), 347.

42. F. P., "Peinture: Panorama d'Alger, par M. Ch. Langlois," *Le Moniteur Universel*, 2nd supp., no. 59 (28 February 1833): 557.

43. This point was first made by Petit, "L'Oeuvre algérois," 1:157. It is noteworthy that the critiques of the *Panorama d'Alger* were often listed under the rubric of "Beaux-Arts," or even "Peinture," demonstrating that a distinct cultural category had not emerged into which panoramas could be fit. The most interesting rubric, from the *Memorial encyclopédique et progressif des connaissances humaines*, vol. 1 (1833), 113–14, is "Théâtre-Tableaux," emphasizing the double nature of the panorama as both image and spectacle.

44. Petit, "L'Oeuvre algérois," 1:166, suggests that this anonymous reviewer may well be Ludovic Vitet, because his regular column did not appear that day and because he was knowledgeable about optics in general and panoramas in particular.

45. "M. Langlois me paraît avoir poussé le genre panorama, en ne voulant plus en fair exclusivement un trompe-l'oeil. Il l'a haussé au rang de la grande peinture, en idéalisant et en embellissant la réalité": Eusèbe de Salle, "Le Panorama d'Alger," *Revue de Paris,* April 1833, 175.

46. Ibid. The critic makes several references to his own experiences in Algeria in the course of his review. As a further means to establish his authority, he even corrects the informational booklet edited by Jal (177–78).

47. Ibid., 176.

48. These changes are reported in a later review of the panorama: Ch. L., *Le Cabinet de Lecture*, no. 303 (19 December 1833), ii.

49. Petit, "L'Oeuvre algérois," 1:151.

50. "Triste condition des panoramas et qui en fixe la limite, que pour donner l'idée de la nature vivante, on soit contraint de l'y réduire aux seules apparences de la nature morte." Anon., "Beaux-Arts: Panorama d'Alger par M. Ch. Langlois," *La France Nouvelle*, 20 March 1833.

51. François Robichon, "Les Panoramas en France au XIXe siècle" (thèse du troisième cycle, Université de Paris X, Nanterre, 1982), 1:317.

52. Petit, "L'Oeuvre algérois," 1:61.

53. Walter Benjamin, *The Arcades Project*, trans. Howard

Eiland and Kevin McLaughlin, ed. Rolf Tiedemann (Cambridge: Harvard University Press, 1999). His essay "Paris—Capital of the Nineteenth Century" first appeared in 1935.

54. John Urry, *Consuming Places* (London: Routledge, 1995), 29.

55. Xavier Yacono, *Histoire de l'Algérie de la fin de la Régence turque à l'insurrection de 1954* (Versailles: Éditions de l'Atlanthrope, 1993), 86.

56. Walter Benjamin, "Paris–Capital of the Nineteenth Century" (1935 exposé), in *The Arcades Project*, 3.

57. Oettermann, *The Panorama,* 155.

58. Ann Bermingham, "Introduction: The Consumption of Culture; Image, Object, Text," in *The Consumption of Culture, 1600–1800: Image, Object, Text,* ed. Ann Bermingham and John Brewer (London: Routledge, 1995), 14.

59. Rolland Munro, "The Consumption View of Self: Extension, Exchange, and Identity," in *Consumption Matters: The Production and Experience of Consumption*, ed. Stephen Edgell, Kevin Hetherington, and Alan Warde (Oxford: Blackwell, 1996), 26. For a recent wide-ranging study of cultural consumption, see John Storey, *Cultural Consumption and Everyday Life* (London: Arnold, 1999).

60. Freud's concept of the fetish is relevant here. See Sigmund Freud, "Fetishism," trans. James Strachey, in *On Sexuality: Three Essays on the Theory of Sexuality,* ed. Angela Richards (New York: Penguin), 345–57.

Chapter 2

The epigraph to this chapter—"C'est le triomphe du people écrit sur les murs d'un palais par la main d'un roi!"—is drawn from *Le Moniteur Universel,* no. 164 (13 June 1837): 1494. The writer is anonymous.

1. This recreation of the official accounts of the opening of the *galeries historiques* at Versailles was generated by the author.

2. Thomas W. Gaehtgens, *Versailles: De la résidence royale au musée historique: La Galerie des batailles dans le musée historique de Louis-Philippe,* trans. Patrick Poirot (Paris: Albin Michel, 1984), 65–85.

3. On Vernet's Algerian works at the Museum of French History, see Valérie Bajou, "'Le Desert a pris place dans le palais de Versailles,'" in *De Delacroix à Renoir: L'Algérie des peintres* (Paris: Institut du Monde Arabe, 2003), 72–75.

4. See David O'Brien, *After the Revolution: Antoine-Jean Gros, Painting, and Propaganda Under Napoleon* (University Park: Pennsylvania State University Press, 2006). O'Brien brings to a new level the consideration of propaganda in large-scale military history painting of the nineteenth century, but there are differences between Napoleonic propaganda and that made under the patronage of Louis-Philippe, which will be discussed below.

5. "Désormais et pour toujours française," quoted in Dominique Bernasconi, "L'Image de l'Algérie dans l'iconographie française, 1830–1871" (mémoire de maîtrise, L'Institut d'Etudes Politiques de l'Université de Paris, 1970), 49.

6. Louis-Philippe, who inherited the Algerian conquest from the Restoration government of Charles X, seems to have been concerned predominantly with the international response to the seizure of Algiers. Historians of the French colonization of Algeria, such as Julien and Montagnon, devote precious little attention to him. See Charles-André Julien, *Histoire de l'Algérie contemporaine*, 2nd ed., vol. 1, *La Conquête et les débuts de la colonisation (1827–1871)* (Paris: Presses Universitaires de France, 1979), and Pierre Montagnon, *Histoire de l'Algérie des origines à nos jours* (Paris: Pygmalion, 1998).

7. The *galeries historiques* are known in English as the Museum of French History, and these two terms will be used interchangeably in this chapter. Michael Marrinan, *Painting Politics for Louis-Philippe: Art and Ideology in Orléanist France, 1830–1848* (New Haven: Yale University Press, 1988), 164. A very useful contemporary guide to the museum is *Galeries historiques du palais de Versailles* (Paris: Fain et Thunot, 1842). See also Gaehtgens, *Versailles.*

8. Nabila Oulebsir has written on Dauzats' journey to Algeria and the imagery that resulted. Nabila Oulesbir, "Paysage et patrimoine: Lieux et monuments de l'Algérie dans les années romantiques," in *De Delacroix à Renoir,* 100–107.

9. Although Dauzats was commissioned in 1836 by Louis-Philippe to produce *La Bataille d'Almanza, 25 avril 1707,* it was apparently not completed until the Salon of 1842 and was not included in the *grand galerie des batailles* of the recently formed *galeries historiques.* Documentation, *Musée national de Versailles*, MV 6679.

10. Charles Nodier, J. Taylor, and Alphonse de Cailleux, *Voyages pittoresques et romantiques dans l'ancienne France,* 20 vols. (Paris: Firmin Didot, 1820–78).

11. Charles Nodier, *Journal de l'expédition des Portes de Fer* (Paris: Imprimérie royale, 1844). This work will be the subject of the next chapter.

12. This point has been amply demonstrated in the

case of French painting under Napoléon by O'Brien, *After the Revolution,* and Darcy Grimaldo Grigsby, *Extremities: Painting Empire in Post-Revolutionary France* (New Haven: Yale University Press, 2002).

13. In 1930, the Gouvernement générale de l'Algérie dated the first *official* attempt at colonization to 18 April 1841, when Général Bugeaud issued a decree concerning the military adminstration's dispensation of land to colonists. See Gouvernement général de l'Algérie, Direction de l'agriculture et de la colonisation, *1830–1930: Cent Ans de la colonisation française en Algérie* (Algiers: Victor Heintz, 1930).

14. See Amédée Desjobert, *La Question d'Alger* (Paris: P. Dufart, 1837) and Général Duvivier, *Quatorze observations sur la dernière mémoire du général Bugeaud* (Paris: Gaultier-Laguionie, 1842).

15. Julien, *Histoire de l'Algérie contemporaine,* 1:132–35, and Montagnon, *Histoire de l'Algérie,* 173–82.

16. I have come across precious few references to the unsuccessful campaign in bibliographical references and have found it even more difficult to locate them in public collections in France today. To some degree, abbreviated accounts of this battle were publicly sanctioned as introductions to the subsequent victorious battle of 1837. For a contemporary account of the siege of 1836, I rely upon Un officier de l'armée de l'Afrique, "Expédition de Constantine," *Revue de Paris* 37 (January 1837): 193–202. L'Abbé Lammenais also addressed this failure directly in his weekly column in *Le Monde* and used it strategically in his attempt to rally against the conquest and colonization of Algeria. F. Lammenais, *Politique à l'usage du peuple* (Paris: Paguerre, 1839), 1:67–74, 2:2–9. While 1836 marks a low point in the number of publications on the subject of Algeria, such publications greatly increased in 1837 and 1838. Sir Lambert Playfair's bibliography of Algeria lists only five brief accounts that discuss the "disaster of Constantine," almost all published anonymously, whereas he notes more than twenty-five accounts of the siege of 1837, not to mention a flurry of writings about the potential colony and its relation to France in these years. See Playfair, "A Bibliography of Algeria," in *Royal Geographical Society—Supplementary Papers* (London: Royal Geographical Society, 1889), 175–82.

17. Julien, *Histoire de l'Algérie contemporaine,* 1:1–20.

18. C. M. Andrew and A. S. Kanya-Forstner, "Center and Periphery in the Making of the Second French Colonial Empire," *Journal of Imperial and Commonwealth History* 16, no. 3 (1988): 9–34.

19. The first reference I have come across to "l'Algérie," as opposed to "la Régence d'Alger" or simply "Alger," is from a work published in 1836 by Armand Pignel entitled *Guide du voyageur et du colon de Paris à Alger et dans l'Algérie* (Paris: Debécourt, 1836). This is but one of three references to "l'Algérie" made in book and periodical titles before 1838, when "l'Algérie" is suddenly the predominant term referring to the region under French military occupation. Bernasconi, "L'Image de l'Algérie," 133, dates the official origin of the term "l'Algérie" to a discourse in the Chamber of Deputies on 18 December 1837.

20. Gabriel Esquer, *Iconographie historique de l'Algérie* (Paris: Plon, 1929), 1:xxx. Also see Service historique de l'armée de Terre, Vincennes, 1 H 227.

21. This was the most important treaty between the French and the Algerians in which Abd-el-Kader, the leader of the Arab population of Algeria, recognized French sovereignty and agreed to respect it as long as the French agreed to certain territorial limits. Because Abd-el-Kader felt that the French had violated this treaty with the Expédition des Portes-de-Fer, he sent forces to destroy French settlements in the Mitidja, the fertile plain just outside Algiers, in November 1839.

22. Though the Bugeaud plan was not published independently until 1842, it was already the target of Genty de Bussy, *De l'établissement des français dans la régence d'Alger et des moyens d'en assurer la prospérité,* in 1839. Genty de Bussy was a former Intendant civile of Algiers who criticized the military's bungling of diplomacy with the native population and suggested a plan of civil colonization.

23. The most notable general countering Bugeaud was Général Duvivier, *Quatorze observations.* Prosper Enfantin, *Colonisation de l'Algérie* (Paris: Bertrand, 1843). Originally, Enfantin was a member of the Scientific Commission of Algeria, but he did not ultimately produce an official volume.

24. Le Centre des archives d'outre-mer (CAOM), Aix-en-Provence, F80, 1586.

25. Alexis de Tocqueville, *Oeuvres,* vol. 1, ed. André Jardin, Françoise Mélonio, and Lise Queffélec (Paris: Gallimard, 1981), 659–759. This journey led de Tocqueville to produce a "Travail sur l'Algérie" in October, 1841.

26. Two examples of this sort of writing are Eugène Buret, *Question d'Afrique et la double conquête de l'Algérie par la guerre et la colonisation* (Paris: Ledoyen, 1842) and J. Czynski, *Colonisation d'Alger* (Paris: L. Bouchard-Huzard, 1839).

27. A list of the works written on the topic of Algerian

colonization between 1837 and 1844 would be too extensive to be of much use. Some of the more significant works I have consulted and not yet cited include Evariste Bavoux, *Alger: Voyage politique et descriptif dans le nord d'Afrique* (Paris: Brockhaus et Avenarius, 1841); Jérôme-Adolphe Blanqui, *Algérie: Rapport sur la situation économique de nos possessions dans le nord de l'Afrique* (Paris: W. Coquebert, 1840); Thomas-Robert Bugeaud, *L'Algérie: Des Moyens de conserver et d'utiliser cette conquête* (Paris: Dentu, 1842); Amédée Desjobert, *L'Algérie en 1838* (Paris: P. Dufart, 1838); Alfred Franque, *Synthèse de la question d'Afrique* (Paris: Corréard, 1840); and François LeBlanc de Prébois, *L'Algérie prise au sérieux* (Paris: Gaultier-Laguionie, 1842). For a more complete bibliography, see Playfair, "A Bibliography of Algeria."

28. Most notably Amédée Desjobert, Député de la Seine-Inférieur, but Xavier de Sade had also argued against the colonization of Algeria in 1834 and remained an opponent to the *colonistes.*

29. This position was exemplified by the most well-informed and carefully reasoned approaches penned by authors such as Tocqueville, Jérôme Blanqui, Genty de Bussy, and LeBlanc de Prébois, among others.

30. The date of 18 April 1841 was the start of official colonization in Algeria. A decree was issued by Bugeaud, then governor-general, specifying the terms of government land concessions. The settler at first received a provisional concession and had to fulfill a list of stipulations, such as residing upon and working the land, in order to keep it. *Cent Ans de colonisation française en Algérie*, 19.

31. Twenty-four battle paintings by Vernet are listed in the catalogue of paintings of the palace of Versailles. Claire Constans, *Musée national du château de Versailles, catalogue des peintures* (Paris: Réunion des musées nationaux, 1980), 131–32.

32. The most recent text focusing exclusively on the Museum of French History is Laurent Gervereau and Claire Constans, eds., *Le Musée révélé: L'Histoire de France au château de Versailles* (Paris: Robert Laffont, 2005). See also Gaehtgens, *Versailles.*

33. Documentation Musée de Versailles, MV 2021–3. This commission for seven paintings was made on 30 April 1838 for a total of 220,000 francs.

34. This title would, of course, serve as a direct translation of the Vatican's Sala di Constantina by Raphael and his studio (1520), and the similarity is no coincidence.

35. Marrinan would perhaps disagree with my evaluation of Louis-Philippe's weakness for bombast, though Vernet's paintings speak for themselves and he was commissioned to produce them time and again. Nevertheless, Marrinan's argument about *juste-milieu* painting, though it leaves aside a possible "Golden Mean" translation, is worth quoting here: "When the accessible, didactic, and journalistic formulas of small-scale genre historique compositions were reformatted to a heroic scale and infused with the persuasive power of popular art for the grand public gallery spaces of Versailles, Louis-Philippe created—with a premeditated, selectively focused fusion of pragmatic, noncosmic concerns—a history picture which might appropriately be called *juste-milieu.*" Marrinan, *Painting Politics,* 210–11. See also Léon Rosenthal, *Du romantisme au Realisme: Essai sur l'évolution de la peinture en France de 1830 à 1848* (Paris: H. Laurens, 1914), and Albert Boime, *The Academy and French Painting in the Nineteenth Century* (London: Phaidon, 1971) and *Art in an Age of Counterrevolution (1815–1848)* (Chicago: University of Chicago Press, 2004).

36. Of course, Vernet was not the kind of painter to let political regimes obscure his renown. He must have been very crafty indeed, for he received his first medal inducting him to the Légion d'honneur from Napoléon, painted the portrait of Charles X in 1828, and, after the July Monarchy, painted portraits of Cavaignac and Louis Napoléon during the Second Republic. Eventually, Napoléon III invented a new level in the Légion d'honneur to honor his contribution to France in 1863, the year of his death. Henri Roujon, *Horace Vernet* (Paris: Pierre Lafitte, 1910). On Vernet, see also J. Bertholon and C. Lhote, *Horace Vernet à Versailles, au Luxembourg et au Louvre: Critique et biographie* (Paris: Librairie Cournol, 1863); Charles Blanc, *Une Famille d'artistes: Les Trois Vernet, Joseph, Carle, Horace* (1898; Paris: Librarie Renouard, 1928); and *Horace Vernet, 1789–1863* (Paris: École nationale supérieure de beaux-arts, 1980).

37. Vernet's works were reviewed by a variety of critics, including Prosper Merimée, "Salon de 1839," *Revue des Deux Mondes;* Dréolle, "Salon de 1839," *La Revolution littéraire* (June 1839): 146; and Amans de Ch . . . et A . . . , *Examen du Salon de 1839, de l'état actuel de l'art en France, et des moyens d'améliorer le sort des artistes* (Paris: Bureau intermédiare de journaux, 1839), 6. Other reviews are discussed below.

38. "Quoi! l'on vous donne cinquante pieds de toile à couvrir, cinquante pieds de toile! ce qu'un peintre peut rêver de plus beau et vous ne faites qu'un procès-verbal à l'huile, vous ne traduisez tout simplement un entre-filet du *Moniteur*

Parisien!" Charles Blanc, "Salon de 1839," *Revue de Progrès Politique, Sociale, et Littéraire* 1, no. 5 (15 March 1839): 348.

39. "[J]ournaliste . . . il fait des articles coloriés sur les conquêtes du jour, il illustre les bulletins." Théophile Gautier, "Salon de 1839, X," *La Presse*, 18 May 1839.

40. *Paris Salon de 1839* (New York: Garland, 1977), 218–19.

41. Grigsby, *Extremities*; O'Brien, *After the Revolution*.

42. Christian Delporte, "Louis-Philippe réinvente l'histoire de France," in *Le Musée révélé*, 31.

43. Bertholon and Lhote, *Horace Vernet à Versailles*, 6.

44. Esquer, *Iconographie historique*, 1:xv.

45. Vernet was the director of the French Academy in Rome from 1828 until 1835, and he originally embarked for Algeria from Rome. Vernet would have had ample opportunities to study the Vatican and other palaces where the Italian masters of the Renaissance produced monumental propaganda for their powerful and rich patrons. See Roger Diederen, ed., *French Artists in Rome: Ingres to Degas, 1803–1873* (New York: Dahesh Museum of Art, 2003), and *Horace Vernet, 1789–1863*.

46. François Robichon et al., *Jean-Charles Langlois (1789–1870): Le Spectacle de l'histoire* (Caen: Musée des Beaux-Arts, 2005), 19. In fact, Langlois also produced a panorama study and two monumental paintings for the Museum of French History that were featured at the Salon of 1839 (see *Paris Salon de 1839*, 131).

47. Guy Debord, *The Society of the Spectacle*, trans. Donald Nicholson-Smith (New York: Zone Books, 1994), 12.

48. Roujon, *Horace Vernet*, 78. It should be noted that this work intended to celebrate Vernet, not criticize him. Including a book on him in Pierre Lafitte's series of single-artist books places him beside not only old masters but widely acknowledged modern ones as well.

49. Blanc, "Salon de 1839," 348.

50. Frédéric Goupil-Fesquet, *Voyage d'Horace Vernet en Orient* (Paris: Challamel, 1843). This book, which describes a journey that took place in 1839, establishes Vernet's early use of the daguerreotype. See also Nissan N. Perez, *Focus East: Early Photography in the Near East (1839–1885)* (New York: Harry N. Abrams, 1988).

51. This point is refuted by Walter Benjamin in "The Work of Art in the Age of Mechanical Reproduction," in *Illuminations*, trans. Henry Zohn (New York: Schocken Books, 1986).

52. J. B. Deperthes, *Théorie du paysage* (Paris: chez Lenormant, 1818). This work, which explores the visual depiction of landscape in broadly theoretical terms, is largely indebted to the teachings and writings of Pierre-Henri de Valenciennes, *Elemens de perspective pratique* . . . (Paris: Desenne and Duprat, Year VIII [1800]), and the writings of Roger de Piles on visual attention and the elements of landscape painting. See Roger de Piles, *Cours de peinture par principes* [1708], ed. T. Puttfarken (Paris: Gallimard, 1989).

53. Descriptions of these terms can be found in Deperthes, *Théorie du paysage*.

54. John Barrell, *The Dark Side of the Landscape: The Rural Poor in English Painting, 1730–1840* (Cambridge: Cambridge University Press, 1980).

55. "[S]i vous avez tant de scruples, il faut alors compter les pierres et faire ce qu'a fait M. Langlois au Panorama, dans une intention bien autrement louable." Blanc, "Salon de 1839," 348.

56. "On sent bien, en voyant l'uniformité d'effet de ces compositions, que l'artiste n'a pas assez pensé avant de faire, qu'il n'a pas éprouvé la difficulté de l'art; mais s'il l'eût mieux sentie, nous n'aurions pas ces trios étonnantes representations." Amans de Ch . . . et A . . . , *Examen du Salon*, 6.

57. Two works likely made in Algeria are listed by Ghislaine Plessier in *Adrien Dauzats, ou, La Tentation de l'Orient: Catalogue raisonné de l'oeuvre peint* (Bordeaux: Musée des Beaux-Arts, 1990): figs. 26 and 36a. The letters are discussed in the next chapter.

58. Documentation, Musée du château de Versailles, MV 2662–2666. This commission for five watercolors at a price of 1800 francs (less than 1 percent of Vernet's commission) was made on 30 June 1840.

59. Nicole Garnier, *Delacroix au Maroc: L'Orientalisme au Musée Condé* (Chantilly: Musée Condé, 1992), 9–11.

60. While it is unquestionably rare to see watercolors measuring a meter in length in this period, there was a tradition of large-scale watercolors depicting the landscapes of Algeria by this point. In her discussion of Gaspard Gobaut, Isabelle Bruller notes that the War Ministry set out certain specifications for the representation of Algerian landscapes under his sponsorship, and the size is delimited as approximately 60 x 90 cm. Thus Dauzats' watercolors fit roughly the scale demanded for military commissions. Isabelle Bruller, *L'Algérie romantique des officiers de l'armée française, 1830–1837* (Vincennes: Service historique de l'armée de Terre, 1996), 54.

61. *Galeries historiques du palais de Versailles*, 1004.

62. This is the only composition that appears in the Versailles series but not in the Chantilly series. Its full title is *Les Soldats atteignent la seconde muraille calcaire des Portes-de-Fer* (Salon of 1841). It needs to be noted that there are discontinuities between the various sequences given in the three sets of images (Versailles, Chantilly, and the *Journal de l'expédition des Portes de Fer)*. This image is the second in the Versailles series, but the first in the *Journal*. I was assured by the curator at Versailles, Xavier Salmon, that the frames of the Dauzats watercolors, which feature the titles, have never been removed. Therefore, the Versailles titles must be original despite the fact that the sequence does not match the others.

63. Baron Taylor published his *Voyages pittoresques* between 1819 and 1878, but most appeared during the July Monarchy. Dauzats began collaborating on them in 1827 and continued to work with Taylor until 1847. See Jean Adhémar, *Les Lithographies de paysage;* Gordon Nichols Ray, *The Art of the French Illustrated Book, 1700 to 1914,* 2 vols. (New York: The Pierpont Morgan Library, 1982); and Segolène Le Men, "Book Illustration," in *Artistic Relations: Literature and the Visual Arts in Nineteenth-Century France,* ed. Peter Collier and Robert Lethbridge (New Haven: Yale University Press, 1994). Six *voyages pittoresques* of Algeria were published before 1841, when Dauzats exhibited the Versailles watercolors at the Salon, and two more appeared before the *Journal* was published in 1844. See Esquer, *Iconographie historique.* I will consider the Passage des Bibans compositions in relation to these related works in the next chapter.

64. This comparison of the soldiers to ants in relation to the landscape was first employed by an anonymous critic in 1841. See "Salon de 1841: Dessins, aquarelles et pastels," *L'Artiste*, 2nd ser., 7 (1841): 348.

65. Plessier lists two extant and one lost oil painting of this subject, as well as another watercolor that does not belong to the two series under discussion. Plessier, *Adrien Dauzats,* 96–98.

66. On early Orientalist painter/travelers, see Lynne Thornton, *Les Orientalistes: Artistes-Voyageurs, 1828–1908* (Paris: ACR Éditions, 1983); Christine Peltre, *L'Atelier du voyage: Les Peintres en Orient au XIXe siècle* (Paris: Gallimard, 1995); and Peltre, *Orientalism in Art,* trans. John Goodman (New York: Abbeville, 1998).

67. "S'il faut le dire, nous n'attendions pas l'aquarelle cette admirable vigeur; il paraît qu'elle endurçit la guerre." Wilhelm Ténint, *Salon de 1841: Collection des principaux ouvrages exposés au Louvre* (Paris: Challamel, 1841), 26.

68. This idea and the suggestion that Dauzats illustrated a combat without an enemy were first articulated by Peltre in *Orientalism in Art,* 52–55.

Chapter 3

The epigraph to this chapter is drawn from Jean Adhémar, "Les Lithographies du paysage en France à l'époque romantique," *Les Archives d'Art Français*, 4th ser., 19 (1938): "Né presque au premier jour de la lithographie, et mort avec elle, le paysage pittoresque est peut-être le meilleur symbole. Ces images charmantes, d'une exactitude souvent discutable, mais d'une écriture amusante, légère et toujours séduisante, ont amusé et instruit les Français pendant plus d'un demi-siècle. Leur influence sur les moeurs et les idées, la littérature et le tourisme, valent à elles seules la peine d'être étudiées."

1. D'Eylac, "Essai bibliographique sur un grand livre illustré du XIXe siècle," *Revue Biblio-Iconographique*, 9e année, 3, no. 7 (July–October 1902): 321.

2. Charles Nodier, J. Taylor, and Alphonse de Cailleux, *Voyages pittoresques et romantiques dans l'ancienne France,* 20 vol. (Paris: Firmin Didot, 1820–78).

3. Maréchal Valée, "Rapport sur l'Expédition des Portes de Fer," *Le Moniteur Universel,* no. 316 (12 November 1839): 2007.

4. In a letter that Dauzats wrote to his former master, Gué, dated 8 August 1839, the artist informs his correspondent that he has been invited to participate in the expedition by the duc himself, and that naturally he accepted such a flattering proposition. Dauzats also wrote that he would collect drawings from the trip and compose them into an album "qui servir à lui rappeler les souvenirs de *cette promenade*" (emphasis mine). Archives municipales, Bordeaux, fonds Meaudre de Lapouyade.

5. D'Eylac's article reprints a document written by A. Poullain, a minister of the royal family, from 25 July 1844. This document states that on his return in 1839, the duc decided "de consacrer le souvenir de l'expédition des Bibans par un ouvrage qui rappelerait les faits d'armes et les principaux événements de cette compagne." D'Eylac, "Essai bibliographique," 321.

6. D'Eylac gives numerous details of the book's production (ibid., 320–40). For the classic description of illustrated book production and marketing during this period, see Jean Adhémar, *Les Lithographies de paysage en France à l'époque romantique,* Archives de l'Art Français 19 (Paris:

Armand Colin, 1938), 260–67 and, more recently, Gordon Nichols Ray, *The Art of the French Illustrated Book, 1700 to 1914* (New York: The Pierpont Morgan Library, 1986), and Roger Chartier and Henri-Jean Martin, *Histoire de l'édition française: Le Temps des éditeurs, du Romantisme à la Belle époque,* vol. 3 (Paris: Fayard, 1989).

7. Though their culture had adopted many aspects of the Islamic faith, the Kabyles retained enough of their distinct way of life—including a rough equivalent of private ownership of property and even their own written language—for them to be considered significantly different from the Arabs and Moors by French scholars of the period. See Patricia Lorcin, *Imperial Identities: Stereotyping, Prejudice, and Race in Colonial Algeria* (London: I. B. Tauris, 1995).

8. Valée, "Rapport sur l'Expédition," 2007–8.

9. Nodier, *Journal,* 256. The information transmitted in the illustrated volume is corroborated by many other journals that reported on the events, but the *Journal* offers the most comprehensive account of the expedition. See note 10.

10. The French press reported the expedition as it evolved. See *Le Moniteur Universel*, nos. 284–317 (11 October–13 November); *Le Constitutionnel*, nos. 312–18 (8–14 November 1839); *Journal des Débats Politiques et Littéraires* (22 October–13 November 1839), and *La Presse,* 29 October and 7 and 14 November 1839.

11. *Le Constitutionnel,* no. 318 (14 November 1839).

12. "Enfin, après avoir marché pendant plus de dix minutes dans une sorte de corridor formé de rochers énormes, dont le surplomb va toujours s'exhaussant, et après avoir tourné à droite, à angle droit, dans le lit même du torrent, nous descendons au fond d'un ravin étroit dominé de toutes parts, d'où la moindre résistance serait impossible contre les défenseurs du défilé, s'il s'en présentait quelques-uns. Là se trouve la première porte. C'est une ouverture de huits pieds de large pratiquée perpendiculairement entre deux de ces couches de roches parallèles, rouge dans le haut et d'un gris de fer vers leur base" (Nodier, *Journal,* 262).

13. Baron Taylor had been dispatched to Egypt by Louis-Philippe to guarantee that Mehemet-Pacha would deliver the promised obelisk. This was the same obelisk erected six years later in the Place de la Concorde in Paris. Ghislaine Plessier, *Adrien Dauzats, ou, La Tentation de l'Orient: Catalogue raisonné de l'oeuvre peint* (Bordeaux: Musée des Beaux-Arts, 1990), 19. See also Todd Porterfield, *The Allure of Empire: Art in the Service of French Imperialism, 1798–1836* (Princeton: Princeton University Press, 1998), 13–42.

14. Letter from Dauzats to A. Mayer, CAOM, 18 X 23.

15. Documentation, *Musée national de Versailles*, MV 3183. The commission for five watercolors at a price of 1800 francs was recorded on 30 June 1840. They were eventually paid for by the prince on 3 June 1841.

16. Nodier, *Voyages pittoresques.* On Dauzats' contribution to this project, see Anita Spadafore, "Baron Taylor's *Voyages pittoresques,*" Ph.D. diss. (Northwestern University, 1973), and Bruno Foucart, ed., *Adrien Dauzats et "Les Voyages pittoresques et romantiques dans l'ancienne France" du baron Taylor* (Paris: Fondation Taylor, 1990).

17. "Plus libre, plus original, plus rapide que le burin, le crayon hardi du lithographie semble avoir inventé pour fixer les inspirations libres, originales et rapides du voyageur qui se rende compte de ses sensations." Nodier et al., *Normandie,* 1:10.

18. "Ce voyage n'est donc pas un voyage de découvertes; c'est un voyage d'impressions, s'il est permis de s'exprimer ainsi" (ibid., 5).

19. Colin Campbell, *The Romantic Ethic and the Spirit of Modern Consumerism* (Oxford: Blackwell, 1987), 89.

20. Nodier, *Voyages pittoresques, Auvergne* (1829), vol. 1, plate 21.

21. Nicholas Green, *The Spectacle of Nature: Landscape and Bourgeois Culture in Nineteenth-Century France* (Manchester: Manchester University Press, 1990), 88.

22. D'Eylac, "Essai bibliographique," 340.

23. Adhémar, *Les Lithographies de paysage,* provides a comprehensive list of lithographic illustrated books between 1817 and 1856. Other sources on illustrated books in the period include a chapter on the *Voyages pittoresques et romantiques dans l'ancienne france* in Michael Twyman, *Lithography, 1800–1850: The Techniques of Drawing on Stone in England and France and Their Application in Works of Topography* (London: Oxford University Press, 1970), 226–56; Paul-Henri Michel, "The French Book in the XIXth Century," in *The Art of the French Book from Early Manuscripts to Present Time,* ed. André Lejard (Paris: Les Éditions du Chêne, 1947), 87–112; and, more recently, Ray, *The Art of the French Illustrated Book,* and Segolène Le Men, "Book Illustration," in *Artistic Relations: Literature and the Visual Arts in Nineteenth-Century France*, ed. Peter Collier and Robert Lethbridge (New Haven: Yale University Press, 1994).

24. Alexandre Dumas and Adrien Dauzats, *Quinze jours au Sinaï* (Paris, 1839).

25. Paul Blanchard and Adrien Dauzats, *San Juan d'Ulùa ou Relation de l'expédition française au Mexique, sous les ordres de M. le contre-amiral Baudin* (Paris: chez Gide, 1839).

26. See Paul Guinard, *Dauzats et Blanchard, peintres d'Espagne romantique* (Bordeaux: Feret, 1967).

27. There are two relevant prototypes worth noting here. The first is Pierre-Paul Denniée's *Précis historique et administratif de la campagne d'Afrique* (Paris: Fain, 1830), which contained some illustrations by Eugène Isabey. The second is le vicomte de la Thouane, *Album pittoresque de la frégate la Thétis et de la corvette l'Espérance: Collection de dessins relatifs à leur voyage autour du monde en 1824–26, sous les ordres de M. le baron de Bougainville* (Paris: Langlumé, 1827–28). In both cases the prints are separate from the texts, and neither of these works is as comprehensive.

28. The first illustrated book with images inserted into the text was A.-R. Lesage's *Histoire de Gil Blas de Santillane*, released by the publisher Paulin in 1835 with six hundred woodcuts by Jean Gigoux. Michel, "The French Book," 90.

29. Two examples of such works are Denniée, *Précis historique*, with illustrations by Eugène Isabey, and Captain Rozet, *Voyage dans la Régence d'Alger ou Description du pays occupé par l'armée française* (Paris: Bertrand, 1833).

30. An example of this phenomenon is Général Marey, *Expédition de Laghouat: Dirigée en mai et juin 1844* (Algiers: Bastide, 1845), with illustrations by La Tour du Pin.

31. Some examples of these texts I have consulted include E. Lessore and W. Wyld, *Voyage pittoresque dans la Régence d'Alger pendant l'année 1833 par M.M. E. Lessore et W. Wyld* (Paris: Charles Motte, 1833–35); Adolphe Otth, *Esquisses africaines, dessinées pendant un voyage à Alger et lithographié par Adolphe Otth* (Berne: Wagner, 1838); and the most significant, Adrien Berbrugger's *L'Algérie historique, pittoresque et monumentale ou recueil de vues, costumes et portraits faits d'après nature dans les provinces d'Alger, Bône, Constantine et Oran*, 4 vols. (Paris: J. Delahaye, 1843).

32. Gabriel Esquer lists twelve illustrated books on Algeria published between 1830 and 1850. See Esquer, *Iconographie historique de l'Algérie jusqu'à 1871* (Paris: Plon, 1929), 1:xxviii–xxxii.

33. In fact, Taylor wrote to Dauzats before his departure for Algeria, instructing him to return with drawings of particular sites in Constantine and Algiers. Bibliothèque nationale, Département des Manuscrits occidentaux, Naf 23192 (letter dated 23 September 1839). See also Plessier, *Adrien Dauzats, ou, La Tentation de l'Orient: Catalogue raisonné de l'oeuvre peint* (Bordeaux: Musée des Beaux Arts, 1990).

34. In the Bibliothèque nationale, Département des Estampes, the collection of Dauzats' drawings includes one drawing dated "8 août 1841" of the Maison carrée (fort Arabe) with a note to Raffet that makes clear that Dauzats was providing Raffet with a background for a figure composition. For more on Raffet, see the recent catalogue from the exhibition at Boulogne-Billancourt: François Robichon, ed., *Auguste Raffet* (Paris: Herscher, 1999), particularly the essay by Michèle Lefrançois, "Raffet et la conquête de l'Algérie."

35. The most comprehensive treatment of Decamps in recent years is Dewey Mosby, *Alexandre-Gabriel Decamps, 1803–1860* (New York: Garland, 1977).

36. "Ainsi nos lecteurs seront mis à même de connaître les contrées dont le panorama va se dérouler devant eux dans les tableaux intéressantes, d'autant plus exacts qu'ils ont été tracés sur les lieux par des hommes aussi habiles qu'impartiaux" (Berbrugger, *L'Algérie historique*, 1:v).

37. CAOM, F80, 645, undated letter.

38. Ségolène Le Men, however, has pointed out that reading illustrated books could be a collective enterprise. Le Men, "Book Illustration," 102.

39. 1843 was also the year that *L'Illustration* was launched, the first large-format illustrated journal produced in France.

40. I assume that the print that appears in Clausolles' book was copied from a lithograph made after one of Dauzats' watercolors from the Salon of 1841 by Imp. Petit & Bertauts (reproduced in Plessier, *Adrien Dauzats*, 65) because Clausolles gives his illustration the title of the *Seconde muraille*, as the print did, when this image actually features the *première muraille*.

41. Quetin, *Guide en Orient: Itinéraire scientifique, artistique et pittoresque* . . . (Paris: L. Maison, 1844), 645.

Chapter 4

The epigraph to this chapter is drawn from Charles Baudelaire, *Salon de 1859* (Paris, 1859): "Mais la lumière et la chaleur, qui jettent dans quelques cerveaux une espèce de folie tropicale, les agitent d'une fureur inapaisable et les poussent à des danses inconnues, ne versent dans son âme qu'une contemplation douce et reposée. C'est l'extase plutôt que le fanatisme. Il est présumable que je suis moi-même atteint quelque peu d'une nostalgie qui m'entraine vers le soleil; car de ces toiles lumnieuses s'élève pour moi une vapeur envirante, qui se condense bientôt en desires et en regrets. Je me surprends à envier le sort de ces homes étendus sous ces ombres bleus, et dont les yeux, qui ne sont ni éveillés ni endormis, n'expriment, si toutefois ils expriment quelque chose, que l'amour de repos et le sentiment du bonheur qu'inspire une immense lumière."

1. "C'est une sorte de clarté intérieure qui demeure, après le soir venu, et se refracte encore pendant mon sommeil. Je ne cesse pas de rêver de lumière; je ferme les yeux et je vois des flammes, des orbs rayonnants ou bien de vague réverbérations qui grandissent, pareils aux approches de l'aube; je n'ai, pour ainsi dire, pas de nuit. Cette perception du jour, même en l'absence du soleil, ce repos transparent traversés de lueurs comme les nuits d'été le sont de météores, ce cauchemar singulier qui m'accorde aucun moment d'obscurité, tout cela ressemble beaucoup à la fièvre." Eugène Fromentin, *Un Été dans le Sahara* [1857], in *Oeuvres complètes,* ed. Guy Sagnes (Paris: Gallimard, 1984), 128.

2. Peter Benson Miller has pointed out that the imagery produced during the Second Empire often contradicted Napoléon III's idealistic notions of engagement with the native population. Peter Benson Miller, "La Vision officielle de l'Algérie sous la règne de Napoléon III," in *De Delacroix à Renoir: L'Algérie des peintres* (Paris: Institut du Monde Arabe, 2003), 152–63.

3. Fromentin, *Oeuvres complètes*, 1370.

4. The first expedition to Laghoaut, directed by Général Marey in 1844, was peaceful, and the French successfully placed a local tribe loyal to their interests in power. In the ensuing years, the imbalance of power in the region, fostered both by the French and by their first adversary, Abd-el Kader, allowed France's opponents, led this time by Mohammed ben Abdallah, to gather strength and eventually seize control of the entire region. Général Marey, *Expédition de Laghouat: Dirigée en mai et juin 1844* (Algiers: Bastide, 1845), and Charles-André Julien, *Histoire de l'Algérie contemporaine*, 2nd ed., vol. 1, *La Conquête et les débuts de la colonisation (1827–1871)* (Paris: Presses Universitaires de France, 1979), 390–93. The official account of the siege is provided in the "Journal des opérations de la colonne expéditionnaire de M. le général Yusuf, du 10 septembre à la fin du décembre 1852," in 1H214, Société Historique de l'Armée de Terre, Vincennes. An account of the history of the region, and of the siege of 1852 in particular, is also featured in *Un Été dans le Sahara.*

5. Fromentin, *Un Été dans le Sahara,* 77–84.

6. This comment is from a foreword penned for the 1874 reissue of Fromentin's two Algeria travel narratives, *Un Été dans le Sahara* (1857) and *Une Année dans le Sahel* (1859). It is reprinted in Fromentin, *Oeuvres complètes*, 4.

7. The project to obtain this commission was actually undertaken by Fromentin's friend Armand du Mesnil, who petitioned the minister personally. While the title of the proposed work was left blank, the minister made it clear that his preference was for a military subject, featuring a "fait des armes" of Général Daumas or Général Canrobert. The final work was not a military landscape and was paid in January 1857. Archives Nationales (CARAN), Paris, F21, 81.

8. The authors of the monograph on Fromentin report the final work as titled *Halte des voyageurs à l'entrée au désert du Sahara.* It has disappeared and no reproduction of it is available. James Thompson and Barbara Wright, *La Vie et l'oeuvre d'Eugène Fromentin* (Paris: ACR Éditions, 1987), 164. See also James Thompson and Barbara Wright, *Eugène Fromentin, 1820–1876: Visions d'Algérie et d'Égypte* (Paris: ACR Éditions, 2008).

9. In an exchange of letters between the artist and the military administration, Fromentin makes clear his need of a military escort and letters from the governor-general. The government's response was to invite Fromentin to call directly upon the governor-general. Le Centre des archives d'outre-mer (CAOM), Aix-en-Provence, 53 S 1.

10. Jean-Pierre LaFouge, *Étude sur l'orientalisme d'Eugène Fromentin dans ces "récits algériens"* (New York: Peter Lang, 1988), 86.

11. Thompson and Wright, *La Vie et l'oeuvre d'Eugène Fromentin,* 114–15.

12. This point, while it expands the field of social relations to include colonialism, echoes the interests expressed by T. J. Clark in his chapter "On the Social History of Art" in *Image of the People: Gustave Courbet and the 1848 Revolution* (London: Thames and Hudson, 1973), 9–20.

13. The discursive formation established by Orientalist travel literature in the nineteenth century has been famously analyzed by Edward Said, *Orientalism: Western Representations of the Orient* (New York: Vintage, 1978), and a short list of works relevant to Fromentin would include Alphonse de Lamartine's *Souvenirs, impressions, pensées et paysages pendant un voyage en Orient (1832–33)* (1854), Gérard de Nerval's *Voyage en Orient* (1851), Théophile Gautier's *Voyage pittoresque en Algérie* (1845), and Gustave Flaubert's *Voyage en Égypte* (1849). When Fromentin published *Un Été dans le Sahara*, he had volumes sent to Lamartine and Gautier, among others.

14. This drawing is reproduced in Anne-Marie Christin, *Fromentin conteur d'espace* (Paris: Le Sycomore, 1982).

15. Thompson and Wright address the artist's use of grey paper in *La Vie et l'oeuvre d'Eugène Fromentin,* 117.

16. Fromentin, *Un Été dans le Sahara*, 92.

17. Ibid., 90.

18. For a discussion of alpine landscape imagery in the eighteenth and nineteenth centuries, see *Le Paysage et la question du sublime*, Musée de Valence (Paris: Réunion des musées nationaux, 1997).

19. Fromentin, *Un Été dans le Sahara,* 123.

20. Ibid., 90. This is also reported by MacCarthy, "Laghouat," 349.

21. Fromentin, *Un Été dans le Sahara*, 77: "Telle est la vue complète d'El-Aghouat du côté du nord; la première était plutôt une vision; celle-ci, plus étendue et dont je crois ne rien omettre, je te la donne pour une *vue*" (emphasis in original).

22. Christin, *Fromentin conteur d'espace*, 36.

23. Besides Christin and Thompson and Wright, the sketches have been addressed by Guy Barthèlemy, *Fromentin et l'écriture du desert* (Paris: L'Harmattan, 1997).

24. "Le ciel était d'un bleu de cobalt pur, l'éclat de ce paysage stérile et enflammé le rendait plus extraordinaire . . . je vis apparaître au-dessus d'une plaine frappée de lumière, d'abord, un monticule isolé de rochers blancs avec une multitude de points obscurs, figurant en noir violet les contours supérieurs d'une ville armée de tours, au bas s'alignait un fourré de vert froid, compact, légèrement hérissé comme la surface barbue d'un champ d'épis. Une barre violette, et qui me parut sombre, se montrait à gauche, presque au niveau de la ville reparaissait à droite, toujours aussi raide, et fermait l'horizon." Fromentin, *Un Été dans le Sahara*, 75–76.

25. "Là commence, dans ces étendues où disparaît le motif 'pittoresque,' la confrontation essentielle avec un autre espace où seule s'offre à l'oeil la nudité des terrains." Peltre, *L'Atélier du voyage,* 76.

26. In most climates, a thick stroke of pigment would take months to become completely dry. Fromentin reported that, while sketching in Laghouat at midday, his painting cracked like burning wood. Fromentin, *Un Été dans le Sahara,* 125.

27. Fromentin, "Preface," *Oeuvres complètes*, 7.

28. Christin, *Fromentin conteur d'espace*, 25, and Anne-Marie Christin, "Fromentin et le monde Arabe à travers *Un Été dans le Sahara* et *Une Année dans le Sahel*," *Colloque Eugène Fromentin* (Lille: Publications de l'Université de Lille, 1979).

29. Anne-Marie Christin, "Space and Convention in Eugène Fromentin: The Algerian Experience," trans. Richard M. Berrong, *New Literary History* 15 (1983–84): 567.

30. See the work of Barthèlemy, *Fromentin et l'écriture du desert;* Vladimir Kapor, "La Couleur anti-locale d'Eugène Fromentin," *Nineteenth Century French Studies* 34, nos. 1–2 (2005–2006): 63–74; Isabelle Daunais, *L'Art de la mesure ou l'invention de l'espace dans les récits d'Orient (XIXe siècle)* (Vincennes: Presses Universitaires de Vincennes, 1996); Elwood Hartman, *Three Nineteenth-Century French Writers and the Magreb* (Tubingen: Gunter Narr Verlag, 1994); LaFouge, *Étude sur l'orientalisme;* and Fouad Marcos, *Fromentin et l'Afrique* (Montréal: Éditions Cosmos, 1973).

31. Barbara Wright, ed., *Correspondance d'Eugène Fromentin* (Paris: CNRS, 1995), 1:969, letter of 9 September 1853.

32. Ibid., 1:960.

33. "La nécessité de les écrire à distance, après des mois, après des années, sans autre ressource que la mémoire et dans la forme particulière propre aux souvenirs condensés, m'apprit, mieux que nulle autre épreuve, quelle est la *vérité* dans les arts qui vivent de la nature, ce que celle-ci nous fournit, ce que notre sensibilité lui prête." Fromentin, preface to *Oeuvres complètes*, 7; emphasis in original.

34. E. Carette, "Recherches sur la géographie et la commerce de l'Algérie méridonale," and E. Renou, "Notice géographique sur une partie de l'Afrique septentrionale," in *Exploration scientifique de l'Algérie: Sciences historiques et géographiques,* vol. 2 (Paris: Imprimérie royale, 1844).

35. Gabriel Esquer, *Iconographie historique de l'Algérie* (Paris: Plon, 1929), 1:xxx and CAOM, F80, 1590–8.

36. The *Exploration scientifique de l'Algérie* was unquestionably inspired by Napoléon's wildly ambitious project for the *Description d'Égypte*, which employed 150 scholars to study and catalogue all aspects of Egypt and published 22 volumes between 1809 and 1822. In opposition to the lushly illustrated texts provided in the *Description d'Égypte*, the volumes of the *Exploration scientifique de l'Algérie* are for the most part not illustrated and favor a more statistical presentation of material. Such is the case with Carette and Renou's volume.

37. Eugène Daumas, *Le Sahara algérien: Études géographiques, statistiques et historiques sur la région au sud des établissements français en Algérie* (Paris: Crapelet, 1845).

38. Daumas produced a number of texts on Algeria designed for the French market. The most popular was his study of horses: Eugène Daumas, *Les Chevaux du Sahara* (Paris: F. Chamerot, 1851).

39. LaFouge, *Étude sur l'orientalisme,* 86.

40. Adding credence to LaFouge's argument is the fact that Fromentin's entries to the Salon of 1851 were accompanied by quotations from another text co-authored by Daumas, *Le Grand Désert,* which appeared in 1848. Thompson and Wright, *La Vie et l'oeuvre d'Eugène Fromentin,* 94.

41. LaFouge, *Étude sur l'orientalisme,* 88–102.

42. This man's name was Cheggeun, and he was from the Saharan Chambas tribe. Fromentin, *Oeuvres complètes*, 1299.

43. CAOM, 53 S 1.

44. Marcos, *Fromentin et l'Afrique,* 90–93.

45. Barthèlemy, *Fromentin et l'écriture du desert,* 136. Fromentin, *Oeuvres complètes*, 1261.

46. "C'est encore un essai d'un autre genre, pour regagner un peu de publicité, puisque aussi bien, par ma faute, ou autrement je l'ai bien et bel tout à fait perdue." Fromentin, *Correspondance*, 1:1004.

47. Thompson and Wright, *La Vie et l'oeuvre d'Eugène Fromentin,* 155.

48. Ibid., 157.

49. Fromentin, *Correspondance*, 1:1077–8, letter of 23 January [1857]: "en vous faisant à peu près souvenir que je suis peintre."

50. All three articles appeared in *L'Artiste.* The two pieces on *Un Été dans le Sahara* were published on 22 February and 1 March, and the Salon review appeared on 1 November 1857.

51. George Sand's response to *Un Été dans le Sahara* was very positive and created the basis for a lasting friendship between the two. Fromentin's third and most famous work, *Dominique,* is dedicated to her. She also published a favorable review of *Un Été* in *La Presse*, 8 May 1857.

52. Fromentin, *Oeuvres complètes*, 1355.

53. Eugène Fromentin, "Alger: Fragments d'un journal de voyage," *L'Artiste* 2 (26 July, 2 and 9 August 1857).

54. "Cette tache lointain d'alfa s'aperçoit à peine dans l'ensemble de ce paysage. . . . Elle leur a fait voir que le but est d'exprimer, et que pour y arriver, les moyens les plus simples sont les meilleurs. Elle leur a dit que l'idée est légère et demande à être peu vêtue. . . . Devais-je donc venir si loin du Louvre chercher cette importante exhortation de voir les choses par le côté simple, pour en obtenir la forme vraie et grande?" Fromentin, *Un Été dans le Sahara*, 56–57.

55. Eugène Fromentin, *Une Année dans le Sahel,* in *Oeuvres complètes*, 313: "profils de montagnes, formes de rochers avec le multiple détail intérieur des stratifications."

56. See Fromentin, *Oeuvres complètes.* This work has also been translated as Eugène Fromentin, *The Old Masters of Belgium and Holland,* trans. Mary C. Robbins, intro. Meyer Schapiro (New York: Schocken Books, 1963).

57. Eugène Fromentin, "Notes sur la genre dans la peinture," in *Oeuvres complètes,* 921–24, 1672–73.

58. Fromentin, *Une Année dans le Sahel*, 317–19.

59. A few recent publications on this painting include Todd Porterfield, *The Allure of Empire: Art in the Service of French Imperialism, 1798–1836* (Princeton: Princeton University Press, 1998), 117–41; Darcy Grimaldo Grigsby, "Orients and Colonies: Delacroix's Algerian Harem," in *The Cambridge Companion to Delacroix,* ed. Beth S. Wright (Cambridge: Cambridge University Press, 2001), 69–87; and *De Delacroix à Renoir.*

60. Fromentin, *Une Année dans le Sahel*, 313–27.

61. Thompson and Wright, *La Vie et l'oeuvre d'Eugène Fromentin,* 148–65.

62. W. J. T. Mitchell, in an attack on Gombrich's formulation of landscape, defines "pure landscape" as "a representation or perception of nature, 'for its own sake.' In art-historical terms, pure landscape is a painting in which natural scenery is depicted with no adulteration of narrative, allegory, drama, or other textual elements; ideally, in its purest form, pure landscape is even free of any human figures that might suggest an interpretable situation, a readable scenario beyond the pure display of natural forms for their own sake. . . . Pure landscape, like pure painting, is unreadable as a text, and unusable as a rhetorical or ritual object." W. J. T. Mitchell, "Gombrich and the Rise of Landscape," in *The Consumption of Culture, 1600–1800: Image, Object, Text,* ed. Ann Bermingham and John Brewer (London: Routledge, 1995), 104.

63. It should be noted that this geographical conception was predated by a similar argument in the art-historical analyses of Hippolyte Taine. Taine asserted, in a less scientific mode, that regional characteristics and social conditions determine the pictorial productions of artists. See Hippolyte Taine, *Philosophie de l'art* (Paris: Baillière, 1865).

64. Lucien Gallois, "Les Dombes," *Annales de géographie* (January1892). Gallois' system, which increased the scientific character of the discipline of geography, was based on geological analysis. See also Vincent Berdoulay, *La Formation de l'école française de géographie (1870–1914)* (Paris: Bibliothèque nationale, 1981), and Olivier Soubeyran, "Imperialism and Colonialism Versus Disciplinarity in

French Geography," in *Geography and Empire,* ed. Anne Godlewska and Neil Smith (Oxford: Blackwell, 1994), 244–64.

65. Despite my repeated attempts to contact the owners of this work and receive permission to see it, I have never seen this picture in person. My description of it is taken from a reproduction of the work in the catalogue for the sale at Christie's London (18 March 1994), Lot 138, and from factual descriptions offered by contemporary commentators.

66. Unfortunately, these studies, which were recorded and compiled by Barbara Wright during her work on the monograph, are now lost. I have seen slides of them in the descendants' collection.

67. "Evidemment amoreux de lumière et de couleur, M. Fromentin excelle à rendre l'une et l'autre et à les marier dans une harmonie extraordinairement plaisante . . . sa peinture nerveuse et profondément sentie . . . court légèrement sur la toile comme des couches d'air et communique une vive et durable impression. C'est bien l'Orient, l'Orient saharien avec ses nuances blondes comme du miel et ses immensités d'horizon que nul oeil n'a pu sonder." Maxime Du Camp, *Le Salon de 1857* (Paris: Libriarie Nouvelle, 1857), 127.

68. This view was not shared by Edmond About, who felt that Fromentin's use of impasto qualified him as a victim of Decamps. Edmond About, "Le Salon de 1857, XVI," *Le Moniteur Universel,* no. 248 (5 September 1857): 973.

69. Ibid.: "nous transportent commodément au sein d'une civilisation curieuse."

70. Théophile Gautier, "Le Salon de 1857, XVIII," *L'Artiste* 2 (1 November 1857): 129–30.

71. Jean Alazard, *Initiation à l'Algérie* (Paris: Adrien-Maisonneuve, 1957), 352–53.

72. Gautier, "Salon de 1857," 130: "Il n'y a là cependant ni sujet ni drame."

73. "Devant cette village sauvage qui a couté tant de sang à nos soldats et qui est maintenant une ville française, quoiqu'il n'en ait guère l'air avec son aspect de cimetière où l'on n'enterre plus. Toute cette nature étrange, invraisemblable, est rendu avec telle sentiment de réalité, qu'on la voit sur la toile comme si l'on était le peintre lui-même en face du site qu'il a représenté" (ibid.).

74. Fromentin, *Un Été dans le Sahara,* 109–10.

75. Gautier, "Salon de 1857," 129. This assertion is likely based on his reading of *Un Été dans le Sahara* and thus would demonstrate the critic's tendency to read the travel narrative as representative of the artist's experience.

76. Thompson and Wright title this work "Autoportrait en Arabe," though they note, "Il n'est pas certain que ce dessin soit un autoportrait, bien que sa resemblance avec Fromentin soit frappante; même s'il s'agit d'un Arabe, la similitude d'aspect physique en dit long sur l'affinité qui unissait l'artiste aux nomades du désert." Thompson and Wright, *La Vie et l'oeuvre d'Eugène Fromentin,* 145.

77. Of the seven, there were three hunting scenes, three caravan/merchant scenes, and one image of the *diffa.* Thompson and Wright (ibid., 157) have suggested that a small work entitled *La Caravane,* currently in the collection of the Musée St. Denis, Reims, could be the work that was entered into the Salon of 1857 as *Marchands Arabes en voyage.* Unfortunately, the records of the proportions of the works submitted to that Salon are not available at the Archives des musées nationaux, so it is impossible to establish this with any certainty.

78. Julien, *Histoire de l'Algérie contemporaine,* 1:394–95.

79. Thompson and Wright, *La Vie et l'oeuvre d'Eugène Fromentin,* 182.

80. On 14 April 1857, Fromentin wrote to the Minister requesting a commission for another painting of southern Algeria, and the official commission was granted on 23 January 1858 for "un tableau de paysage." The commission was paid on 7 April 1859, and though this document does not list the title, *Une Rue à Laghouat* was the only work bought by the state from Fromentin in 1859. An initial report by an inspector described the work as a "vue prise dans la ville du El-Aghouat." CARAN, Paris, F 21 81.

81. Jean Rousseau, "Salon de 1859, IV," *Le Figaro,* no. 444 (17 May 1859), 3–4.

82. Paul Mantz, "Le Salon de 1859," *Gazette des Beaux-Arts* (1 June 1859): 291: "paraît mettre une certaine coquetterie à publier un volume à l'ouverture de chaque exposition."

83. Alexandre Dumas, *L'Art et les artistes contemporains au Salon de 1859* (Paris: Librairie Nouvelle, 1859), 125–30.

84. Henri Dumesnil, *Salon de 1859* (Paris: Ve. J. Renouard, 1859), 59.

85. "Cette ombre des pays de lumière, tu la connais. Elle est inexprimable; c'est quelque chose d'obscur et de transparent, de limpide et de coloré; on dirait un eau profonde. Elle paraît noir, et, quand l'oeil y plonge, on est tout surpris d'y voir clair. Supprimez le soleil, et cette ombre elle-même

deviendra du jour. Les figures y flottent dans je ne sais quelle blonde atmosphère qui fait évanouir les contours. Regardez-les maintenant qu'elles y sont assises; les vêtements blanchâtres se confondent presque avec les murailles; les pieds nus marquent à peine sur le terrain, et sauf le visage qui fait tache en brun au milieu de ce vague ensemble, c'est à croire à des statues pétries de boue et, comme les maisons, cuites au soleil. Par moments seulement, un pli qui se déplace, un geste rappelant la vie, un filet de fumée qui s'échappe des lèvres d'un fumeur de *tekrouri* et l'enveloppe de nébulosités mouvants, révèlent une assemblée de gens qui se reposent." Fromentin, *Un Été dans le Sahara*, 106.

86. Rousseau, "Salon de 1859, IV," 3.

87. Perhaps this begins with Edmond Duranty's attack on Fromentin in "La Nouvelle Peinture" (1876), reprinted in Charles S. Moffett et al., *The New Painting: Impressionism, 1874–1886* (Geneva: Richard Burton SA, 1986), 37–50.

88. Gary Tinterow and Henri Loyrette, *Origins of Impressionism* (New York: Metropolitan Museum of Art, 1994), 387.

89. Gautier, "Salon de 1859," 613.

90. Paul de Saint-Victor, "Salon de 1859, IX," *La Presse*, 25 June 1859, 2.

91. Gautier, "Salon de 1859," 613. Gautier had made previous references to an ethnographic movement in the visual arts attached to artist/travelers in his "Salon de 1857," 129. The fact that this term was first applied to Fromentin's landscapes may seem odd to a current reader, since ethnographic art currently denotes Orientalist artists such as such as Jean-Léon Gérôme and Charles-Henri Cordier, who were very attentive to the kinds of genre details Fromentin was careful to avoid.

92. "La vapeur n'a pas tué l'art, et c'est peut-être elle qui le sauvera en lui ouvrant des horizons nouveau et en le portant en quelques jours au seuil des contrées vierges où s'est réfugié le pittoresque exilé de la civilisation. . . . Aujourd'hui la nature a remplacé le paysage historique, et les peintres se sont aperçus qu'il y avait d'autres hommes que les modèles d'académie; . . . et le Sahara voit maintenant se déployer autant de parasols de paysagistes qu'autrefois la forêt de Fontainebleau." Gautier, "Salon de 1859," 613.

93. Ali Behdad has termed this phenomenon "belated Orientalism," because travelers like Fromentin had to search further for an authentic experience abroad. See Ali Behdad, *Belated Travelers: Orientalism in the Age of Colonial Dissolution* (Durham: Duke University Press, 1994).

94. "J'avais visité l'Algérie à plusieurs reprises; je venais d'y pénétrer plus loin et d'habiter posémont . . . une sorte d'acclimation intime et définitive." Fromentin, preface to *Oeuvres complètes*, 4.

95. Denis Cosgrove, "Prospect, Perspective, and the Evolution of the Landscape Idea," *Transactions of the Institute of British Geographers* 10 (1985): 57.

96. Gautier, "Salon de 1857," 129.

Chapter 5

This epigraph is drawn from Ernest Lacan, "L'Algérie photographiée," *Le Moniteur Universel*, no. 343 (9 December 1858): 1493. "Mazagran, Beni-Mered, Zaatcha disparaîtront sans doute un jour, ou tout au moins seront absorbés dans l'envahissement de notre colonisation; mais le penseur, le poëte ou l'historien pourrent les retrouver avec leur aspect primitif dans le portefeuille de M. Moulin."

1. The most in-depth treatment of Moulin to date has been Estelle Fredet's master's thesis, "*L'Algérie photographiée* de Félix-Jacques-Antoine Moulin, et la politique algérienne de l'Empire" (mémoire de maîtrise sous la direction de M. Marc Michel, Directeur de I.H.P.O.M., 1993–94). Moulin's photographs of studio nudes have been examined in Elizabeth Anne McCauley, *Industrial Madness: Commercial Photography in Paris, 1848–1871* (New Haven: Yale University Press, 1994), and his works were included in the recent exhibition *De Delacroix à Renoir: L'Algérie des peintres* (Paris: Institut du Monde Arabe, 2003), *Photographes en Algérie au XIXe siècle* (Paris: Musée-Galerie de le Seita, 1999), as well as *Regards sur la photographie en France au XIXe siècle* (Paris: Petit Palais, 1980).

According to Moulin's letter to the journal *La Lumière*, dated 14 March 1856, Moulin made photographs in Algeria with two different processes, using "grands plaques," meaning glass negatives with wet collodion and also stereographic views. Only the former seem to have survived, however. "La Photographie en Algérie," *La Lumière* 6, no. 12 (22 March 1856).

2. Moulin made two panoramas of Constantine, and the other one was taken from the opposite side of the city and presents its more picturesque aspect.

3. Abigail Solomon-Godeau has written, "photography was a method of comprehending the world in terms of its exterior appearance. Photography itself was the technical analogue to the absolute belief in the legibility of appearances, a belief whose philosophical expression was, of course, positivism and whose artistic expression was realism

and naturalism." Abigail Solomon-Godeau, "A Photographer in Jerusalem, 1855: Auguste Salzmann and His Times," *October* 18 (Fall 1981): 98. This claim goes a long way toward explaining the significance of photography for the natural sciences, though I am not entirely convinced by her associations between photography and realism in painting.

4. Joel Snyder, "Territorial Photography," in *Landscape and Power*, ed. W. J. T. Mitchell (Chicago: University of Chicago Press, 1994), 181.

5. Ibid.

6. See Chapter 2 for a more complete description of Vernet's Salle de Constantine at the *galeries historiques*.

7. For more on the details of the siege, see Chapter 2. Other images of the city are discussed below.

8. French colonial urban planning in Algeria in the nineteenth century is a topic that has not been fully investigated by scholars. Zeynep Çelik has worked significantly on the city of Algiers, but her comprehensive study concentrates on the twentieth century. See Zeynep Çelik, *Urban Forms and Colonial Confrontations: Algiers Under French Rule* (Berkeley and Los Angeles: University of California Press, 1997), and Çelik, "Colonial/Postcolonial Intersections: Lieux de mémoire in Algiers," *Third Text* 49 (Winter 1999/2000). In his work focusing on the city of Bône, David Prochaska has also illuminated the French transformations of this city during the Third Republic. See David Prochaska, *Making Algeria French: Colonialism in Bône, 1870–1920* (Cambridge: Cambridge University Press, 1990).

9. Along with the previously cited work by McCauley, the most complete analysis of the development of photography in relation to the social transformations of mid-nineteenth-century France is André Rouillé, *L'Empire de la photographie: Photographie et pouvoir bourgeois* (Paris: Le Sycomore, 1982).

10. Ibid., 130.

11. Both of these images had an afterlife in guidebooks and illustrated journals and as prototypes of popular imagery. See Dominique Bernasconi, "L'Image de l'Algérie dans l'iconographie française (1830–1871)" (mémoire de maîtrise, L'Institut d'Études Politiques de l'Université de Paris, 1970). For example, the anonymous woodcut appears in 1865 in Achille Fillias, *Nouveau Guide général du voyageur en Algérie* (Paris: Garnier frères, 1865), and Jung's view is featured in Adrien Berbrugger, *L'Algérie historique, pittoresque et monumentale ou receuil de vues, costumes et portraits faits d'après nature dans les provinces d'Alger, Bône, Constantine et Oran,* 4 vols. (Paris: J. Delahaye, 1843).

12. Curiously, this image of the "attack" features precious few soldiers, who appear minute in this composition.

13. This album is conserved at the Archives de l'armée de Terre, Vincennes.

14. The first was the review by Lacan that provided the epigraph to this chapter: Ernest Lacan, "L'Algérie photographiée," *Le Moniteur Universel,* no. 343 (9 December 1858): 1493; G. Julien, "L'Algérie photographiée," *L'Illustration* 787, vol. 31 (27 March 1858): 200–201, and "L'Algérie—Publication nationale—M. Moulin," *Revue Photographique*, 3e année, no. 32 (5 June 1858): 80–82. Quotation from Julien, "L'Algérie photographiée," 200.

15. "L'Algérie—Publication nationale—M. Moulin," 81.

16. Both of these works are discussed in Chapter 3. Charles Nodier, J. Taylor, and Alphonse de Cailleux, *Voyages pittoresques et romantiques dans l'ancienne France*, 20 vols. (Paris: Firmin Didot, 1820–78) and Charles Nodier, *Journal de l'expédition des Portes de Fer* (Paris: Imprimérie royale, 1844).

17. William Henry Fox Talbot claimed to have invented photography, and he did invent the calotype in 1840, which made possible the multiple reproduction of prints from a single negative. His book *The Pencil of Nature* was originally published in 1844.

18. Implicit in his notion of landscape is a viewer who perceives and orders. Denis Cosgrove, *Social Formation and Symbolic Landscape* (London: Croom Helm, 1984), 27.

19. Rouillé, *L'Empire de la photographie,* 131–36.

20. James R. Ryan, "Imperial Landscapes: Photography, Geography, and British Overseas Exploration, 1858–1872," in *Geography and Imperialism, 1820–1940*, ed. Morag Bell, Robin Alan Butlin, and Michael Heffernan (Manchester: Manchester University Press, 1995), 73.

21. Newly planted deciduous trees are ubiquitous in the Algerian albums of Moulin and of another photographer I shall discuss below, the marquis de Courcival. They function as a sign of French colonial presence in the Algerian landscape.

22. According to Jammes and Janis, de Beaucorps employed the calotype method of printing, using waxed paper negatives. He exhibited this view of Constantine in 1859 at the Société française de photographie. Andre Jammes and Eugenia Parry Janis, *The Art of French Calotype: With a Critical Dictionary of French Photographers, 1845–1870* (Princeton: Princeton University Press, 1983), 148.

23. The whiteness of the building and the distinct architectural configuration visible in the original photo-

graph mark this building as both new and French, as opposed to the more traditional dwellings visible on the left side of the image.

24. The colonial context is also not immediately apprehensible here, because this image strongly resembles photographs of hill towns in southern France and northern Italy.

25. In the catalogue of a recent exhibition of Algerian photographs, this image is described as having been made with wet collodion and a glass negative. *Photographes en Algérie au XIXe siècle* (Paris: Musée-Galerie de la Seita, 1999), 76. Moulin employed the same process.

26. Fredet, "*L'Algérie photographiée* de Félix-Jacques-Antoine Moulin," 102. This fact leads her to the following conclusion: "Insensible à l'actualité, assez peu observateur, Moulin semble être guidé par une conception générale, préalablement élaborée par d'autres, sur la situation en Algérie" (106).

27. Malcolm Daniel, *The Photographs of Édouard Baldus* (New York: Metropolitan Museum, 1994).

28. Walter Benjamin, *The Arcades Project,* trans. Howard Eiland and Kevin McLaughlin, ed. Rolf Tiedemann (Cambridge: Harvard University Press, 1999), 465.

29. Daniel, *Photographs of Édouard Baldus.*

30. I employ this word as a direct translation of the French term "vulgarisation" despite the derogatory connotations it imports, because in the context of photography, where reproductions are multiple, the resulting depictions are at once more widely available and less precious than artistic depictions in which the hand of an author is in evidence. Vulgarization is also useful because it implies that the ideal, or original, has been somehow sullied in the process.

31. This point has been made most effectively by Walter Benjamin, "The Work of Art in the Age of Mechanical Reproduction," in *Illuminations*, trans. Harry Zohn (New York: Schocken Books, 1968), 217–52. While Benjamin is concerned with the loss of aura in the perception of works of art, and the loss of their unique character, I am interested in the way in which spaces are perceived differently when rendered photographically.

32. "Publication nationale, sous les auspices de S. Exc. le Ministre de la guerre. . . . Cette publication destinée à populariser l'Algérie, a été accueillie avec faveur par S. M. Napoléon III, qui a bien voulu en accepter la dédicace; elle comprend les principales villes, ruines romaines, sites pittoresques, oasis et villages arabes les plus intéressants des trois provinces." F. Moulin, *L'Algérie photographiée,* 6 vol. (Paris: Goubaud, [1858]). As far as I know, only four volumes of the album are extant (vols. 1, 3, 4, and 5), leading me to believe that they were the only ones that were ever published. McCauley notes that Moulin did produce another photographic album commemorating the trip made by Napoléon III to Constantine as part of his tour of Algeria in 1865. McCauley, *Industrial Madness,* 307.

33. Because there was no official commission or mention of Moulin's trip in any official source, Estelle Fredet concludes that the journey was the result of Moulin's opportunistic initiative and that the authorities tolerated but did not actually endorse the trip. Fredet, "*L'Algérie photographiée* de Félix-Jacques-Antoine Moulin," 36.

34. E. Lacan, "Exposition photographique de Bruxelles," *La Lumière* 6, no. 49 (6 December 1856), 189.

35. Fredet, "*L'Algérie photographiée* de Félix-Jacques-Antoine Moulin," 45.

36. The only critical remarks on Moulin's contributions to any of these exhibitions is E. Lacan, "Exposition photographique (II)," *La Lumière* 9, no. 24 (11 June 1859), 93.

37. Fredet, "*L'Algérie photographiée* de Félix-Jacques-Antoine Moulin," 77; see also Charles Baudelaire, "The Modern Public and Photography," *Salon of 1859*, in *Art in Paris, 1845–1862: Salons and Other Exhibitions*, trans. Jonathan Mayne (Ithaca: Cornell University Press, 1981), 149–55. See also Félix Nadar, *Quand j'étais photographe* (Paris: Flammarion, [1900]).

38. As a point of comparison, Baldus' most ambitious compendium—the *PLM Album*, which featured images of the Paris-Lyon-Mediterranée rail line—contained only sixty-nine images. Daniel, *Photographs of Édouard Baldus,* 241.

39. This is reported in a letter written by the Moulin to the editor of *La Lumière,* Ernest Lacan. "La Photographie en Algérie," *La Lumière* 6, no. 12 (22 March 1856).

40. Fredet, "*L'Algérie photographiée* de Félix-Jacques-Antoine Moulin," 58. In fact, there are 448 prints numbered at the Bibliothèque nationale, but many are missing and some may have been taken when Moulin returned to Algeria in 1865 to photograph the emperor's visit.

41. By decree of the Second Republic in 1848, Algeria was divided administratively into three distinct provinces: Algiers, Constantine, and Oran.

42. 138 of 297, by Fredet's count. Fredet, "*L'Algérie photographiée* de Félix-Jacques-Antoine Moulin," 58.

43. At this point, Frederic Chassériau, cousin of the

Orientalist painter Théodore Chassériau, was busy redesigning Algiers for a massive construction project that would be completed in 1860, for the visit of Napoléon III and Empress Eugénie. The main result of this rebuilding of the city was a large boulevard running along the quays that strongly resembled the Rue de Rivoli in Paris. It was entitled Boulévard de l'Impératrice.

44. In Moulin's album, the photographs are affixed to thick sheets of paper that are removable, and each volume contains a group of fifty photos. The panoramas I have already discussed are composed of two distinct photographs, each mounted on a separate sheet of paper and stuck together. These images appear without captions. However, most of the other images are accompanied by captions in typeface on narrow strips of paper affixed on each page below the image. Where appropriate, I address these captions in conjunction with the images.

45. Shortly after the French conquest at Constantine, Philippeville was created by Maréchal Valée at the site of an ancient Roman settlement. This site provided the most direct route inland to Constantine and thus quickly became a center of trade. See Nodier, *Journal,* and Charles-André Julien, *Histoire de l'Algérie contemporaine*, vol. 1, *La Conquête et les débuts de la colonisation (1827–1871)* (Paris: Presses Universitaires de France, 1964), 147.

46. Fillias, *Nouveau Guide général,* 187–88. This woodcut image serves as an illustration for this early guidebook, meant to provide "tous les renseignements nécessaires aux voyageurs" (title page).

47. Ibid.

48. "Nous n'y avons pas trouvé le plus petit village indigène." Moulin, *L'Algérie photographiée,* vol. 3, no. 132.

49. His full name was Gustave Alexandre Maurice Thimoléon Stellaye Baigneux de Courcival. France Duclos has explored this figure in two publications: *Les Voyageurs photographes et la Société de la Géographie, 1850–1910* (Paris: Bibliothèque nationale, 1998) and *Photographes en Algérie au XIXième siècle* (Paris: Musée-Galerie de la Seita, 1999), 71–74.

50. The photographs in this album (We 25) range from 10–15 cm in height and 15–21 cm in length. Another, smaller album is in the collection of the Archives de la Société de géographie (We 21); it contains forty-one images, many of them identical to the images from We 25. Courcival's album is composed like Moulin's, with the photographs affixed to removable sheets of paper. There are no typeface captions. Rather, the numbers and titles, as well as occasional descriptions, are inscribed by hand.

51. An exception to this claim would be the realm of industrial photography. In this case, it is possible to read de Courcival's image as a hybrid of landscape and industrial photography, an epithet that could be applied to Baldus' bridge pictures (e.g., fig. 57). It would be immediately apparent, however, that Baldus' image is far more conventional, featuring industrial forms elegantly framed and even integrated in the landscape. The only photographs of the period whose imagery approaches the disjunctive abstract forms that characterize de Courcival's picture of Sétif are photographs of industrial constructions produced for engineers by photographers such as Hippolyte Collard. See McCauley, *Industrial Madness*, 195–232.

52. Presumably, the album was composed by the photographer and numbered when it was donated to the archive, though the exact succession of images does not really concern me.

53. France Duclos, "Gustave Alexandre Maurice Thimoléon Stellaye de Baigneux de Courcival," in *Photographes en Algérie au XIXe siècle* (Paris: Musée-Galerie de la Seita, 1999), 72–73, and Service historique de l'armée de Terre, Vincennes, 5Yf 23030.

54. Needless to say, documentation on a figure such as de Courcival is lacking. His military record is basically all there is to go on, although he did join the Société française de photographie after his return to France (he was listed on their rolls in 1869 and again in 1885 and 1894). He thus had some interest in interacting with other photographers after his time in Algeria, but he was never listed as an exhibitor. Pierre Marc Richard, *La Société française de photographie: Membres-correspondants-amateurs-exposants: Index 1854–1876* (Paris: Editions du Palmier et Zinc, 1990). In one of his letters from Algeria reprinted in *La Lumière*, Moulin notes that several army officers were experimenting with photography in Algeria, so de Courcival's photographic expedition should not be seen as an isolated incident. "La Photographie en Algérie," *La Lumière* 6, no. 26 (28 June 1856), 102.

55. Eugène Fromentin, *Un Été dans le Sahar*a (1857), in *Oeuvres complètes*, ed. Guy Sagnes (Paris: Gallimard, 1984), 18. This text originally appeared on 1 June 1854 in the *Revue de Paris* and thus predates Moulin's photograph (*Oeuvres complètes,* 1269).

56. "Franchissez cette limite, et vous trouvez d'autres

hommes, d'autres moeurs, d'autres usages, d'autres productions. Le palmier remplace les céreales, l'eau devient le symbole de la vie. Vous traversez des espaces immenses sans végétation. . . . Sitôt que vous avez traversé le pont romain, vos yeux, habitués à une nature triste, sont émerveillés par l'aspect enchanteur du village; un fôret de palmiers se déroule à vos pieds, vous oubliez vos fatigues, et avez hâte d'entrer dans ce paradis terrestre." Moulin, "Gorge d'El-Kantara et le pont romain," in *L'Algérie photographiée,* vol. 4, no. 158.

57. James R. Ryan, *Picturing Empire: Photography and the Visualization of the British Empire* (Chicago: University of Chicago Press, 1997), 72. Ryan's use of the term "landscape aesthetics," as I read it, is an attempt to describe a variety of integrated practices of spatial organization included in the term "landscape," including landscape gardening and landscape painting, among others. Thus landscape aesthetics are not based on the developments of any single practitioner, but the term seeks to describe the general activity of aestheticizing space, or the act of perceiving space as a form of aesthetic appreciation.

58. See Chapter 3; Nodier, *Journal.*

59. Though images deriving from Moulin's photographs appeared on numerous occasions in *L'Illustration*, the only topographical views appeared in G. Julien, "L'Algérie photographiée," 200–201.

60. "Pour ceux qui ont habitée [in Algeria] et pour ceux qui sont avides de renseignements sur ce pays si peu connu qui mérite tant de l'être." Moulin, *L'Algérie photographiée,* frontispiece.

61. "The travel and tourist industry will account for 8.2 percent of worldwide gross domestic product (GDP) in 1998, and this will grow to 8.7 percent by 2010. . . . For a number of countries, tourism is the largest commodity in international trade. In many others, it ranks among the top three industries." See Charles R. Goeldner, J. R. Brent Ritchie, and Robert W. McIntosh, *Tourism: Principles, Practices, Philosophies*, 8th ed. (New York: John Wiley and Sons, 2000), 7–8. Jean Adhémar was the first to connect the development of tourism to the production of imagery: Adhémar, *Les Lithographies de paysage en France à l'époque romantique* (Paris: Armand Colin, 1938), 189–283. More recently, many scholars have written on the development of tourism in the nineteenth century, including Ali Behdad, *Belated Travelers: Orientalism in the Age of Colonial Dissolution* (Durham: Duke University Press, 1994); James Buzard, *The Beaten Track: European Tourism, Literature, and the Ways to Culture, 1800–1918* (Oxford: Clarendon Press, 1993); Robert L. Herbert, *Monet on the Normandy Coast: Tourism and Painting, 1867–1886* (New Haven: Yale University Press, 1994); John Urry, *The Tourist Gaze: Leisure and Travel in Contemporary Societies* (London: Routledge, 1990); and Urry, *Consuming Places* (London: Routledge, 1995). Deborah Bright discusses the implications of tourism related to landscape photographs in this period in her essay "Souvenirs of Progress: The Second Empire Landscapes," in *Image and Enterprise: The Photographs of Adolphe Braun* (London: Thames and Hudson, 2000), 92–119.

62. Nicholas Green, *The Spectacle of Nature: Landscape and Bourgeois Culture in Nineteenth-Century France* (Manchester: Manchester University Press, 1990). Though Green does not discuss photography in his study of nature and the urban experience, he articulates the way in which early tourist imagery, such as the *Voyages pittoresques et romantiques dans l'ancienne France*, framed city-dwellers' visual conception of nature. He further draws connections between subjective experience and the effects of nature.

63. Urry, *The Tourist Gaze*, 3.

64. Colin Campbell, *The Romantic Ethic and the Spirit of Modern Consumerism* (Oxford: Blackwell, 1987).

65. Jean-Baptiste Alary and Jean Geiser were the predominant tourist photogaphers installed in Algiers during this era. For a discussion of their Algerian imagery, see *Photographes en Algérie au XIXe siècle,* 62–66 and 85–95. The Maison Bonfils, originally based in Lebanon, constituted the most prominent source of photographs of the Near East in the second half of the nineteenth century, mostly for tourists. See Carney E. S. Gavin, *Image of the East: Nineteenth-Century Near Eastern Photographs by Bonfils* (Cambridge: Harvard University Press, 1992), and Nissan Perez, *Focus East: Early Photography in the Near East (1839–1885)* (New York: Harry N. Abrams, 1988), 141.

66. "Les baigneurs trouverent les buts de promenades, de distractions et toutes les choses nécessaires à la vie." Moulin, *L'Algérie photographiée,* vol. 4, no. 199.

67. Lacan, "*L'Algérie photographiée,*" 1493.

68. "C'est l'histoire,—et de l'histoire vivant,—que le practicien dont nous parlons, a pris sur le fait dans cette Algérie qui, destinée à devenir une nouvelle France, ne doit plus avoir rien d'inconnu pour les habitants de la mère-patrie." "L'Algérie—Publication nationale—M. Moulin," 80.

69. The figures in de Courcival's panorama are more or less invisible in the reproduction, but they are posed with horses on the far left in the foreground.

70. In his article on Laghouat, Oscar MacCarthy listed Bou-Saâda beside Laghouat as one of the cities on the southern limit of the French empire. Like Laghouat, it would have been economically significant for the development of trade routes across the Sahara, and this accounts for the profusion of French buildings in this outlying village. Oscar MacCarthy, "Laghouat," *Revue de l'Orient de l'Algérie et des Colonies* 15 (1854): 346.

71. To be fair, it is important to note that de Courcival took these pictures near the end of his journey. He was most likely running low on pure water at this point, which is absolutely necessary to produce photographs and would have been unavailable in Bou-Saâda. It is likely that Moulin did not journey so far into Algeria's interior, despite voyaging in the colony for eighteen months, because of the lack of necessary materials available there.

72. Eugenia P. Janis, "Photography," in *The Second Empire, 1852–1870: Art in France Under Napoléon III,* ed. Joseph J. Rishel, Kathryn B. Heisinger, et al. (Philadelphia: Philadelphia Museum of Art, 1978), 402.

73. One explanation is suggested in Joel Snyder's argument about Timothy O'Sullivan's topographical photographs of the American West. Referring to O'Sullivan's photographs of the Great Basin, Snyder writes: "They repeatedly deny what [Carleton] Watkins's photographs characteristically confirm, namely, the possibility of comfortable cohabitation, of an agreeable relation of humans to the natural landscape. They portray a bleak, inhospitable land, a godforsaken, anesthetizing landscape." Snyder, "Territorial Photography," 191. See also Joel Snyder, *American Frontiers: The Photographs of Timothy H. O' Sullivan, 1867–1874* (New York: Aperture, 1981), 49.

Chapter 6

The epigraph to this chapter is drawn from Henri Lefebvre, *The Production of Space*, trans. Donald Nicholson-Smith (Oxford: Blackwell, 1991), 389.

1. The most comprehensive text on this period of colonial history in Algeria is Annie Rey-Goldzeiguer, *Le Royaume arabe: La Politique algérienne de Napoléon III, 1861–1870* (Algiers: Société nationale d'édition et de diffusion, c. 1977). See also Charles-Robert Ageron, *Histoire de l'Algérie contemporaine,* 10th ed. (Paris: Gallimard, 1994), 25–32, and Charles-André Julien, *Histoire de l'Algérie contemporaine,* vol. 1, *La Conquête et les débuts de la colonisation (1827–1871)* (Paris: Presses Universitaires de France, 1964), 396–415.

2. Henri Lefebvre, *The Production of Space*, trans. Donald Nicholson-Smith (Oxford: Blackwell, 1991), 288.

3. This reading follows that of Derek Gregory, who refers to a "decorporalization of space" in Lefebvre's thought. Derek Gregory, *Geographical Imaginations* (Oxford: Blackwell, 1994), 382–95.

4. Michael J. Heffernan, "The Desert in French Orientalist Painting During the Nineteenth Century," *Landscape Research* 16, no. 2 (1991): 41.

5. Ibid., 42.

6. Michèle Salinas has produced a remarkable graph incorporating French writers' associations with the Algerian desert. See Salinas, *Voyages et voyageurs en Algérie, 1830–1930* (Toulouse: Privat, 1989), 136–37.

7. The sense of the term implied here derives from W. J. T. Mitchell, "Gombrich and the Rise of Landscape," in *The Consumption of Culture, 1600–1800: Image, Object, Text,* ed. Ann Bermingham and John Brewer (London: Routledge, 1995), 103–18.

8. Donald A. Rosenthal, *Orientalism: The Near East in French Painting, 1800–1880* (Rochester, N.Y.: Memorial Art Gallery, 1982), 89, 102.

9. Philippe Jullian, *The Orientalists: European Painters of Eastern Scenes*, trans. Helga and Dinah Harrison (Oxford: Phaidon, 1977), 102.

10. Robert Rosenblum, "L'Orientalisme," in *Les Peintures du Musée d'Orsay* (Paris: Nathan, 1989), 176.

11. Théophile Gautier, "Le Salon de 1868," *Le Moniteur Universel,* 2 May 1868, 2.

12. See Gustave Guillaumet, *Tableaux algériens* (Paris: Plon, 1888).

13. "Sénatus-consulte de 22 avril 1863," reprinted in Rodolphe Dareste, *De la propriété en Algérie,* 2nd ed. (Paris: Lainé et Havard, 1864). Dareste is my source for the history of property law in Algeria during this period. He also reprints in full the *sénatus-consulte* and the instructions for its application.

14. See Chapter 4. For a more complete discussion of Arab stereotyping, particularly by scholars working on Algeria, see Patricia Lorcin, *Imperial Identities: Stereotyping, Prejudice, and Race in Colonial Algeria* (London: I. B. Tauris, 1995).

15. These are the critiques leveled by Warnier and Duval, among others, in a number of works that I will attend to below.

16. Lorcin, *Imperial Identities,* 80.

17. Auguste Warnier, *L'Algérie devant l'Empereur* (Paris: Challemel aîné, 1865), 25.

18. Ibid., x.

19. The ratio of ten to one recalls John Locke's chapter "Of Property," part of his *Second Treatise of Government.* This text, which provided a rationalization for both enclosure in England and territorial seizure in the American colony, is perhaps the fundamental text in which an abstract concept of property is elaborated in relation to another abstract concept, money. At one point, Locke argues that one acre of enclosed and cultivated land is worth ten acres of unused land held in common. John Locke, *Second Treatise of Government,* ed. C. B. Macpherson (Indianapolis: Hackett, 1980), 23.

20. This term was first coined by Louis Napoléon (Napoléon III) in 1860 on his first visit to Algeria. Consequently, this period in Algerian history is known in France as Le Royaume arabe.

21. This spirit can be surmised from a portion of the emperor's proclamation to the indigenous inhabitants of Algeria on his visit, dated 5 May 1865: "Vous connaissez mes intentions; j'ai irrévocablement assuré dans vos mains la propriété des terres que vous occupez; j'ai honoré vos chefs, respecté votre religion, je veux augmenter votre bien-être, vous faire participer de plus en plus à l'administration de votre pays comme aux bienfaits de la civilisation." Reprinted in Florian Pharaon, *Voyage en Algérie de Sa Majesté Napoléon III* (Paris: Plon, 1865), 11.

22. Patricia Lorcin has explored this issue in depth: see Lorcin, *Imperial Identities.* Warnier's text fits into this trend.

23. "Instructions générales pour l'exécution du Sénatus-consulte du 22 avril 1863 et du règlement de l'administration publique du 23 mai suivant," reprinted in Dareste, *De la propriété en Algérie,* 279.

24. Ibid.

25. A brief contemporary article sought to refute this point of view by rounding up Islamic scholars who lent their support to the *sénatus-consulte* by declaring it legal within the context of Koranic law. E. Vaysettes, "La Question de la propriété, jugée par les docteurs de la loi musulmane," *Revue Africaine* 7, no. 41 (September 1863): 353–56. In the same vein, Rey-Goldzeiguer describes the responses of Muslim tribal leaders to the legislation in strictly positive terms, even assuring us that the *bureaux arabes* sources she quotes did not just write such things for political reasons. Rey-Goldzeiguer, *Le Royaume arabe,* 249–53.

26. This view is in evidence in Warnier, *L'Algérie devant l'Empereur,* iv–v, and in Jules Duval, *Réflexions sur la politique de l'Empereur en Algérie* (Paris: Challamel aîné, 1866), 133.

27. Jules Duval, *Des rapports entre le géographie et l'économie politique* (Paris: Bertrand, 1864). This work was excerpted from the *Bulletin de la Société de Géographie* in 1863 and was originally presented to the Society in that year. Duval's work remains unknown or considered insignificant by historians of geography and political economy, with the exception of Dominique Lejeune's recent work, *Les Sociétés de géographie en France et l'expansion coloniale au XIXe siècle* (Paris: Albin Michel, 1993), 69–77. In this work, Lejeune mentions Duval's influence on the Société de la géographie of Paris without discussing this figure in any detail. Otherwise, I have found only two brief bibliographies on Duval in recent literature: Roman d'Amat, ed., *Dictionnaire de biographie française,* vol. 12 (Paris: Librairie Letouzey et Ané, 1970), 979–80, and in Rey-Goldzeiguer, *Le Royaume arabe,* 120–21. The latter notes: "L'Orientalisme de bazar de Gautier sonne aussi faux que les palabres d'éonomiste desséché de Jules Duval, car pour l'un que pour l'autre, il s'agit d'intégrer l'Algérie à un cadre qui lui est étranger" (121).

28. Jules Duval, "Politique coloniale de la France, Algérie," *Revue des Deux Mondes* 20 (15 April 1859): 891–930, and 22 (15 May 1859): 257–300.

29. Jules Duval and Dr. Auguste Warnier, *Bureaux arabes et colons* (Paris: Challamel aîné, 1869).

30. Duval, "Politique coloniale de la France, Algérie."

31. Duval, *Des rapports,* 11.

32. E. Carette, "Recherches sur la géographie et la commerce de l'Algérie méridonale" and E. Renou, "Notice géographique sur une partie de l'Afrique septentrionale" in *Exploration scientifique de l'Algérie: Sciences historiques et géographiques,* vol. 2 (Paris: Imprimérie royale, 1844); Eugène Daumas, *Le Sahara algérien: Études géographiques, statistiques et historiques sur la région au sud des établissements français en Algérie* (Paris: Crapelet, 1845).

33. Duval, *Des rapports,* 77 and 78.

34. Duval, *La Politique de l'Empereur en Algérie,* 21 and 22.

35. "Instructions générales," 282.

36. Michel de Certeau, *The Practice of Everyday Life*, trans. Steven R. Rendall (Berkeley and Los Angeles: University of California Press, 1984), 121.

37. For more on Fromentin's voyages to Algeria, see Chapter 4, and James Thompson and Barbara Wright, *Eugène Fromentin (1820–1876): Visions d'Algérie et d'Égypte* (Paris: ACR Éditions, 2008).

38. Ibid., 240.

39. Heffernan, "The Desert in French Orientalist Painting," 40.

40. Linda Nochlin, "The Imaginary Orient," *Art in America* 7, no. 5 (1983): 125.

41. Eugène Mouton, introduction to Gustave Guillaumet, *Tableaux algériens* (Paris: Plon, 1888), 21.

Epilogue

1. At the beginning of the Third Republic, in 1871, the three provinces of Algeria—Algiers, Oran, and Constantine—were declared to be actual provinces of France, thus ending Algeria's colonial status in a legislative sense. In 1873 indigenous Algerians were invited to partake of French citizenship, though precious few took advantage of this offer.

2. See Roger Benjamin, *Orientalist Aesthetics: Art, Colonialism, and French North Africa (1880–1930)* (Berkeley and Los Angeles: University of California Press, 2003), 190–220.

Selected Bibliography

Archival Sources

Archives de la Société de géographie, Bibliothèque nationale de France, Paris

Archives des Musées nationaux

Archives du Louvre, Paris

Archives municipales, Bordeaux

Bibliothèque nationale de France, Département d'Estampes, Paris

Bibliothèque nationale de France, Département des Cartes et plans, Paris

CAOM (Le Centre des archives d'outre-mer), Aix-en-Provence

CARAN (Archives nationales), Paris

Société française de photographie, Paris

Service historique de la Marine, Vincennes

Service historique de l'Armée de Terre, Vincennes

Documentation sections of the following museums:

Musée Condé, Chantilly; Musée de la Chartreuse, Douais; Musée de l'Armée, Paris; Musée des Beaux-Arts, Bordeaux; Musée des Beaux-Arts, Caen; Musée d'Orsay, Paris; Musée du Louvre, Départements de Peintures et de Dessins, Paris; Musée national du château de Versailles, Versailles

Journals Consulted

L'Akhbar

L'Artiste

Le Bulletin de la Société de Géographie

Le Constitutionnel

L'Économiste

Le Figaro

L'Illustration

La Lumière

Le Magasin Pittoresque

Le Moniteur Algérien

Le Moniteur Universel

Revue Coloniale

Revue de l'Orient, de l'Algérie et des Colonies

Revue de Paris

La Revue des Deux Mondes

Revue Photographique

La Tour du Monde

Works Cited

Achille-Etna Michallon. Paris: Réunion des musées nationaux, 1994.

Adams, Steven. *The Barbizon School and the Origins of Impressionism.* London: Phaidon, 1994.

Ageron, Charles-Robert. *Modern Algeria: A History from 1830 to the Present.* Translated and edited by Michael Brett. London: Hurst, 1991.

———. *Politiques coloniale au Magreb.* Paris: Presses Universitaires de France, 1972.

Alazard, Jean. *Initiation à l'Algérie.* Paris: Adrien-Maisonneuve, 1957.

———. *L'Orient et la peinture française.* Paris: Plon, 1930.

Amans de Ch . . . et A. . . . *Examen du Salon de 1839, de l'état actuel de l'art en France et des moyens d'améliorer le sort des artistes.* Paris: Bureau intermédiare de journaux, 1839.

d'Amat, Roman, ed. *Dictionnaire de biographie française.* Vol. 12. Paris: Librairie Letouzey et Ané, 1970.

Andrew, C. M., and A. S. Kanya-Forstner. "Center and Periphery in the Making of the Second French Colonial Empire." *Journal of Imperial and Commonwealth History* 16, no. 3 (1988): 9–34.

Angrand, Pierre. "L'État mécène—Période autoritaire du Second Empire (1851–1860)." *Gazette des Beaux-Arts* 71 (May 1968): 303–48.

Aperçu historique, statistique et topographique sur l'état d'Alger, à l'usage de l'armée expéditionnaire d'Afrique. Paris: Ch. Piquet, 1830.

Appleton, Jay. *The Experience of Landscape.* London: Wiley, 1975.

———. *The Symbolism of Habitat: An Interpretation of Landscape in the Arts.* Seattle: University of Washington Press, 1990.

Aubert, Maurice. *Souvenirs du Salon de 1859.* Paris: Jules Tardieu, 1859.

Bajou, Valerie. "'Le Desert a pris place dans le palais de Versailles.'" In *De Delacroix à Renoir: L'Algérie des peintres,* 72–75. Paris: Institut du Monde Arabe, 2003.

Barchou de Penhoën, Auguste Théodore Hilaire. *Mémoires d'un officier d'état-majeur, expédition d'Afrique.* Paris: Charpentier, 1835.

Baroli, Marc. *La Vie quotidienne des français en Algerie, 1830–1914.* Paris: Hachette, 1967.

Barrell, John. *The Dark Side of the Landscape: The Rural Poor in English Painting, 1730–1840.* Cambridge: Cambridge University Press, 1980.

Barrows, Susanna. "Alcohol, France, and Algeria: A Case Study in the International Liquor Trade." *Contemporary Drug Problems* (1982): 525–43.

———. *Distorting Mirrors: Visions of the Crowd in Late Nineteenth-Century France.* New Haven: Yale University Press, 1981.

Baudelaire, Charles. *Art in Paris, 1845–1862: Salons and Other Exhibitions.* Edited and translated by Jonathan Mayne. London: Phaidon, 1965.

———. *The Painter of Modern Life and Other Essays.* Edited and translated by Jonathan Mayne. London: Phaidon, 1964.

Bavoux, Evariste. *Alger: Voyage politique et descriptif dans le nord d'Afrique.* Paris: Brockhaus et Avenarius, 1841.

Beaulieu, Jill, and Mary Roberts, eds. *Orientalism's Interlocutors: Painting, Architecture, Photography.* Durham: Duke University Press, 2002.

Beaume, Georges. *Fromentin.* Translated by Frederic Taber Cooper. New York: Frederick A. Stokes, 1913.

Behdad, Ali. *Belated Travelers: Orientalism in the Age of Colonial Dissolution.* Durham: Duke University Press, 1994.

Bell, Morag, Robin Alan Butlin, and Michael J. Heffernan, eds. *Geography and Imperialism, 1820–1940.* Manchester: Manchester University Press, 1995.

Bellanger, Claude, et al. *Histoire générale de la presse française.* 5 vols. Paris: Presses Universitaires de France, 1969–76.

Benjamin, Roger. *Orientalism: Delacroix to Klee.* Melbourne: Art Gallery of New South Wales, 1997.

———. *Orientalist Aesthetics: Art, Colonialism, and French North Africa (1880–1930).* Berkeley and Los Angeles: University of California Press, 2003.

———. *Renoir and Algeria.* Williamstown, Mass.: Sterling and Francine Clark Art Institute, 2003.

Benjamin, Walter. *The Arcades Project.* Translated by Howard Eiland and Kevin McLaughlin. Edited by Rolf Tiedemann. Cambridge: Harvard University Press, 1999.

———. "The Work of Art in the Age of Mechanical Reproduction." In *Illuminations,* translated by Henry Zohn, 217–51. New York: Schocken Books, 1986.

Berbrugger, Adrien. *L'Algérie historique, pittoresque et monumentale ou recueil de vues, costumes et portraits faits d'après nature dans les provinces d'Alger, Bône, Constantine et Oran. . . .* 4 vols. Paris: J. Delahaye, 1843.

Berdoulay, Vincent. *La Formation de l'école française de géographie (1870–1914).* Paris: Bibliothèque nationale, 1981.

Bermingham, Ann. *Landscape and Ideology: The English Rustic Tradition, 1740–1860.* Berkeley and Los Angeles: University of California Press, 1986.

Bermingham, Ann, and John Brewer, eds. *The Consumption of Culture, 1600–1800: Image, Object, Text.* London: Routledge, 1995.

Bernasconi, Dominique. "L'Image de l'Algérie dans l'iconographie française (1830–1871)." Mémoire de maîtrise, L'Institut d'Études Politiques de l'Université de Paris, 1970.

Bertholon, J., and C. Lhote. *Horace Vernet à Versailles, au Luxembourg et au Louvre: Critique et biographie.* Paris: Librairie Cournol, 1863.

Betts, Raymond. *Assimilation and Association in French Colonial Theory, 1890–1914.* New York: AMS Press, 1966.

Bhabha, Homi. *The Location of Culture.* London: Routledge, 1994.

Biass-Fabiana, Sophie. *Photographies de la collection de Félix Ziem.* Martigues: Musée Ziem, 1998.

Blanc, Charles. *Une Famille d'artistes: Les Trois Vernet, Joseph, Carle, Horace.* 1898. Paris: Librarie Renouard, 1928.

———. "Salon de 1839." *Revue de Progrès Politique, Sociale, et Littéraire* 1, no. 5 (15 March 1839): 268–73, 341–49.

Blanchard, Paul, and Adrien Dauzats. *San Juan de Ulùa ou Relation de l'expédition française au Mexique, sous les ordres de M. le contre-amiral Baudin.* Paris: chez Gide, 1839.

Blanqui, Jérôme-Adolphe. *Algérie: Rapport sur la situation économique de nos possessions dans le nord de l'Afrique.* Paris: W. Coquebert, 1840.

Boime, Albert. *The Academy and French Painting in the Nineteenth Century.* London: Phaidon, 1971.

———. *Art in an Age of Counterrevolution (1815–1848).* Chicago: University of Chicago Press, 2004.

Bouillon, Jean-Paul. "Sociétés d'artistes et institutions officielles dans le seconde moitié du XIXe siècle." *Romantisme* 54 (1986): 89–113.

Bouillon, Jean-Paul, et al., eds. *La Promenade du critique influent: Anthologie de critique d'art en France, 1850–1900.* Paris: Hazan, 1990.

Bouret, Jean. *The Barbizon School and Nineteenth-Century French Landscape Painting.* Greenwich, Conn.: New York Graphic Society, 1973.

Bourseul, E. Charles. *Biographie du Colonel Langlois, fondateur et auteur des panoramas militaires.* Paris: Dupont, 1874.

Brookner, Anita. *Genius of the Future: Studies in French Art Criticism.* London: Phaidon, 1971.

Bruller, Isabelle. *L'Algérie romantique des officiers de l'armée française, 1830–1837.* Vincennes: Service historique de l'Armée de Terre, 1994.

Brunschwig, Henri. *French Colonialism, 1871–1914: Myths and Realities.* Translated by William Granville Brown. New York: Praeger, 1966.

Bugeaud, Général. *L'Algérie: Des Moyens de conserver et d'utiliser cette conquête.* Paris: Dentu, 1842.

Buret, Eugène. *Question d'Afrique et la double conquête de l'Algérie par la guerre et la colonisation.* Paris: Ledoyen, 1842.

Burty, Philippe. *Vingt-cinq dessins d'Eugène Fromentin, réproduits à l'eau-forte par E. L. Montefiore.* Paris: Librairie d'Art, 1877.

Buzard, James. *The Beaten Track: European Tourism, Literature, and the Ways to Culture, 1800–1918.* Oxford: Clarendon Press, 1993.

Campbell, Colin. *The Romantic Ethic and the Spirit of Modern Consumerism.* Oxford: Blackwell, 1987.

Cantrel, Emile. "Salon de 1859, XIII." *L'Artiste* 7 (3 July 1859): 145–48.

Carette, E. "Recherches sur la géographie et la commerce de l'Algérie méridonale." In *Exploration scientifique de l'Algérie: Sciences historiques et géographiques,* vol. 2. Paris: Imprimérie royale, 1844.

Casey, Edward S. *Representing Place: Landscape Painting and Maps.* Minneapolis: University of Minnesota Press, 2002.

Casid, Jill H. *Sowing Empire: Landscape and Colonization.* Minneapolis: University of Minnesota Press, 2005.

Caussé, Jeanne, and Bruno de Cessole, eds. *L'Algérie, 1830–1962: Les Trésors retrouvés de la Revue des deux mondes.* Paris: Maisonneuve et Larose, 1999.

Çelik, Zeynep. "Colonial/Postcolonial Intersections: Lieux de mémoire in Algiers." *Third Text* 49 (Winter 1999/2000): 63–72.

———. "Framing the Colony: Houses of Algeria Photographed." *Art History* 27, no. 4 (2004): 616–26.

———. *Urban Forms and Colonial Confrontations: Algiers Under French Rule.* Berkeley and Los Angeles: University of California Press, 1997.

Chabert, Philippe-Gérard, and Patrick Wintrebert. *Léon Belly: Retrospective.* St.-Omer: Musée Sandelin, 1977.

Chartier, Roger, and Henri-Jean Martin. *Histoire de l'édition française: Le Temps des éditeurs, Du Romantisme à la Belle époque.* Vol. 3. Paris: Fayard, 1989.

Cherry, Deborah. "Algeria In and Out of the Frame: Visuality and Cultural Tourism in the Nineteenth Century." In *Visual Culture and Tourism,* edited by David Crouch and Nina Lübbren, 41–58. Oxford: Berg, 2003.

———. "Earth into World, Land into Landscape: The Worlding of Algeria in Nineteenth-Century British Feminism." In *Orientalism's Interlocutors: Painting, Architecture, Photography,* ed. Jill Beaulieu and Mary Roberts, 103–30. Durham: Duke University Press, 2002.

Christin, Anne-Marie, ed. *Un Été dans le Sahara,* by Eugène Fromentin. Paris: Le Sycomore, 1981.

———. *Fromentin conteur d'espace.* Paris: Le Sycomore, 1982.

———. "Fromentin et le monde arabe à travers *Un Été dans le Sahara* et *Une Année dans le Sahel.*" In *Colloque Eugène Fromentin.* Lille: Publications de l'Université de Lille, 1979.

———. "Space and Convention in Eugène Fromentin: The Algerian Experience." Translated by Richard M. Berrong. *New Literary History* 15 (1983–84): 559–74.

Clancy-Smith, Julia. *Rebel and Saint: Muslim Notables, Populist Protest, Colonial Encounters (Algeria and Tunisia, 1800–1904).* Berkeley and Los Angeles: University of California Press, 1994.

Clark, T. J. *The Absolute Bourgeois: Artists and Politics in France, 1848–1851.* London: Thames and Hudson, 1973.

———. *Image of the People: Gustave Courbet and the 1848 Revolution.* London: Thames and Hudson, 1973.

———. *The Painting of Modern Life: Paris in the Art of Manet and His Followers.* Princeton: Princeton University Press, 1984.

Clausolles, P. *L'Algérie pittoresque ou histoire de la Régence d'Alger depuis les temps les plus reculés jusqu'à nos jours. . . .* Toulouse: J.-B. Paya, 1843.

Clifford, James. "On Orientalism." In *The Predicament of Culture: Twentieth-Century Ethnography, Literature, and Art,* 255–76. Cambridge: Harvard University Press, 1988.

Collingham, H. A. C. *The July Monarchy: A Political History of France, 1830–48.* London: Longman, 1988.

Colloque Eugène Fromentin. Amsterdam: Maison Descartes, 1976.

Constans, Claire. *Musée national du château de Versailles, cata-*

logue des peintures. Paris: Réunion des musées nationaux, 1980.
Corner, James, ed. *Recovering Landscape: Essays on Contemporary Landscape Architecture.* Sparks, Nev.: Princeton Architectural Press, 1999.
Cosgrove, Denis, ed. *Mappings.* London: Reaktion Books, 1999.
———. "Prospect, Perspective, and the Evolution of the Landscape Idea." *Transactions of the Institute of British Geographers* 10 (1985): 45–62.
———. *Social Formation and Symbolic Landscape.* London: Croom Helm, 1984.
Cosgrove, Denis, and Stephen Daniels, eds. *The Iconography of Landscape: Essays on the Symbolic Representation, Design, and Use of Past Environments.* Cambridge: Cambridge University Press, 1988.
Crary, Jonathan. *Techniques of the Observer: On Vision and Modernity in the Nineteenth Century.* Cambridge: MIT Press, 1990.
Cronon, William. *Changes in the Land: Indians, Settlers, and the Ecology of New England.* New York: Hill and Wang, 1983.
Crow, Thomas. *Painters and Public Life in Eighteenth-Century France.* New Haven: Yale University Press, 1986.
Curtis, Atherton. *Catalogue de l'oeuvre lithographié d'Eugène Isabey.* Paris: Paul Prouté, n.d.
Czynski, J. *Colonisation d'Alger.* Paris: L. Bouchard-Huzard, 1839.
Daniel, Malcolm. *The Photographs of Édouard Baldus.* New York: Metropolitan Museum, 1994.
Dareste, Rodolphe. *De la propriété en Algérie.* 2nd ed. Paris: Lainé et Havard, 1864.
Daumas, Eugène. *Le Sahara algérien: Études géographiques, statistiques et historiques sur la région au sud des établissements français en Algérie.* Paris: Crapelet, 1845.
———. *The Ways of the Desert.* Translated by Sheila M. Ohlendorf. Austin: University of Texas Press, 1971.
Daunais, Isabelle. *L'Art de la mesure ou l'invention de l'espace dans les récits d'Orient (XIXe siècle).* Vincennes: Presses Universitaires de Vincennes, 1996.
Davis, John. *Landscape of Belief: Encountering the Holy Land in Nineteenth-Century American Art and Culture.* Princeton: Princeton University Press, 1996.
Debord, Guy. *The Society of the Spectacle.* Translated by Donald Nicholson-Smith. New York: Zone Books, 1994.
de Certeau, Michel. *The Practice of Everyday Life.* Translated by Steven R. Rendall. Berkeley and Los Angeles: University of California Press, 1984.
De Delacroix à Renoir: L'Algérie des peintres. Paris: Institut du Monde Arabe, 2003.
Denniée, Pierre Paul. *Précis historique et administratif de la campagne d'Afrique.* Paris: Fain, 1830.
Deperthes, J. B. *Théorie du paysage.* Paris: chez Lenormant, 1818.
de Piles, Roger. *Cour de peinture par principes.* 1708. Edited by T. Puttfarken. Paris: Gallimard, 1989.
Deschamps, Léon. *Histoire de la question coloniale en France.* Paris: Plon, 1891.
Description d'Égypte ou recueil des observations et des recherches qui ont été faites en Égypte pendant l'expédition de l'armée française. 22 vols. 1809–22. Cologne: Benedikt Taschen, 1994.
Desjobert, Amédée. *L'Algérie en 1846.* Paris: P. Dufart, 1846.
———. *La Question d'Alger.* Paris: P. Dufart, 1837.
Desvoisins, V. *Expéditions de Constantine: Accompagnées de reflexions sur nos possessions d'Afrique.* Paris: Roret, 1840.
Diederen, Roger, ed. *French Artists in Rome: Ingres to Degas, 1803–1873.* New York: Dahesh Museum of Art, 2003.
Dorbec, Prosper. *L'Art du paysage en France: Essai sur son évolution de la fin du XVIIIe siècle à la fin du Second Empire.* Paris: H. Laurens, 1925.
Dubbini, Renzo. *Geography of the Gaze: Urban and Rural Vision in Early Modern Europe.* Translated by Lydia G. Cochrane. Chicago: University of Chicago Press, 2002.
Du Camp, Maxime. *Egypte, Nubie, Palestine et Syrie, dessins photographiques recueillis pendant les années 1849, 1850 et 1851. . . .* Paris: Gide et J. Baudry, 1852.
———. *Le Salon de 1857.* Paris: Librairie Nouvelle, 1857.
———. *Le Salon de 1859.* Paris: Libriarie Nouvelle, 1859.
Duclos, France. *Les Voyageurs photographes et la Société de la Géographie, 1850–1910.* Paris: Bibliothèque nationale, 1998.
Dumas, Alexandre, and Adrien Dauzats. *Quinze jours au Sinaï.* Paris, 1839.
Dumas, Alexandre. *L'Art et les artistes contemporains au Salon de 1859.* Paris: Librairie Nouvelle, 1859.
Dumesnil, Henri. *Salon de 1859.* Paris: Ve. J. Renouard, 1859.
Duranty, Edmond. "La Nouvelle Peinture (1876)." In *The New Painting: Impressionism, 1874–1886,* ed. Charles S. Moffett et al., 37–50. Geneva: Richard Burton, 1986.
Duval, Jules. *Des rapports entre le géographie et l'économie politique.* Paris: Bertrand, 1864.
———. "Politique coloniale de la France, Algérie." *Revue des Deux Mondes* 20 (15 April 1859): 891–930; 22 (15 May 1859): 257–300.

———. *Réflexions sur la politique de l'Empereur en Algérie.* Paris: Challamel aîné, 1866.
Duval, Jules, and Dr. Auguste Warnier. *Bureaux arabes et colons.* Paris: Challamel aîné, 1869.
Duvivier, Général. *Quatorze observations sur le dernier mémoire du général Bugeaud.* Paris: Gaultier-Laguionie, 1842.
Eckstein, Marie-Anne. *La Rôle du souvenir dans l'oeuvre d'Eugène Fromentin.* Zurich: Jules Verlag, 1970.
École Polytechnique. *Livre du centenaire, 1794–1894.* 3 vols. Paris: Gauthier Villars et fils, 1897.
Egyptomania: Egypt in Western Art, 1730–1930. Paris: Réunion des musées nationaux, 1994.
Enfantin, Prosper. *Colonisation de l'Algérie.* Paris: Bertrand, 1843.
Esquer, Gabriel. *Iconographie historique de l'Algérie depuis le XVI siècle jusqu'à 1871.* 3 vols. Paris: Plon, 1929.
Evans, Arthur Robert Jr. *The Literary Art of Eugène Fromentin: A Study in Style and Motif.* Baltimore: Johns Hopkins University Press, 1964.
d'Eylac. "Essai bibliographique sur un grand livre illustré du XIXe siècle." *Revue Biblio-Iconographique* 9, no. 7 (1902): 329–46.
Fanon, Frantz. *The Wretched of the Earth.* Translated by Constance Farrington. New York: Grove Press, 1967.
Fillias, Achille. *Nouveau Guide général du voyageur en Algérie.* Paris: Garnier frères, 1865.
Flaubert, Gustave. *Voyage en Égypte.* Edited by Pierre-Marc de Biasi. Paris: Grasset, 1991.
Franque, Alfred. *Synthèse de la question d'Afrique.* Paris: Corréard, 1840.
Fredet, Estelle. "*L'Algérie photographiée* de Félix-Jacques-Antoine Moulin, et la politique algérienne de l'Empire." Mémoire de maîtrise sous la direction de M. Marc Michel, Directeur de I.H.P.O.M., 1993–94.
Fromentin, Eugène. "Alger: Fragments d'un journal de voyage." In *Oeuvres complètes*, edited by Guy Sagnes. Paris: Gallimard, 1984. Originally published in *L'Artiste* 2 (1857).
———. *Une Année dans le Sahel.* 1859. In *Oeuvres complètes*, edited by Guy Sagnes. Paris: Gallimard, 1984.
———. *Un Été dans le Sahara.* 1857. In *Oeuvres complètes*, edited by Guy Sagnes. Paris: Gallimard, 1984.
———. "Notes sur le genre dans la peinture." In *Oeuvres complètes*, edited by Guy Sagnes. Paris: Gallimard, 1984.
———. "Salon de 1845." In *Oeuvres complètes*, edited by Guy Sagnes. Paris: Gallimard, 1984. Originally published in *Revue organique des départements de l'Ouest,* April–May 1845, 194–208, 258–72.
Fromentin: Le Peintre et l'écrivain, 1820–1876. La Rochelle: Bibliothèque municipale et Musée des Beaux-Arts, 1970.
Foucart, Bruno, ed. *Adrien Dauzats et "Les Voyages pittoresques et romantiques dans l'ancienne France."* Paris: Fondation Taylor, 1990.
Foucault, Michel. "Questions on Geography." In *Power/Knowledge.* New York: Pantheon, 1980.
Frond, Victor. *Panthéon des illustrations francaises au XIXe siècle: Dauzats.* Paris: Lemercier, 1865.
Gaehtgens, Thomas W. *Versailles: De la résidence royale au musée historique: La Galerie des batailles dans le musée historique de Louis-Philippe.* Translated by Patrick Poirot. Paris: Albin Michel, 1984.
Galassi, Peter. *Before Photography.* New York: The Museum of Modern Art, 1981.
———. *Corot in Italy: Open-Air Painting and the Classical Landscape Tradition.* New Haven: Yale University Press, 1991.
Galeries historiques du palais de Versailles. Paris: Fain et Thunot, 1842.
Gallois, Lucien. "Les Dombes." *Annales de géographie* (January 1892).
Garnier, Nicole. *Delacroix au Maroc: L'Orientalisme au Musée Condé.* Chantilly: Musée Condé, 1992.
Gautier, Théophile. *L'Orient.* In vol. 20 of *Oeuvres complètes.* 26 vols. Paris: Charpentier, 1880–1903.
———. "Salon de 1839, X." *La Presse,* 18 May 1839.
———. "Salon de 1857, XVIII." *L'Artiste* 2 (1 November 1857): 129–30.
———. *Voyage en Algérie.* Edited by Denise Brahimi. Paris: La Boîte à Documents, 1989.
Gavin, Carney E. S. *Image of the East: Nineteenth-Century Near Eastern Photographs by Bonfils.* Cambridge: Harvard University Press, 1992.
Genty de Bussy, M. P. *De l'établissement des français dans la régence d'Alger et des moyens d'en assurer la prospérité.* 2nd ed. 2 vols. Paris: Firmin Didot frères, 1839.
Gervereau, Laurent, and Claire Constans, eds. *Le Musée révélé: L'Histoire de France au château de Versailles.* Paris: Robert Laffont, 2005.
Goeldner, Charles R., J. R. Brent Ritchie, and Robert W. McIntosh. *Tourism: Principles, Practices, Philosophies.* 8th ed. New York: John Wiley and Sons, 2000.
Gonse, Louis. *Eugène Fromentin: Peintre et écrivain.* Paris: Quantin, 1881.

Goupil-Fesquet, Frédéric. *Voyage d'Horace Vernet en Orient.* Paris: Challamel, 1843.
Gouvernement général de l'Algérie, Direction de l'agriculture et de la colonisation. *1830–1930: Cent ans de colonisation française en Algérie.* Algiers: Victor Heintz, 1930.
Grandville. *Un Autre Monde.* 1844. Reprint, Paris: Les Librairies Associés, 1963.
Grate, Pontus. *Deux critiques d'art de l'époque romantique: Gustave Planche et Théophile Thoré.* Stockholm: Almquist & Wiksell, 1959.
Green, Nicholas. "'All the Flowers of the Field': The State, Liberalism, and Art Under the Early Third Republic." *Oxford Art Journal* 10, no. 1 (1987): 71–84.
———. *The Spectacle of Nature: Landscape and Bourgeois Culture in Nineteenth-Century France.* Manchester: Manchester University Press, 1990.
Gregory, Derek. *The Colonial Present: Afghanistan, Palestine, Iraq.* Malden, Mass.: Blackwell, 2004.
———. *Geographical Imaginations.* Oxford: Blackwell, 1994.
Grigsby, Darcy Grimaldo. *Extremities: Painting Empire in Post-Revolutionary France.* New Haven: Yale University Press, 2002.
———. "Rumor, Contagion, and Colonization in Gros's *Plague-Stricken of Jaffa.*" *Representations* 51 (Fall 1995): 1–46.
Grunchec, Philippe. *The Grand Prix de Rome: Paintings from the École des Beaux-Arts, 1797–1863.* Washington, D.C.: National Gallery of Art, 1984.
Guégan, Stéphane, and Jean-Claude Yon. *Théophile Gautier, la critique en liberté.* Paris: Réunion des musées nationaux, 1997.
Guégan, Stéphane, et al. *Théodore Chassériau, 1819–1856: The Unknown Romantic.* New York: Metropolitan Museum of Art, 2002.
Guillaumet, Gustave. *Tableaux algériens.* Paris: Plon, 1888.
Guinard, Paul. "Adrien Dauzats, peintre et voyageur romantique." *Medécine de France* 116 (1968): 17–28.
———. *Dauzats et Blanchard, peintres de l'Espagne romantique.* Bordeaux: Feret, 1967.
Hamdani, Amar. *La Vérité sur l'expédition d'Alger.* Paris: Balland, 1985.
Hardt, Michael, and Antonio Negri. *Empire.* Cambridge: Harvard University Press, 2000.
Hartman, Elwood. *Three Nineteenth-Century French Writers and the Magreb.* Tubingen: Gunter Narr Verlag, 1994.
Haskell, Francis. "A Turk and His Pictures in Nineteenth-Century Paris." *The Oxford Art Journal* 5, no. 1 (1982): 40–47.
Heffernan, Michael J. "The Desert in French Orientalist Painting During the Nineteenth Century." *Landscape Research* 16, no. 2 (1991): 37–42.
Heilbrun, Françoise, Bernard Marbot, and Philippe Néagu. *L'Invention d'un regard (1839–1918).* Paris: Réunion des musées nationaux, 1989.
Herbert, Robert L. *Barbizon Revisited.* Boston: Museum of Fine Arts, 1962.
———. "City vs. Country: The Rural Image in French Painting from Millet to Gauguin." *Artforum* 8, no. 6 (1970): 44–55.
———. *Impressionism: Art, Leisure, and Parisian Society.* New Haven: Yale University Press, 1988.
———. *Monet on the Normandy Coast: Tourism and Painting, 1867–1886.* New Haven: Yale University Press, 1994.
Herold, J. Christopher. *Bonaparte in Egypt.* New York: Harper and Row, 1962.
Hobsbawm, Eric J. *Nations and Nationalism Since 1780.* Cambridge: Cambridge University Press, 1990.
Holt, Elizabeth. *The Art of All Nations, 1850–73: The Emerging Role of Exhibitions and Critics.* Princeton: Princeton University Press, 1981.
———. *Triumph of Art for the Public, 1785–1848: The Emerging Role of Exhibitions and Critics.* Princeton: Princeton University Press, 1979.
Horace Vernet, 1789–1863. Paris: École nationale supérieure des beaux-arts, 1980.
Hyde, Ralph. *Panoramania! The Art and Entertainment of the "All-Embracing" View.* London: Trefoil Publications, 1988.
Une Invention du XIXe siècle: La Photographie: Collections de la Société française de la photographie. Paris: Bibliothèque nationale, 1976.
Irlam, Shaun. "Gerrymandered Geographies: Exoticism in Thomas and Chateaubriand." *MLN* 108 (1993): 891–912.
Jacquot, Félix. *Expédition du général Cavaignac dans le Sahara algérien en avril et mai 1847: Relation du voyage, exploration scientifique, souvenirs, impressions, etc.* Paris: Gide et J. Baudry, 1849.
Jammes, Andre, and Eugenia Parry Janis. *The Art of French Calotype: With a Critical Dictionary of French Photographers, 1845–1870.* Princeton: Princeton University Press, 1983.
Janin, Jules. "Le Salon de 1840: Quatrième article." *L'Artiste* 5 (1840): 217–224.

Janis, Eugenia P. "Photography." In *The Second Empire, 1852–1870: Art in France Under Napoléon III,* ed. Joseph J. Rishel, Kathryn B. Heisinger, et al., 401–33. Philadelphia: Philadelphia Museum of Art, 1978.

Jouin, Henri. *Adrien Dauzats, peintre et écrivain.* Paris: L'Artiste, 1896.

Jourdan, Louis. *Les Peintres français: Salon de 1859.* Paris: Librairie Nouvelle, 1859.

Julien, Charles-André. *Histoire de l'Algérie contemporaine.* Vol. 1, *La Conquête et les débuts de la colonisation (1827–1871).* Paris: Presses Universitaires de France, 1964.

Julien, G. "L'Algérie photographiée." *L'Illustration* 787, no. 31 (27 March 1858): 2001.

Jullian, Philippe. *The Orientalists: European Painters of Eastern Scenes.* Translated by Helga and Dinah Harrison. Oxford: Phaidon, 1977.

Kapor, Vladimir. "La Couleur anti-locale d'Eugène Fromentin." *Nineteenth Century French Studies* 34, nos. 1–2 (2005–2006): 63–74.

Krauss, Rosalind E. *The Originality of the Avant-Garde and Other Modernist Myths.* Cambridge: MIT Press, 1986.

Lacan, Ernest. "L'Algérie photographiée." *Le Moniteur Universel,* no. 343 (9 December 1858): 1493.

———. "Exposition photographique (II)." *La Lumière* 9, no. 24 (11 June 1859): 93.

———. "Exposition photographique de Bruxelles." *La Lumière* 6, no. 49 (6 December 1856): 189.

———. "La Photographie de genre: Epreuves de M. Moulin." *La Lumière* 3, no. 34 (20 August 1853): 135.

———. "Revue photographique: MM. Disdéri, Moulin." *La Lumière* 4, no. 24 (17 June 1854): 95.

LaFouge, Jean-Pierre. *Étude sur l'orientalisme d'Eugène Fromentin dans ces "récits algériens."* New York: Peter Lang, 1988.

Lagrange, André. *L'Art de Fromentin.* Paris: Editions Dervy, 1952.

Lamartine, Alphonse de. *Souvenirs, impressions, pensées et paysages pendant un voyage en Orient, 1832–1833.* Paris: Pagnerre, V. Lecon et Furne, 1854.

Lammenais, F. *Politique à l'usage du peuple.* 2 vols. Paris: Paguerre, 1839.

Laspinasse, L. N. *Traité du lavis des plans, appliqué principalement aux reconnaissances militaires.* Paris: chez Magimel, Anselin et Pochard, 1818.

Leduc-Adine, Jean-Pierre. "L'Orientalisme et la critique d'art sous le Second Empire." In *Exotisme et création,* 231–43. Lyon: Actes du colloque international, 1983.

Lefebvre, Henri. *The Production of Space.* Translated by Donald Nicholson-Smith. New York: Blackwell, 1988.

Lejeune, Dominique. *Les Sociétés de géographie en France et l'expansion coloniale au XIXe siècle.* Paris: Albin Michel, 1993.

Lemagny, Jean-Claude, and André Rouillé, eds. *A History of Photography: Social and Cultural Perspectives.* Translated by Janet Lloyd. Cambridge: Cambridge University Press, 1987.

Le Men, Segolène. "Book Illustration." In *Artistic Relations: Literature and the Visual Arts in Nineteenth-Century France,* ed. Peter Collier and Robert Lethbridge, 94–110. New Haven: Yale University Press, 1994.

Leroy-Beaulieu, Pierre Paul. *De la colonisation chez les peuples modernes.* Paris: Plon, 1874.

Lessore, E., and W. Wyld. *Voyage pittoresque dans la Régence d'Alger pendant l'année 1833 par M.M. E. Lessore et W. Wyld.* Paris: Charles Motte, 1833–35.

Locke, John. *Second Treatise of Government.* Edited by C. B. Macpherson. Indianapolis: Hackett, 1980.

Lorcin, Patricia. *Imperial Identities: Stereotyping, Prejudice, and Race in Colonial Algeria.* London: I. B. Tauris, 1995.

Loti, Pierre. *The Desert.* Translated by Jay Paul Minn. Salt Lake City: University of Utah Press, 1993.

Lowe, Lisa. *Critical Terrains: French and British Orientalisms.* Ithaca: Cornell University Press, 1991.

Loyer, François. *Paris in the Nineteenth Century: Architecture and Urbanism.* Translated by Charles Lynn Clark. New York: Abbeville, 1988.

MacCarthy, Jacques. *Voyage dans la régence d'Alger, ou description géographique, physique, philologique, etc., de cet état par le Docteur Shaw.* Paris: Marlin, 1830.

MacCarthy, Oscar. "Laghouat." *Revue de l'Orient de l'Algérie et des Colonies* 15 (1854): 346–53.

MacKenzie, John M. *Orientalism: History, Theory, and the Arts.* Manchester: Manchester University Press, 1995.

MacMahon, Maréchal. *Mémoires du maréchal de MacMahon, duc de Magenta: Souvenirs d'Algérie.* 9th ed. Paris: Plon, 1932.

Magri, Véronique. *Le Discours sur l'autre: A travers quatre récits de voyage en Orient.* Paris: Honoré Champion, 1995.

Mainardi, Patricia. *Art and Politics of the Second Empire: The Universal Exhibitions of 1855 and 1867.* New Haven: Yale University Press, 1989.

———. *The End of the Salon: Art and the State in the Early Third Republic.* Cambridge: Cambridge University Press, 1993.

Marcos, Fouad. *Fromentin et l'Afrique.* Montréal: Éditions Cosmos, 1973.

Marey, Général. *Expédition de Laghouat: Dirigée en mai et juin 1844.* Algiers: Bastide, 1845.

Marrinan, Michael. *Painting Politics for Louis-Philippe: Art and Ideology in Orléanist France, 1830–1848.* New Haven: Yale University Press, 1988.

Marseille, J. "The Phases of French Colonial Imperialism: Towards a New Periodization." *Journal of Imperial and Commonwealth History* 13, no. 3 (1985): 127–41.

Marx, Karl. *The Eighteenth Brumaire of Louis Bonaparte.* Translated by Daniel de Leon. New York: Mondial Books, 2005.

Masson, André. "L'Opinion française et les problemes coloniaux à la fin du Second Empire." *Revue Française d'Histoire d'Outre-mer* 50, nos. 3–4 (1962).

Matisse in Morocco: The Paintings and Drawings, 1912–1913. Washington, D.C.: National Gallery of Art, 1990.

McCauley, Elizabeth Anne. *Industrial Madness: Commercial Photography in Paris, 1848–1871.* New Haven: Yale University Press, 1994.

McClintock, Anne. *Imperial Leather: Race, Gender, and Sexuality in the Colonial Contest.* London: Routledge, 1995.

McWilliam, Neil. "Opinions professionnelles: Critique d'art et économie de la culture sous la Monarchie de Juillet." *Romantisme* 71 (1991): 19–30.

Michel, Paul-Henri. "The French Book in the XIXth Century." In *The Art of the French Book from Early Manuscripts to Present Time,* edited by André Lejard, 87–112. Paris: Les Éditions du Chêne, 1947.

Miel, E. F. A. M. *Essai sur les beaux-arts, et particulièrement sur le Salon de 1817, ou examen critique des principaux ouvrages d'art exposés dans le cours de cette année.* Paris: Didot le jeune, 1817–18.

Miller, Peter Benson. "By the Sword and the Plow: Théodore Chassériau's Cour des Comptes Murals and Algeria." *Art Bulletin* 87, no. 4 (2005): 690–718.

———. "Théodore Chassériau and the French Colonial Project in Algeria." Ph.D. diss., New York University, 2003.

Miquel, Pierre. *Eugène Isabey, 1803–1886: La Marine au XIXe siècle.* Maurs-La-Jolie: Editions de la Martinelle, 1980.

Mitchell, Claudine. "What Is to Be Done with the Salonniers? A Review Essay of *A Bibliography of Salon Criticism in Second Empire Paris* by Christopher Parsons and Martha Ward." *Oxford Art Journal* 10, no. 1 (1987): 106–115.

Mitchell, Timothy. *Colonizing Egypt.* Berkeley and Los Angeles: University of California Press, 1991.

Mitchell, W. J. T., ed. *Landscape and Power.* Chicago: University of Chicago Press, 1994.

Montagne, D.-J. *Physiologie morale et physique d'Alger, 1833.* Marseille: Camoin, 1834.

Montagnon, Pierre. *La Conquête de l'Algérie, 1830–1871.* Paris: Pygmalion, 1986.

———. *Histoire de l'Algérie des origines à nos jours.* Paris: Pygmalion, 1998.

Mosby, Dewey. *Alexandre-Gabriel Decamps, 1803–1860.* New York: Garland, 1977.

Moulin, Félix-Jacques-Antoine. *L'Algérie photographiée.* 6 vols. (4 extant). Paris: Goubaud, 1858–60.

———. "La Photographie en Algérie." *La Lumière* 6, no. 12 (22 March 1856).

Munro, Rolland. "The Consumption View of Self: Extension, Exchange and Identity." In *Consumption Matters: The Production and Experience of Consumption,* ed. Stephen Edgell, Kevin Hetherington, and Alan Warde, 428–73. Oxford: Blackwell, 1996.

Musée de Valence. *Le Paysage et la question du sublime.* Paris: Réunion des musées nationaux, 1997.

Nerval, Gérard de. *Voyage en Orient.* Paris: Garnier-Flammarion, 1980.

Nochlin, Linda. "The Imaginary Orient." *Art in America* 7, no. 5 (1983): 119–31, 187–89.

———. *The Politics of Vision: Essays on Nineteenth-Century Art and Society.* New York: Harper and Row, 1989.

Nodier, Charles. *Journal de l'expédition des Portes de Fer.* Paris: Imprimérie royale, 1844.

Nodier, Charles, Baron Taylor, and Alphonse de Cailleux. *Voyages pittoresques et romantiques dans l'ancienne France.* 20 vols. Paris: Paris: Firmin Didot, 1820–78.

Novak, Barbara. *Nature and Culture: American Landscape Painting, 1825–1875.* Oxford: Oxford University Press, 1980.

O'Brien, David. *After the Revolution: Antoine-Jean Gros, Painting, and Propaganda Under Napoleon.* University Park: Pennsylvania State University Press, 2006.

Ockman, Carol. *Ingres' Eroticized Bodies: Retracing the Serpentine Line.* New Haven: Yale University Press, 1995.

Oettermann, Stephan. *The Panorama: History of a Mass Medium.* Translated by Deborah Lucas-Schneider. New York: Zone Books, 1997.

Un officier de l'armée de l'Afrique. "Expédition de Constantine." *Revue de Paris* 37 (January 1837): 193–202.

Orwicz, Michael, ed. *Art Criticism and Its Institutions in*

Nineteenth-Century France. Manchester: Manchester University Press, 1994.

Osbourne, Michael A. *Nature, the Exotic, and the Science of French Colonialism.* Bloomington: Indiana University Press, 1992.

Otth, Adolphe. *Esquisses africaines, dessinées pendant un voyage à Alger et lithographié par Adolphe Otth.* Berne: Wagner, 1838.

Oulesbir, Nabila. "Paysage et patrimoine: Lieux et monuments de l'Algérie dans les années romantiques." In *De Delacroix à Renoir: L'Algérie des peintres,* 100–107. Paris: Institut du Monde Arabe, 2003.

Pagden, Anthony. *Lords of All the World: Ideologies of Empire in Spain, Britain, and France, c. 1500–c. 1800.* New Haven: Yale University Press, 1995.

Pandolfo, Stefania. *Impasse of the Angels: Scenes from a Moroccan Space of Memory.* Chicago: University of Chicago Press, 1997.

Peltre, Christine. *L'Atelier du voyage: Les Peintres en Orient au XIXe siècle.* Paris: Gallimard, 1995.

———. *Orientalism in Art.* Translated by John Goodman. New York: Abbeville, 1998.

Perez, Nissan N. *Focus East: Early Photography in the Near East (1839–1885).* New York: Harry N. Abrams, 1988.

Perrot, Aristide Michel. *La Conquête d'Alger, ou Relation de la campagne d'Afrique.* Paris: H. Langlois, 1830.

Petit, Marie-Paule. "L'Oeuvre algérois de Jean-Charles Langlois." 3 vols. Thèse de troisième cycle, Université de Paris I, [c. 1983].

Pharaon, Florian. *Voyage en Algérie de Sa Majesté Napoléon III.* Paris: Plon, 1865.

Photographes en Algérie au XIXe siècle. Paris: Musée-Galerie de le Seita, 1999.

Pignel, Armand. *Guide du voyageur et du colon de Paris à Alger et dans l'Algérie.* Paris: Debécourt, 1836.

Pinkney, David H. *Napoléon III and the Building and Rebuilding of Paris.* Princeton: Princeton University Press, 1958.

Playfair, Sir Lambert. "A Bibliography of Algeria." In *Royal Geographical Society—Supplementary Papers.* London: Royal Geographical Society, 1889.

Plessier, Ghislaine. *Adrien Dauzats, ou, La Tentation de l'Orient: Catalogue raisonné de l'oeuvre peint.* Bordeaux: Musée des Beaux-Arts, 1990.

Plessis, Alain. *De la fête impériale au murs des fédérés, 1852–71.* Paris: Éditions du Seuil, 1973.

Porch, Douglas. *The Conquest of the Sahara.* New York: Alfred A. Knopf, 1984.

Porter, Dennis. "Orientalism and Its Problems." In *The Politics of Theory: Proceedings of the Essex Conference on the Sociology of Literature, July 1982,* ed. Francis Barker et al., 179–91. Essex: University of Essex, 1983.

Porterfield, Todd. *The Allure of Empire: Art in the Service of French Imperialism, 1798–1836.* Princeton: Princeton University Press, 1998.

Priestly, Herbert Ingram. *France Overseas: A Study of Modern Imperialism.* New York: Appleton-Century, 1938.

Prochaska, David. *Making Algeria French: Colonialism in Bône, 1870–1920.* Cambridge: Cambridge University Press, 1990.

Pugh, Simon, ed. *Reading Landscape: Country-City-Capital.* Manchester: Manchester University Press, 1990.

Pyenson, Lewis. *Civilizing Mission: Exact Sciences and French Overseas Expansion, 1830–1940.* Baltimore: Johns Hopkins University Press, 1993.

Quetin. *Guide en Orient: Itinéraire scientifique, artistique et pittoresque. . . .* Paris: L. Maison, 1844.

Ray, Gordon Nichols. *The Art of the French Illustrated Book, 1700 to 1914.* New York: The Pierpont Morgan Library, 1986.

Regards sur la photographie en France au XIXe siècle. Paris: Petit Palais, 1980.

Renou, E. "Notice géographique sur une partie de l'Afrique septentrionale." In *Exploration scientifique de l'Algérie: Sciences historiques et géographiques,* vol. 2. Paris: Imprimérie royale, 1844.

Rey-Goldzeiguer, Annie. *Le Royaume arabe: La Politique algérienne de Napoléon III, 1861–1870.* Algiers: Société nationale d'édition et de diffusion, c. 1977.

Richard, Jean-Pierre. *Littérature et sensation.* Paris: Éditions du Seuil, 1954.

Richard, Pierre Marc. *La Société française de photographie: Membres-correspondants-amateurs-exposants: Index 1854–1876.* Paris: Editions du Palmier et Zinc, 1990.

Richter, Melvin. "Tocqueville on Algeria." *Review of Politics* 25 (1963): 362–98.

Rishel, Joseph J., and Kathryn B. Heisinger, et al., eds. *The Second Empire, 1852–1870: Art in France Under Napoléon III.* Philadelphia: Philadelphia Museum of Art, 1978.

Robert, Jules. *Album du Salon de 1840.* Paris: Challamel, 1840.

Robichon, François, ed. *Auguste Raffet.* Paris: Herscher, 1999.

———. "Le Panorama, spectacle de l'histoire." *Le Mouvement Social* 131 (April–June 1985): 65–86.

———. "Les Panoramas en France au XIXe siècle." 3 vols. Thèse de troisième cycle, Université de Paris X, Nanterre, 1982.
Robichon, François, et al. *Jean-Charles Langlois (1789–1870): Le Spectacle de l'histoire.* Caen: Musée des Beaux-Arts, 2005.
Rosenblum, Robert. "L'Orientalisme." In *Les Peintures du Musée d'Orsay.* Paris: Nathan, 1989.
Rosenthal, Donald A. *Orientalism: The Near East in French Painting, 1800–1900.* Rochester, N.Y.: Memorial Art Gallery, 1982.
Rosenthal, Léon. *Du romantisme au realisme: Essai sur l'évolution de la peinture en France de 1830 à 1848.* Paris: H. Laurens, 1914.
Rouillé, André. *L'Empire de la photographie: Photographie et pouvoir bourgeois.* Paris: Le Sycomore, 1982.
———. "Exploring the World by Photography in the Nineteenth Century." In *A History of Photography: Social and Cultural Perspectives,* ed. Jean-Claude Lemagny and André Rouillé, trans. Janet Lloyd, 53–59. Cambridge: Cambridge University Press, 1987.
Roujon, Henri. *Horace Vernet.* Paris: Pierre Lafitte, 1910.
Rozet, Captain. *Voyage dans la Régence d'Alger ou description du pays occupé par l'armée française.* Paris: Bertrand, 1833.
Ruedy, John. *Land Policy in Colonial Algeria: The Origins of the Rural Public Domain.* Berkeley and Los Angeles: University of California Press, 1967.
Ryan, James R. "Imperial Landscapes: Photography, Geography and British Overseas Exploration, 1858–1872." In *Geography and Imperialism, 1820–1940,* ed. Morag Bell, Robin Alan Butlin, and Michael Heffernan, 53–79. Manchester: Manchester University Press, 1995.
———. *Picturing Empire: Photography and the Visualization of the British Empire.* Chicago: University of Chicago Press, 1997.
Said, Edward. *Culture and Imperialism.* New York: Vintage, 1993.
———. *Orientalism: Western Representations of the Orient.* New York: Vintage, 1978.
———. "Orientalism Reconsidered." *Cultural Critique* 1 (Fall 1985): 89–108.
Saint-Victor, Paul de. "Salon de 1859, IX." *La Presse,* 25 June 1859, 1–2.
Salinas, Michèle. *Voyages et voyageurs en Algérie, 1830–1930.* Toulouse: Privat, 1989.
Samuels, Maurice. *The Spectacular Past: Popular History and the Novel in Nineteenth-Century France.* Ithaca: Cornell University Press, 2004.
Sandoz, Marc. *Cahiers Théodore Chassériau.* 2 vols. Paris: Editart-Quatre Chemins, 1982.
———. *Théodore Chassériau, catalogue raisonné des peintures et des estampes.* Paris: Arts et métiers graphiques, 1974.
Schapiro, Meyer. "Fromentin as a Critic." *Partisan Review* 16 (January 1949): 25–51.
Schneider, William H. *An Empire for the Masses: The French Popular Image of Africa, 1870–1900.* Westport, Conn.: Greenwood Press, 1982.
Schwartz, Joan M., and James R. Ryan. *Picturing Place: Photography and the Geographical Imagination.* London: I. B. Tauris, 2003.
Smith, Bernard. *European Vision and the South Pacific.* 2nd ed. New Haven: Yale University Press, 1985.
Snell, Robert. *Théophile Gautier: A Romantic Critic of the Visual Arts.* Oxford: Oxford University Press, 1982.
Snyder, Joel. *American Frontiers: The Photographs of Timothy H. O'Sullivan, 1867– 1874.* New York: Aperture, 1981.
———. "Territorial Photography." In *Landscape and Power,* ed. W. J. T. Mitchell, 175–202. Chicago: University of Chicago Press, 1994.
Solomon-Godeau, Abigail. "A Photographer in Jerusalem, 1855: Auguste Salzmann and His Times." *October* 18 (Fall 1981).
Soubeyran, Olivier. "Imperialism and Colonialism Versus Disciplinarity in French Geography." In *Geography and Empire,* ed. Anne Godlewska and Neil Smith, 244–64. Oxford: Blackwell, 1994.
Spadafore, Anita. "Baron Taylor's *Voyages pittoresques.*" Ph.D. diss., Northwestern University, 1973.
Stafford, Barbara Maria. *Voyage into Substance: Art, Science, Nature, and the Illustrated Travel Account, 1760–1840.* Cambridge: MIT Press, 1984.
Stevens, MaryAnne. *The Orientalists: Delacroix to Matisse; European Painters in North Africa and the Near East.* London: Royal Academy of Arts, 1984.
Storey, John. *Cultural Consumption and Everyday Life.* London: Arnold, 1999.
Taine, Hippolyte. *Philosophie de l'art.* Paris: Baillière, 1865.
Talbot, William Henry Fox. *The Pencil of Nature.* 1844. New York: Da Capo Press, 1969.
Ténint, Wilhelm. *Salon de 1841: Collection des principaux ouvrages exposés au Louvre.* Paris: Challamel, 1841.
Thomas, Greg M. *Art and Ecology in Nineteenth-Century France: The Landscapes of Théodore Rousseau.* Princeton: Princeton University Press, 2000.

Thompson, James. "Un Autre Fromentin." *Revue de l'Art* 74 (1986): 29–36.
———. *The East: Imagined, Experienced, Remembered: Orientalist Nineteenth-Century Painting.* Dublin: National Gallery of Art, 1988.
———. *Eugène Fromentin au Musée des Beaux-Arts de La Rochelle.* La Rochelle: Musée des Beaux-Arts, 1988.
Thompson, James, and Barbara Wright. *Eugène Fromentin (1820–1876): Visions d'Algérie et d'Égypte.* Paris: ACR Éditions, 2008.
———. *La Vie et l'oeuvre d'Eugène Fromentin.* Paris: ACR Éditions, 1987.
Thomson, Richard, ed. *Framing France: The Representation of Landscape in France, 1870–1914.* Manchester: Manchester University Press, 1998.
Thornton, Lynne. *Les Orientalistes: Artistes-Voyageurs, 1828–1908.* Paris: ACR Éditions, 1983.
Thouard, Valérie. "Eugène Fromentin: Entre Sahel et Sahara, entre écriture et peinture." *L'Écrit-Voir* 2 (January 1983): 41–53.
Tinterow, Gary, and Henri Loyrette. *Origins of Impressionism.* New York: Metropolitan Museum of Art, 1994.
Tocqueville, Alexis de. "Notes de voyage en Algérie de 1841." In *Oeuvres*, vol. 1, ed. André Jardin, Françoise Mélonio, and Lise Queffélec, 657–88. Paris: Gallimard, 1981.
———. "Rapports sur l'Algérie (1847)." In *Oeuvres*, vol. 1, ed. André Jardin, Françoise Mélonio, and Lise Queffélec, 795–905. Paris: Gallimard, 1981.
———. "Voyage en Algérie (novembre–décembre 1846)." In *Oeuvres,* vol. 1, ed. André Jardin, Françoise Mélonio, and Lise Queffélec, 761–93. Paris: Gallimard, 1981.
Todorov, Tzvetan. *On Human Diversity: Nationalism, Racism, and Exoticism in French Thought.* Translated by Catherine Porter. Cambridge: Harvard University Press, 1993.
Trachtenberg, Alan, ed. *Classic Essays on Photography.* New Haven: Leete's Island Books, 1980.
Tucker, Paul Hayes. *Monet at Argenteuil.* New Haven: Yale University Press, 1982.
Twyman, Michael. *Lithography, 1800–1850: The Techniques of Drawing on Stone in England and France and Their Application in Works of Topography.* London: Oxford University Press, 1970.
Urry, John. *Consuming Places.* London: Routledge, 1995.
———. *The Tourist Gaze: Leisure and Travel in Contemporary Societies.* London: Routledge, 1990.
Valée, Maréchal. "Rapport sur l'Expédition des Portes de Fer." *Le Moniteur Universel,* no. 316 (12 November 1839): 2007.
Valenciennes, Pierre-Henri de. *Elemens de perspective pratique. . . .* Paris: Desenne and Duprat, Year VIII [1800].
Vallois, Marie-Claire. "Exotic Femininity and the Rights of Man: *Paul et Virginie* and *Atala*, or the Revolution in Stasis." In *Rebel Daughters: Women and the French Revolution,* ed. Sara E. Melzer and Leslie W. Rabine, 178–97. Oxford: Oxford University Press, 1992.
Vaysettes, E. "La Question de la propriété, jugée par les docteurs de la loi musulmane." *Revue Africaine* 7, no. 41 (September 1863): 353–56.
Vidal-Bué, Marion. *Alger et ses peintres, 1830–1960.* Paris: Hazan, 2000.
Voisin, Georges. *L'Algérie pour les algériens.* Paris: Michel Lévy frères, 1861.
Wagner, Anne. "Courbet's Landscapes and Their Market." *Art History* 4, no. 4 (1981): 410–30.
Warnier, Auguste. *L'Algérie devant l'Empereur.* Paris: Challamel aîné, 1865.
Warnke, Martin. *Political Landscape: The Art History of Nature.* Translated by David McLintock. London: Reaktion Books, 1994.
Weber, Eugen. *Peasants into Frenchmen: The Modernization of Rural France, 1870– 1914.* Stanford: Stanford University Press, 1976.
Williams, Raymond. *The Country and the City.* Oxford: Oxford University Press, 1973.
Wollen, Peter. "Out of the Past: Fashion/Orientalism/The Body." In *Raiding the Icebox: Reflections on Twentieth-Century Culture,* 1–34. Bloomington: Indiana University Press, 1993.
Wright, Barbara, ed. *Correspondance d'Eugéne Fromentin.* 2 vols. Paris: CNRS, 1995.
———. *Croquis et dessins inédits d'Eugène Fromentin: Promenades en Aunis, Saintonge et Limousin.* Paris: CNRS, 1987.
———. *Eugène Fromentin: A Life in Art and Letters.* New York: Peter Lang, 2000.
Wright, Beth S., ed. *The Cambridge Companion to Delacroix.* Cambridge: Cambridge University Press, 2001.
———. "'That Other Historian, the Illustrator': Voices and Vignettes in Mid-Nineteenth-Century France." *Oxford Art Journal* 23, no. 1 (2000): 113–36.
Wright, Gordon. *France in Modern Times.* 5th ed. New York: W. W. Norton, 1995.

Yacono, Xavier. *Histoire de l'Algérie de la fin de la Régence turque à l'insurrection de 1954*. Versailles: Éditions de l'Atlanthrope, 1993.

Zarobell, John J. "Abstracting Space: Remaking the Landscape of Colonial Algeria in Second-Empire France." In *Modern Art and the Idea of the Mediterranean,* ed. Vojtěch Jirat-Wasiutyński and Anne Elizabeth Dymond, 61–83. Toronto: University of Toronto Press, 2007.

———. "Fragments of a Dream (History)." Review of *Jean-Charles Langlois, 1789–1870: Le Spectacle de l'histoire. Nineteenth-Century Art Worldwide* 5, no. 1 (2006): n.p.

———. "Framing French Algeria: Colonialism, Travel, and the Representation of Landscape, 1830–1870." Ph.D. diss., University of California, Berkeley, 2000.

———. "Jean-Charles Langlois's Panorama of Algiers (1833) and the Prospective Colonial Landscape." *Art History* 26, no. 4 (2003): 638–68.

Index

Page numbers in *italics* refer to illustrations.